The Therapeutic Situation in the 21st Century

Extending the themes of *Contemporary Psychoanalytic Foundations, The Therapeutic Situation in the 21st Century* offers a systematic reformulation of fundamental psychoanalytic concepts, such as transference, therapeutic action, and the uses of psychotropic drugs, in the light of recent developments in postmodernism, complexity theory, and neuroscience. Leffert offers formulations of areas not previously considered in any depth by psychoanalysts, such as power relations in the analytic couple, social matrix theory, and narrative theory informed by considerations of archaeology, genealogy, complexity, memory, and recall. He also considers new areas, such as the role of uncertainty and love in the therapeutic situation. This book is part of an ongoing effort to place psychoanalysis in the current century, and looks to outside as well as inside areas of thought to inform how we work and how we think about our work.

Mark Leffert, M.D., has been on the faculty of five psychoanalytic institutes and has been a Training and Supervising Analyst at four of them, most recently the New Center for Psychoanalysis. He has taught and supervised for 35 years. He is the author of many papers and a previous book, *Contemporary Psychoanalytic Foundations*. His interests focus on an interdisciplinary reformulation of psychoanalysis, drawing on postmodernism, neuroscience, complexity, and network studies. His future work will center on the self, subjectivity, and the way our understanding of both is impacted by a statistical understanding of heuristics and biases. He maintains a private practice centered around psychoanalysis, psychotherapy, and telephone therapy in Santa Barbara, California.

The Therapeutic Situation in the 21st Century

Mark Leffert

Routledge
Taylor & Francis Group
NEW YORK AND LONDON

First published 2013
by Routledge
605 Third Avenue, New York, NY 10017
4 Park Square, Milton Park, Abingdon, Oxon OX14 4RN

Routledge is an imprint of the Taylor & Francis Group, an informa business

Library of Congress Cataloging in Publication Data
Leffert, Mark.
The therapeutic situation in the 21st century / Mark Leffert.
p. cm.
Includes bibliographical references and index.
ISBN 978-0-415-88335-1 (hardback) — ISBN 978-0-415-88336-8 (paperback)
— ISBN 978-0-203-84473-1 (e-book) 1. Psychotherapy. I. Title.
RC475.L44 2012
616.89′14—dc23

2012008551

ISBN: 978–0–415–88335–1 (hbk)
ISBN: 978–0–415–88336–8 (pbk)
ISBN: 978–0–203–84473–1 (ebk)

Typeset in Minion
by RefineCatch Limited, Bungay, Suffolk

Dedication

For

Nancy,

Jonathan, and Jeremy

And, of course,

For

Sammy

Contents

Acknowledgments

I am grateful to a number of people who helped turn a first draft into a book worthy of publication. My two friends and colleagues, Jeff Seitelman and Jimmy Fisher, read and commented on various chapters of the book and were always available to discuss their thoughts with me.

If I have become somewhat familiar with the arcane process of writing a book and bringing it to publication, I still want to especially thank Kristopher Spring, my associate editor at Routledge, for his readiness to discuss any and all questions that came up during my writing and editing process. There is nothing that I can say to adequately express my gratitude to my wife, Nancy Leffert, Ph.D., for her help and support. In the past, she has read every word I have published but, since assuming the Presidency of the Santa Barbara campus of Antioch University, this has no longer been possible. For the present volume I turned to Susan Stewart for language and copyediting; I have found her suggestions to be uniformly helpful.

With one exception this has been a new text, written from scratch for the present purpose. Chapter 5, "Reading (or not Reading) Freud in the 21st Century," began life as a short commentary in the *Journal of the American Academy of Psychoanalysis and Dynamic Psychiatry, 38*, 2010, pp. 441–450. I am grateful to Doug Ingram, its Editor, for permission to revise it for the present volume.

Introduction

In a previous book, *Contemporary Psychoanalytic Foundations* (2010a), I offered a basic science approach to psychoanalysis at the beginnings of the 21st century. I discussed the relationship of the modern to the postmodern, the advent of neuroscience, and the role of complexity theory in the psychoanalytic endeavor. I also argued that *all* of these broad areas could be used interreferentially to inform each other *and* our understanding of the psychoanalytic situation. Such thinking had not found much of a place in psychoanalytic thought or that of the people working in these disparate disciplines. I used tools derived from an exploration of these areas and their interrelatedness to study a number of issues with which psychoanalysis has struggled with only limited success during its long existence. In particular, I looked at consciousness, unconsciousness, memory, power relations in psychoanalytic organizations, and therapeutic action.

However, one thing that *Contemporary Psychoanalytic Foundations* did not attempt to offer was any sort of consistent approach to clinical psychoanalysis, to the therapeutic situation if you will. In that area, it did not go beyond offering a radical critique of the standing of individual named metapsychologies.[1] I plan to offer the beginnings of such an approach here, a rudimentary textbook of clinical psychoanalysis in a different language.

In the still early days of Relational Psychoanalysis and Intersubjectivity Theory, Mitchell (1992b), in volume 2 of *Psychoanalytic Dialogues* (of which he was the first editor), offered the observation that:

1 I use *metapsychology* as a kind of shorthand to denote any of the named schools of psychoanalytic theory and practice and the implicit claims of standing that follow from such namings.

> In [his] view, the battle against orthodoxy has been largely won; the real vitality and creativity in the field have shifted to efforts . . . to develop postclassical, broadly relational approaches to mind, development, and the analytic situation. Because the battle has been won, it is now less interesting to recount the deficiencies of the classical model than to explore the subtle but quite important differences among postclassical perspectives.
>
> (p. 43)

I would suggest that neither of the assertions made in this perfectly reasonable sounding introduction to Mitchell's paper is correct. They fail in a general way because "the battle against orthodoxy" has not been so much won as elided: Orthodoxy, despite its serious deficiencies, does continue to have things to offer psychoanalysis, even relational psychoanalysis, and the differences "among postclassical perspectives," while undoubtedly real, are perhaps, when all is said and done, in 2011, not so important after all. The secular problem with Mitchell's paragraph and its assertions is greater still and lies in the fact that he continues to position the development of psychoanalysis as determined by the changing outcomes of dueling metapsychologies. The evolutionary course of psychoanalysis still follows from the prioritizing of protagonists and the outcome of the struggle, civilized by a shift in metaphor from battles being won to subtle differences being explored.

Of course, authors developing and elaborating the theory and technique of psychoanalysis have always done so while working within the framework of some metapsychology. They have achieved, over the decades, major therapeutic advances and both learned and understood much about psychological functioning and psychopathology. We continue to use many of their ideas and discoveries in our clinical work with patients. Mitchell's work under the broad relational umbrella and the narrower umbrella of the Relational School[2] is but one recent example of this. Whether the various metapsychologies that were developed alongside of these advances were truly necessary components of them or whether they even interfered with and constrained the therapeutic gains that were realizable by them are important questions that have never been addressed. Proceeding beyond Gill and Holtzman's (Gill, 1976; Gill & Holtzman, 1976) formulation that metapsychology is not psychology and that there are in fact two psychoanalytic theories, a powerful clinical one and a dubious metapsychological one, I would answer both of those questions in the affirmative. What will be offered here has been formulated outside of and independently of any metapsychology.

2 For the sake of clarity, I use capitals when designating the various metapsychological schools.

Looking back over perhaps the past 20 years, I gradually became aware that metapsychology, of whatever denomination, had essentially disappeared from my clinical work as well as my thoughts about that work. (I have no way of knowing how true this is for other analysts and psychotherapists, or whether this disappearance is in fact what lies behind some describing themselves as "eclectic.") I remained bilingual, however, able to speak or teach most metapsychology as circumstances warranted. An attendant change was that I no longer identified myself with the signifier of a named school to other professionals who did not know me or to informed lay people whom I met socially and who asked about my occupation. I was surprised to find that my unwillingness to safely identify myself as (metapsychologically) Freudian, Relational, or whatever, was often met by anxiety rather than interest. What's in a name is safety, apparently, and they would not take "no" for an answer. This is not a safe book; in the best postmodern sense, it is subversive. It implicitly and at times explicitly offers a radical critique of psychoanalysis as it is thought about and to a lesser extent how it has been practiced.

What I have retained, for lack of a better term, is an ontology of the clinical situation. For example, I continue to interpret defense (or not, as circumstances dictate) but I did not retain metapsychological ego psychology as a basis for doing so. Or, I will help a patient internalize their experience of my normative failings and imperfect self, and metabolize the ensuing small narcissistic injuries without reference to any concept of a bipolar self, or any psychological construct of a self. Transference remains a cornerstone of the clinical experience but, as will be talked about in chapters 3 and 6, it is a much more complex and nuanced one than is generally acknowledged.

This book, picking up where I left off in 2010 with *Contemporary Psychoanalytic Foundations*, develops and explores a clinical psychoanalysis, a psychology in Gill and Holtzman's (Gill, 1976; Gill & Holtzman, 1976) terms, free of metapsychology. This is not to say that it is atheoretical; it draws on a wide range of interdisciplinary studies and creates theory of its own—but it is not *meta-theory* and makes no such claims. The book is organized around six short monographs or long chapters addressing areas of fundamental importance to the therapeutic encounter, followed by an essay that attempts to take stock of where we find ourselves. I stress at a number of points (perhaps too many) that this is a preliminary effort. It is not meant to be all-inclusive, but as I hope the text will demonstrate, it addresses areas of great relevance to clinical work that are seldom thought of in connection with it, and offers a systematic approach to navigating them.

The chapters are reasonably independent of each other and could be read out of sequence. When earlier chapters do contribute to some argument or point made later in the book, they are always referenced as doing so. I *have* ordered them to provide some sense of a building argument; this is certainly true for chapters 6 and 7.

Throughout the book I use the terms *psychotherapist* and *psychoanalyst* more or less interchangeably. I use them at all only because therapists tend to identify themselves with one term or another and my thinking attempts to be as inclusive as possible. By psychotherapist and psychotherapy I mean here to refer to therapists whose orientation is significantly informed by psychoanalytic ideas and whose therapeutic work is similarly informed. Analysts who define themselves as graduates of psychoanalytic institutes (or at times of particular psychoanalytic institutes) may well be unhappy with this position, but it is necessary, I believe, for two reasons. A true clinical distinction between psychotherapy and psychoanalysis is in practice extremely difficult to draw and of at best limited utility. We must also recognize that in the wider world of therapists there are many who identify themselves as psychoanalysts based on their individual modes of study and reflection rather than formal attendance at a psychoanalytic institute. Since this is how psychoanalysts first began to *be* psychoanalysts a century ago, who is to say that they may not do so, except in the State of New York where the term is licensed and denotes certain specific credentials.

I have previously discussed in *Contemporary Psychoanalytic Foundations* (2010a) the interdisciplinary literature on power, drawing on sources in the fields of sociology, psychology, and postmodernism. This material had not, until then, been considered in the psychoanalytic literature. It deals with the dynamics of power in groups and the formation of ruling elites and dominated underclasses. How these groups are defined, how they constitute themselves and how they remain connected, are subjects that I saw as highly relevant to the pathological behavior of psychoanalytic organizations and their politics.

I discussed power relations as they have manifested themselves over the history of American psychoanalysis and in the current political battles within the American Psychoanalytic Association (APsaA)—battles that have sadly continued, as of this writing, largely unabated. I posited that in both venues, the historical and the contemporary, ruling elites struggled to hold on to power and control over depreciated and dominated classes of psychoanalysts. Power resides specifically in the elites of APsaA's Board on Professional Standards (BoPS) that has so far resisted attempts to make APsaA an egalitarian, power-neutral organization.

What I did not consider then was the way in which power is exerted and plays out within the therapeutic relationship, how it mostly goes unidentified if not unnoticed, and how it can cripple analytic results or therapeutic action. This is the subject of chapter 1. It offers a brief review of the power relations literature discussed in the previous volume and goes on to consider works germane to the clinical situation, and the role of power in the hands of the therapist. Foucault's *History of Madness* (1961/2006a) has relevance for current clinical practice, as does *Discipline and Punish* (1979/1995). The chapter also reviews literature on clinical hypnosis that, perhaps surprisingly, has bearing on the psychoanalytic situation. Much of the chapter goes on to address power relations as they appear in four clinical vignettes, two drawn from the analytic literature and two from my practice.

In *Contemporary Psychoanalytic Foundations*, a chapter was devoted to current concepts of memory that drew heavily on neuroscience. I went on to consider narrative and metanarrative as they were addressed in clinical practice. Postmodern thought and critiques of both forms of narrative informed these discussions. There, I put forward a clinical theory of working with memory and narrative.

What were not considered were theories of knowledge and how they inform our ideas about memory, narrative, and experience. That is what we will do in chapter 2. I will posit that all individuals have personal epistemologies, personal rules of knowledge and discursive practice that govern both what they can think about, the very nature of the thoughts they are capable of having, and what they can remember. These discussions will draw upon Foucault's concepts of the archaeology and genealogy of knowledge. They will be organized around a long case vignette describing the analysis of Susan, a patient I have discussed previously. To readers having only limited experience with postmodern ideas, their language can at first seem strange-sounding or arcane, and thus daunting. I have tried to describe them in more accessible language. These ideas will offer new tools for understanding issues relating to patients' rules of knowledge, rules that have been mischaracterized and misaddressed as resistance.

We all have developed characteristic rules for how we formulate knowledge. Those rule sets, called discursive practices, can be relatively effective or ineffective in allowing us to access the world and the relationships we have in it. They shape not only how we know but what we are able to know. The chapter will consider how these rules develop and how they can result in the inability to formulate particular thoughts about how people or things actually are. It will further explain how such people can only characterize them in unrealistic ways, requiring often-dysfunctional responses.

Although it has been relatively easy to talk about patients' feelings (even though early on analysts weren't all that interested in them), it is much harder to talk about our own. We have had only two categories in which to place them: countertransference and boundary violations. (Each of these was met with enormous resistance from within our profession; the battle over countertransference was fought in the 1950s and the battle over acknowledging the existence of therapist–patient sex is still with us.) There is now a sparse but growing literature on a different kind of feeling, that of therapists loving their patients, a feeling that does not fall into either of these categories.

Chapter 3 will consider this literature and these feelings, but with a number of caveats. In these early days it is very hard to make generalizations about loving feelings, where they belong, what they consist of, what to do with them. Writing about these feelings requires a considerable degree of courage, as I found out for myself. It also requires overcoming one's internal resistance to exploring and talking about feelings we were taught to view as countertransference at best, psychopathology at worst. The *only* criticism I would offer about the literature we do have is that its authors draw as yet unwarranted conclusions and offer generalizations about the nature of these feelings that lack sufficient evidence to support them.

One such generalization that cannot yet be made concerns whether or not the therapist should discuss these feelings with her patient (as you will see, I do not think it useful to do so). In the chapter, I will describe my own experiences as just that, my own experiences, and try to relate them to the literature. I do not consider them, at this time, a path to wider truth. The literature on therapists' loving feelings will develop over time with two possible outcomes in the future. One is that as psychotherapists and analysts digest it, they will begin to mull over their own feelings and some will write about them. It may then emerge that some generalizations *are* warranted. The other is that it may turn out that the way analysts experience and handle loving feelings is highly individual. The two need not be mutually exclusive and eventually I would expect us to come to both; some generalizations are possible, but ways of handling these feelings are more individual than with most issues of technique.

In trying to better understand and place these loving feelings for patients we will look outside of psychoanalysis to the neurobiology of love and, in particular, Jaak Panksepp's (1998) work on affective neuroscience. In this context we will also consider the relationship between love and attachment, and Alan Schore's (2003b, 2009) location of therapeutic action in the areas of affect and affect regulation.

Psychoanalysts have always struggled with theories of cure that have, in effect, amounted to metapsychologies of cure. Much less thought or writing has gone into defining the *object* of analysis. For Freudian, and for that matter Kleinian, analysts and psychotherapists, that object explicitly or implicitly is the ego, an element of psychic structure. It is at once problematic for this point of view that structures such as the ego are constructs, that they are arbitrary and of uncertain ontology. Their further instability is evidenced by Anna Freud's (1936/1966) observation that, in the absence of conflict, elements of psychic structure cannot be distinguished.

Both Winnicott (1955) and Kohut (1977) address the self as the object of analysis. For Winnicott it is the self of the true self/false self dilemma, and for Kohut it is the bipolar self and its "restoration." The issues here are that both of these putative selves are, once again, constructs, and that they are entirely psychical.

If we are going to describe (not construct) a self that actually exists, that *has* ontology, it has to be a holistic self that includes its inseparable and indistinguishable physical aspects. Such a self can stand as its own subject and the object of therapeutic action; chapter 4 will be taken up with its description.

Psychoanalysts and, for that matter, general psychologists have endlessly confused self-representation (I prefer self-schema) and self; an understandable difficulty if both are considered psychical. The chapter will consider these difficulties. There are two ways of doing this. One is to consider the neurobiology of the holistic self and how it operates both inside and outside of the brain. The other is to see what neuroscience can tell us about functional representations of the self and how the self maintains such essential schemata.

The relations of the self to the world in which it finds itself through its perceptions and its connections to other selves are of great importance. The latter have been of interest to psychoanalysts at least since the 'teens of the last century (Freud, 1914/1957b, 1917/1957a). We know the study of these connections as object relations theory. But an entirely different way of knowing them involves the recognition that each self is embedded in its own social network and the study of that embedding can be informed by postmodern thought and the relatively new discipline of Network Studies. Chapter 4 will also look at these connections in some detail.

Freud and his writings, known to nearly all American clinicians and academics through *The Standard Edition of the Complete Psychological Works of Sigmund Freud*, produced under the general editorship of James Strachey, have been shunned by some and clung to by others, probably the former more often than the latter. Chapter 5 has things to say that are likely to trouble both groups.

The chapter has two goals. The first is to consider the many broad issues that must be addressed if one is to truly apprehend Freud's work and get something out of it that is as consistent as possible with what he actually said in his original texts. Freud wrote in vernacular prose and received the Goethe prize, a prestigious literary award of which he was the fourth recipient, in 1930. If such outside corroboration were required, one should be led to presume that exactly what he said and how he said it are of some importance, and any translation of his work should initially be viewed with a degree of skepticism, benign or otherwise.

Getting at the meaning contained in Freud's work, its *Deutung*, is a difficult and demanding task. These days, the difficulties mostly go unnoticed. This chapter will lay out the difficulties, deconstruct them if you will, and suggest solutions and coping strategies. Doing so involves considering the episteme in which Freud wrote, that of *fin-de-siècle* Vienna, and understanding how things meant in that time and place. Then there are the problems inherent in translating Freud and the problems with the translations that do exist. There are questions surrounding claims of his work constituting a science and, if it is a science, what sort of science it is. This chapter is really a study of meaning and how things mean as applied to Freud's work. It will draw on many of the concepts discussed in chapter 2, exploring the archaeology of meaning in a wider social sense. Freud used his work to assert power over the psychoanalytic movement and it has been used for similar purposes by generations of orthodox American psychoanalysts. Finally, novel suggestions for reading and teaching Freud are offered in this chapter.

The other goal is perhaps a strange one; I want to convince you to try reading, rereading, or teaching Freud. But I want you to try it in a very different way, in changed contexts and in lesser volumes. The chapter will show you how to do it. The aim is to use it as part of a wider perspective on contemporary psychoanalytic thought as opposed to reading Freud chronologically for Freud's sake.

As the chapters unfold I hope it will become clear that I am laying the groundwork for a novel approach to therapeutic action. I took the subject up at some length in chapter 1 of *Contemporary Psychoanalytic*

Foundations by offering a review of its development linked to the history of the various schools of metapsychology in which the various theories of therapeutic action arose. *Contemporary Psychoanalytic Foundations* also offered a conservative postmodern critique of metapsychology based on its representing a species of metanarrative where metanarratives generally produce artificial constraints on meaning—constraints that limit the freedom of ideas to enter a text and allow for *différance.*

In the intervening two years, I have in retrospect found that my thinking about metapsychology has grown more radical, as has the critique I would now level against it. I have chosen therapeutic action as the site for this argument because it is the most essential part of psychoanalysis, the point at which our discipline succeeds or fails, colloquially, where the rubber meets the road. Chapter 6 is mostly, but not all, about stripping metapsychology from therapeutic action and then, more importantly, looking at what remains. It too must be taken as a preliminary effort requiring further development.

It begins innocuously enough with two surveys of the psychoanalytic literature on therapeutic action. The first is a historical survey of the literature of the past 50 years, but one structured to sample *all* of that literature. The second is still more novel. Using the tools gleaned from Network Studies in chapter 4 (Albert, Jeong, & Barabási, 1999; Barabási & Bonabeau, 2003) and *Psychoanalytic Electronic Publishing*, we will create a social network of the literature on therapeutic action and then study its hubs and connections. These two complementary approaches offer a surprisingly rich survey of the psychoanalytic literature. It is a survey of what the community of psychotherapists and psychoanalysts has been writing and reading about therapeutic action.

The chapter goes on to posit that concepts of therapeutic action in psychoanalysis act at different levels of inquiry, micro, mid-, and macro, and failing to recognize this point obfuscates any discussion of them. I would posit that while psychoanalytic process is best described on a micro level, therapeutic action is best described on a macro level.

I will argue here that all psychoanalytic therapies, regardless of the professed theoretical orientations of their practitioners, are relational (small *r*). While this statement is of course trivially true, I mean much more by it. Even if we should come to agree that all therapies are significantly relational, we would not accept that the therapeutic relationship is enough to yield a successful analysis. Something more must be required to morph a relationship into an analysis. Arguably this book has largely been taken up with that "something more," a discourse on emotion, narrative, and meaning.

Chapter 6 concludes with a discussion of four areas of clinical psychoanalytic thought (this should not be taken to be an exhaustive list) that must bear on therapeutic action. These include transference, resistance, conflict, and hermeneutics. What makes this consideration necessary is that all therapists take an explicit position on each of them, explicit to themselves and at least implicit to their patients. Any consideration of therapeutic action must address and take positions on them, how they are defined, and whether they require metapsychology to explain them.

This book is about opening up a wide range of ideas about psychoanalysis and, almost by definition, would not lend itself to a final chapter of synthesis aimed at tying things up and cutting off loose ends. Instead, chapter 7 will, after some brief stock-taking, offer six essays, some of which approach the length of short chapters. Three—power, therapeutic action, and the self—will revisit earlier chapter topics from the perspective of the now complete discourse. The remaining three—on therapeutic discourse, uncertainty, and support, palliation, and care—are quite new and will address issues that have been only implied or hinted at in places throughout the book. They leave much room for further elaboration in the future.

The section of chapter 7 on uncertainty makes explicit a central theme of the book: that we must function as psychoanalysts and psychotherapists in a world that manifests both limits on the possible degree of knowability and the absence of any ontological basis for certainty. What masquerades as certainty is only a manifestation of the synthetic functions of the self, functions that yield a necessary self-cohesion and continuity that operate in part by hiding from us the discontinuities in our knowledge of the world. I want to say here, in a point that I will develop later, that certainty is, and always has been, the greatest single enemy of psychoanalysis. By psychoanalysis I mean to include three interreferential areas: the therapeutic situation, the creation of theory, and politics (power relations).

L'âme d'autrui est une forêt obscure où il faut marche avec precaution

(The soul of another is a dark forest in which one must tread carefully)

Claude Debussy, Letter, 1891

1

Power Relations in the Office

Introduction

The subject of power as it plays out in the therapeutic situation has come rather late to the psychoanalytic literature (Leffert, 2010a, especially chapters 1 and 7). However, its relevance to the wider areas of the treatment of people termed mentally ill and its presence in social relations generally has been a subject of inquiry and discourse in other disciplines for many decades. Foucault (1961/2006a), in his monumental work *History of Madness*, offers a history of society's dealings with both madness (*folie*) and the mad (*fou*) from the 17th to the beginnings of the 19th century. Trained as a clinical psychologist as well as a philosopher, he portrays the relationship in terms of power and fear of contagion. The *fou* are to be corrected, linking them to the second of Foucault's (1979/1995) great concerns, the prison and the imprisoned.

More or less simultaneously, the psychoanalyst Thomas Szasz, in *The Myth of Mental Illness* (1961) and *The Manufacture of Madness* (1970/1997), independently approached the same problem, but without clearly identifying the issue of power relations.[3] He went on (1965/1969) to posit a psychotherapy, psychoanalytic in content but organized as a game involving two players that is governed by rules that ensure equality and is otherwise quite post-structural (Szasz does not refer to post-structuralism as he does not refer nakedly to power). The game involves contracts freely entered into and, if successfully played, has two winners. Szasz's ideas fit well with the episteme of the 1960s and, although they

3 Nor did Szasz consider that, in denying the existence of schizophrenia, on the surface a very postmodern thing to do, he was taking a position with the same power implications as that of a psychiatrist in a state hospital.

found a place within the therapeutic community movement, they did not long survive as a governing principle in the practice of psychotherapy.

A trickle of publications appearing in the psychoanalytic literature has dealt with issues of power (often not named as such) as they involve psychoanalytic training, the selection of candidates, the training analysis, and the relations among the members of analytic institutes and societies. An issue of *Psychoanalytic Inquiry* (Lichtenberg, 2004) was devoted to the topic of power arising in psychoanalytic organizations. The presence of power issues embedded in the politics of national and international psychoanalytic macro-organizations has begun to be considered and has produced a significant literature outside the bounds of clinical psychoanalysis (Hale Jr., 1995; Kirsner, 2000, 2009; Reeder, 2004). It is a matter of some curiosity that, with rare exceptions, all of these authors seem unfamiliar with the extensive literature on power developed over the last century in the disciplines of postmodernism, sociology, political science, and literary criticism.[4]

It is of equal interest that the therapeutic situation has received almost no attention as a locus of power relations between therapist and patient. When power relations *are* mentioned, it is usually only in passing or secondarily to other contexts such as race and gender issues or training analyses (Aron, 1997; Balsam, 1994; Benjamin, 2000; Cavalcanti de Albuquerque, 1993; Celenza, 2006; Coen, 2002; Cushman, 2005; Davies, 1996; Goldner, 1991; Harris, 1997, 2009; Jimenez, 1989; Silverman, 2003; Stern, 2003; Wolstein, 1977b; Zeddies, 2001). Kernberg (1996) and Hoffman (1996, 1998) are exceptions in that they discuss problems with power in the therapeutic setting in a thoughtful, although in the case of the former, a descriptive way.

Although power relations stand outside the scope of any particular metapsychology,[5] they inhabit all of them equally and become of concern when they are taken out of the various scholarly settings (texts, journals, seminars, scholarly meetings, and supervision) and into the therapist's office. Their presence there then goes unrecognized or, if recognized, is not viewed as problematic. I think that our resistance to looking at power relations in the therapeutic setting is twofold. Firstly,

4 For a thorough treatment of all of this material see chapter 7 of *Contemporary Psychoanalytic Foundations* (Leffert, 2010a).

5 I use the term *metapsychology* to denote the differing schools of psychoanalytic theory rather than in its original sense, limited to the varying theoretical points of view within Freudian psychoanalytic theory.

as therapists we do not think of ourselves as wielding power over our patients. The idea of doing so is abhorrent to the great majority of us who think of ourselves instead in terms of being there to help or to heal. Unfortunately, this quite understandable tendency robs us of the opportunity to examine how we are inadvertently exerting power over our patients. Some therapists also claim for themselves, as part of their therapeutic role, the right and perhaps even the obligation to wield a power characterized as "benign" in the therapeutic situation. Such a designation is questionable. The notions of knowing what is right or of protecting the patient, perhaps from himself, can stand as a rationalization for such a stance.

Secondly, there is some degree of resistance directed at examining how and when our patients may exert power over us. I can see many analysts and therapists reacting with amazement to such a proposal. Their response would be along the lines of: "Well, patients may *attempt* to control us as an expression of transference, but that is simply being a patient, it doesn't really affect us and we deal with it, we *interpret* it." I don't believe it is anywhere nearly as simple as that, or as manageable. When patients do exert power over us, and we have all had such experiences, it involves an element of narcissistic injury we prefer not to think about. When a patient fails to appear for an appointment, I know that I do not like it. I can understand its meaning much of the time, I'm being paid for my time, the feeling is a mild one, but I still don't like it; I've suffered a very small narcissistic injury. The fact that I also understand the transaction in terms of power relations further mitigates it. I imagine it is possible, although not to my mind desirable, to suppress such reactions altogether.

The exercise of power by patients over their therapists can, in cases of severe psychopathology, reach epic proportions. Kernberg (1968) describes the treatment of a patient with borderline personality disorder (a case he supervised). The patient had broken off two previous treatments and exerted total sadistic control over her current therapist, immobilizing him for months. She would respond to unwelcome questions with either a raised eyebrow or the phrase "watch it" and felt she had the right to be secretive or uncommunicative. For his part, the therapist did not confront her, fearing either rageful outbursts or her leaving. When, as a result of the supervision, he did attempt to set limits with her she indeed did leave and the therapy, that wasn't a therapy, ended.

In this chapter, I propose to do a number of things. I plan to review the interdisciplinary literature on power relations from the perspective of how they play out in the relationship of the therapeutic couple rather than from that of how power operates politically in groups (as I did in Leffert, 2010a, chapter 7). For this purpose, the therapeutic relationship might be considered a member of a class of intimate relationships, existing between an expert and an individual in need of that expertise, involving significant inequalities, and extending over time. This review will involve the usual suspects, postmodernism, sociology, political science, and literary criticism. It will also include neuroscience, and that unwelcome relative, long confined to the psychoanalytic attic, clinical hypnosis. (We will also have to consider *its* relative, suggestion, which cannot be so confined.) Finally, the question of benign power will have to be discussed.

The actual discussion of power as it appears in the therapeutic situation divides into a number of sub-topics. They include identifying power transactions initiated by either the therapist or the patient and the related subject of abusive (or abuses of) power. Then there is the topic of power relations as the subject of analysis, *not* simply as an aspect of some overarching metapsychological framework. This does not appear to have ever been considered in the literature. Lastly, there is the therapist's personal study and reflections on power relations resulting in a modification, or correction, really, of her general clinical stance that serves to mitigate the power issues that inevitably arise in an intimate, unequal relationship. Clinical material will be used to illustrate all of these topics.

A considerable literature on power has appeared in several disciplines, directed primarily at describing relationships between societal groups identified as dominant and their respective dominated classes, or between dominant individuals (or small groups) and their respective dominated groups (or larger groups). This literature is, perhaps surprisingly, easily applicable to the particular group of two comprised of a patient[6] and a therapist and to the larger groups of which they are both members. Thus, there exists a class of individuals identified by therapists as patients and a class of therapists who are members of social networks of varying sizes and manifesting varying degrees of separation. Christakis and Fowler (2009) have argued that such networks

6 I will use the term *patient* throughout to refer to the people who seek us out for therapy and analysis. I do so for two reasons. The first is that, as a physician, it's the term I grew up with and with which I feel most comfortable. The second is that I find *client* too general, signifying the recipient of any of a wide variety of services rather than help with illness or impairment. I would wish that the term could be used by members of all the helping professions.

(see chapter 4) pass experiential information regarding subjects such as power across varying degrees of separation, allowing individuals to unknowingly pass information to other network members who receive it, also unknowingly. They term the process *network contagion.* A ready example of this is how the power dynamics of an institute can get into a particular therapeutic relationship and distort it.

Foucault and Said

Foucault on Madness and the Therapist's Power

As I have discussed elsewhere (Leffert, 2010a, especially chapters 7 and 8), Foucault came at the concepts of power, freedom, and knowledge from the margins of society, considering the mad, the criminal, and the sexually outcast, as well as from where they were frequently housed, the asylums and the prisons (Foucault, 1979/1995, 2000, 1961/2006a). At first, it might appear that these margins manifest a kind of feculence that is far removed from the consulting room occupied by an upper-middle-class client and a clinical expert. However, they are not really so very separate. Foucault concerned himself mostly with matters of power and freedom and their relations to knowledge, all terms that, as we shall reconstruct, lose something both in translation and in a shift from Foucault's particular usage. For him power, *pouvoir*, has to do with the ability of an individual or individuals to assert dominance over other individuals. Foucault struggled with the possibility of a differentiation between dominant power and a collection of capabilities including strength, ability, and agency. Such a distinction is far easier to discuss than it is to maintain in its exercise. In his discussions of knowledge, Foucault has struggled to formulate an essential distinction between two broad kinds of "knowledge" based on how they encompass power. The one, *savoir*, is intimately bound up with power while the other, *connaissance*, is fixed and free of it; it represents something like recognition and familiarity, things known but not part of any system of *savior*, hence free of power but unusable. His position on this distinction shifts, based on whether he is speaking out from the margins against power or reflecting on it from within the academy. However, the holism that is *pouvoir–savoir* exists for Foucault in that no knowledge is ever developed or deployed for reasons *not in some way connected to the wielding of power*. Foucault describes this interreferentiality least opaquely in *Discipline and Punish* (1979/1995):

> Power produces knowledge (and not simply by encouraging it because it serves power or by applying it because it is useful); that power and knowledge directly imply one another; that there is no power relation without the correlative constitution of a field of knowledge, nor any knowledge that does not presuppose and constitute at the same time power relations . . . In short, it is not the activity of the subject of knowledge that produces a corpus of knowledge, useful or resistant to power, but power–knowledge, the processes and struggles that traverse it and of which it is made up, that determines the forms and possible domains of knowledge.
>
> (pp. 27–28)

I would posit that this dilemma faces all of us as therapists and the only way out of it is the repeated deconstruction of accruing power relations in the therapeutic situation.

To identify and characterize as power relations activities taking place between patient and therapist, Foucault (2000) would require the presence of five areas of relational constraint between the participants. There must be a *differentiation* between the participants, in this case based on the possession of particular knowledges and experiences. Personal *objectives* (such as income or status) that lead one person to act upon another must be present. Particular *modalities* (speech, implicit or explicit rules, records) that allow one person to act upon the other must also be present. Some *formal institutionalization* such as schedules, the creation of a closed system by one of the participants with its own special rules and procedures, all of which the other agrees to participate in,[7] must exist as the locus of the relationship. Finally, there has to be a *rationale*, a reason for the system to exist and an outcome of its operations that is, or appears to be, beneficial to both parties.

In his *History of Madness* (1961/2006a),[8] Foucault studied madness and unreason in the Classical Age, roughly defined as 1650–1800. In a series of lectures (Foucault, 2003/2006b) on psychiatric power delivered at the Collège de France in 1973–1974, he continues the story with the medicalization of madness and the rise of the psychiatrist in the 19th century. During much of the Classical Age, madness was not an illness but a kind of animality, a loss of humanness that fulfilled a social purpose similar to that of leprosy in earlier ages. It was not something to which the concept of cure became relevant until the Enlightenment, and cure was not then defined as a medical treatment but rather as an

7 A central part of Foucault's thesis is that a power relation requires an object who is free to act; a slave in chains and its owner does not constitute a power relationship since it is static, there is no place for either dominance or rebellion to act.

8 The full title in French is *Folie et Déraison: Histoire de la Folie à l'Âge Classique.*

attempt to restore humanness through potion or panacea. As Gutting (2003) describes Foucault's position, madness was one member of the class of unreason. The mad were idle; this in turn was equated with a refusal to work, with sloth, and this made madness, on religious grounds, an ethical and moral matter. For Foucault, the mad were thus in a state of rebellion (against power) and their grouping with the other *déraisonnés*, sexual offenders, the religiously profane, and the free-thinkers (*les libertines*), made good power-relations sense.

The Great Confinement of the *déraisonnés* (Foucault, 1961/2006a) that ushered in the Classical Age (for example, over the span of a few years, 5000–6000 persons, roughly 1% of the population of Paris, were so confined) served to justly punish, another of Foucault's great themes, these moral reprobates. A sub-purpose of confinement was to protect the Church and the bourgeoisie from the contagion of the *déraisonnés*. As with his other positions, Foucault's views of the history of the mad became the subject of intense criticism. Surely what he described as a uniform Western European process varied significantly from country to country.

Gutting (2003) responds that Foucault was not so much interested in verifying the empirical data as he was in attempting to construct the underlying system of categories that led to these at-times diverse practices. Foucault is seeking to define a *dispositif*, a term that one of his translators, Graham Burchell (Foucault, 2003/2006b), correctly describes as untranslatable. It encompasses "a configuration or arrangement of elements and forces, practices and discourses, power and knowledge, that is both *strategic* and *technical*" (p. xxiii).[9]

Foucault (1961/2006a) speaks generally of the relations between doctors and patients during the Classical Age. As he observes, "the world of the cure [was] organized along principles which are in a certain sense peculiar to it [the Classical Age], and which medical theory, physiological analysis and even the observation of symptoms [did] not always control perfectly" (p. 297). There were a variety of nostrums, potions, compounds and herbs—mercury, antimony, and opium prominent among them—however, the search was always for the elusive panacea, which no man can know, that was not so much a cure as an almost magical or supernatural substance that would return the body to its natural state, *regardless of what was wrong with it*. The panacea became a sort of compromise between nature herself that cures (acts against

9 As can be seen, the term *dispositif* is both an expansion and a refinement of the term *episteme*, which has come much more into common postmodern usage.

counter-nature) and something that acts on the disease. Efficacy of the drug is linked always to the theme of nature, just as *les déraisonnés* were linked to unnature. Potions and mystical compounds ultimately became central to the treatment of madness. Doctors did little of the direct treatment, which was left to "empirics," nuns, monks, charlatans, druggists, and herbalists. (Here read, in the 21st century, the pharmaceutical industry, but note carefully the distinction between psychopharmacology per se and the power the industry has claimed for itself in the prescribing of medication, a role in decision making co-opted from the physician.)[10] Doctors in fact came very late to the treatment of the mad; when the asylums went up in France in the 18th century, treatments were first carried out by the guards. "The constant and reciprocal relation between theory and practice was supplemented by an immediate confrontation between doctors and patients" (p. 307). The physician came up with remedies and, from a position of power, deployed them on the patient; the patient was acted upon by the physician. There was no psychological medication, no place for consolation, reason, or empathy. The mad lost not only their autonomy but their very personhood, they became instead *objects of treatment*.

"The essential function of psychiatric power [around 1840] is to be an effective agent of reality, a sort of intensifier of reality to madness" (Foucault, 2003/2006b, p. 143). Recovery in turn was expected as an automatic response to four elements: first, isolation in the asylum; second, treatment with psychiatric medications (i.e., opiates); third, a series of restraints, discipline, and enforced obedience to regulation; and fourth, a kind of punitive "medication," forced cold showers, the rotary swing, and, although Foucault does not mention it, corporal punishment. (One can only hope that the second lessened the mortification of the fourth.) These procedures shared a common function: to immediately create a power relationship with the doctor in control of his patient. The patient is subject to the "foreign will" (p. 147) of the doctor, the goal of which is to induce a state of docility in the patient; he is forced to accept the doctor's treatments. If the *fou* is conceptualized as being in a state of rebellion, of maniacal omnipotence, he must be broken if he is to be cured. The object of and the producer of the cure is the patient's administrative submission, his acknowledgement of the *reality of his madness*. Foucault posits that the asylum is a kind of curing

10 They have done so by controlling the information that doctors receive about the products they prescribe through the funding and publication of "research" and the deployment of their agents, known as detail persons.

apparatus in which the doctor's action operates on the same level as its regulations and its very buildings. It is a great machine filled with structures whose major function is supervision (*surveillance*).

I would not deem it surprising if, at this point, someone were to ask: What on earth does this have to do with a patient (a *client* even) and a doctor sitting in a consulting room in 2012 for the purpose of psychotherapy or psychoanalysis? The answer is twofold. Up until a generation ago (Foucault's time), the inpatient mental health system was not all *that* different from what he described as taking place in 1840.[11] Foucault knew this; he worked for a time in that system, at l'Hôspital Sainte-Anne in the 1950s (Foucault, 1961/2006a). Significant elements of that system exist in an albeit milder form into the present. More importantly, what I have been presenting is a genealogy of all the psychological and psychiatric therapies that we have in the present, one that is carried forward in the cultural memories of all of us and brought into that office by the participants. An article in a recent *New Yorker* magazine (Menand, 2010) in effect describes all psychotherapy and psychopharmacology as absurd exercises in power and economic gain. Power relations issues may well determine why some prospective patients seek out psychologists over psychiatrists, social workers and marriage and family counselors over psychologists, and women therapists over men, while others simply go where they are sent. Fear not, power relations are very much alive and well in the therapy machine of the 21st century.

Foucault (1961/2006a) concluded that madness and unreason are constructions of meaning that have changed over time and reflect the particular *dispositifs* in which they find themselves.[12] As with any psychological problem, the language we use in talking about it can be problematic because it specifies more than we might wish. Foucault credits Freud with returning language to madness and its treatment. He saw Freud as re-humanizing the *fous* and the *déraisonnés* who had been considered at the time to be at best neurologically degenerate (for reasons mostly thought to be due to hereditary or toxic exposure). Freud did not, according to Foucault, "set out to bring a major addition to the list of psychological treatments of madness, but restored instead the possibility of a dialogue with unreason to medical thought" (p. 339). We will turn

11 For a 20th century version of this discourse between asylum and patient, one need only turn to Ken Kesey's (1962/2002) novelization of asylum life, *One Flew over the Cuckoo's Nest*.

12 Foucault's position should not be confused with Szasz's (1961) that mental illness as such does not exist. Foucault was not questioning the existence of madness but rather offering a social and power relations critique of its usages.

next to Edward Said's (1979, 1994) work which, at first glance, hardly seems relevant to the problem of power in the therapeutic situation at all.

Said and Orientalism

Edward Said's work is inseparable from his life. He was born into a wealthy Christian Palestinian family that was forced to flee Jerusalem for Egypt in 1948 as a result of the first Arab–Israeli War (Morris, 2008). He was educated in the United States and became variously a social/cultural/literary critic, a journalist, and a neo-Marxian philosopher. He was also a passionate supporter of Palestinian independence. He is perhaps best known for his singular contribution to power-relations theory, the concept of Orientalism (Said, 1979). Briefly stated, "it is a view of the Orient as exotic, mysterious, old, decadent, and inferior to the point of dysfunction that justifies colonial domination; its location is ontologically unstable, based on the utility and convention of the moment" (Leffert, 2010a, p. 205).

It should be clear that so little stretch is required to get from the other (*autre*) of the oriental to the *autre* of the mad that there at first seems little purpose in discussing it. The point is that Said (1994) then proceeds to discuss the literature of Orientalism and Imperialism (19th and early 20th century English, Continental, and American literature), and *these* discussions shed an interesting light on the psychoanalytic literatures of psychopathology and clinical case material. I would suggest that although psychoanalysts and psychotherapists have sometimes claimed that the differences between their patients and themselves are ones of degree, this position is often not honored in the breach; our literature tends toward a qualitative shift when it talks about patients versus when it talks about therapists.[13] With the advent of the two-person psychologies, relationalism and intersubjectivity, a significant change *has* taken place, one that we will want to assess in greater detail.

13 I would hasten to add that this is nothing like what persists in contemporary psychiatry. If one strips away the considerable degree of sanitization that has of course taken place in how psychiatrists go about their treating and their writing, what one finds is quite indistinguishable from what Foucault (2003/2006b) wrote about as existing in the 19th century. A not insignificant number of contemporary psychiatrists still safely ensconce themselves in white coats with a desk between themselves and their patients. A vestige of this remains in psychoanalysis, manifested in how an analyst arranges the chairs and couch in his office. When I was a resident, a supervisor of mine had a large rectangular office; he placed his chair and his patient chair in opposite corners, at least 25 feet apart.

Said (2001a), like Foucault (1980, 2000), is concerned with knowledge and its relations to power, but also with its acquisition and maintenance. To understand the world, in this case the psychoanalytic world, one must do scholarship and, for Said (1996/2001b), doing scholarship involves the study of past *dispositifs*—in our case, this means the Freudian, Kleinian, and others' pasts—in order to fully comprehend the relational, intersubjective, and interdisciplinary present. As Said puts it "It's [past scholarship] not something you can just blow away and say it's all dead white males or [some] clap-trap" (p. 263). This, I fear, is a point that has become lost on too many contemporary therapists, analysts, and their students. It must also be stressed that scholarship operates in two directions. Although scholarship of past *dispositifs* necessarily informs present knowledges, it is equally true that, if scholarship has created knowledges that have supported prevailing orthodoxies, new scholarship can deconstruct such structures and shed light on the needs that originally gave rise to them.

Said always stood to the side in his work; he did not want to produce students who thought and did as he did, something that has plagued psychoanalysis from its beginnings, with endless schools named after one person or another or one concept or another.[14]

Said's (1979) discussions of the nature of knowledge, texts, and the writing of texts are of particular relevance to the case reports that we write and the purposes that lead us to seed our literature with case material. I have previously (Leffert, 2010a) described the points that are central to his arguments and my own.

> Said wanted to separate the use of a knowledge from its truth standing but at the same time could not do so. He makes a series of methodological points critical of even the possibility of an objective approach to a text (here a codified form of knowledge). First, Said describes a "strategic location," where an author positions himself in relation to a text, his own or another's. Second, "strategic formation" depicts how texts are aggregated (or are woven) into positions that acquire power-knowledge. Third, there is no set point of departure from which to begin a text (or, I would add, a set point from which to conclude a text); such a set point is *chosen* and it enables some things and bars others from inquiry. Finally, he acknowledges the inseparability of the author from the starting point; who we are determines what we write.
>
> (p. 207)

14 At a recent conference, the presenter observed that, in his immediate psychoanalytic community, he could always tell who someone's analyst was by listening to their answering machine message.

So, what would Said have to say about our psychoanalytic literature taken as a whole? Specifically, what does his work tell us about how that literature manifests evidence of power relations in the therapeutic situation, and what kind of power relations would that be? The first thing that jumps out about our clinical literature is that the clinical part of it, the part that describes what the participants are actually doing, saying, thinking and feeling, is at least 90% about the patient, at most 10% describes the therapist in a similar way. As will be seen again when Lukes (2005) is discussed, Said (1979, 1994) would see this inequality as clear evidence for the presence of a dominated class and a significant power differential (the Relational and Intersubjective schools demonstrate less of an inequality in their clinical literature and in fact do struggle with it, albeit without naming it). With the exception of a few books (Leuzinger-Bohleber & Target, 2001; Tessman, 2003; Yalom, 1996; Yalom & Elkin, 1974) and a recent popular television series, there has been little focus in our literature on the other therapeutic partner, that is, us.

Case Illustrations

To illustrate the various points of Said's and Foucault's theses and what they tell us about our power relations with our patients, I am going to offer three clinical vignettes: one drawn from, for lack of a better term, the orthodox Freudian literature, one from the relational literature, and one from my own practice.[15] I am going to describe this material in ways that explicitly honor the premise I share with Said (1979, 1994), Foucault (1980, 2000), and, as we shall see later, Lukes (2005), that no knowledge or text can exist independently from the circumstances attendant to its creation or subsequent usage. Try not to treat this as an exercise in comparing metapsychologies or clinical theories of cure, but rather pay attention to the nature and structure of the texts and what they say about how the therapist views her role and her patient's role in the therapeutic situation. This is not a discussion of cases, of relative therapeutic efficacy, theory, or technique; it is a study of three texts and what the writing reveals about the *dispositifs* of the writers. The texts tell us what the writers deem necessary to tell us. We are interested in why it is necessary for them to tell us these things, how they go about the telling, and what we can learn about them from what they do not tell us. In the first

15 For purposes of confidentiality, all of my case material, presented as illustrations not evidence, will consist of composites drawn from clinical work.

vignette (Abend, Porder, & Willick, 1983), the authors have 16 pages, more than ample room to include all they might find necessary.

Let me make some epistemological observations about this enterprise. By presenting you with these vignettes, I am embedding them in my text and thus their meaning is changed for you; it is different from the subjective meaning they would have had if you happened upon them in the course of your own reading. While I am presenting them as illustrations, I am doing so because I want to convince you that there exists an inevitable power differential between patient and therapist that appears in the text;[16] in clinical practice such differentials can only be addressed and dealt with, they can never be eradicated.

The first two vignettes are too long to quote in their entirety; I have inevitably chosen parts of them to illustrate the points I am trying to make. There is then an inevitable subjectivity in my text, in my accounts of the authors' texts. In each case, the author of the vignette has his own political (read power) reasons for presenting it. Finally, this text and the publications from which the vignettes are taken support each therapist as a member of a network of clinicians, a network of *savoir* that serves to reinforce the dominant position of the therapist vis-à-vis the patient (who is only an unknowing member of that network and has none of his own).

Case One

This first vignette is taken from *Borderline Patients: Psychoanalytic Perspectives* (Abend et al., 1983). At the beginning of this book, we are told that it is a monograph of the Kris Study Group of the New York Psychoanalytic Institute (NYPI). In 1983, Freudian orthodoxy was the predominant theoretical model present in American Psychoanalytic Association (APsaA) institutes and the NYPI probably still stood at its theoretical epicenter. The Kris Study Group in turn stood at *its* theoretical center. The authors make use of this in their introduction to claim standing for themselves and, in describing their process, to establish their scholarly credentials. Their goal is to examine the borderline concept with particular reference to the work of Otto Kernberg (then much in vogue). They disclose that some members were predisposed to discard the concept and none predisposed to accept it. I remember

16 This is an unusual statement to find in an analytic text. The motivation is not at all unusual; it is, after all, what we all do in such writing. What is unusual is that I am making it explicit.

reading the book when it first came out with some sense (speaking only for myself) that the game was, nevertheless, rigged.[17]

The authors spend 55 pages, roughly 20% of the book, presenting material taken from four analytic cases[18] suggesting they believed that such presentations had evidential rather than mere illustrative standing. They describe the case material as presented in a "*descriptive*" (italics as quoted) and "phenomenological" (p. 19) manner. All this is relevant as a deconstruction of the matrix in which it is to be presented, the reasons for the creation of this knowledge. The whole, case and matrix, are then embedded in *my* text and become a new knowledge created for my own purposes.[19]

We are introduced to Miss W, an unmarried research assistant who "complained of recurrent depressive periods, of an increased use of non-prescription drugs to help her sleep and lift her spirits, of poor relationships with men, and of a fear of being hurt by others" (Abend et al., 1983, p. 34). She was lonely, ate compulsively, and only much later told her analyst (who remains genderless for several pages) of her bulimia. She speaks superficially and sees herself and women generally as inferior to men. Her father began leaving her mother periodically; at some point he left for good. When she was four and a half, he left and she was told she cried for days. Her mother told her that she was supposed to have been a boy; she believed in her father's disappointment and that it might have contributed to the break-up of the marriage.

We are told that the patient was "a tall, sandy haired, attractive, moderately overweight young woman who dressed casually and was smiling and pleasing during the initial interviews" (Abend et al., 1983, p. 67). Once on the couch, she felt great pressure to tell everything,

17 In the interests of full disclosure (although I bring my own agenda to this discussion of the case material, often at considerable odds with theirs) my own conclusions about the term *borderline* are similar to theirs: that it is amorphous, ontologically unstable, and not of great clinical value.

18 The cases were all treated by relatively inexperienced candidates in supervision. Copious written notes were thus available. This knowledge was created for a different purpose, the supervisory process, as were the supervisor's notes—a further sub-matrix. The material was then further worked over by being presented in clinical conferences over the years. Then the treating analysts prepared the case summaries for the book. I then condensed the material still further for the purpose of this text. Who can know *where* the poor patient actually is in all of this. That is another reason why I say that this is all really about texts and is very separate from real-world experience.

19 This paragraph may likely seem odd, perhaps even precious. However, its purpose is to make explicit what we usually gloss over when we read analytic texts—that the relationship between what is presented as case material and what actually went on in the consulting room is tenuous at best and driven by the author's motivations. I am also trying to be as forthright about my motivations as possible.

however embarrassing, as if she had lost her privacy. In the instantaneous transference, the strong, G-d-like analyst would rescue her from her crazy father. In the first session, she "hallucinated" his laughing at her. His silence "was seen as cold and critical" (p. 67) and his interpretations made her feel she was a "faker" (her word); everything she said was worthless. She would see herself and her analyst as alternatively exalted or degraded, polar views that could reverse from moment to moment. She nevertheless brought in relevant material and dreams that *she* (italics mine) could work with "whenever the state of the transference permitted" (p. 68).

During the first year, a sadomasochistic paternal transference became intense; the analyst became a "Nazi" jailor and then roles reversed. She was also by turns seductive. The analyst interpreted a repetition of feelings about her father. There were episodes of explosive rage. Nighttime phone calls demanding answers or relief from panic were common. The patient threatened to quit or transfer. The only effective interpretation was that she was torturing her analyst much as her father had done to her (no historical material is presented to substantiate this). She was defiant and withholding around separations.

During the second year, *whatever work was done* involved the above transference and her rage at genital differences. "Her behavior in the analysis *deteriorated* further" (Abend et al., 1983, p. 69, italics added). She took pleasure in sullen silences, threatening to leave, belittling her analyst and making many phone calls "openly to annoy him" (p. 69). "Attempts to interpret this behavior failed, and the telephone calls were finally *interdicted*" (p. 69, italics added). She felt "butchered" and "castrated."

The analysis continued in this manner into the third year. What is described as primal scene material appeared. We are introduced to her loving relationship with a married girlfriend, who gave birth to a daughter; she is intensely jealous and fantasizes nursing like the baby. The girlfriend announces that she is leaving her husband and moving to another city. There is rage at the girlfriend, remembered fears that her mother would leave her and rage at her analyst for not stopping this.

We are told that despite this regressive state, the patient's life outside of the analysis matures while her transference neurosis became even more bitter. "Her bitter isolation remained refractory to any intervention" (Abend et al., 1983, p. 71), she repeatedly threatened to change analysts and, after months of apparent stalemate, "the analyst began to consider this threat a reality and raised the question of a consultation" (p. 71). The patient was shocked that the "analyst could give her up and stop trying to control her" (p. 71). We are told that the analyst's countertransference feelings reached "a crescendo" that contributed to the consultation. From the start, he had felt bullied and buffeted by her feelings. Her behavior provoked his anger about which he felt guilty.[20] This led to rescue fantasies, seeing the analysis through, etc. He would soon be attacked and the cycle would begin again. "There was no question that the analyst was thus experiencing what the patient had felt at the hands of her father" (p. 72).[21]

"The transference crisis finally softened" (Abend et al., 1983, p. 72) and a critical maternal transference developed, in which the analyst was cold, critical, judgmental, and frightening. He (she?) in fantasy could be a maniac who would murder her. A primal scene is reconstructed and, "with the re-working of the Oedipal material, her life began to change even more" (p. 73). I will break off here. The analysis continued stormily around infantile sexual material, a planned termination took place (we are told nothing about it), and the analyst describes it as a qualified success.

Following Polsby (1963/1980), I would for our purposes here define a power relation as existing when an individual or group has influence and control over another. In this case illustration the two members of the therapeutic dyad are members of subordinated groups; Miss W is a patient and a control case, and Dr.? (he doesn't get a designation and is genderless for half of the material) is a psychoanalytic candidate early in his training and under supervision. Dr.? is subject to the control and influence of his supervisor and his institute; Miss W is subject to him and through him to his institute. She had to submit to a variety of unpleasant procedures, interviews, possibly in the context of case conferences, and suchlike; such submission was a requirement of being chosen.[22]

But what about the *text*? First, it styles itself implicitly as objective. It says in effect that there is a knowable reality to the case and to the activities of the participants and this is it. It meets our earlier test; 13 pages are about the patient, one *paragraph* is about the analyst. Beyond the paragraph describing how the analyst got very angry and guilty about the

20 It is unclear why these feelings are considered to be countertransference.

21 It should be noted that nowhere in the history is any "kernel of truth" concerning the origins of the patient's transference experiences to be found, and an iatrogenic component cannot be ruled out.

22 I am describing procedures so familiar to us that we tend to forget about them. Noting them offers a partial deconstruction that frees them up; it is then possible to consider the effect of these power-relations on the participants and how they might feel about their situation.

patient and saying he interpreted this or that he is otherwise a cipher, it has been deemed unnecessary to say anything about him. The patient never speaks in the text. It has not been deemed necessary for her to speak, to feel, to talk to us; her voice has been taken away. It is actually her very personhood that has been taken away[23] because it is irrelevant to the purposes of the text, to consider her borderline credentials. It is unnecessary to know what she thinks and feels; she is an object.[24] Yet her presence is voluntary; Foucault (2000) requires this freedom for someone to be truly dominated. (A slave in chains is not free and cannot thus submit to be dominated.) However, the analyst is equally dehumanized. If Miss W cannot speak, he cannot think or question, he only interprets and suffers, all in the third person. As in any power relation, the dominant member is just as bound by it as is the submissive one. This is as close to a hermeneutic circle as psychoanalysis can get. As a whole, although describing intense feelings and events, the text somehow feels dead and lifeless, there is no humanity to it.

The text does include two central transactions about power that are both central to it, yet go unnoticed by its author and his colleagues. The patient misbehaves by repeatedly telephoning the analyst to "annoy" him. After interpretation fails, "they [the calls] were finally interdicted" (Abend et al., 1983, p. 69). The problem with the text here is in what the *choice* of wording reveals: to interdict, which carries meanings of to both authoritatively forbid and to destroy (*Merriam-Webster's Collegiate Dictionary*, 2004, p. 652). Make no mistake, this is power language and the patient understands it *perfectly*, even if the analyst does not, she says that she feels "butchered" and "castrated" (Abend et al., 1983, p. 69).

In the second power transaction the patient became "even more bitter and negativistic" (p. 71). She is grieving, we are told, the loss of her friend. She is "refractory to any intervention" (p. 71) and threatens to change analysts. In this "apparent stalemate" (p. 71), the analyst suggests a consultation. Again, the patient understands perfectly, she "is incredulous that her analyst could give her up and could stop trying to 'control' her" (p. 71). We are next told of the analyst's anger and that "the transference crisis [then] finally softened" (p. 72). In terms of the power

23 Only the fragment, "a tall, sandy-haired, attractive, moderately overweight young woman" (Abend et al., 1983, p. 67), survives.

24 In particular, she never speaks about herself, about what she makes of her predicament, the analysis, and how she understands herself. In other words, the text does not treat her as a participant in her own analysis, i.e., the search for meaning that is at the core of every analysis and distinguishes it from other therapeutic endeavors.

dynamics of this particular analytic couple, Miss W heard the threat and began behaving herself.

These observations could easily be described as unfair; perhaps they are to a degree. All of the participants, analyst, patient, supervisor, study group members, are, as much as I am able to tell from the text, sincere, honest people—the professionals experienced, well-trained, and seeking the best outcomes for the multiple agendas that the text sets forth. It is rather that, in deconstructing it, another level of meaning is revealed, one that the participants are by and large unaware of. It is this other level of meaning, I would contend, not necessarily what the patient brings to the encounter, that often makes a particular therapeutic situation so problematic or untenable.

Case Two

The second case vignette is drawn from *Unformulated Experience: From Dissociation to Imagination in Psychoanalysis* (Stern, 1997). Stern defines the latter as "the uninterpreted form of those raw materials of conscious, reflective experience that may eventually be assigned verbal interpretations and thereby brought into articulate form" (p. 37). It follows from this concept that meaning is constantly being created anew (*reformulated* might be a better term) rather than already there, waiting around to be discovered or rediscovered as it is in Freud's metapsychology. This amounts to a theory of therapeutic action. The book presents Stern's personal take on Relational psychoanalysis. The discussion of this is beyond our scope here except insofar as it informs our study of texts, how they are structured, and what power relations issues their structure reveals.

Stern offers a number of clinical vignettes throughout the book to illustrate the concepts he is discussing. They all manifest the same textual properties and it was not difficult to choose one that was representative. Stern tends to structure his case vignettes in more or less the same way; an interaction between him and his patient is taking place, a problem arises, he thinks and feels his way through it and then brings the patient on board. This particular vignette is meant to illustrate the "analyst's unformulated experience of the patient" (p. 185), the title of the chapter. However, Stern has a further agenda in the chapter. He wants to describe what he calls the two possible attitudes towards the patient, the autocentric and the allocentric, that I would rather term the two ways of being with the patient. Citing Schachtel (1959), Stern describes the autocentric in the clinical setting as experiencing the patient in a subjective, routinized way, being able to step outside of the clinical relationship and look at the behavior of the two participants, while the allocentric involves experiential embeddedness, curiosity, and openness.

Stern (1997) tells us about a "young professional man" (p. 197), early in treatment who tells him that he will not be coming to the next session. He has the day off, he explains, and wants to have it completely off, without responsibilities. He is matter-of-fact about it and assumes that he will be charged for the missed session. Stern says that his "immediate response was frustration and annoyance" (p. 197). He goes on to say that he inquired "routinely" (by which I construe that his heart wasn't in it and that he was behaving autocentrically) about what the patient liked about having no responsibilities and why the therapy was experienced as an obligation. However, Stern thinks the real issue is about why the patient feels oppressed by him and why he can't think of a non-adversarial way to bring this up. Whenever Stern has brought it up, the patient has broken off the discourse, becoming "overtly compliant but secretly sullen" (p. 197). He was oppressed by Stern's inquiry into his feeling oppressed. Stern's experience was of a micro-stalemate; he describes his reaction at this point as autocentric; he felt the patient would not let him do his job.

Stern (1997) posits that his position remains autocentric until he formulates (again, I would say reformulates) the experience; then it becomes allocentric. Schachtel (1959) writes, and Stern quotes him here, that the autocentric mode provides valuable information about the patient so long as it can also be treated allocentrically. The therapeutic situation "would probably have spiraled" (p. 198) (out of control) had he not been able to ask himself why he had not simply accepted the patient's lead and awaited further developments. Instead, he had been attached to a particular outcome: "I wanted the patient to come to that session," Stern says. "Actually, I realized, it was not only the idea of missing the session that had annoyed me, it was the matter-of-fact tone of the patient's voice" (p. 198); it was *insistently* matter-of-fact. Stern saw it as setting him up; he could not question without oppressing. He avoided direct questioning, but "apparently" resented the patient's control over him. He responded to the "challenge," and *became* the oppressor, "a silent power struggle seemed to be taking place" (p. 198).

Stern (1997) then asks the patient if he was feeling "pushed around," offering "some" (p. 198) of the above reflections as the reason for asking. The patient is "somewhat wary" about his intentions, but said he was feeling "pushed around" (p. 199), and volunteers that this had happened before and that at such times he felt that Stern was less responsive to him. The patient says he had never considered that he had some role in evoking Stern's reaction. Stern asks if the patient could remember anything from the previous hour that made him feel that Stern was "lording it over him" (p. 199). The patient does remember something, "hardly 'lording' . . . but that was the word [Stern] had used with him" (p. 199).

The vignette concludes with "further questions were raised" (Stern, 1997, p. 199). How might he have attempted to control the patient? Was the patient's collaboration real or was it simply another, subtler, version of the oppressor–oppressed relationship? Was he eager not to disappoint Stern, so he tried to please him and hated himself for doing so? Stern is not explicit about whether these questions were raised with the patient or reserved for his own reflections. This is a rather important distinction. He suggests the latter when he says, "All of these possibilities were plausible, given what I knew about the patient, and, eventually I could feel that I knew whether they were true" (p. 199). Stern ends with the observation that such transactions are repeated over and over again, but each such resolution leads both parties to an increasing freedom of articulation as the therapy progresses.

The first, striking observation is how different this text is from that of Case One. It is at once clear that it is drawn from the Relational literature, while the other is from that of Freudian orthodoxy. A premise that is implicit in such a comparison of the rules governing the formulation of clinical texts is that we can know a case better through a micro-analysis of how patient and therapist interact, think, and feel about each other than we can through a lengthy description of events.[25] Much of the vignette consists of Stern's (1997) thoughts and feelings about his patient, "a young professional man" (p. 197), and his quite noble struggles to understand their interaction at a particular point in the treatment. Stern does not name him, a convention he seems to follow in his case writing. However, if he began, for example, with "John, a young professional man . . ." we would of course know that John was not his real name. But he would seem more human; since we know Stern's name, the absence of a name makes the patient less so.

Stern (1997) does not offer us words (as Abend et al., 1983, also do not), none of the patient's and only two remarks of his own—to wit, he

25 One might argue that the length of the text is determined by the author's purpose in each case were it not for the fact that Stern has never seen the need to offer a lengthy descriptive account in his writings. Abend et al. (1983), however, believe that providing such lengthy accounts is a tool for claiming epistemological standing; evidence of a very different *dispositif.*

asks the patient if he felt "pushed around" (p. 198) and if he felt Stern was "lording it over him" (p. 199). These are both unusually powerful and the whole "lording" transaction described above is never explained. It does say something about Stern, but we are left to only guess at its connection to unacknowledged power. We could know both Stern and his patient better if we knew their words (we knew Miss W and *her* analyst not at all) and might have been able to formulate answers to the questions Stern raises towards the end of the vignette.

The purpose of the vignette is to illustrate shifts in the analyst between autocentric and allocentric knowing of the patient. In this context, Stern does a very strange thing. He has already discussed these terms in the material immediately preceding the vignette and cited their origins in Schachtel's (1959) seminal work. Stern goes on to cite him again for much the same reasons, as part of the case material. Why does he do this? The point he quotes Schachtel as making could as easily have been included in the original pre-case discussion. It appears here as some kind of additional claim of standing that Stern is making for his position and that such additional claims are necessary.

There are two aspects to the vignette in which we can observe the presence of an unacknowledged power differential. The first is that Stern does not grant the patient the option of also moving into an autocentric position, of also initiating a process whereby he steps outside to observe the therapy and himself. (It is not that Stern does not know that patients do this; I'm quite sure he does. It is the meaning of his not mentioning it in the text that indicates the differential.)

The second has to do with a statement that Stern makes after raising a series of questions about the patient's motivations, whether or not he was truly collaborating, or still feeling oppressed, etc. that he could not then answer. He says, "eventually I could feel that I knew whether they were true" (p. 199). Such an absolute claim is never about knowledge; it is always about power.[26] Stern is sensitive to the problem of power relations in the therapeutic situation, however he limits his concern to what he describes as "the unconscious workings of power" (p. 82) that compromise the ideal of "egalitarianism." The latter is a complex term that refers to a spirit of equality, but it is not the same as saying the participants are equal. Unconscious or otherwise, power is power

26 I could not imagine making such a claim myself and, in discussing a patient elsewhere (Leffert, 2008), raise similar questions and go to some pains to stress that they are unanswerable. Such certainty is never possible; some future event can always come along and show us just how wrong we were.

(Leffert, 2010a) and such an ideal is a false one; the therapeutic relationship is not equal and does not approach equality. It is perhaps unnecessary to repeat that this has been a critique of Stern's text, *not* his work. The work comes through as both sensitive and thoughtful, very much in the patient's interest.

Case Three

I crafted this text, a composite from my own work, to illustrate the power differentials inevitably present in any treatment situation and how one might acknowledge and manage instances of them as they come up. However, I believe that the differential always remains. Shanaz is an Irani family-practice resident who recently called for an appointment. She had gotten my name from a former therapist, an analyst in the Midwest. In the call, she mentioned depression and concern about whether her insurance would cover her seeing me. She subsequently cancelled, then remade the appointment around this issue.

I practice at home; my office is quite separate from the rest of the house and a secluded patio serves as my waiting room. I gave Shanaz directions to the patio that have rarely proved problematic, only to get a call from her at the time of the appointment that she had found herself at the back of the house rather than the front. I thought to walk out to meet her. I usually introduce myself and hold out my hand at a first meeting, but she walked with her head down, turned slightly away from me, without making eye contact. She seemed vulnerable to me, small and fragile. I thought, "She's having trouble with this" and, sharing her silence, showed her into my office.

This assessment governed my approach to her throughout the session. I did not offer any comment about how she presented herself; I did not *know* anything to say about it, but more importantly, did not want to begin the relationship by claiming the powerful role of interpreter. *She*, not I, knew more about how she was feeling. She told me that she felt depressed and had trouble doing her work; it went slowly she said and took far more time than it should, particularly preparing to take the National Board exam. She also told me that she had tried continuing with her original therapist by phone, but stopped after a year, adding "It was not enough."

She had seen a therapist here for some months, but ended it because "she was too friendly." I heard friendly in the sense of not attending to meaning and not allowing her enough space and said, "Not like your therapist in Chicago," to which she nodded. She spoke at times haltingly. She seemed to be telling me she was not getting what she needed, that it was too little, then too much. I felt this as her plight, but to empathize seemed again like an intrusion, and a more direct comment could only amount to telling her she was too picky. I felt like she was establishing a situation in which I could not do very much and I decided to just be with this rather than *make* something happen.

She described her parents, also haltingly, in an insightful way that made them come alive and then, seeming to take stock of the session up until then, said, a bit anxiously "I really haven't been able to tell you very much" (I'm not doing the work here either). Feeling quite the opposite to be the case, I spontaneously contradicted her, saying, "I thought you told me quite a lot and maybe you surprised yourself and were a little anxious." She accepted this, but went on to talk more about insurance problems, obstacles to doing therapy (although she had *been* in therapy here under the same financial circumstances). She then looked directly at me and said, "I have never been in therapy with a man, never thought of it." And then, after a pause, "There is no *recognition*." This got my attention at once. What was she really saying to me? I thought of the French *connaissance*. Did she know the word and was she in effect translating it? I would eventually want to talk more about this "recognition" and its absence with a man, but, again, not now. I nodded my understanding and said that if someone tells me they want to see a woman therapist, I don't question it (of course there *are* questions, but in such a context they inevitably become power transactions and such a choice is the patient's to make) but take it at face value.

She asked for the name of a woman therapist and I gave it to her. It turned out it was someone she had seen/talked to. "There was no [fit]." I had been feeling that this was probably not going to "go" as a therapy and that there wasn't anything that could or *should* be done about it.[27] I did not attempt to solve this as a problem or take it up with the patient. Her ambivalence, if that's what it was, was not approachable as such. She then told me that what caused her the most trouble (with therapists) was that they made cultural assumptions rather than tried to find out about her. I again spontaneously told her that I was indeed interested in how she had dealt with her cultural passage, but that the passage was not

27 I know that other therapists feel differently about this (on one occasion I was even on the receiving end of it) and start making interpretations. But you see, they are not really interpretations but simply power moves aimed at limiting the patient's autonomy and exacting compliance.

her. She seemed to consider this. The session ended with a need to further clarify her insurance situation. She told me not to expect to hear from her for several days because she would be on call and would not have time to look into the matter. I did not expect to hear from her again and regretted it; I was interested in working with her. To my surprise, she called again a week later. She told me about the insurance and asked if a reduced fee was a possibility. I told her what I could do and she asked again for time to think about it.

This text was not written to display my work as an analyst or showcase my writing abilities. It is, of course, clinically unsatisfying. Its purpose is twofold: to demonstrate how one navigates power transactions when one is aware of them and to illustrate the limits of knowability present in any therapeutic situation to a greater or lesser extent. It is worse than useless to fill in the blanks and navigation does not imply removal. Whenever someone comes to us as a patient, a power differential exists and continues to exist. I describe what I and the patient said and what I thought; I say nothing about what the patient thought because, in this session, I don't know what she was thinking; it would only be conjecture. The vignette also illustrates what I did *not* do. I did not become technically active. I had nothing to act *on*. To act would have involved a shift in goals from a therapeutic goal to a power relations goal, to pressure this at best ambivalent, putative patient into "therapy" by whatever means possible. All that could be done therapeutically in this particular first session is to try to avoid interactions that dominate, and to treat the power as a subject of reflection. Nor is there any guarantee of being completely successful in carrying out even this limited agenda. The outcome of this encounter is really for the patient to judge. Lukes' (2005) work will serve to make this clearer and to clarify more about why I took this kind of a stance and what exactly I wanted to avoid.

Lukes on Power

I have already discussed in some detail (Leffert, 2010a, especially chapter 7) how Lukes' study of power bears on the understanding of the behavior of organizations in general and of psychoanalytic organizations in particular. At first glance, power relations in the intimacy of the therapeutic situation seem subtler and more manageable, or even nonexistent, but that is only at first glance. It is that very intimacy that makes power more dangerous and its expression more direct. Rather than discuss Lukes' ideas in a discrete block, I will discuss them in the context of those areas present in any therapeutic situation that carry with them the risk of turning a therapeutic relationship into one of dominance and submission.

Lukes (2005) offers what he calls a three-dimensional theory of power that describes the behavior and relations of ruling social elites and dominated groups. His ideas are applicable to all relationships, among them those of therapist and patient. As therapists and psychoanalysts, we are not at all accustomed to thinking about our relationships with our patients in terms of power and find the idea of the latter representing a dominated class both ridiculous and abhorrent.

In applying Said's (1979, 1994, 2001a, 1996/2001b) work to clinical material written for publication, careful textual analysis revealed considerable evidence of power relations in the way the case illustrations were structured. Relational analysts (e.g., Elliott & Spezzano, 1996; Greenberg, 1999, 2001; Hoffman, 1996, 1998; Mitchell, 1998; Stern, 1997) are variously aware of the risks of the dominating potential of power in the therapeutic situation. Some (e.g., Stern) tend to see them as largely unconscious on the part of the analyst. They often formulate them in terms of the analyst's authority (e.g., Hoffman), which shifts the discussion away from the harsher, naked, term *power*.

It is frequently argued that the shift to a Relational perspective brings with it a lessening of the dangers of power in the therapeutic setting.[28] However, a study of the power relations literature leads one to a less sanguine conclusion. (Intersubjective authors do not appear to have considered power relations as a dimension of the analytic relationship.)

Lukes' (2005) first dimension follows Dahl (1957, 1958), who posits three tests to determine the presence of a power relationship. Applied to the therapeutic situation they are: 1) the participants must have defined roles, 2) the preferences of one must run counter to those of the other, and 3) one of them must consistently prevail in realizing those preferences. Most therapeutic relationships "fail" this test, but some do not. Bill, a lawyer in his 40s, had had a previous analyst who expected him to schedule his vacations to coincide with his own; he would be charged if he did not do so. The analyst would often not settle on a date until two or three weeks before his proposed annual vacation. Bill's protests were met with silence and *he felt that he could only acquiesce.*[29]

28 An exception to these generalizations is the psychoanalytic literature on gender, feminism, race, and gay and lesbian studies (e.g., Abel, Christian, & Moglen, 1997; Corbett, 2001; Dimen, 2003; Layton, 2000; Walton, 1997).

29 We usually ascribe such behaviors on the part of an analyst to unanalyzed character pathology, but in doing this, we miss the power component that frequently goes on to queer the analysis.

A colleague of mine was notoriously late with all of his patients. He would arrive late to the office and take no breaks between hours. Occasionally, he would short a patient's time to get back on schedule. He limited his responses to patients' complaints to genetic interpretations or silence; the patients felt they had no choice but to submit. His analytic results were always limited and his patients often sought re-analyses, partly, I think, to deal with the unnamed power relations.

Lukes then takes up the question of why someone accepts such a subordinate position and cites Tilly's (1991) checklist of possible reasons for their acquiescence. All of these can be found in analytic relationships:

1. The premise is false; patients often rebel in such situations, but in covert ways.
2. The patient gets things that make acquiescing worth it most of the time.
3. The patient has some other valued end (such as occurs in a training analysis) that leads him to accept a situation that exploits or oppresses him.
4. As a result of suppression or the unavailability of alternate ways of viewing a therapeutic situation, a patient may be unaware of her true interests.
5. Inertia holds the patient in place.

Lukes (2005) cites Bachrach and Baratz (1970) for the second dimension of power. In it, *A* limits the subjects of discourse with *B* to those that are acceptable to her. She does so by creating barriers to unacceptable discourse through overtly or covertly setting agendas and creating or modifying language that directs or limits how a conflict in a relationship may be identified or discussed. Covertly teaching a patient metapsychology is but one tool for doing so. Silence is another. A third is the use of language to create and confer titles upon *A* that make *B* believe that it is really in his interest to acquiesce to *A*.

There is a growing body of neurocognitive evidence that the shaping of discourse can produce changes in the brain (Doidge, 2007) that alter its perceptions and how it reacts to values, ideas, and cognitive information.[30] A simple analytic example is when the patient asks a question

30 This concept, neuroplasticity, is one of the hottest areas of research in the neurosciences. It refers to the ability of the nervous system to structurally change itself as a result of experience.

only to be greeted by the analyst's silence. After a couple of repetitions of such a narcissistic injury, the patient stops asking; he still covertly wants to ask and thinks the analyst unfair or controlling, but he doesn't. After a while, this acquiescence is no longer perceived and the patient forgets about asking questions. The way to prevent such a power transaction from becoming rooted in an analysis is for the analyst never to use silence in this way, to always say something, even if it is limited to a statement that she doesn't think answering such a question would be productive or useful.

Lukes (2005) criticizes these first two dimensions for defining power as existing only in its exercise and for requiring the existence of observable conflict. These points led him to posit a third dimension, "*A* may exercise power over *B* by getting him to do what he does not want to do, but he also exercises power over him by influencing, shaping or determining his very wants" (p. 27). It is seldom considered how *A* becomes as much a prisoner of the power relationship as is *B*. An aspect of the problem not considered by Lukes is how wants may be shaped through the application of language, narrative, and metanarrative generationally or multigenerationally, that then bias how the present is experienced.

Psychoanalysts are at particular risk due to the nature of our training with its accompanying *training* analysis that imparts a *conviction of legitimacy* to our thinking and to our approach to patients. Psychoanalytic education is further burdened by *its* multigenerational loading with theoretical and historical metanarrative. Political warfare based on theoretical differences has become a part of institute cultures (Leffert, 2010a) and provides independent corroboration of the presence of self-proclaimed elitism. This elitism easily becomes problematic in the clinical setting (Kirsner, 2009).

Many therapists and analysts view concerns about the presence of dominating power in therapeutic relationships with skepticism, believing them to be overly alarmist. Their argument would go something like this: We are aware of such concerns, but they don't apply to us. We always treat the patient with respect and carefully monitor our countertransference to make certain that such dominance doesn't occur. However, other analysts are cognizant of the problem posed by power.

Greenberg (1999), for example, comments that "temptation and restraint are built into the analytic relationship" (p. 39). He observes that "it can be a small step from saying that authority is granted in the transference to saying that the patient is submitting to the analyst passively or masochistically . . . Analytic authority—and analysis itself—can come to look like a collusive arrangement worked out by a needy patient and a power-mad analyst" (p. 28). Greenberg goes on to suggest that the analyst's embedding in her professional community exerts a mitigating effect on potential power relations issues, but expresses some doubt concerning this hypothesis; he does not consider the possibility that the community may implicitly collude with the analyst and constitute a *source* of the power relations problem. Even more problematic for us as analysts is Lukes' (2005) observation that "power is real and effective in a remarkable variety of ways, some of them indirect and some hidden, and that, indeed, is at its most effective when least accessible to observation, to actors and observers alike" (p. 64). We all too easily remain unaware of exerting dominating power on a patient when we are doing so.

No such discussion can be complete without taking up the possibilities of legitimate power. Lukes (2005) follows a well-trod path when he talks about power in terms of its strength, productiveness, and transformative capability. As I have discussed elsewhere (Leffert, 2010a), it is very difficult to actually separate productive from dominating power. Lukes further takes the position that there is no domination in hierarchical relations that are consensual and lack a conflict of interest. This would seem to point to a solution to the problem of power in the clinical setting, were it not for the "consensual" requirement.

However, a patient nearly always seeks us out at a time when they or their lives have broken down to a greater or lesser extent. They mostly lack a clear sense of where a treatment will take them or what its costs will be, emotional as well as financial. They may well "get worse" before they get better. Related to the latter point is the question of therapeutic regression (I say question because I believe a case can be made for its constituting an iatrogenic illness of power that will be discussed shortly). It must be questioned whether, based on these issues, informed consent is truly possible at the beginning of a therapy. The problem is rarely acknowledged by psychoanalysts or psychotherapists yet it must be addressed, however imperfectly, in order to avoid future power relations difficulties in a treatment. So informed consent is at best approximate. We know this, but to present all of these caveats will distort the very process of the treatment we are proposing to begin; we can only offer at best an approximation, but we must offer it nonetheless.

An area that has not been much considered in connection to power is that of sexual boundary violations, or, to put it baldly, therapists who abuse their patients sexually. It is surprising how little thought has been given to the role of power and suggestion in these one-sided transactions between therapist and patient. After decades of psychoanalytic denial, a robust literature on boundary violations (e.g., Celenza, 2006; Celenza & Gabbard, 2003; Gabbard, 1994b, 1995; Gabbard & Peltz, 2001) *has* developed that includes an issue of *Psychoanalytic Inquiry* (Lichtenberg, 1997) devoted to the subject. The problem with that literature is that it largely fails to see past the sex and past a consideration of the psychological makeup of the perpetrating therapist. The latter *is* important in addressing issues of organizational response and rehabilitation.

Dimen (2003), for example, is aware of the relationship of sex and power, but she (2011) does not bring it up in a lengthy and courageous paper in which she describes her own experience of such a violation by her then analyst. Sexual boundary violations are a species of rape; they are mostly about *power* in the therapeutic situation, *not* sex.[31] The feminist literature on rape (e.g., Brownmiller, 1993; Buchwald, Fletcher, & Roth, 2005) is quite clear on the preeminence of power relations in sex crimes.

The one paper that I was able to find in the psychoanalytic literature that actually deals with sexual abuse in the therapeutic setting as being largely about power is Wohlberg's (1997) paper in the *Psychoanalytic Inquiry* issue (Lichtenberg, 1997) on sexual boundary violations. In it, Wohlberg describes herself "as a victim of sexual abuse by a psychotherapist ... who has, over the past 8 years, come into contact with several hundred other victims" (p. 329). She herself is not a psychotherapist. As she puts it:

> Extending personal power appears to be a driving force for many abusive therapists. Through a variety of subtle and not-so-subtle manipulations, the abuser undermines the patient's ego strength and widens the gap between controller and controlled. Many victims do research or writing for the therapist's professional papers, run errands, do house or office work, or otherwise serve their abusers. The ultimate measure and acknowledgement of the therapist's power and control is sexual servitude.
>
> (pp. 336–337)

Wohlberg's paper is discussed by other participants in this issue of *Psychoanalytic Inquiry* (Lichtenberg, 1997), who are impressed (as am I) by her courage, but do not consider the power relations abuse that has gone so awry. After that, Wohlberg goes uncited until Pinsky's (2011) recent paper. She describes Wohlberg's discussion of power at some

31 Minnesota understood this in the 1990s and prosecutes therapist–patient sex as a felony, first-degree assault.

length, but ultimately backs away from it, calling the sexual abuse of patients "failures in ethical conduct" (p. 364). Nowhere in the psychoanalytic literature on the subject is there *any* consideration of the interdisciplinary literature on power that I have discussed here.

If the therapeutic situation were not already sufficiently problematic as a power relations venue, it is made more so by the necessary therapeutic praxis of implicitly teaching the patient our own inevitably subjective sense of what constitutes an analytic therapy and how we will both participate in it. But a moment's reflection is required to see that such a necessary education lies irreducibly at the cusp of productive and dominating power. There can be no question of true equality here; the best we can offer is Stern's (1997) "egalitarianism" (p. 82).

Much of the above must assume a thoughtful, well-informed, and well-intentioned therapist. Before offering a series of suggestions for navigating the power relations pitfalls of the therapeutic encounter, we have to discuss the legacy of power handed down to us by that often forgotten psychoanalytic ancestor, clinical hypnosis.

Psychoanalysis, Hypnosis, and Suggestion

We prefer not to dwell very much on the fact that hypnosis and suggestion[32] first led Freud into psychoanalysis. (Gay, 1988, devoted only a few of the more than 800 pages of his biography of Freud to the subjects of hypnosis and suggestion.) The reasons for this must lie, I think, in our discomfort with the fact that a hypnotized patient has given up control of herself to her therapist and is completely under his control as well as in our wish that psychoanalysis should epitomize conscious discourse. The difference between hypnosis and suggestion is one of degree, not kind and, as Gay observed, Freud continued to use suggestion for a number of years after he had abandoned formal hypnosis.

Kihlstrom (2008) views the domains of hypnosis, hypnotizability, and suggestion as intertwined and interreferential. I initially had the thought that looking into the neuroscience of the hypnotic state would be relevant to a discussion of power in the therapeutic setting. In thinking about it, I realized that I was not particularly knowledgeable about clinical hypnosis. In retrospect, I recognize that I was already struggling with another concern. A few days later, it came to me that

32 *The Shorter Oxford English Dictionary* (Trumble, 2007) defines *suggestion* as "the introduction of a belief or impulse into the mind of a subject by words, gestures, etc." (p. 3098).

what I was actually wondering about was the degree to which suggestion was a factor in everyday therapy or analysis, most likely without any awareness on the part of the clinician that he was employing it. If so, it would raise additional concerns about the power relations in the clinical situation. I took my question to my colleague David Wark, a past president of the American Society of Clinical Hypnosis. He coined the term "inadvertent suggestion"[33] (personal communication, February 25, 2010) for what I was talking about and consulted with a number of *his* colleagues, who graciously supplied me with references relevant to my inquiry. (Wark and his colleagues do believe that inadvertent suggestion does exist in the psychotherapies.)

The hypotheses generated by this question would go something like this: Do suggestible and hyper-suggestible states exist in the therapeutic situation, unbeknownst to either participant? And if so, did the therapist self-teach himself how to generate them out of years of patient interaction, or did he learn them, again unconsciously, from his own analyst or supervisors or some combination of all three? If either of these is true, then these techniques would be expected to reside somewhere in the therapist's conceptual-procedural memory[34] (Schacter, 1996). Finally, how do the answers to these questions bear on power relations and the presence of dominating power in the therapeutic situation?

A discussion of these questions falls naturally in two areas: the psychoanalytic writings on suggestion and the writings in the quite separate hypnosis literature on suggestion. We will consider what each has to tell us about psychoanalysis as it is currently practiced.

Psychoanalytic Writing on Hypnosis and Suggestion

There *is* a psychoanalytic literature on hypnosis and suggestion, albeit a sparse one. Freud wrote on hypnosis at a number of points in his career

33 The crucial distinction between inadvertent suggestion and the work of clinical hypnosis is that, in the latter, the patient consents to have a *specific* procedure performed upon him for a *specific* purpose; power relations are not involved.

34 The term *procedural memory* has typically been used to describe learned motor tasks such as bike riding, but there are also many verbal or cognitive procedures, for example how one greets someone, how one orders in a restaurant, or how one goes about writing a text. As is often the case with memory (Leffert, 2010a, especially chapter 4), such common functionality need not represent anatomic commonality. Procedures and memory will be discussed again in the next chapter.

(1905/1953c, 1921/1955c, 1892–1893/1966a, 1891/1966b). Many of his writings on the subject have been cordoned off by the editors of the *Standard Edition* in Volume 1 under the epigraph of "Pre-Psychoanalytic Writings." The other volumes of the *Standard Edition* have headings that simply list one or more of the works they contain; "Writings on Hypnosis" would be comparable. "Pre-Psychoanalytic Writings" seeks to change meaning to get us to think about the text in a particular way (Said, 1994). The wish to create a separation between psychoanalysis and hypnosis, particularly suggestion, although understandable, is entirely arbitrary and we are under no obligation to accept it.

Freud (1891/1966b) was aware, almost from the start, of the potential risks to a patient of the inherent power differential between hypnotist and subject. He considered but ultimately rejected the possibility of introducing a third party into the sessions as a "measure [that] would be desirable to protect the patient from an abuse of hypnosis" (p. 107). He also thought about "the misuse of hypnosis for illegitimate purposes—a possibility that exists for every other therapeutic method" (p. 113). Notably, he did not consider the risks of dominating power inherent to psychoanalysis as well, as he so amply demonstrated in his work with "Dora" (1905 [1901]/1953a).

Silverstein and Silverstein (1990) review Freud's theories of hypnosis beginning with his work of the 1880s and 1890s (Freud, 1892–1893/1966a, 1891/1966b, 1888 [1888–1889]/1966c) and continuing with later works (1905/1953c, 1921/1955c) not usually associated with hypnosis. In the introduction to his translation of Bernheim's *de la Suggestion* (Freud, 1888 [1888–1889]/1966c), Freud accepted with reservations the connection of the hypnotic state to sleep, but in the later works he came to view it as a manifestation of transference. In *Three Essays on the Theory of Sexuality* (1905/1953c), Freud saw hypnosis as resulting from a displacement of a masochistic libidinal fixation, while later, in "Group Psychology and the Analysis of the Ego" (1921/1955c), he considered it the product of desexualized libido.

However, Freud had more to say about suggestion in "Group Psychology and the Analysis of the Ego" (1921/1955c). He posited that "there is no doubt that something exists in us which, when we become aware of signs of an emotion in someone else, tends to make us fall into the same emotion" (p. 89)[35] and that this formed the basis of both

35 We now know that the shared processing system that is responsible for such behavior resides primarily in an area of the right pre-frontal cortex known as the mirror neuron system (MNS). It will be discussed further in chapter 4.

suggestion and group behavior. He considered "suggestion [to be] actually an irreducible, primitive phenomenon, a fundamental fact in the mental life of man" (p. 89). He compared hypnosis to falling in love, both being states that put the object in place of the ego.

There are a number of important points to be made here. Freud had accepted Bernheim's contention that suggestibility was universal, although more pronounced in neurotics (i.e., patients). He discussed hypnosis and suggestion in two of the *Introductory Lectures on Psychoanalysis* (1916–1917/1963): Lecture XXVII on Transference and Lecture XXVIII on Analytic Therapy. In the former, he defined a continuity between suggestibility and transference, in the process asserting a similar continuity between hypnosis and psychoanalysis. In the latter, he takes up the objection that analysis would then be considered a form of direct suggestion. Direct suggestion aims at symptom removal and covering things up, he argues, while psychoanalysis is explorative. Freud posited at that time that the essential function of an analysis was the overcoming of resistance. However, he did *not* abandon suggestion altogether: "the patient has to accomplish [the overcoming of resistance] and the doctor makes this possible for him with the help of suggestion in an *educative* sense" (p. 451).[36] Freud does not say more about "educative suggestion," does not consider its power implications, and leaves us to decide just what sort of animal it is. He continued to write about suggestion and its attendant concerns, although his remedy—"any danger of falsifying the products of a patient's memory by suggestion can be avoided by prudent handling of the technique" (Freud, 1923 [1922]/1955f, p. 251)—strikes me as far too sanguine and assumes far more conscious control of our clinical actions than we have.

Etheredge (1980) appears to be the first to baldly state that the relationship between hypnotist and subject is a power relationship. He looks at the role of the hypnotic state in groups, particularly the power of charismatic figures (he uses Hitler and Mao Tse-tung as examples) to form a group and radically determine their behavior. He also discusses the relationship between hypnotist and subject. He sees both uses of hypnosis as exercises in compliance where power, apparent expertise, and rapport figure prominently. He notes that "hypnotic power relationships in social settings are stronger and more pervasive than is immediately obvious" (p. 430), citing Orne (1970), and observes that "often the hypnotic relationship operates indirectly and implicitly by affecting the symbolic 'construction' of reality, the definition of a

36 What Freud did abandon was the *formal* use of hypnosis in his analytic technique.

situation" (p. 431). (Note the similarity of Etheredge's position on hypnosis to that of Bachrach & Baratz, 1970, and Lukes, 2005, on power.)

Etheredge (1980) does not have much to say about the role of suggestion in the psychoanalytic situation, but his comments and Freud's (1921/1955c) do illuminate some highly problematic aspects of the group behavior of psychoanalysts. Specifically, there is the intense factionalism that plagues our profession that I have written about elsewhere (Leffert, 2010a, especially chapter 7) in which groups coalesce around a charismatic leader. Both leader and group form ostensibly because of a theoretical discovery that is closer to the truth, and they maintain themselves via mutual suggestion. These groups can often be unstable, resulting in further schisms.

Even more destructive are the situations in which a training analyst makes disciples of his or her former and sometimes current analysands, only to lead them into political battles. I think we all know of such situations, but have thought of them more in terms of boundary violations and under the rubric of inadequate personal analyses.

The Hypnosis Literature on Suggestion

There are a number of different ways of classifying suggestion that are relevant to our concerns about its place in therapy and analysis. First, it can be used in either a trance or an awake state. Suggestion can be direct or indirect, depending on whether or not it proceeds from an explicit command. It can also be deemed advertent or inadvertent, depending on whether the therapist was aware that she was employing suggestion. We will be concerned with inadvertent suggestion in an awake state, but must recognize that it can be either indirect or direct. (A direct but inadvertent suggestion is one that a therapist makes without being aware that it represents a form of hypnotic suggestion rendered in the awake state.[37])

As an example of indirect suggestion that I believe to have been inadvertent, we will turn to Zev, a psychologist in his 40s, who consulted me some years after a brief second analysis with Sam Klein, a highly respected psychoanalyst in the Midwest. He mentioned depression in his phone call, but said he wasn't sure that he needed or wanted to begin another therapy. I occasionally encounter such ambivalence and responded as I always do; I invited him to come in for a session so that

37 Direct and indirect hypnotic suggestion (see, for example, Erickson & Rossi, 1980) offered purposefully in the awake state will be discussed in more detail below.

we could think about it together or, if he preferred, he could think about it for a while and call me back if he wanted to proceed. He responded that he would like to make an appointment and so we began to work together.

It turned out that Zev had had cancer of the prostate, had been essentially cured of it but couldn't shake his fear of a recurrence and had become depressed over it. What turned out to be his ambivalence about entering therapy had to do with a fear of being controlled by another man. After a few months, during which he never mentioned it, I decided to ask him about his work with Sam Klein and how it had ended. He told me what then seemed to me a rather strange story. Zev had called Klein, much as he had called me. (This was before the cancer.) He mentioned some questions left over from his first six-year analysis in another city, some anxiety, and the same uncertainty about starting a treatment. He said, "You know it was funny, I never remembered what Sam had said then, something about anxiety, but I felt *compelled* to make an appointment with him and did so. I never forgot that feeling and never brought it up. I didn't like it. When I had the prostatectomy I had to interrupt the analysis and well, I just never went back. I didn't think much about it. I think now that it had to do with that feeling that he had done something to me at the start and I resented it." (Klein had called him once, after the surgery, to ask how he was, but did not call again.)

Zev felt the work had answered some questions he had had about the first analysis, but had otherwise not been helpful. At the time (more than a decade ago), I had no idea what to make of this and could only say something along the lines of this being more of a burden than any analysis could carry and be successful. That first contact, along with his ambivalence and anxiety over being controlled by a man went into the mix that we came to understand—a mix that included an ambivalent, masochistic, homosexual submission to a powerful father. His analysis with me lasted four years and ended in a planned termination; we both felt good about the work. I have rare organizational contacts with him still and he continues to do well. The experience stuck with me and I continued to puzzle over his first contact with Klein and how different an outcome Zev and I had had.

I believe that our understanding of his core issues was correct, but now see his initial contact with Klein as an instance of suggestion. Klein said something to Zev for the explicit purpose of getting him to make the appointment, so it was certainly direct. However, I'm quite certain that he knew nothing about hypnotic suggestion, that the usage was *inadvertent*, and that he would have been horrified at the idea. I suspect that Sam had naively taught himself or been taught to do something like this in handling a first contact with an ambivalent patient. However, of greater concern are those instances of inadvertent suggestion that are not easily detectable because they are indirect.

From the earliest days of clinical hypnosis, Bernheim (1887/1973) worked with patients in the waking as well as the trance state. However, it was Milton Erickson (1980; Erickson & Rossi, 1980) who introduced a wider range of methods for using hypnosis in his clinical work. Among them was indirect suggestion "where the relation between the operator's suggestion and the subject's response is less definite or obvious" (Erickson & Rossi, 1980, p. 452). Of particular relevance to our concerns is his citation of Forel's view that "suggestion is the stronger the more concealed it is" (p. 455). Erickson posited that indirect suggestion brings the subject's life experience and personality into the treatment, that the usual "psychodynamics of learning" (p. 455) are brought into play at the level of the unconscious and that, because it bypasses conscious reflection, can be more effective than direct suggestion.

Erickson (1980) also saw indirect suggestion as initiating an unconscious search on the part of a patient that results in surprise at what she come up with and, in the process, obscures the presence of the suggestion. Particular techniques of indirect suggestion that Erickson talks about are the use of questions that focus, suggest, or reinforce, and paradoxical suggestions or double binds that shock or surprise the patient. This formulation raises issues concerning a therapeutic technique often used by relational analysts, that of "throwing the book away"[38] (e.g., Greenberg, 1991, 1999; Hoffman, 1998; Spezzano, 1998). I would posit that throwing the book away is a species of inadvertent, indirect suggestion and that it exerts power over a patient *without her knowledge or consent.*

Hoorwitz (1989) describes methods of indirect hypnotic induction that also brush up against psychoanalytic technique. In one, a very slow induction is accomplished through the therapist's tuning into the patient's most subtle responses distinguished by "a synchrony between hypnotist and subject" (p. 11). In another, very slow shifts in the therapist's body and motion (that can also be inadvertent) cannot be consciously followed by the patient, but can *unconsciously* attract and

38 Throwing the book away involves a sudden radical change in the therapist's speech or actions, a conscious enactment that acts paradoxically to place the patient in a kind of double bind. The therapist is the therapist but is also not the therapist, and as the patient attempts to relate to this her thinking also is changed and requires new ways of being.

maintain his attention to suggestion. Both could easily operate in the therapeutic situation.

Tasso and Perez (2008) describe what they call everyday suggestibility while Barabasz and Barabasz (2008) refer to "spontaneous hypnosis and its occurrence as a part of everyday life for hypnotizable persons" (p. 338). They also note, "Hypnosis can occur within social contexts such as heterohypnotic inductions with or without the use of the word hypnosis, or spontaneously without any social influence or hypnotic context" (p. 338). Tasso and Perez support this position when they observe that we in fact have very little ability to identify what is influencing our ongoing experience, an observation that is also consistent with the findings of cognitive neuropsychology (Schacter, 1996, 2001).[39] Their view is consistent with the neuropsychological observation that the great majority of mental function takes place out of the realm of awareness (Leffert, 2010a).

The question we now have is a serious one, as it directly impacts our understanding of the therapeutic situation. Simply put, does some significant part of a therapy or analysis take place with the patient in a suggestible hypnotic state, unbeknownst to either participant? If so, as therapists, we certainly need to rethink what we do with our patients. This question has not been studied, but there is relevant literature on two closely related subjects that bears on it: witness testimony and false memory syndrome.

Kihlstrom (2008) has described a hypnotic state called "*interrogative* suggestibility" (p. 26) that manifests itself in the responses of witnesses and patients, among others, to leading questions. He goes on to cite a number of relevant references (Doris, 1991; Eisen, Quas, & Goodman, 2002; Gudjonsson, 1984; Shobe & Kihlstrom, 2002). Schacter (1996) has discussed witness testimony from the perspective of the cognitive neuropsychology literature (Ceci & Bruck, 1993, 1995).

The psychology of eyewitness testimony has hatched a vast literature of interest to the legal, judicial, and law enforcement professions (e.g., Lindsay, Ross, Read, & Toglia, 2006–2007). Researchers working on this problem from these two lines of inquiry, hypnotic suggestion and memory, seem unaware of each other; still another failure of interdisciplinary communication. What is at issue for both of them is the fact that the way someone is questioned about something that has happened to them profoundly affects what they remember, and such questioning can produce permanent changes in memory (Leffert, 2010a, especially

39 Confirmations of these observations from an entirely different source (Nisbett & Wilson, 1977) will be discussed in chapter 7.

chapter 4). Extreme cases can lead to false memory syndrome (Schacter, 1996, 2001), in which *an event that never happened* is remembered; most prominent among these "remembered" events in the therapeutic situation are instances of supposed childhood sexual abuse. It is but a small step to conclude that such suggestion can take place on a much more subtle level in therapeutic discourse, both consciously and unconsciously. It could produce significant distortions, telling the therapist what she wants to hear (that her hypotheses are correct), confirming her theoretical orientation, not telling her what it would be inconvenient for her to know (e.g., that she has just acted out her countertransference), or some combination of these.

So what's an analyst to do? I would posit that inadvertent suggestion is to some extent universal and unavoidable. The first thing is to be aware of the idea of it. There is not much to be done about the parts of it that operate beyond our awareness. However, we can certainly add inadvertent suggestion to the long list of things we think about in connection with the way we talk to our patients, both during the talking and afterwards, once removed. An area of particular concern is that of offering our patients reconstructions, purported descriptions of emotionally charged events they experienced in the distant past. I had already developed some concerns about offering reconstructions when I originally wrote about memory (Leffert, 2010a, especially chapter 4). I found that while some memories can be stable over decades, others—particularly ones involving conflict—can be fragile and subject to permanent damage. I reduced the frequency with which I offered reconstructions as a result of this work but, when the possibility of inadvertent suggestion is considered, I think it is probably best to refrain entirely from using them. This is no doubt a controversial recommendation, one that would upset some therapists more than others. The dictum, *primum non nocere*, would seem to apply.

How Concerns about Power Relations Influence Therapeutic Technique

Let us return briefly to the question of legitimate power. Some psychoanalysts and psychotherapists will say that no problem exists here. They would say something along the lines of "we are competent, well-meaning professionals who bring our expertise to our work and whose authority[40]

40 Put another way, psychoanalysts of all ilks claim cultural authorization for their work with patients.

is a necessary part of the therapeutic situation. We are not interested in dominating anyone and do not do so." This is an appealing argument; furthermore, as we saw, it is one that Lukes (2005) also has made. He argues that "we have seen [many] ways in which power over others can be productive, transformative, authoritative and compatible with dignity" (p. 109). He goes on to state that the problem is not with power at all, but with those whose interests lie in securing compliance with domination. Lukes raises two further questions: "How do the powerful secure the compliance of those they dominate?" (p. 110) and "Who is to say who is dominated and on what basis [do they make that claim]?" (p. 112). It is fair to say that these two sorts of things, productive power and dominating power, do exist and that Lukes' questions are fundamental to the problem; *there is no reliable way to separate them.*

In the subjective interreferential world of the therapeutic relationship in which so much goes on beyond the awareness of either participant, it is even more impossible to separate them. Colleagues have said to me on occasion, "When I'm right, I'm right" and "I'm in charge." Such certainty is both arbitrary and unsustainable and leads to dominating power. However, patients do come to us for our expertise and competent power, and endow us with authority. Much of the time things do seem to turn out well in spite of these considerations (as at other times they do not), but this is really no answer at all. How then, are we to deal with power as it comes up in the therapeutic setting?

What we can do is to think seriously about the problem and think about our technique and the way we structure the analytic situation in the light of our concerns. Some things are simple. With a nod to the intervening 80 years, Ella Sharpe's (1950 [1930]/1968) dictum should be amended to "treat the patient as an informal guest in your office." It should be followed. The nuts and bolts of a therapeutic contract should be made explicit in the first hours. When are the patient's hours, what is the therapist's fee? How will he bill the patient and how and when does he expect to be paid? What is the patient's responsibility for missed sessions? What about holidays and vacations? What about contacts with the therapist between sessions? As long as these matters are arranged in advance and are not exploitative, the therapist can set them up in whichever way he prefers. The patient should be asked if any of this is problematic for him and, if there are difficulties, they should be explored, answered and, where possible, negotiated.

Therapists should avoid any activity that reduces to the exercise of power. A controversial example I would offer is the use of and response to silence in the therapeutic hour. In Case One (Abend et al., 1983) we saw that the patient lapsed into "sullen silences" and was unresponsive to interpretation. There are instances when the patient is deep in silent reverie (Ogden, 1997) that can be sensed intuitively and the appropriate response is a kind of co-reverie. Otherwise, to meet silence with silence is simply to engage in a power struggle; to interpret into the silence, except in the most tentative of ways, becomes a power maneuver aimed at making the patient talk.

The best approach is to check in with the patient a few times during the silence by asking a question or sharing a thought. This invites the patient to talk, it shows you are not abandoning him, but leaves the power in his hands. I have to observe that in 35 years of psychoanalytic practice I have never had patients be silent for more than a few minutes. This leads me to suspect that lengthy silences represent iatrogenic problems of power relations. The interpretations or statements I make to patients are always just a little tentative. I often explicitly couch them in terms of what I think and do not force them on patients. I ask lots of questions; most analysts do not. It is part of the way I help the patient to deconstruct the ways they organize narrative knowledge that may or may not lead to reformulations of it. I ask about inconsistencies; I do not ask leading questions that change narratives, perhaps irreparably. If something about power in the session does not sit well with me, during or, more usually after, I bring it up as a subject of analysis. I also apply these techniques to power moves originating from the patient.

A significant power relations problem revolves around the therapist's use of her particular metapsychology (regardless of flavor) to drive and shape therapeutic technique. Most of us have what amounts to a theoretical belief system comprised of a series of constructs that we have been taught, or learned, in our own professional training or analyses. We then proceed to treat these constructs (structural theory or the Kohutian concept of the self can serve as but two examples) as knowledge. Although they do not possess the truth or standing that is claimed for them and are subject to deconstruction, this need not in itself become a clinical problem.[41] It becomes a clinical problem, and one of dominant power, when the therapist uses metapsychology to drive therapeutic discourse, teaches it to his patient, and, as a result, literally controls what can and can't be thought or talked about.

Merton Gill (1976, 1982, 1994) was, during his lifetime, the most passionate critic of the clinical repercussions of the use of metapsychology

41 For a thorough discussion of the role and nature of metapsychologies, see Leffert (2010a, especially chapters 1 and 2).

in the consulting room, although he lacked the language to frame the problem as I have done in terms of power and epistemology. He and other "pre-postmodern" critics wrote about it in a volume, *Psychology versus Metapsychology* (Gill & Holtzman, 1976), a festschrift in honor of George Klein. Again, many analysts will not see this as a problem. Others, without conscious thought about what they were doing or why they have, over the years, simply dropped metapsychology from their clinical vocabularies. That is what happened to me during the years before I began to study power relations and the nature of psychoanalytic knowledges. Self-reflection on the issue, if a clinician is willing to undertake it, can be of use here.

I have also become very skeptical of the concept of "therapeutic regression." All too often, it represents an iatrogenic regression in the face of the therapist's power and is harmful. Transference is not transference if the therapist is actually behaving as the patient thinks he is; it is power and "interpreting" that leads to iatrogenic regression or pulling back. If transference *is* transference, then it is fair game, as is whatever regression goes along with it.

I do not understand the place of "resistance" in the therapist's clinical vocabulary. It is a power term that invites penetration or grinding away. Patients do protect themselves from knowledge that is frightening, painful, or narcissistically injurious, they do not resist, unless the couch becomes a dentist's chair or an operating table. The therapeutic task then becomes one of helping a patient who is frightened, in pain, or narcissistically injured and dealing with the affects and motivations that ensue.

A power issue that frequently arises involves a patient's need to imbue their analyst with power and authority. The need is to experience, sometimes for the first time, a power figure who is not corrupt. The danger is that the therapist might not be up to the job. She has to recognize that the patient is doing this and needs to accept it—on a temporary and conditional basis. The therapist needs to hold the power entrusted to him and return it to the patient at what he judges to be the appropriate time. I believe that Hoffman (1998) was trying to talk about this when he coined the phrase "the analyst's ironic authority." However, I don't think this quite works for the patient in the allocentric mode, particularly when power is usually deadly serious.

These are preliminary suggestions; there is a great deal of room for further study of power relations and how to approach them in the therapeutic situation. However, if followed they will clear away much of the potential for dominance in the therapeutic setting. The next chapter moves on to consider some of the meat of the clinical encounter, the exploration of memory and how it is linked to a patient's individual ways of acquiring, processing, and using knowledge. A patient's history of memory and of knowledge will be conceptually informed by a study of their archaeologies and genealogies.

2

Archaeology, Genealogy, and Memory

Introduction

Memory, relationships, and feelings, our patients' and our own, are the stuff of therapy and psychoanalysis. As psychoanalysts and psychotherapists, our interest in memory first takes us to autobiographical memory. We are interested in a patient's life history from the start, that is, their nuanced personal narrative, and in different pieces of that narrative as a treatment progresses.

Such memory is not a database but rather a living, breathing, entity in a state of flux. It is not filed, but is rather dynamically constructed and reconstructed, processed and re-processed. Some elements of it are recoverable after decades, while others are lost or changed in moments. It has the properties of a complex, holistic system. It is self-organizing; it manifests both plasticity and stability over time. It is searchable, a process more usually termed recall or retrieval; our "search engines" are the subject of much interest. However, blanks remain; we do not understand, for example, how personal algorithms might be involved in recall. Memory is a contingent property of the mind/brain; it is state-dependent on the immediate circumstances of recall; we can never enter into exactly the same memory twice.

Tulving (1985/2003) terms this memory subsystem *autonoetic*, or self-knowing, that is it relates to autonoetic consciousness. It is not that autobiographical memory is conscious, but rather that its contents can become conscious, sometimes at will, when they are brought into working memory.[42] Tulving termed the ability to bring up such

42 Working memory is that part of the memory system capable of temporarily retaining a limited amount of information in awareness.

memories of the past "mental time travel" (p. 583). Autonoetic memory is also capable of taking us into the future via simulation (Addis, 2008; Leffert, 2010a; Schacter, Addis, & Buckner, 2008). We view one of the tasks of therapy, and an aspect of its therapeutic action, as the expansion of either autobiographical memory or an increase in its searchability.[43] One issue connected with such a formulation is that some psychoanalytic authors (e.g., Fonagy, 1999a; Fonagy & Target, 1996) believe that important memories, like those of early traumas, were never laid down in the first place.

I'm going to begin this chapter with two suggestions. The first is that autobiographical memory does not constitute a discrete, isolated system in the same way that other kinds of memory do not constitute discrete isolated, systems. This view flies in the face of much neuroscientific research, based on ablation, injury, and contemporary imaging technologies that places such declarative memory in the medial temporal lobe of the cerebral cortex (see, for example, Shrager & Squire, 2009; Zola & Squire, 2000). However, my position is consistent with that of other neuroscientists (e.g., Fuster, 1997; Nyberg & Cabeza, 2000) who argue that memory is a distributed property of neural networks residing in far-reaching areas of the brain (Rumelhart & McClelland, 1986).

I would posit that memory can be *talked about* and studied anatomically and cognitively as comprised of subsystems for heuristic purposes, as atomic elements of a holistic system in general systems language (Laszlo, 1972/1996), but these subsystems are not autonomous. Although particular memory functions can be lost through injury or ablation, that does not mean either that they function independently or that all the components necessary for their function reside in some particular anatomical area. In order to talk about autobiographical memory, we will have to talk about memory function across these multiple inseparable memory subsystems.

My second suggestion is that the therapeutic goal of mining autobiographical memory for more data to increase what we and our patients know about ourselves and in theory to increase personal freedom ignores other equally important information about the narrative past stored in these subsystems.

43 It should be noted that I am avoiding such terms as *repression* and an *unconscious* and am instead beginning to offer a phenomenologically based theory of memory informed by postmodernism and the neuroscience. I previously (Leffert, 2010a, especially chapter 5) concluded that both of these terms—*unconscious* and *repression*—signify unsustainable constructs that have little to do with how memory actually works.

Foucault's concepts of archaeology and genealogy (1969 & 1971/1972, 1966/1994) and their epistemic extensions can serve to direct one aspect of an investigation of how these different kinds of memory flesh out autobiography. They also support the general systems approach to human memory. However, where Foucault is talking about an archaeology of science and of knowledge, I want to talk about an archaeology of the self.[44] The resulting linkage of knowledge to the self, which will be discussed more fully in chapter 4, offers a postmodern view of Tulving's (1985/2003) linkage between autonoetic memory and consciousness.

After a discussion of the neuroscience and psychoanalysis of memory, I will offer a case vignette illustrating how different sorts of memory appear in the clinical process and how these ideas bear on understanding and working with it. Following the vignette, these postmodern concepts will be discussed and then applied to the case material to find out whether they further illuminate our understanding of the patient and her memories.

Cognitive neuroscience is currently at the very beginnings of considering its domain in the light of complexity theory (e.g., Gazzaniga, Doron, & Funk, 2009).[45] However, some authors in the cognitive sciences, notably Freeman (1995a, 1999; Freeman & Barrie, 2001; Freeman, Chang, Burke, Rose, & Badler, 1997), Gottman (1991; Gottman, Murray, Swanson, Tyson, & Swanson, 2002/2005), and Zeeman (1987a, 1976/1987b), who are less well known to the bulk of neuroscientists, have been working for decades in the areas of complexity, chaos, and catastrophe theory at high levels of sophistication. Memory is an example of a complex system with some chaotic properties; strange attractors play a major role in its organization and stability. As I have discussed elsewhere (Leffert, 2008), complexity and postmodernism brush up against each other around issues of knowability and that commonality is relevant to the understanding of memory.

Different Kinds of Memory?

While cognitive neuroscientists have classified memory both descriptively and anatomically as a basis for conducting research, they have not worried much about the ontological problems inherent in such

44 *Self* is being used in the sense of the totality of what we each of us are, not in the usual psychoanalytic sense of some sort of cognitive construct or schema.

45 Some authors confuse a modular systems theory with true complexity theory.

taxonomy, nor the fact that it is following the rules of knowledge (the episteme) of the 17th and 18th centuries rather than the 21st. As a result, they construe a number of domains of memory that they treat as an all-inclusive list of identity categories. In contrast to the Aristotelian position that categories are irreducible absolutes, postmodern thought views categories as unstable, artificial entities without epistemological standing, and as such, are appropriate subjects of deconstruction.[46] The mutual interaction between memory domains, the fact that memories are constructed, not stored, and the current status of memory research that provides few clues concerning precisely what *is* stored,[47] all favor Nyberg and Cabeza's (2000) view of memory as a distributed property of the mind/brain. These findings would all seem to argue against offering the descriptively different kinds of memory and the standing of discrete identity categories. In keeping with their position (which I strongly share), Freeman's (1995a) observations about the location of meaning and its biology apply equally to that of memory in a distributed system. He elaborates on this holism:

> The biology of meaning includes the entire brain and body, with the history built by experience into bones, muscles, endocrine glands, and neural connections. A meaningful state is an activity pattern of the nervous system and

46 I have written elsewhere (Leffert, 2007a) that "the term 'deconstruction' requires some explication. On a surface level, it refers to any operation that takes apart a text, breaking it into pieces. An immediate result is to be able to observe what has been added or lost by combining these pieces in the first place. Postmodern critics, however, go beyond this. Deconstruction involves the removal of structure from a text that is seen as opening it to expanded meaning. Derrida (see, for example, Malabou & Derrida, 1999/2004; Norris, 2002) sees deconstruction as a way of freeing a text from structure while preserving particular aspects of meaning, often contrary aspects, lost in the reliance on that structure, which he refers to as *différance* (a term he refused to define that combines a sense of differ and of defer) and otherness. Structure imposes a regulative framework that provides focus but at the price of freezing and narrowing meaning, forfeiting its interplay and plurality, seeking commonality at the cost of *différance*. The unacceptable price of commonality is the loss of the other (*autre*), the *contre allée* or counter path. The other, by its presence, enhances the meaning of the primary text, part of which would be lost without it" (p. 181). Deconstruction serves to at once identify and neutralize meta-narrative, freeing and opening the subject. I have since come to realize that deconstruction also can involve a number of discursive practices employed for specific purposes; among them are the practices of archaeology and genealogy.

47 We understand memory storage on the micro and macro levels. That is, on the level of individual neurons, we understand how information is encoded on a cellular level through changes in synaptic activity and protein and RNA synthesis (Kandel, 2001) and we understand the coming into being of the memory of the wonderful birthday cake mother baked us for our twelfth birthday. However, we know little about the mid-level of the system; what goes on between the neurons and the birthday cake that lights up the functional magnetic resonance image (fMRI).

> body that has a particular focus in the state space of the organism, *not* in the physical space of the brain.
>
> (p. 121, italics added)

Such a general theory of memory can only lessen the importance and standing of distinctions between conscious and unconscious memory, a position that most psychoanalysts would find controversial. It is, however consistent with Klein's (1966, 1976b) critique of metapsychology in which he observed that it is not thought, nor, I would add, memory that is conscious or unconscious, but the self that is or isn't conscious of particular thoughts or memories.

Memory researchers define three discrete long-term memory systems: episodic memory, semantic memory, and procedural memory (Schacter, 1996). Episodic memory refers to the memory of the events that have occurred in one's life; their sum is a personal autobiography. Semantic memory is knowledge memory, the storehouse for what we know. Both forms of memory are declarative or explicit, terms that cognitive neuroscientists use in order to avoid dealing with the concepts of consciousness and the Freudian unconscious and the research problems they would cause. We are able to become conscious of episodic and semantic memories, more or less at will, when these memory systems are functioning normally. (Obviously there are times and reasons for their not functioning "normally.")

The medial temporal lobe of the cerebral cortex has a great deal to do with episodic and semantic memory. This is a more modest claim than that made by some memory researchers (Shrager & Squire, 2009; Zola & Squire, 2000) and derives from an epistemological and ontological critique of the localization and modularization of mental function (Leffert, 2010a, especially chapter 4) that persists to the present day in neuroscience research (e.g., Doidge, 2007; Gazzaniga et al., 2009). Episodic memory is at once more complicated still.

The hippocampus (named for its anatomical resemblance to a sea horse) and surrounding structures serve as a kind of processing/indexing center for episodic memory. Anatomically close to it is another structure, the amygdala, which has much to do with emotion and emotional memory; it influences the functioning of the hippocampus. (These two anatomical structures, along with some others constitute what is called the limbic system.) The hippocampus has widespread afferent and efferent connections, but how and where long-term memory is stored (remember, discrete memories are constructed not stored) and what is done to it that culminates in conscious recollection is not known or understood (Markowitsch, 2000). If the hippocampus is lost through damage or ablation, the ability to form and remember recent events is lost (anterograde and retrograde amnesia), but curiously, complete bilateral damage to it or other limbic structures need not interfere with the recovery of old memories (Markowitsch, 2000).[48] On the other hand, retrograde amnesia for older memories (more than weeks or months old) is functionally heterogeneous and can be produced by lesions in the medial temporal lobe as well as other areas of the forebrain (Mayes, 2000).

Procedural memory is an even messier and more far-flung affair, one whose claim to systemhood or modularity is even more dubious than that of episodic or semantic memory. It is in one respect simpler in that it is by nature implicit[49] or non-declarative; in other words, it is unconscious and requires no explanation of how its contents get *into* consciousness.

The first problem is that procedural memory comes in two flavors, cognitive and motor, that involve different parts of the brain. Procedural memory for motor tasks refers to things like riding a bicycle or golf, and correlates with activity in the cerebellum, the area of the brain responsible for tasks that require smooth and finely tuned motor control. Although originally thought to be engaged exclusively in motor activities, recent evidence has shown the cerebellum to be active in cognitive activities that include memory retrieval (Nyberg & Cabeza, 2000). This has led Doya (2000) to argue that the cerebellum is less about motor or cognitive function per se than it is about a particular kind of learning and information processing that is parsed among its anatomically repeating modules. In a review article, Schacter and colleagues (Schacter, Wagner, & Buckner, 2000) observe that procedural memory is incrementally learned and becomes independent of episodic and semantic memory. As procedures are learned, beginning with activity in a naive state, there is a change in what pathways are observed to be active in serial functional magnetic resonance imaging (fMRI) recorded when the activity is taking place. "This basic observation—alternative pathways are adopted during overlearned performance—appears to be quite general in studies of procedural memory" (p. 637).

Cognitive procedural memory involves learned skills; reading and writing are but two examples. It also involves other habit-like functions

48 This is only to say that the hippocampus is involved in anterograde rather than retrograde functions with respect to old memories. The part of the brain that is essential (necessary, not sufficient) for the retrieval of remote information is the right prefrontal cortex (Ardila, 1984).

49 For a radical and to my mind damning critique of the whole category of implicit memory, see Willingham and Preuss (1995).

that can have affective components, such as the particular nature and quality of a person's object relations and their formation. Shrager and Squire (2009) assign a central function to the striatum, which in turn entails the basal ganglia, in cognitive procedural memory. (Again, I would only go so far as to say that its activity, like that of other structures in other functions, is of importance to procedural memory.) However, given the work of Nyberg and Cabeza (2000) and Doya (2000), it would seem necessary to include the cerebellum in this area of procedural memory as well. Having offered a very concise description of long-term memory from a neuroscience perspective, the next step is to discuss how psychoanalysts and psychotherapists work with memory.

How Psychoanalysts and Psychotherapists Think about Memory

Memory has played a central role in classical psychoanalysis, as it does in the present day. The theory of technique during the *classical age*[50] of psychoanalysis had a twofold focus: the interpretation of transference and the recovery of primal scene memories, their derivatives, or other traumatic memories through the undoing of repression via interpretation and reconstruction. As with so many other aspects of clinical psychoanalysis, it is unclear how many modern-day psychoanalysts still cleave to working with memory primarily in this way.[51]

50 The period of time during which psychoanalytic theory and practice were more or less dominated by Freud's teachings and thoughts. The period dates, of course, from the beginnings of psychoanalysis; its rough endpoint would be a matter of some controversy; arguments could be made for placing it anywhere from the late 1930s to the 1960s.

51 Drawing on a group of authors from multiple neurocognitive disciplines, including psychoanalysis (Klein, 1966, 1970, 1969/1976a, 1976b; Ringo, Doty, Demeter, & Simard, 1994; Schacter, 1996; Tulving, Kapur, Craik, Moscovitch, & Houle, 1994), I have elsewhere (Leffert, 2010a, chapter 5) mounted a radical critique of repression as any sort of singular or discrete process and also concluded that there was no evidence for the existence of any sort of psychoanalytically discrete or dynamic unconscious. Positron Emission Tomography (PET) and fMRI studies demonstrate that being unable to remember something, whether or not it is emotionally charged or significant, correlates with possible action or inaction in one of several separate areas of the brain involving different mental functions. Repression would have to involve a host of different functions that interfere with many different processes. If the term is to be retained, and I can't imagine most psychoanalysts giving it up, it can only be as a recognizable label with phenomenological standing referring to any difficulty in recovering specific contents from episodic or semantic memory. Psychoanalytic technique aimed at the undoing of a repression would thus not seem to have any particular specificity, but rather simply to represent an instance of the generally observed neurocognitive phenomena that talking about associative links to a memory that cannot be recalled is likely to result in its recall (e.g., Neisser & Libby, 2000; Schooler & Eich, 2000).

Autobiographical Memory

A second kind of clinical work with memory involves the expansion of a patient's autobiographical narrative.[52] This would include, but not be limited to, the incorporation of traumatic events that are recalled in isolation as "flash bulb" memories. It is again unclear how many psychoanalysts and psychotherapists view the expansion and fleshing out of personal narrative (as opposed to the recovery of specific memories) as an important aspect of clinical work, but the relative sparseness of literature on the subject would suggest it is not an area that has sparked any great degree of interest. Nonetheless, expansion of autobiographical narrative would be expected to occur naturally as a byproduct of any good therapeutic process. The question, then, really amounts to whether therapists act to support its occurrence or whether it is an aspect of therapeutic action that goes on outside of the therapist's active consideration. We do know that greater access to autobiographical narrative and the analysis of corrupting distortions contained within it would have to be freeing, stabilize the identity of the self (Covington, 1995), and would participate in new character formation (Blos, 1968).

Memory Distortion

It is important to say something about the risk of memory distortion occurring as a result of the therapist's interventions and reconstructions. False memory syndrome is perhaps the most severe, best known, and least understood of these distortions. For the purpose of this discussion, we will limit our considerations of false memories to those instances arising in the therapeutic situation in which a therapist, based on little or no clinical history, informs a patient that s/he is a victim of childhood sexual abuse. After being so informed, some suggestible sub-population of patients take up such ideas and make them a part of their own memory, as if they had been recalled rather than told. This observation has been interpreted by some as a claim that childhood

52 Although autobiographical narratives do contain some ancient memories, they are mostly composed of later versions stitching together new editions of these memories that fluctuate as they are recalled. Testing reveals that these narratives are not continuous; the left cerebral hemisphere provides us with an *experience* of continuity, the absence of which is highly dysphoric. Gazzaniga (1998) has even named the non-specified area that provides this function "the interpreter." Were I to guess, I would expect this function to reside in the left pre-frontal cortex.

sexual abuse is a matter of fantasy rather than fact,[53] which it is not. There is evidence corroborating the accuracy of patients' spontaneous reports of having suffered childhood sexual abuse and the accuracy of some such memories recovered in therapy (Neisser & Libby, 2000). There is also evidence that suggestions made by therapists can lead to patients developing false memories (Ofshe & Watters, 1994).

Neurocognitive research supports these clinical studies. Nader (2009) describes how recent memories show considerable lability; they can be influenced by subsequent events or suggestions. They undergo a process of consolidation that makes them a stable part of long-term memory; it seems likely that the hippocampus is involved in consolidation and it is known that it involves new protein and RNA synthesis. These memories become labile upon recall, and a process of reconsolidation involving a recapitulation of protein synthesis is required to restabilize them. Reconsolidation is a major focus of current neuroscientific memory research. Nader has in effect offered a process model of memory that addresses its two conflicting properties; stability over decades and fragility in the face of external suggestion.

Clinical Recommendations

Two clinical recommendations emerge from what has so far been discussed. In keeping with the work of Blinder (2007) and Covington (1995), the expansion of the autobiographical self through that of autobiographical memory should be at least a background goal of any therapeutic process. As therapists, we maintain autobiographical schemata of our patients. It is well worth remembering that our patients, during the early to middle periods of a treatment, do not necessarily share these schemata; their growing ability to do so is perhaps an index of the progress of a therapy.

The second recommendation follows from the considerable research on the instability of individual memories. It would seem wise to reconsider how much information we put into a patient, either through questioning some of the memories our patients tell us (and not asking questions about others) or by offering reconstructions (that are actually only constructions). These clinical activities not only have the potential for distorting patients' autobiographical memories, but can

53 Freud's abandonment of the seduction hypothesis (1985b) has been understandably used in support of this argument.

also interfere with a future therapy by offering the new therapist a distorted clinical picture. I have elsewhere (Leffert, 2010a) used art restoration as a metaphor for clinical work. To the extent possible (recognizing that this can be quite limited), the therapeutic work we do with a patient should be discretely recognizable or, more likely, capable of becoming so as a new therapy unfolds.

Transference

Although we do not think of it as such, transference is very much a kind of procedural memory with affective components. A reasonable question might well be asked: Is there any advantage to thinking about transference in this way? The advantage is threefold: It offers a wider understanding of what transference is, places it in a wider social and neurocognitive perspective, and suggests a basis for working with it consistent with knowledges developed by other disciplines. The term *transference* as well as *The* Transference (always followed by a second or so of respectful silence) is another constituent of our arcane psychoanalytic lexicon that separates us from other disciplines and allows us to pay insufficient attention to its ontological moorings. To those psychoanalysts who hew to their work with a hermeneutic bent, this may not seem a problem, but, in the 21st century, it just won't do. We know a lot about working with transference, but not very much about its ontology. We know how to use transference as it occurs in the therapeutic situation, as a tool to reach the infantile relations from which it arose and free a patient from their hold upon her. We understand how transference can overwhelm and distort the experienced reality of contemporary relationships with disastrous consequences. We know that some equally arcane process called "working through" can free those relations and root them instead in the present. Although we don't really know just what working through consists of, we are nonetheless somehow able to accomplish it. We treat transference as a separate entity arising out of the projection or displacement of early infantile object relations onto the person of the analyst or therapist.

Transference is not a separate entity. When we talk about it as such, we do so for heuristic purposes and elide its lack of separateness from the many forms of relating. Similarly, it is not confined to the therapeutic situation; transference is everywhere and interacts with the transferences of others as an aspect of unconscious relating. We think it is more prevalent in low-data relationships (hence therapeutic "neutrality") and we have discussed in the previous chapter how it certainly *is* more prevalent in power relationships where one individual is forced into a state of regression by another.

If we don't know about some of these things, does cognitive neuroscience have anything to offer us? A great deal *is* known about how cognitive and motor procedures are acquired (Schacter et al., 2000). Neuroscientists study the acquisition of procedures like word generation tasks rather than object relations because they are far simpler systems to study. But the basic observation that the process occurs as a result of multiple repetitions or experiences, that it is incremental, and that its progress is accompanied by the adoption of alternate pathways in the brain, is the same for verbs as it is for infants and mothers. (Although attachment is an aspect of the process, I am not talking about it per se, but rather the cumulative affective, procedural development of the unique way in which an individual relates to and conceptualizes others.)

What, then, can neuroscience tell us about transference? Again, it turns out that a great deal has been written about how procedural knowledge gets *transferred* from one procedure to another. In a review article, Kimball and Holyoak (2000) describe transfer as a basic process of learning and that various forms of expertise can involve transfer to naïve domains. They cite Hatano and Inagaki (1986), who refer to such transfer of expertise as "adaptive" to distinguish it from the transfer of more usual and routine expertise of simple and familiar tasks. Although transfer is studied in relation to task and procedural learning, it involves, particularly as the tasks become more complex, the same kinds of operations that occur in transfer*ence* when it is a particular object relation that is transferred. When, for example, what is being transferred becomes more complex, the process can take place unconsciously rather than consciously. Transfer, like transference, is more likely to occur in cases where people are given some hint concerning the similarity between the original learned task and the task the learning is being transferred to. A therapist's turn of phrase or familiar burst of feeling would, for a patient, constitute such a hint.

The neuroscience suggests a number of technical strategies for addressing transference clinically. The first involves interventions that would shift neural activity back to the original pathways that were active as the original cognitive procedure, that is the infantile object relation, was incrementally learned (Schacter et al., 2000). This would involve moving the transference back to episodic and semantic memory, what we already do when we talk to patients about their transferences and their origins. If we think of transference as a learned procedure, then we would want to replace it with a contemporary procedure. This is the same process that Gill (1982) was talking about in his critique of clinical psychoanalysis for failing to engage the transference in the present, the here-and-now transference. It is the same process that Loewald (1960) was talking about in his oft-quoted paper when he wrote of the analyst becoming a new object. Since the neuroscience points to the development of transference as incremental, it would suggest not intervening clinically until it is fully developed in order that it not be partially excluded from therapeutic action. If one accepts that the therapeutic situation is inevitably a two person psychology with multiple indirect participations by members of the participants' respective social networks (see chapter 4), then the therapeutic task would seem to center around maintaining a dialectical relationship between it and the here-and-now transference.

I believe that this suggestion constitutes a change in the technique of psychotherapy and analysis as it is usually practiced. It would still be taken as a given that the engagement of the transference involves the interreferential development of countertransference that can be employed as another tool in the therapeutic process. However, the neuroscience also confirms that, if the *original* behavior of the therapist has important elements in common with the pathological behavior of the early objects, the therapy will fail and serves instead to increase the hold that these objects maintain on the patient's life.

Let's move on to a narrative of a treatment that illustrates some of the points I have been making in this chapter and also paves the way for a consideration of archeology and genealogy, concepts that are less familiar to us as analysts and therapists but that offer important insights into memory, autobiography, and the self.

Case Vignette: Susan

Susan, a patient I originally discussed elsewhere (Leffert, 2007a, 2010a) for the purpose of illustrating the interplay of narrative and metanarrative[54] over the course of an analysis, was an attractive corporate

54 Metanarratives are brief overarching statements about how the world works. Postmoderns view them as subjects for deconstruction. They range from practical statements such as "stop your car when a traffic light is red" to more complex and at-times problematic rules such as "men (or women) are dangerous and untrustworthy."

executive in her early 50s who first sought analysis because of a string of failed relationships. An earlier analysis had proved only moderately helpful and left her with a mixture of ill-defined feelings for her older, chronically ill analyst. Recurrent or chronic illness was a theme that reverberated through much of her childhood. Susan was the only child of a mother from a well-to-do family who underwent successful surgery for the removal of a temporal lobe astrocytoma when Susan was six months old. Susan's father was a bright but passive man who felt entitled to great success and blamed everyone but himself when his efforts failed due to his chronic lack of perseverance and assertiveness. She knew all of this except for the reasons for his failures when she first consulted me; she had always sided with her father against the "injustices" he described to her.

Susan's mother was disabled by a series of postoperative complications (the surgery had been extensive and, performed in the 1940s, caused problems) until Susan was three. She was cared for by a series of nursemaids; the one she bonded with most closely was suddenly dismissed when she was 18 months old for "showing her too much affection." Her first memories were of her third birthday party, a party given for adults and family to thank them for their help during her mother's illness. Mother, however, had been emotionally damaged by the traumas of her surgery and recovery; she remained focused on her health and suffered severe headaches along with other ill-defined problems.

At age four, Susan began suffering repeated sore throats and fevers that were treated with painful penicillin injections. A ritual developed beginning with the family doctor's house call, the decision that an injection was called for, the boiling and sterilizing of the syringe in a special pot reserved for such purposes as Susan looked on with dread, and finally, Susan's being held down by her mother on the couch, screaming, while the penicillin was injected into her buttocks. The details were etched in her mind, accompanied by an anxiety so intense she described it strangely as "liquid."

At age five, Susan was told that her parents were taking her to a special toy store. The toy store turned out to be a hospital where Susan was surprised with a tonsillectomy; she was later told that it was done that way "for her own good" to spare her from getting "too upset." (This was a grudge she held against her parents and brought to her analysis.)

Susan entered middle childhood with two sequelae from her childhood traumas: a severe needle phobia that only resolved in her analysis with me and a separation anxiety that caused school avoidance and then cleared spontaneously when she consolidated a narcissistic character with defensive obsessional features in adolescence (Blos, 1968). Intelligent and precocious, Susan became a confidante to both her parents, who freely discussed their adult problems with her.

In spite of her own preoccupations, Susan's mother cared deeply for her, applauded her successes, and told her that she could succeed at anything. As often happens with such talented children, this became a self-fulfilling prophecy. Her father publicly took both pride in and credit for her successes; beneath the surface, this unreflective man blamed her for her mother's illness and never directly praised her. Susan was an isolated child who kept herself entertained and had few friends; she grew into an equally reserved adult.

Susan attended college and business school and easily found employment at a Fortune 500 company, where she quickly rose through the ranks. Her success, and her outbursts of rage at slights both real and imagined, were discussed elsewhere (Leffert, 2007a, 2010a). The recommendation of a mentor who cared about her enough to tolerate her anger led to her first analysis. Her analyst, a well-known, mildly arrogant man, was largely silent and mostly left her to her own devices in her analysis (I had had enough contact with him in professional circles to confirm Susan's view), much as her parents frequently did.

Susan used the three years she spent with him to assemble the autobiographical narrative she brought to her work with me, a mixture of component memories and stories her parents had told her about her childhood at her request. Although she had her story, she had little sense of what its components meant to her; what she felt mostly were the narcissistic gratifications she had assembled to compensate herself for the injuries she had suffered as a child and an adult. Relationships with men had not gotten better. She realized that she had felt as if *she* were the parent who'd had to take care of her mother and father. She remained unaware of any anger at them and, although she realized her father had a lot to do with her career choice, she had no sense that her success was a way of sticking it to him. Predictably, she became periodically angry with her first analyst, an aspect of maternal transference that had to do with the injections. Whether he endured or tolerated her anger was not clear, but he never commented on it and, in consequence, she had thought little about it.

Probably the most important therapeutic action to take place, or, as it turns out, to not take place, in that first analysis was that he did not retaliate against her or symbolically immobilize her in response to these angry outbursts. The anger at work lessened considerably, seemingly as a result of this experience. Susan had had similar problems in relationships with men, including a brief caretaking marriage that ended in divorce. Modest improvements occurred here as well. Susan pronounced herself satisfied with these results and a date to conclude the analysis was agreed upon. The termination was marked by a resurgence of separation anxiety that related to the traumatic maternal separations occurring early in her life. She was able to work with the separation and left with positive feelings for her analysis and her analyst that proved to be excessive.

Some years passed and Susan found herself on the wrong side of a political battle that she had helped to precipitate at work. Forced out of her job, she was able to find another roughly similar position but, deeply shaken by the experience, she decided to resume her analysis. Her analyst had since retired and she was referred to me.

Perhaps because of my level of activity, asking questions and offering comments where her first analyst had remained silent, this analysis went very differently from the start. (As we will see, interpretations initially seemed to have only limited effects.) Susan spent months talking about how lonely and isolated she had always felt. A question or comment was all that was needed for her to continue and she seemed surprised that I was interested in her or her feelings. She was also surprised by the depths of her feelings of isolation and aloneness. She then, characteristically, began to find fault with me; I was late, I wasn't listening, I was looking out the window (she seemed unaware that she had no information about the last two). After listening to her angry outbursts for some time, I asked her why she was so angry at me. It seemed like a reasonable question, yet she seemed shocked that I would ask it. To my surprise, she burst into tears and started talking about how her parents never cared about what she was feeling, only about themselves and their unhappiness. She gradually became aware of just how angry she was at them; they were supposed to take care of *her*. Similarly, it became clear that she was wounded and angered by receiving little help or support from her bosses in her work. While engendered by her independence, competence, and aloofness, it led to her angrily provoking them, often with disastrous results.

What seemed to be a primal scene memory emerged. She was knocking on the door of her parents' bedroom at around age four, her mother in a yellow nightgown, and then her father took her to her room and spanked her. First, she laughed to show him he couldn't hurt her, behavior that became typical throughout her life, but then she cried bitterly when the pain became too great. I interpreted her being frightened by what she had burst in on and then being beaten rather than cared for.

This led to her describing other medical conditions she had had in childhood and adolescence. She had perhaps a half dozen incapacitating headaches a year that, in retrospect, were clearly migraines, but was given only aspirin and never saw a doctor for them. A moderate case of acne was also never treated. A case of plantar warts accompanied by pain and bleeding went untreated for months. Susan and I concluded that, in this medically aware household, she had been quite neglected. The exceptions were the traumatic injection-ridden upper respiratory infections, the traumatic tonsillectomy, and massive dental caries in her deciduous teeth that were filled without benefit of local anesthetic.

Susan began to wonder at what she began to see as her parents' sadism and linked it to her mother's suffering and need to make her suffer. (I had wondered about this for some time, but waited—it was *not* a reconstruction I would make; the risk for distorting her memories if I was wrong would have been too great.) As she explored how her parents had failed to care for her, she began to look at her first analyst's behavior in the same way. He was often ill and there were frequent cancellations. She now saw how he had failed to help her deal with or understand her anger and the emotional price she had paid for it. Her migraines had continued through the first analysis (they disappeared when a calcium channel blocker prescribed for hypertension coincidentally provided migraine prophylaxis); in one of his few direct interventions, he insisted that she not take any medications for relief, but instead to try to understand them as an identification with her mother and her neurosurgery. This "understanding" brought no relief.

As the current successful analysis moved towards termination, Susan could reformulate a more positive, although realistically mixed, relationship with her mother. The central factor for her was her mother's support and belief in her that she had constantly conveyed to Susan throughout her childhood. Her father was experienced in a much more negative light. She grasped his failures, his sucking her success out of her to feed himself while he praised her to others and spoke critically to her. She also saw that she had succeeded both for him, but also as a way of showing him she had surpassed him. Her work had become much more satisfying and less conflicted; she had begun, tentatively, to again explore having relationships with men.

Aside from representing a narrative of a nice analysis containing Susan's personal narrative, one could be forgiven for wondering why it is situated here. Any analysis, like any series of events, is open to many different narrative possibilities as it explores both present and past. This narrative form was chosen to inform a different sort of inquiry into the past, one that involves what we will come to know as the archaeology and genealogy of the self.

Archaeology and Genealogy

Psychoanalytically informed therapy has explored memory and the past largely through the vehicles of narrative or episodic memory and transference interpretation. I have suggested (Leffert, 2007a, 2007b) that metanarratives, overarching statements about how the world works, along with family and individual myths, shape narrative and play an important role in the therapeutic process. These are all content-based aspects of memory. The case vignette, as described up to this point, illustrates the recovery of these memories and their assembly into an autobiographical narrative. Except for this focus, it is not particularly unusual.

Postmodern thought about the nature and influence of the past, particularly Foucault's (1969 & 1971/1972, 1966/1994) concepts of archaeology and genealogy, offers a processual and post-processual approach to memory and its effects on a contextual rather than a content-based present. They indeed go a step further in demonstrating how context can determine whether specific contents can even be perceived. Foucault conceptualized archaeology and genealogy as referencing the functions of society and its institutions at different points in time in a project that Flynn (2003) aptly referred to as the "mapping of history" (p. 29). The purpose here is not to translate psychoanalytic concepts into postmodern ones or vice versa. It is rather to address these concepts as they apply to the history and development of the individual and how they form and define her present, then to use them as a part of the psychoanalytic process. The archaeology and genealogy of the individual are aspects, not modules, of the distributed, holistic memory system.

Archaeology

Archaeology (Foucault, 1969 & 1971/1972) as a form of inquiry is not about the knitting together of ideas, knowledge, or history into a logical narrative of events and dates. Archaeology seeks to elucidate through epistemological inquiry the discursive and non-discursive formations and practices that lie beneath and determine the shape of these narratives. Its aim then is quite different from mine was when I put together a history of events to offer a narrative (however incomplete) of my patient Susan's life and analyses.

Archaeology is a kind of unconscious knowledge, inaccessible to the individual, that provides the rules and structures that, for Foucault, underlie the theories of science. He described these rules of knowledge as comprising an episteme and posited that every age could have but a single episteme. For example, the episteme of the Classical Age (roughly the 17th and 18th centuries) was mathematics and taxonomy. Foucault saw the limitations inherent in seeking such a unifying principle and began using the term *dispositif* later in his career. Although hard to translate, a *dispositif* is a plurality; it subsumes the collection of rules and propositions for knowing and discourse, a formation that operates at a given moment in time and is subject to change.

Before proceeding with this discussion of archaeology, and the subsequent one on genealogy, it is important to ask the related questions: Just what, exactly, are discursive and non-discursive practices and how do they relate to Susan, her life, and my clinical work with her? Discursive formations are groups of consistent practices that encompass how things are, their regularity, the way one correlates with another, the particular rule set or order that governs them. They exist in society and time; I am positing that sets of discursive practices exist as well for the individual, the self, and the time. Such formations arise out of the sum of discourse on a given subject. Discourses are texts that consist of either literal discussions or of defined bodies of statements about a particular thing (*chose*) (Foucault, 1966/1994). They do not refer to things in the way that signs and symbols designate objects that exist independently of language. Instead, they embody their own objects about which they provide information.

The central feature about discourse and discursive formations is not that they are structures of subjectivity, but rather that they set out the underlying positions and rules, mostly unconsciously, that establish and formulate an *individual's* subjectivity. For purposes of illustration, on a societal level, "neurosis" is a discursive formation. It includes a series of statements concerning descriptions of behavior, psychopathology, development, and intrapsychic conflict that display a high degree of correlation. It identifies individuals as possessing particular roles—patients, clients, therapists, doctors, psychoanalysts, social service workers—and defines the particular circumstances in which these individuals act on each other. Finally, the discursive formation *neurosis* exists side by side with other discursive formations such as the *DSM-IV* (American Psychiatric Association, 1994) that, although they share some domains, have their own discursive practices. Non-discursive formations are societal components such as organizations, parts of governments, and widely influential events.

Let me describe one of Susan's discursive formations that often had destructive consequences for her at work. In a variety of contexts, she would offer colleagues or superiors compilations of information as part of her job. Not infrequently, someone would suggest that one item or another was different from, or had a different meaning than, the one Susan ascribed to it. She would first feel that what was being suggested was incorrect, without considering even for a moment the possibility that it was valid. In her practice, no such possibility existed! She assumed that the person had simply not understood her and would expand her exegesis on the subject. If the person was not someone she regarded as a political enemy, this part of the practice was devoid of emotion and unconsciously executed, although she would remember the *content* of what was said to her for long periods of time. If the person then let it go (and they usually did), so be it. But if they persisted, in her practice they became an enemy, Susan would coldly attack them, leaving her the victor and sole occupant of the abandoned field.

It took a long time to clarify the practice I have just related. Susan never spoke of it, although she did speak of being attacked at work, unjustly she felt. It was only when this practice appeared in her analysis that we were able to get at it. Susan had an enthusiastic interest in collecting American Indian art. In one session, she was telling me about a Zuni fetish figure of a bear she had just acquired. She told me, among many details, about its heart line. Not being particularly knowledgeable about Indian art, I asked her about it (it seems that in a fetish figure there is a graven line running from the tail and ending in an arrowhead roughly over the chest). I recalled that Susan had told me that a few years ago, she had been successfully treated for ventricular tachycardia. Although she owned many pieces of Indian art that did not feature a heart line, I did inquire (I would scarcely call it an interpretation) whether she thought there was any connection between the fetish and the ventricular tachycardia. She told me in a cautious, neutral way that there wasn't; she of course had had ventricular tachycardia (which she mentioned matter-of-factly from time to time in her work with me) and went on to describe the characteristics of the piece once more. I thought this was probably defensive, but saw no useful way to pursue it.

A bit later, an incident arose at work when she insisted on developing a project in a way she thought best, against the suggestions offered by a subordinate who had then become visibly upset. I asked her if she had thought about, as she had described at other times, how important it was for her to be right. She responded that her plan had been best and explained to me again why it was. This time I did pursue it and wondered neutrally if she felt threatened by the subordinate. She became visibly angry and told me she was surprised that I would say something that made so little sense; I wasn't as smart as I thought I was. I noted and resisted an impulse to attack her in turn and simply asked her why she had attacked me. She became reflective and told me she had felt fearful of being attacked. For the rest of the hour I explored, with her active participation, genetic possibilities based on her history that might have given rise to her response as transference. Susan considered the possibilities I raised, but none of them led to a *process* response. As a result, it seemed to me that her actions had to do with discourse, not with transference, and that they could best be approached archaeologically, not interpretively.

This discursive formation rested on a number of practices that Susan had developed over the course of her life. She needed to be prepared to defend herself against her expectation of being attacked and controlled (or immobilized and injected). She also felt she might be unfairly criticized at work for things that she hadn't done. Related to both of these was a sense that her colleagues could and did at times become hostile to her. She had no idea why they would do so, nor that she could have done anything to bring such responses about.

These practices illustrate a subjectivity of language that is unconscious. It is not dynamically so and has no connection to repression. (It involved the way she chose words and constructed stories.) They are contents of the holistic memory system that are concentrated in procedural and semantic memory and had to do with, if you will, her epistemology of anxiety, attack, and retaliation. Some of these practices sound paranoid, but Susan was not paranoid. They appeared in response to the discursive practices of others. Susan was able to trust and confide in people in most situations. She did not read things into what people said to her; she simply responded to them. Her colleagues could become hostile to her, but she did not experience them as plotting or malevolent.

Looking back on her history, we can observe a series of events: the painful penicillin injections that were forced on her, her parents' neglect, and her bonding with her father over the way others had (as she then believed) driven him from business. These experiences led to the development of the various discursive practices we have described. What is important here is that they had become linguistic practices completely independent of their origins.[55] As such, *they are not subject to interpretation*. Appealing to those origins or drawing Susan's attention to them would not affect them or move her emotionally. This is not to say for a moment that approaching someone's past is not essential or therapeutic, but rather that archaeology represents a new area that we have not explicitly engaged in our clinical work with patients.[56] Archeological problems are procedural and semiotic, they do not involve latent meaning or repressed meaning; rather they create linguistic and discursive situations that exclude meaning. I would posit that such problems are, in fact, fairly common but have so far escaped our notice. Instead, we have tended to misunderstand their outcomes as defensive, which they are not, and to label them as resistance.

Clinically, what we are likely to first notice is that something that strikes us as obvious about what a patient is saying to us is not at all obvious to her. Questioning it, let alone interpreting it, does not lead to a process response as opposed to *apparently* similar situations in which a fruitful exploration does ensue. The presence of some particular discursive formation or, sometimes more importantly, the absence of others, then leads to the lack of response that may well be what we have (mistakenly) identified as resistance, denial, disavowal, or repression.

Foucault (Flynn, 2003) wrote archaeologies of madness, clinical medicine, and the human sciences. I am suggesting that a part of our work as therapists and psychoanalysts is to write archaeologies of our patients, their rules of knowledge as extant at different points in their lives. Doing so takes place when we are in an autocentric as opposed to an allocentric mode (Schachtel, 1959) vis-à-vis our patients. We must step outside the two-ness of the therapeutic situation for a bit if we are to see, let alone to study, them. Foucault's archaeology is not about the "arche," but rather about what he calls the study of the "archive."[57]

55 The relation of practice to origin can be approached, as we will see, through the study of genealogy.

56 As I came to understand archaeology, I realized that I did engage these issues, but have done so implicitly and in a non-systematic way. I suspect that is also true for many psychotherapists and analysts. The advantage of studying the archaeology is that it informs a systematic approach and some explicit additions to clinical theory.

57 Derrida (1995/1998) has also written about archives. Although his analysis of the term is highly sophisticated, he employs it in a manner that is much more consistent with its more general usage: as a storehouse or storehouses of different kinds of knowledge.

Archive is a complicated term. It is the sum of the discursive practices and formations and all of the discourses that have been thought or uttered up to a given time (in this case, by a single person, Susan).[58] It is the discursive practices that underlie the existence of discourse. The word *archive* does not exist in French (*Le Nouveau Petit Robert*, 2009); it only exists in its plural form, archives. Foucault's purpose in using it is to emphasize its *singularity*. His object is the study of the archive, not language, not mental geology, and not beginnings and sequences (hence his need later to posit genealogy). He further complicates matters for us by using the self-contradictory term "historical *a priori*" to refer to the archive; he wishes it to combine the relativistic and the absolute. In the individual, the archive contains the rules and past practices that determine what actions, thoughts, and judgments are possible plus memories of all the statements that have been made based on those rules. Archives are time bound and factual, they refer to different ages of a person's life; they are discovered, not deduced, interpreted, or remembered.

We have dealt with Susan's archive at the time of her second analysis. Histories (genealogies) chart the breaks between ages, the appearance of new practices and, often, the abandonment or demise of old ones. The new practices often appear in areas where old ones were weak or absent.

Foucault (1966/1994) considered chance to be a major factor in these shifts and changes; I believe he would have embraced complexity in this context. The emphasis on practices of exclusion that Foucault posited on a societal level exists in the individual as well. As archaeologist-psychoanalysts, we discover the unspoken and the unspeakable relationships between often disjointed and disparate areas of thought, emotion, and experience. An example in Susan's case was her mother's practice of neglect that determined her unconscious shortcomings as a caretaker. Archaeology can lead people to offer radically different accounts of the same events; it in effect offers a radical critique of a patient's world and self-views. It serves to render biases, beliefs, and necessities contingent; it offers a space where change can occur. Susan did not refuse to believe evidence placed before her, *she simply perceived it differently*. I would often initially accept her perceptions as accurate; the therapeutic task in these cases involved accepting this received opinion and then, as a result of accumulating more information, crafting a new one that reconfigures

58 Archive involves elements of procedural, episodic, and semantic memory. Neuroanatomically, it is distributed, not in any way discrete.

the evidence. This process involves the development of new practice(s) that replace or supplement the old ones.

Foucault struggled with the question of whether the archive expanded as a result of these new practices or whether there was a shift from old practices to new. He argued different positions at different times. I think the answer for our purposes would have to be some of both (with potential shifts from new practices *back* to old). Neuroscience, psychoanalysis, and complexity theory as well as the work of other postmoderns would all support such a view, although none specifically consider archaeology. Transference, also a part of the archive, is relevant to this question; it both changes and remains; it becomes more contingent.

Foucault (1969 & 1971/1972) brings much of his thinking together around his use of the term "historical *a priori*" and the archive. The positivity of a discourse comprises its unity over time. It does not tell us which statements are true, or anything else about them, but does tell us if they are, so to speak, on the same playing field of knowledge, if they are about the same thing or reside in the same conceptual field.[59] It is about history as well as meaning. They rest on a tangled web that is unconscious (descriptively, not dynamically) to the author.

Discourse does not involve just a logical progression of statements, or any particular organization of them for that matter. Rather, there is what Foucault (1969 & 1971/1972) calls a form of positivity (he refers here to discursive formations) that "defines a field in which formal identities, thematic continuities, translations of concepts, and polemical interchanges may be deployed" (p. 127). Such a field does not comprise a condition of the validity of statements but rather a condition of the *reality* of statements. It is an instance of the historical *a priori*. For example, one could say that the displacement of sharecroppers in 1930s America has nothing to do with the displacement of British textile workers in the 1950s. This statement is not valid, but it is real. If one were to substitute Rembrandt's art for the latter phrase in the sentence about sharecroppers, the statement would be true, but would have no reality in discourse. Foucault is making a point about *discursive* reality involving a series of statements that manifest patterns, regularity, order of some sort, location, and function in some particular discourse. Discursive reality does not require the truth or falsity of any statement. The statement that the displacement of sharecroppers has nothing to do with Rembrandt's art is certainly true, but it does not constitute or have

59 In Lyotard (1983/1988) it tells us that the statements are not *différends*.

a place in any sort of discourse; it lacks that form of reality.[60] Susan's attacking her colleagues because she felt they wanted to attack her was also not valid, but had discursive reality. The history of an archive is the record of all the statements that have been said within this particular field, subject to the limits of knowability and memory. It is the group of rules that characterize a person's, in this case Susan's, discursive practices. "*A priori* [the rules] does not elude historicity [the practices]" (p. 127). They are both within the field and are transformable over time.

Different times, different ages (Susan as a child, Susan in her first analysis) have different *a priori*'s and different archives. By the combination of historical and *a priori*, Foucault (1969 & 1971/1972) wishes to include *contingency*, to modify the absolutes of *a priori* in isolation. The archive, this dense system of statements, is "the law of what can be said" (p. 129), but also serves to group what would otherwise be an amorphous mass of statements into discrete figures or systems.

An archive cannot be described or retrieved in its entirety, but only in fragments relevant to a particular discourse. Foucault (1969 & 1971/1972) argues at what I believe is the interface with psychoanalysis that we cannot describe our own archives because they are unconscious formations. I would argue that the analysis and transformation of archive is a modality of therapeutic action. The analysis of archive leads to its differences in time, to the mapping of an individual's past and its transformation into the *a priori* present. The term *archaeology* describes the study of the archive, the searches into it, and the recovery of specific discourses and practices present within it.

Discourses change over time in an effective therapy (even if the process is not identified as such by the therapeutic couple). They do not require temporal succession; archaeology ignores the temporal relations between them and treats history as frozen into particular moments or ages. "Discourse is snatched from the law of development and established as a discontinuous atemporality. It is immobilized in fragments: precarious splinters of eternity" (Foucault, 1969 & 1971/1972, p. 169). This is what our patients bring us; archaeology addresses the discontinuities, gaps, ruptures, and sudden redistribution of discursive practice. It stands in contrast to the history of ideas that seeks to document a logical flow. Susan's archaeology included immobilization for injections (age 2–5), tonsillectomy (age 5), feeling attacked at work (age 30–50), attacking others (age 15–50) and the ideas surrounding each.

60 It has other sorts of reality (one can, for example, utter it and make a recording of that utterance), but that's not what we are interested in here. Any statement we make is real as such, but that doesn't affect the fact it can be either true or false.

A goal of therapeutic practice is to expand the archive and introduce discontinuities in it. The perfect vehicle for doing so is the behavior of the therapist; the therapist responds to his patient in ways different from what she has previously experienced in discourse with others, her later as well as her infantile objects. An example was when I asked Susan how she "knew" I was looking out of the window or knew that I had forgotten something she told me even though I had been silent, saying nothing to make her think that I had. I didn't interpret what she assumed, did not correct it, and did not offer a defensive denial. In effect, what I did was to focus on the discursive practice that led to her assumptions. As is often the case, no new information needed to be provided, the novel concept came from the transformations and rearrangements of what is knowable. Information is either not noticed because it doesn't fit the rules (even though it might objectively be more accurate) or it is noticed but the right questions aren't asked about it. Material may be isolated by the discursive practices at the time an event occurred or an individual may be isolated by being locked into a group of practices from other ages, the ancient or recent past.

The archive of an individual as opposed to the societal archive that Foucault talked about is a component of memory. It is holistic and post-structural. Although its discourses are subject to conscious retrieval, much of it is a part of the 90+% of mental contents that are not directly accessible to consciousness. The archive is subject to unconscious modification occurring as a result of experience, and conscious modification as a result of discourse.[61] We need to talk more about just how history fits in to all of this if it is not a sequential presence in the archive. This will lead us to genealogy and then back to the question of what it all has to do with Susan.

Genealogy

Genealogy, in contrast to archaeology, *is* about the history and the origins of things (*choses*) or ideas. Foucault drew the concept from Nietzsche's *On the Genealogy of Morals* (1887/1969). McGowan (1991) describes Nietzsche's view that the origins of things are not definitive;

61 I am using discourse in the sense of a method of inquiry aimed at furthering an understanding of a subject. It is comprised of cognitive and emotional components and can exist in the form of a solitary reverie or a dialogue between two people. Multiple discourses can exist simultaneously, can intersect, can plagiarize each other, and can become tangled in a web; discourse includes unconscious elements that are unknown to their participants.

changes are only transformations imposed by the temporarily more powerful. He quotes Nietzsche: "the cause of the origin of a thing and its eventual utility, its actual employment and place in a system of purposes, lie worlds apart; whatever exists, having somehow come into being is again and again reinterpreted to new ends, taken over, transformed, and redirected by some power superior to it" (p. 77). Power involves a taking over, a subduing, an adaptation in which previous meaning and purpose are lost and another character or function is just one thing that is produced.

> Genealogy, in this view, names the history of meaning's production and the self, as in any structuralist schema, must be understood as just one among the other meaningful units that have been produced. Power produces history, meaning and selves, and there are no grounds for believing that humans freely choose the forms that these productions take.
>
> (p. 78)

When speaking of the individual, this is very much about development in general and development of the self[62] in particular. We do not have control over our development as children, and adults and our parents have only quite limited control over it, consciously or otherwise. If what is sought in therapy is in part freedom, then the deconstruction of genealogies is a mode of therapeutic action.

Foucault (1979/1995) posited genealogy as a supplement to archaeology in his later writings. He used the term exclusively to refer to power relations and their history. Although power relations as they involve parents, their children, and the influence of society *are* of considerable importance, and have not yet been studied as an aspect of development, we need not limit our considerations of genealogy in this way. Like Nietzsche (1887/1969), he posited that the causes that gave rise to a particular thing have no relation to its subsequent usage or behavior. By offering a genealogy, he is offering a deconstruction that shows history to be discontinuous and often determined by accident. History assigns knowledges to various categories, but there is no fundamental truth or ontological standing to these categories; categories are constructs, also part of archive, that can be deconstructed to produce discourse manifesting increasing degrees of freedom. Deconstruction does not aim at

62 In discussing the self, I make a distinction not much made by psychoanalysts. The self is all of us—body, brain, mind, the works. What we are accustomed to talking about as psychoanalysts is really the self-schema, a discontinuous psychical formation that, although essential to mental function, is still, nonetheless, a schema.

revealing some essence of knowledge, but rather at doing away with particular categories. (As individuals, we create our own categories of, for example, gender, success, or relatedness, which can be similarly limiting.)

Genealogy involves a history of change in function best understood in terms of the behavior of complex systems. Prior meanings do not determine new purpose and function; think of psychopathology here, perhaps of symptoms or characters that arise out of new interactions with the social environment. As therapists, we can and do dialectically construct genealogies of, for example, dependence, depression, or anxiety for individual patients. This genealogical research offers a therapeutic procedure that can be used to increase a patient's understanding of areas in which origins or their causes are not necessarily of primary importance. It also clarifies why the clinical identification and interpretation of those origins is often not therapeutic in and of itself, and why it is the record of the discontinuities and shifts in a life history that are ultimately of greater importance. Before getting back to Susan, it would be worthwhile to see what more postmodernism and complexity theory can tell us about archaeology and genealogy.

Postmodern and Complex Views of Archaeology and Genealogy

Foucault (1969 & 1971/1972, 1979/1995) took two positions about archaeology and genealogy on the societal level (we have posited that both concepts are also applicable and useful on the level of the individual). These positions are relevant to complexity theory as well as to more general post-structural views concerning the accessibility of legitimate knowledge. He described knowledge of archive as discontinuous and fragmented, and he viewed genealogies (Foucault, 1980) in sum as "local, discontinuous, disqualified, illegitimate knowledges . . . [that can never constitute a] unitary body of theory which would filter, hierarchise, and order . . . in the name of some true knowledge and some arbitrary idea of what constitutes a science of objects" (p. 83). He also saw the occurrence of the discontinuities—the histories of which constitute genealogies as well as the shifts from archive to archive—as very much subject to chance. This was as close as he could come at the time to positing a role for complexity theory in understanding the operation of and the changes in archives and genealogies.

A common misreading of postmodernism (which, unfortunately, includes most psychoanalytic critiques of the subject, e.g., Chessick,

1996, 2007; Eagle, 2003; Eagle, Wolitzky, & Wakefield, 2001) equates postmodern views of knowledge with those of neo-pragmatism (e.g., Rorty, 1979, 1982, 1989). Neo-pragmatists largely hold the world to be unknowable, that all knowledge of the world is unstable and, when subject to deconstruction, collapses. Why they maintain such a position and to what extent they actually mean what they say are beyond the scope of the present discussion. The post-structuralists, among whom Foucault (1969 & 1971/1972, 1980, 2000) and Derrida (1978, 1972/1982, 1995/1998) are prominent, view the world as knowable, albeit in discontinuous ways. These knowledges are subject to the limitations of individual perception,[63] subjectivity, and discourse. Further limitations are based on the interreferentiality of at-times conflicting knowledge-claims that can only be tolerated if they are accepted dialectically as *autres* rather than as absolutes. Examination of such claims often reveals their dependency on unstable or arbitrary signifiers and categories. When absolute claims of knowledge and standing are subject to deconstruction, it is only the absoluteness that collapses, not the knowledge. (Absolute claims of knowledge are most often matters of power relations. Post-structuralists do not deny knowability, but they insist, as I do, on its limitations and the degree of standing that can be assigned to it.)

These same limitations exist for archaeology and genealogy. The archive of an individual, in the absence of reflection, and accompanied by the observations of the other (*autre*), is unconscious. In the therapeutic situation, the patient's archive is an appropriate and necessary subject of analysis.[64] If the patient knows nothing about it, we are only able to identify fragments of it; we will only come to know at best a portion of it, and that by dint of very hard work. However, if we acquaint patients with the concept that we all carry around certain "rules for formulating knowledge," and that these rules can also limit or bias what we know and how we perceive and act, then the patient can become a collaborator in this part of the analysis and the work is easier. Therapeutic work on the archive seems inevitably partial and incomplete, at least on a conscious and explicit level. As I have asserted elsewhere (Leffert, 2010a) about other, more usual forms of analytic

63 Should outside confirmation of this statement be required, neuroscience can provide it. Of the information contained in the visual image that we see, roughly 10–15% is provided by the retina through the optic nerve, while the remaining 85–90% comes from the cerebral cortex (Gregory, 1997).

64 This assumes that the therapist's archive has also been the subject of initial and ongoing analysis, which, without the material presented here, can only naively and intuitively be the case.

work, more may be accomplished on a level beyond the awareness of patient and therapist.

Working therapeutically with a patient's genealogy(ies) is quite similar to working generally with narrative. We are focused on the appearance of discontinuities and of changes in function; if some element appears at different times in a patient's story, we have to ask ourselves (and, if necessary, the patient) if it is really the same element or whether it has undergone a change of function or meaning. In Susan's case, being restrained first meant being in danger of being hurt. It later underwent a transformation from the physical to the social and came to represent being denied success. If one were to witness only the latter, there would be no immediate reason to connect it to specific events in Susan's early life. Again, we are limited by what we can know, how accurate our view really is, and the many discontinuities we will not see or not allow ourselves to see.

Complexity theory offers a considerable expansion of Foucault's (1969 & 1971/1972) views on the role of chance in archaeologies and genealogies. Each represents a complex system, and, as such, has certain properties. As I have discussed elsewhere (Leffert, 2008, 2010a especially chapter 3), the behavior of a complex system is not equal to the sum of the behaviors of its individual parts and is not knowable based on them. Although these parts can be discussed individually for heuristic purposes, they cannot be considered as modules that act in isolation. Although the behavior of these systems can be modeled mathematically and probabilistically, at times with very high degrees of certainty, this should not be confused with any notion that if the behavior of the system were completely known up to some point in time, that the next activity of the system would be knowable.

However, complex systems do display their own kinds of organization, often at high levels of, well, complexity (Freeman, 1995a, 1995b; Freeman & Barrie, 2001; Freeman et al., 1997; Leffert, 2010a; Marion, 1999). We are most interested in the discrete organizers called attractors. There are two sorts of attractors. One kind are stable, and cycle repetitively; they act linearly and are present in linear sciences like Newtonian physics. The other kind also manifest stability but, otherwise, their properties are completely different; they are called strange attractors. (To complicate things still further, complexity theorists generally call these just "attractors" as well.) If strange attractors are displaced or perturbed, they tend to return to their baseline state and, although they do also *seem* to cycle, they never exactly repeat themselves. They are the interactive and nonlinear organizers that are found in biological and social systems.

Attractors attract; they perturb[65] complex systems and organize them. They can elaborate complex organizations or collapse parts of them into closed systems that sequester information. Metaphorically, these can be closed like whirlpools or open like black holes, confined to a limited part of a system or drawing increasing amounts of the system into themselves. Attractors both affect and are affected by other parts of a holistic system in interreferential ways. Finally, they are organized into basins of attractors that influence the behavior of complex systems. If perturbed, these basins will shift. They will tend to return to their previous organizations, but, if the perturbation is great enough, they can undergo a qualitative shift in organization that changes the attractor landscape of parts of the system.

Complexity is highly relevant to archaeology and genealogy of the self. The archive is a distributed part of the holistic memory system that influences it, and is influenced in turn by its rules for formulating knowledges or perceptions (its discursive formations, its *dispositif*) and the ability to recall past discourses. Collections of practices can be thought of as attractor basins that shape memory acquisition, retrieval, and the formulation of new discourses. An archive can remain essentially unchanged in the absence of the kinds of shifts that Foucault talks about, yet its access to past discourses and the operation of its discursive practices still fluctuate unpredictably in smaller ways from moment to moment.

The history of the unpredictable archival shifts that is the business of genealogy to study is very much about complex behaviors of distributed systems. They lead backwards to origins that are sometimes vastly different from the kinds of practices present in different time frames. One striking point of clinical relevance inherent in complex genealogies is that they explain the frequent observation that changes in function for good or ill (for example, freedom from a persistent inhibition or the appearance of a symptom) can appear at some particular point in time for no apparent reason. Rather than representing a failure of clinical observation on our part or the action of countertransference, this is simply business as usual in a complex system. It is important to remember that this is a discussion of the genealogies of individuals, individuals who happen to be patients, and of our own genealogies. Saying that genealogies and archives are complex systems that lack

65 When complex systems are perturbed, they become increasingly out of equilibrium; the more out of equilibrium a system, the more likely it is that the system will change, although the point and degree of change remain unpredictable.

predictability does not mean to suggest that some major life experience—a death, the birth of a child, the loss of job, a change in society—cannot be expected to affect an individual or that the effect is not subject to a rough predictability (we would expect the first and third to be negative, the second positive, and the fourth lacking in sufficient information). It is the accuracy and timing of predictions that are unknowable.

Returning to Susan

It would be useful at this point to return to Susan and look at some of her discursive practices and their genealogy to illustrate the clinical relevance of what has certainly been a highly theoretical and, at times, dense discussion. We will consider two of these practices that, although they were in no sense disabling, did significantly hamper both her work life and her ability to be meaningfully involved in a relationship with a man. Briefly, Susan 1) would never admit to not knowing something, and 2) would never expect people to help her do something; she would never ask. She was vaguely aware of both of these practices. Although she could identify the feelings that accompanied each one—anxiety and low-grade anger respectively—she made nothing of them, saw them simply as the way the world was, and did not even consider that she might be able to change them.

We eventually were able to identify three genealogical shifts in the first practice. It is easier to talk about these shifts in chronological order, although they were not discovered[66] in that way. The initial practice was a kind of helpless vigilance surrounding the inevitable penicillin injections about which she could say or do nothing. A shift occurred in middle childhood (the needle phobia itself continued as a psychodynamic symptom) to the experience with her father that, if she revealed she didn't know something, he would disapprove of her not knowing and say he was disappointed in her. She soon became very careful about what she revealed about what she knew and what she didn't (this did not affect her bond with her father). The second shift took place at her very

66 I have argued extensively (Leffert, 2010a), as have other psychoanalysts (especially Hoffman, 1998; Stern, 1997) influenced by postmodernism, that memories or knowledges of past events do not sit around in complete packages waiting to be discovered, but are constructed anew in each act of recollection. However, archaeologies and genealogies involve established practices and, as such, are the subjects of discovery.

competitive high school. Teachers were unmerciful in their criticisms of students who failed to answer questions correctly in oral discussions. This drove her to work very hard and she became single-mindedly competitive for the first time in her life. (One teacher would never call on anyone who raised her hand; Susan taught herself to raise her hand when she *didn't* know the answer to a question.)

The final shift occurred between her analyses. She was able to observe a colleague at work who felt free to both ask questions and admit he didn't know things at meetings. She noted as well that, if anything, people seemed to respect him all the more for it; Susan herself did. She tried it herself with some apprehension and got the same result. The practice of never admitting that she didn't know something disappeared as a result. No part of this genealogy was a subject of her first analysis. I believe that what must have happened was that some implicit work had been done that allowed Susan a limited amount of reflection on this discursive practice. She could not yet question it herself, but, when someone behaved so differently, she was able to notice it. Similar kinds of discontinuities or shifts were also discovered in the genealogies of the other practice.

My awareness of the second practice, Susan doing things for herself and never asking for help, emerged directly out of the analytic process. I noticed that she never asked me a question[67] and did not seem to directly take up any interpretations I might make, although they might find their way into the process at a later date. I asked her about this on a couple of occasions; she was a bit nonplussed and seemed to have no idea what I was talking about. After briefly feeling irritated, I got interested in what was going on, but could get no further with it. One day, a few weeks later, it rained. As I usually do, I put a little carpet by the door to my office, but did not notice that a corner of it was not lying flat. As I was showing Susan into the office, she tripped and might have fallen; I reflexively reached out for her arm and steadied her. She looked quite shaken as she continued on to the couch. Whether it was because of my intervention or not, she had not been at all close to falling. I thought what I might hear would have to do with her reactions to the physical contact; instead she told me how shocked she was that I had helped her rather than left her to fend for herself. It never had occurred to her that she could expect anyone to do something for her.

67 In my experience, patients usually ask questions; if one meets them with silence, they soon stop, preferring to avoid the narcissistic injury. However, if one answers, or gives the patient an explanation of why answering is not a good idea, in my experience they continue to ask them at varying rates and they become another useful and analyzable part of a therapy.

I asked her then about the interpretations and it struck her that it also hadn't occurred to her that they were for her, for her to use. There *was* a root to this practice, several shifts away, in the parents' neglect of her health on several occasions, but the practice was neither a symptom nor a piece of character. Susan's stumbling and my intervening was an unusual event. Had it not occurred, I can only speculate as to whether we would have gained access to the practice in some other way or not.

Psychoanalytic Precursors to Archaeology and Genealogy

The fact that psychotherapists and psychoanalysts (myself included) have been unaware of the concepts of archaeology and genealogy and their applications to individuals does not mean that we have been completely blind to what they signify. Beginning with Freud and continuing with the work of a number of second-generation psychoanalysts, attempts have been made to explain phenomena similar to those described over the course of this chapter within the context of a general theory of psychoanalysis. Freud (1914/1958d) put forward the term *working through* (of resistance) to signify that some period of time and work was required before a patient could assimilate and make use of an interpretation. Although undoubtedly true in some cases, it seemed to me that the term could also signify implicitly moving from the genetic material that was interpreted to the now separate discursive practice that was its genealogical descendent.[68]

Hartman (1939/1958), Erikson (1950/1963), and Kris (1955) developed concepts describing changes of function that could refer as well to the appearance of discursive practices descended from issues of development or neurotic conflict. Hartman talked about *change in function* and *apparatuses of secondary autonomy*, whereby something born in psychic conflict could become an ego function independent of that conflict and termed the process *adaptation*. Unfortunately, the same could become true of symptoms that became isolated from the conflicts that gave rise to them and made them very hard to treat. Autonomous functioning could also be very similar to discursive practice. Kris' concept of neutralization, whatever one thinks of the linkage of libido theory to psychic energy, is about the same idea of severing ties to original developmental or conflictual situations. Erikson's introduction of

68 An entirely different aspect of working through (Leffert, 2010a) involves addressing the encrustations of meaning that have accrued to some genetic event over the course of a patient's life.

the developmental concept of epigenesis, although not well assimilated by clinicians who largely have not known what to do with it, does again make room for discursive practices and formations.

I did not simply happen upon the idea of applying Foucault's societal concepts of archaeology and genealogy to the individual. For quite a few years I had been observing and working with aspects of what my patients were telling me with no idea of where to put them in any sort of analytic theory. They could have been included in ego psychology, having to do with its synthetic functions or with perception, or as aspects of object relations theory. Doing so is certainly more comfortable, but does not necessarily add meaning.

More recently, I was working with a fairly disturbed patient when I had the thought "Doris lives in a different world than I do." By this I did not mean anything that had to do with socio-economics, race, origins, or gender. It was rather that what she saw of the world she lived in and how she saw and described it to me was very different from what I saw and experienced, and no explanation rooted in psychopathology could explain the difference. Sensitized to the observation, I began to see more subtle manifestations of this difference in most of my patients. More recently, as I became more cognizant of postmodernism in general and Foucault's (1969 & 1971/1972, 1966/1994) two works, *The Archaeology of Knowledge* and *The Order of Things*, in particular, I realized that I was experiencing an archaeology of the individual, and that it had to do with both present functioning and memory.

I have presented a long case vignette of Susan in two parts with some intermittent commentary. The first part describes a not unusual, successful analysis with the text focused on narrative. I have a number of reasons for doing so. The first is to demonstrate that it was *not* an unusual analysis and that the usual elements[69] of an analysis were *not* abandoned to make way for new ideas (i.e., the role of the study of archive and genealogy in an analysis). The second is to provide a point of reference for those ideas and the third is to demonstrate that the usual was also necessary. A fourth reason is to provide the reader with a familiar base of case material from which to understand the new material I am suggesting. The fifth and final reason is to illustrate that there are many ways to describe the same case that offer different knowledges about it, and that these need not conflict with each other.

Psychoanalysis has, over its long history, constructed a number of such categories. They include ego psychology, self psychology,

69 I focused here, as I do in my work, on clinical theory and process material.

intersubjectivity, and relational theory among others. Some of these have been further divided into sub-categories. Postmoderns are, with good reason I believe, deeply suspicious of categories. The fact that different groups of therapists and analysts believe in different categories or groups of categories is cause for further skepticism (Leffert, 2007a, 2007b). In the archive and its study through archaeology and genealogy, we approach at times debilitating psychopathology that lies outside of our familiar categories, but is, as I have argued, an important subject of analysis. They are additions, not replacements. The manner in which I have separated my discussions of Susan was meant to emphasize just that distinction. I would contend that this can be thought of as a new piece of clinical theory that offers an opportunity to supplement the existing ways in which we already work.

Another distinction that might be more obvious in territory less strange is that Archaeology and Genealogy are *modes of study*. They do not reside within the patient, although a patient can become cognizant of them if an analysis or therapy addresses this kind of material and then they gradually become mentalized as discursive practices. It is Archive, the subject of archaeological and genealogical study, that resides in individuals, patients, people, us. If they are taken back into childhood, they can offer a developmental genealogy of archive.

To once again fall back on Foucault (1979/1995), genealogy can reveal elements of power relations in a developmental history of archive. Susan's dealings with her mother around the injections and her provocative behavior with her father around the spanking were both very much about power relations. While continuing to bear in mind knowledge and discursive practice, we will now take up a particular emotion in the therapeutic situation, the therapist's love for his or her patient, a love that I will posit is independent of the transference/countertransference interplay and of the patient's feelings.

3

Love (the Analyst's) in the Office

Introduction

As a first-year psychiatry resident at Bronx Municipal Hospital Center in 1970, many experiences stood out, two of which I did not begin to grapple with, let alone understand, until much later. In those days, in that program, the first year was spent on the wards doing short-term and long-term (six months) inpatient work. Somewhat early on, our chief resident mentioned to the five of us that a patient had recently asked him if he loved him—he had said "no." He regretted this because he realized that he did in fact love his patient, but couldn't say it and the therapy had suffered as a result.

At the end of the year, Stewart, a quiet, withdrawn, young man with a severe thought disorder whom I had treated as an inpatient for six months was ready for discharge. Patients had the option of continuing in outpatient psychotherapy with whichever resident had treated them in the hospital[70]—this was seen as a "win-win" situation and they were encouraged to do so. Although most patients were happy to accept this arrangement, my patient quietly declined. For educational purposes, our patients were interviewed by the attending psychiatrist, Dr. K., while our small group of residents watched through a one-way mirror. In this interview, Stewart was encouraged to continue to see me. He again declined, in a quiet, pleasant way. Dr. K. asked Stewart if he liked me, wondering if he didn't. Stewart replied, with a faint note in his voice suggesting that such a question was absurd, "Like him? I love him." His comment was at once unexpected and disturbing. If I didn't know what

70 Some of these therapeutic relationships lasted for the remaining two years of residency and continued for many years in private practice, usually at a nominal fee.

Stewart was talking about, I did know that it had nothing to do with transference. Did I love Stewart? Had I been brave enough to ask myself the question in that long-ago May, I would have said I didn't know. Asking the question now, given the intervening years of occasional thought and my choice to place Stewart in this current narrative, I would say that I did. In any event, asking him about his comment or further discussion of his continuing in outpatient psychotherapy produced no further information or results. Stewart and I continued to see each other for a few more weeks until he vanished, at least from my purview, into the East Bronx.

In neither instance—not his loving me, not his refusal to continue to see me—did I have much of an idea what any of this was about. I knew that it was not about sex and I knew that I did not know what it was about—not so bad, really, for a first-year resident in 1970. Picking up from where we left off in the last chapter, a genealogy of my knowledge and capabilities as a psychotherapist (e.g., Foucault, 1980, 1979/1995) would lead back to my psychotherapeutic archive circa 1970. By today's standards it is fairly slim, but it did include discursive practices addressing positive and erotic transference and countertransference, as well as what we now refer to euphemistically as boundary violations. However, it contains no discursive practices or formations having to do with a therapist's loving his patients or vice versa. Fortunately, it does contain a "tilt" button that "lit up" whenever a discontinuity in the archive was detected.[71]

Stewart and my former chief resident remained in the back of my thoughts along with the whole question of love and its place in the therapeutic situation until I began rethinking psychoanalysis in the light of postmodernism, complexity theory, and neuroscience (Leffert, 2007a, 2007b, 2008, 2010a, 2010b, 2011a). I had looked at some, but by no means the most important, of Freud's comments in the area (Freud, 1918 [1914]/1955b, 1919 [1918]/1955d). I was familiar with the earlier psychoanalytic brouhahas over the work of Ferenczi (1930, 1919/1952, 1988) and Alexander (1950; Alexander & French, 1946). I had shared the view held by the Novicks (Novick & Novick, 2000) that, although there is a huge literature about the loving and sexual feelings experienced by

71 Although I have never heard it discussed in these terms, I'm fairly certain that at least some analysts possess a similar tilt button. It represents, however, a very different procedure from what goes on when we realize we are not understanding what a patient is telling us. The tilt button signals a realization that it is not the patient we are missing, but rather an area of knowledge about patients *generally*.

patients for their therapists, there had been, with only a few exceptions, almost nothing written about therapist's love for their patients.[72]

It had also seemed to me that of the papers that *had* been written, most had to do with the therapist's boundary violations (e.g., Celenza, 2006; Celenza & Gabbard, 2003; Gabbard, 1995; Gabbard & Peltz, 2001)—in other words, the psychopathology of loving or sexual feelings and actions on the part of the therapist. A smaller number had to do with the ongoing spirited debate over the advisability of the therapist's disclosure to the patient of erotic countertransference feelings (e.g., Davies, 1994, 1998; Gabbard, 1994a, 1998) in the context of the therapeutic work of analysis. Although the importance of the appearance in our literature of a thorough discussion of boundary violations, their evaluation, and possible treatment cannot be overstated, this literature also served inadvertently to reinforce the taboos against having or writing about any loving feelings experienced towards one's patients.[73]

As it turns out, there *is* a little literature on the therapist's loving feelings for his or her patients (e.g., Coen, 1994; Friedman, 2005; Nacht, 1962a; Natterson, 2003; Novick & Novick, 2000; Segal, 1962), but it is still so small that it is hard to determine what weight to assign to it. It should come as no surprise that love in the therapeutic situation is a hard subject to write about, even if it is first stipulated, as I have done, that it is a non-sexual sort of love that is not acted upon, is not an aspect of psychopathology, and does not contain any sort of technical recommendations. It is a remarkably difficult subject to think about, feel about, and talk about. Friedman (2005) observes, "one hardly need ask whether analysts are fond of many patients" (p. 349). Perhaps. However, none of my colleagues or patients has ever spontaneously talked to *me*, or to others in my presence for that matter, about such feelings, so I remain skeptical concerning this presumptive lack of a need to ask.

There are no surveys here, nor would their results necessarily be reliable. I believe that analysts do have loving feelings for their patients, but whether all or nearly all do, whether some do but are largely unaware of them, and to what degree those analysts who are aware of them actually think very much about them, I have no idea. To the extent that some

72 The relational literature, it is true, is much concerned with therapists' feelings towards their patients and the clinical employment of those feelings, but it is not much concerned with the particulars of loving feelings.

73 This is doubly ironic because this literature had itself broken through the taboos against talking about or dealing with colleagues' sexual boundary violations individually or institutionally.

psychoanalysts subscribe to the concept of therapeutic neutrality, it is hard to imagine their being aware of any such feelings. I see nothing for it but to speak for myself concerning such loving feelings as I am aware of, and infer what I can from what other analysts have written about their experiences outside of transference/countertransference[74] interplay.

I'm afraid that readers waiting for a definition of love will be disappointed. It is not that I wish to leave the problem exclusively to poets and philosophers or, as Freud suggested, that "our psychoanalytic flag ought [not] to be raised over the territory of normal love" (Freud & Jung, 1974, p. 287). I believe, to the contrary, that psychoanalysts have a role to play in the discussion of love, alongside the poets and philosophers, but also alongside the neuroscientists and the social network theorists. However, it is a role beyond the scope of a single chapter. I have two reasons for not offering a definition. The first follows Sandler's (1983) rather postmodern argument for the importance of the imprecise and the elastic in psychoanalytic terminology, very much in the spirit of Freud's writing in the original German:

> Elastic concepts play a very important role in holding psychoanalytic theory together. As psychoanalysis is made up of formulations at varying levels of abstraction, and of part-theories which do not integrate well with one another, the existence of pliable, context-dependent concepts allows an overall framework of psychoanalytic theory to be assembled ... The elastic and flexible concepts take up the strain of theoretical exchange, absorbing it while more organized newer theories or part-theories can develop.
>
> (p. 36)

The second reason is more basic. I suspect that love is a "primitive," a term that defies further definition. This will have to do. As will become apparent, even this very partial discussion of love and its place in therapy raises complex issues with uncertain conclusions. In contrast to the limited analytic literature, it is not at all possible at this point to simply offer a theory of therapeutic love, even if illustrated with case material. I think Friedman (2005), whom I take to task for his distancing himself and his work from the subject, is more thoughtful about these limitations than are other authors (e.g., Davies, 1994, 1998; Natterson, 2003; Novick & Novick, 2000) who appear to have little problem making

74 I have found transference and countertransference to be so interreferential that, in the absence of some particular purpose, it seems artificial to refer to them in isolation.

absolute declarative statements about what therapeutic love consists of and where it fits in the therapeutic situation. Given all of these caveats, what is offered here about the therapist's love for her patients is, unlike the other more fully realized chapters of this book, very much a preliminary communication. My plan is to look at these issues, and then turn to postmodernism and neuroscience for some preliminary answers.

Epistemological Problems: More Questions than Answers

Writing about therapeutic love immediately imposes difficulties. The first concerns the very question: do therapists love their patients? I can say for myself that I do and that most therapists probably do as well. I put the question to a few colleagues and found they answered affirmatively in terms of liking their patients or finding something to like in them. I *assumed* that they shied away from the *L*-word because of its sexual and extra-therapeutic connotations, but I did not feel in a position to press them. Like is safer, if less accurate. That leaves those analysts who profess some version of therapeutic neutrality; if *they* were to have such feelings, they could only do so by not thinking about them or by labeling them as countertransference. This certainly is very possible, but not knowable.

However, most of us have heard about or even experienced affectless analysts and how unsatisfactory they and their analytic work prove to be.[75] We sometimes succeed in convincing ourselves for years or even decades that this lack of affect is not a problem; we sometimes even identify with the aggressor (i.e., our analyst) as a way to avoid confronting it. Finally, there are anecdotal reports of something more negative. When I was a resident, a supervisor once told me that he "preferred to work with negative transference," which, based on the supervisory process, seemed to entail provoking it in patients. He contrasted this work with what he termed *unanalytic support*. A colleague once related to me that a relative had told her analyst that she thought he disliked her. He responded that they didn't need to like each other for the analysis to be successful. She wisely terminated the treatment.

I want to posit two things: one, that therapeutic love is not sexual, and two that therapists and analysts are, of course, capable of sexual feelings

75 Tessman (2003) offers clinical material that illustrates this problem.

for their patients. The latter stands quite apart from the former and falls within the province of transference/countertransference. In other words, sexual feelings are a part of clinical process, hopefully subject to analysis, self-analysis, or supervision.[76]

The problem with this assertion is that, in making it, I have had to create a number of identity categories. Love for a patient is assigned to one category, while clinical process is assigned to another. (There is disagreement as to the viability of such a separation even in the limited literature on the analyst's loving feelings.) I also mean to imply that the latter category is relational while the former is not; *it focuses on the analyst as subject of this love not the patient as the object of it.* The problem here is that these categories are constructs; they serve a useful heuristic purpose in allowing us to talk about these different things, but as separations, they are artificial and unstable.[77]

Can a feeling for a patient, in this case love, be entirely uninflected by the two-person therapeutic interaction that is simultaneously going on? We have already said that these categories are to a degree unstable. There has to be some degree of interreferentiality between the occupants of these different categories. The view of loving feelings for patients that I am espousing is quite different from those put forth by other authors (indeed, the more I hear and read, the more I think that such loving remains something of an individual matter); I believe this variance merits a certain degree of tentativeness in my argument.

Questions, Questions, Questions

Other problems lie in the question of just where does the patient fit in as the object of such love. If the patient is expected (or theorized) to possess some complementary feeling, how is this different from the transference/countertransference interplay or its relational analogues? If we were to have such an expectation, would our feelings then limit the patient's freedom to experience or explore the spectrum of negative feelings towards us that most of us feel has a necessary place in an effective analysis? Can we perhaps develop these loving feelings quite independently of a patient's response *in kind* and maintain them in some

76 This is a controversial statement in that some analysts think quite differently about the role of their sexual feelings in an analysis or psychotherapy (e.g., Davies, 1994, 1998).

77 As I have argued elsewhere (Leffert, 2010a), I view the separation of transference/countertransference, the working alliance, and the real relationship as equally unstable.

manner that does not elicit such a response? This does seem at least possible. Loving feelings would then indeed have much more to do with the analyst as subject than with the patient as object and would stand in proximity to her treating or healing role, in her head rather than in the relationship.

Do our patients love us, and if so what kind of love is it? Is it transference love as Freud (1915 [1914]/1958c) taught us? Not always, I think, and not entirely. I have a clear sense that some of my patients feel affection for me, all right, they love me, while with others I don't know, and, with some others, I know they do not. These feelings change, I think, over the course of an analysis. How necessary is our love, or a patient's love, for a successful analytic outcome? I don't feel that I am yet able to answer that question, although some analysts (e.g., Marcus & "Hope," 2007) believe that such a reciprocal bond is necessary for success. I can say that I believe the analyst's love is a curative factor in an analysis. Tessman's (2003) subjects (see chapter 6) who considered their analyses highly satisfying were describing something in their analysts that sounded similar to love, although they did not (were afraid to?) use the word *love*.

An equally troubling problem involves the hard question: If therapists do love their patients, do they do so equally, do they love all of them or only some of them, and what accounts for the differences? And what effect does it have on patients for an analyst to go public about this question? (Although there is justifiable concern about violating confidentiality in a case vignette, I have found no systematic account of the effects of an analyst's writing on his other patients.) Coen (1994), who seems to treat analysts loving their patients as a given (a conclusion that I would see as beyond our ability to know or determine), begins his paper "Barriers to Love Between Patient and Analyst" with his own useful list of questions:

> Is love resistance or vehicle for change? How much love (and how much hatred) must patient and analyst feel toward each other for an analysis to be effective? When and how do such passionate feelings between the analytic couple interfere with analytic change? Are loving feelings between the analytic couple merely neurotic wishes in each which must be relinquished or do they facilitate growth? If loving feelings do assist change, how do they do so?
> (p. 1107)

By the very nature of these questions, it is clear that Coen is pointing towards different givens and answers than I am. At the very least, he locates loving feelings clinically in the specifics of therapeutic action.

Friedman (2005) asks a number of important questions (and prompts me to ask one of my own) that he proceeds to discuss, although he makes no attempt at offering any personal answers. "Do analysts have feelings for patients?" (p. 350). "Are the analyst's feelings a standard part of the treatment?" (p. 351). "Why do analysts think they love their patients?" (p. 352). And, why do "analysts want analytic love to be different?" (p. 354). Without meaning to lessen the importance of these questions, Friedman, in his discussions, has no problem in generalizing about "analysts" from a tiny literature and a microscopic sample; I am unable to follow his example. The presence of so many questions and the coincident lack of clarification about a therapist's love are not new; they go back to Freud's own confusions manifested by the diversity and disorganization of his writings on the subject.

Freud's Dilemma

Freud's views on love are among the least well understood of his works, an instance of emotion foundering on the rocks of metapsychology. Indeed, although he unites love and sex under the rubric of *Eros*, they are neither truly united nor separate. One could read much of his oeuvre with scarcely any sense that a problem exists at all. Freud's central concern was the establishment of psychoanalysis as a movement and a therapeutic discipline; normal emotions like love were of lesser importance. To achieve those goals he was primarily interested in drive theory and the analysis of the drives. As such, his principle interest was in sex and describing it as the fuel cell that drove the mental apparatus.

Sexuality is removed from the picture by displacement in the *Three Essays* (1905/1953c), sublimation in " 'Civilized' Sexual Morality and Modern Nervous Illness" (Freud, 1908/1959a) as well as in the *Three Essays*, and conversion to narcissistic libido in *The Ego and the Id* (1923/1961a). Non-sexual love was left as a watered down version of sexuality that seemed to trace its origins to the baby at the mother's breast (1905/1953c). But this left no place for any other kind of love; in the therapeutic situation such feelings on the part of analysts for their patients remained dangerous and this dangerousness was handed down generationally along with the rest of revealed psychoanalytic wisdom.[78]

78 Freud's concerns about Ferenczi and Jung's sexual activity and, at least in Ferenczi's case, his love for his patients (Gabbard, 1995), must have influenced Freud's views on the subject. Ferenczi's behavior occurred in the context of his developing a more active technique in which

As Bergmann points out (1987/1991), Freud could probably have formulated a more coherent argument concerning *Eros*, love, and sex if he had both acknowledged the contributions of Plato, Nietzsche, and Schopenhauer to his position on *Eros* and sublimation and then went on to develop them further. As it is, we are left with several scattered, but important, comments on Freud's part that move drive theory and the analysis of the drives back to love.

If we look elsewhere in Freud, we find a range of different ideas about love. In "Instincts and Their Vicissitudes" (1915/1957d), he observes "the case of love and hate acquires a special interest from the circumstance that it refuses to be fitted into our scheme of the instincts . . . we are naturally unwilling to think of love as being some kind of special component instinct of sexuality" (p. 133). Love is already special and different. Five years later in "Group Psychology . . ." (Freud, 1921/1955c), he goes on to treat love as a global emotion with multiple referents:

> The nucleus of what we mean by love naturally consists in sexual love with sexual union as its aim. But we do not separate from this—what in any case has a share in the name "love"—on the one hand, self-love, and on the other, love for parents and children, friendship and love for humanity in general, and also devotion to concrete objects and to abstract ideas . . . We are of the opinion then, that language has carried out an entirely justifiable piece of unification in creating the word "love" *with its numerous uses*, and that we cannot do better . . .
>
> (pp. 90–91, italics added)

Finally, in a few sentences of the posthumously published *Outline of Psychoanalysis* (1940 [1938]/1964c), Freud offers a radical reformulation of his concepts of love and *Eros*: "The aim of the first of these basic instincts [*Eros*] is to establish ever greater unities and to preserve them thus—in short to bind together . . . The aim of the second [*the destructive instinct*] is, on the contrary, to undo connections" (p. 148). Libido remains the energy of *Eros*, but "there can be no question of restricting one or the other of the basic instincts to one of the provinces [id, ego, or superego] of the mind" (p. 149). Freud, in effect, leaves us with an open

he encouraged patients to express their feelings (1930, 1919/1952). He advocated a "principle of indulgence" (1930, p. 434). There were references to Ferenczi's kissing patients and allowing them to kiss him; one was in a letter to Freud (Freud & Ferenczi, 1996) and another in a letter from Freud to Ferenczi (Freud & Ferenczi, 2000) in which Freud writes "you have made no secret that you kiss patients and allow them to kiss you" (p. 422). Freud saw this as playing with fire. The legend of Breuer's flight from psychoanalysis because of his reactions to Anna O.'s transference has been served up as a cautionary tale for generations of psychoanalysts. (I say legend because both Novick & Novick, 2000, and Breger, 2009, have researched this story and find little truth in it.)

playing field on which to take the subject of love where we will and leave structural theory on the sideline.

Freud did describe deviations from a position of abstinence in his clinical work that indicated a deep, if understated, caring for his patients. He proposed the first of these (1919 [1918]/1955d) with an uncertain connection to Ferenczi. Freud discusses what he means by *activity* in psychoanalysis.

> We have defined our therapeutic task as consisting of two things: making conscious the repressed material and uncovering the resistances. In that we are active enough, to be sure. But are we to leave it to the patient to deal alone with the resistances we have pointed out to him? Can we give him no other help in this besides the stimulus he gets from the transference? Does it not seem natural that we should help him in another way as well, by putting him into the mental situation most favourable to the solution of the conflict which is our aim? After all, what he can achieve depends, too, on a combination of external circumstances. Should we hesitate to alter this combination by intervening in a suitable manner? I think activity of such a kind on the part of the analysing physician is unobjectionable and entirely justified.
>
> (p. 162)

From what Freud goes on to say in this paper, and from what Rachman (1997) gleans about his technique in this area from several sources, Freud meant two things by activity. The first had to do with caring for his patients when the need arose (e.g., feeding the Rat Man when he was hungry; Lipton, 1977). The second had to do with actively encouraging patients suffering from phobias or obsessions to struggle against them in order to bring them into the analysis. Although Freud did not pursue these points in his subsequent writings, there is no evidence that he did not continue to make use of them in his clinical work. His personal caring for Sergei Pankejeff (also known as the Wolf Man), the responsibility for whom was assumed by Muriel Gardiner, in fact became a psychoanalytic legend. Freud's conversations with Abraham Kardiner (1977) during the latter's analysis reveal a level of intimacy and self-disclosure far beyond what is described in contemporaneous writings on orthodox technique (e.g., Glover, 1931).

If We Do Love Our Patients, Where Have We Put That Love and What Do We Do with It?

It is fair to say that for an analyst to write about loving feelings for his or her patients still, in 2010, is a courageous act. Gabbard (1994a) has observed that this is particularly so for male analysts writing about their loving feelings for female patients. Recently (July 27, 2010), a colleague's internet posting advocating less analytic listening and less constraint (a stance that the current psychoanalytic consumer generally subscribes to) was met by another analyst's immediate rejoinder placing such increased activity in the same category as sexual boundary violations.

A number of authors (Celenza & Gabbard, 2003; Coen, 1994; Davies, 1994; Searles, 1959) have commented on the fact that most of us have been inculcated as part of our analytic *training* with the premise that, beyond the occasional useful bits of countertransference, such loving feelings are simply bad. Coen (1994) notes "our analytic ego ideal may tend to encourage constriction and discomfort for the full range of our loving feelings with analysands and that such closure will interfere with analytic change and growth" (pp. 1108–1109). Similarly, Searles (1959) observes, "my training has been predominantly such as to make me hold rather suspect any strong feelings on the part of the analyst toward his patient, and these particular emotions seem to be of an especially illegitimate nature" (p. 180). (I would suggest that things are not all that different a half-century later.) In spite of this, Searles was able to both experience and write that toward the end of any successful analysis he felt both romantic and erotic feelings for his patients. In each case, they lasted for a number of months and became a subject of self-analysis.

I have noted in myself an increasing awareness of loving feelings for my patients as I have researched and written this chapter. What began as an observation of feelings for a few patients now appears to be much more widespread in my practice. I can only account for this change in the context of my having unconsciously pathologized these feelings. I would posit this to be the case for a great many therapists.

The acknowledgement by analytic authors that they have loving feelings for their patients is accompanied by a somewhat matter-of-fact taxonomy and some particular clinical approach to dealing with them that is not, I believe, at all warranted. Friedman (2005) is perhaps alone in observing that there are a wide range of differing views on the subject that require us to question such certainty. The varying choices made by these authors also carry with them a number of epistemological consequences or problems.

Authors have most commonly chosen to locate loving feelings for their patients in the transference/countertransference. In all of what follows, when I say that analysts locate loving feelings in a particular place, it does not mean that that's where the feelings actually are, only that they have made a decision in the realm of clinical *theory* about where to put them. In other words, they can have the feelings but be quite wrong in their conclusions about where they reside. Although Freud never formulated the concept as such, it seems clear that he would have located what he would have termed his caring feelings for his patients in an *unobjectionable positive countertransference.* Coen (1994), Davies (1994, 1998), Gabbard (1998, 2001), Kernberg (1994), and Searles (1959) all locate loving feelings for the patient in this area with the transference forming an essential part of them.

The centrality of the transference/countertransference to the clinical theory of most analysts no doubt accounts for its popularity as a locale for loving feelings. It allows them to address these feelings in the usual therapeutic manner from wherever they locate themselves on the relational and self-disclosure axes. No real alteration in clinical theory need be considered or developed. It is true that although Coen (1994) seems not to talk about his loving feelings for his patients at all and Davies talks explicitly about her sexual feelings when they arise, neither appear in doing so to be deviating from their own standard techniques.[79] There are problems with choosing the transference/countertransference as a location for the analyst's loving feelings. Transference/countertransference is all about displacement. The true subjects and objects of the feelings are not in the room; they are located far away in space and time. The feelings are, in effect, *imagined.*

Many authors (e.g., Nacht, 1962a; Natterson, 2003; Novick & Novick, 2000; Segal, 1962) do not consider loving feelings to be imagined. Nor is it entirely clear that authors using this location want to consider their loving feelings as imagined; Coen (1994) speaks well of this dilemma. He points out that Freud wanted transference feelings to be both real and genuine, but also unreal (Freud, 1915 [1914]/1958c). As for himself, Coen wants "the freedom to enjoy feeling a variety of passions with [his] patients" (p. 1108), while also identifying his patients and his "own wishes for and defenses against wanting and giving love [as residing] *in*

79 Within the psychoanalytic frame there are certainly a number of different "standard techniques" consistent with the broad theoretical orientations that coexist with at times great difficulty under the umbrella of psychoanalysis (I have elsewhere, Leffert, 2010a, criticized the standing of any such orientations). The fact that Davies (1994) talked explicitly with her patients about her sexual fantasies towards them is, I believe (and most analysts would agree with me), outside the frame. The variations with which analysts conceptualize their loving feelings for their patients particularly suggests that standard technique is probably a very individual thing. While this formulation might be seen as problematic by some, it does allow for the fact that the way in which one analyst works can include successful components that might or might not prove effective if employed by another.

the analytic transference" (p. 1113, italics added). Other problems have to do with a tendency, particularly in older writings and older theories of technique, to assign all feelings arising in the therapeutic situation to the transference/countertransference. This location often does not work very well.

As I have already suggested, assigning the variety of feelings that therapists and patients have for each other to locations in impermeable identity categories that we have constructed is an arbitrary and unstable exercise. By positing that the loving feelings that we are describing are not situated in the transference/countertransference, I do not mean that an absolute separation is possible. Rather, as no transference/countertransference feeling is devoid of reality, so no loving feeling is entirely devoid of transference/countertransference. It would also seem to have to be true that there is a potential for feelings whose character places them in one category to evoke feelings in the other.

Other authors (e.g., Davies, 1998; Gabbard, 1994b; Kernberg, 1994; Searles, 1959) also variously locate the analyst's love along the temporal spectrum of pre-oedipal, oedipal, and post-oedipal development. These locations are problematic in that they introduce fixation, regression, and conflict into this area of the analyst's functioning. That is to say, these feelings, if cast in this way, represent an aspect of the therapist's psychopathology. Many would have it so. They ignore the possibility that their reactions could as easily represent simple reaction formations, themselves evidence of psychopathology.

The Novicks (Novick & Novick, 2000) take a position that successfully addresses these problems, and if I disagree with them at all it is only around the nature of the terrain on which the analytic encounter takes place. They identify two different kinds of love that analysts may experience towards their patients: a mature, adult kind of love and an infantile one. The former occurs as part of an open, reality-oriented, system, while the latter takes place in a closed system, sadomasochistically organized around omnipotent beliefs. It is a response to helpless feelings on the part of the analyst. The latter they place in the countertransference, where it should be the subject of further analysis rather than playing a role in the theory of technique.[80] The first kind of love is what they are interested in as a healthy part of any therapy or analysis. They describe it as developing gradually over the course of an analysis or therapy, beginning around the sharing of knowledge during the evaluation or

80 This kind of love is similar to what is described by Celenza and Gabbard (2003; Gabbard, 1994b) as appearing in some therapists and analysts who commit sexual boundary violations.

opening phase of the treatment. Entirely consistent with their description of it, they find a different place in the therapeutic relationship in which to locate it; the therapeutic alliance. Their aim is "to establish a technical and theoretical space for what [they] call objective love" (p. 204). They also want to "emphasize the ongoing need to distinguish between omnipotent power relations in a closed system of functioning, disguised as love, and the growth-enhancing love that [they] allocate to open-system functioning" (p. 204).

Other authors take a much less structured approach to the nature and importance of the analyst's love in the therapeutic situation. Lear (1990/1998) and Loewald (1988) both view the very act of the analyst's doing analysis with his patient as a manifestation of love. Nacht (1962a), in a panel discussion, is very critical of the effects of a frustrating analyst on a patient who, in childhood, has known frustration at the hands of his parents. He (Nacht, 1962b) observes, after considerable struggle, that "the analyst must bring love to the patient" (p. 233). In the same panel discussion, Segal (1962) responds to Nacht with the observation, "like Nacht, I consider that a good therapeutic setting must include unconscious love in the analyst for the patient" (p. 232).

I want to return to the question of the Novicks' (Novick & Novick, 2000) technical and theoretical space shortly, but we must first address a serious criticism of the whole idea of therapists loving their patients. Many therapists, particularly those subscribing to some version of clinical neutrality, would argue that these loving feelings are a burden to patients that interfere with their developing hateful or angry feelings towards their therapists and instead experience guilt at the idea of feeling this way about their loving analyst. Some might also argue that analysts develop these loving feelings precisely in order to avoid or deflect such an assault or as a defense against *their own* hostile, angry feelings. They are right to raise these concerns. If the feelings were a part of the transference/countertransference (I do not believe that they are), then these concerns would be telling; as it is, they can be answered.

The first point is that the great majority of authors, myself included, do not make these loving feelings an explicit part of the therapeutic encounter but restrict them to their own experience and reflections. They *say* nothing about them. For me, they remain as an implicit tone in the background of my experience during a psychotherapy or analysis. Their presence at that level fluctuates in or out of awareness (they have become more present, perhaps temporarily, as I have been writing about them). They are about me as the subject and not about the patient as the object of love. They could be thought of as having a great deal to do with a holding environment or a containment. We also know that, in and out of the therapeutic situation, love and hate can rather easily both be present. Finally, in my own clinical experience with my loving feelings handled in this way (and in the case vignettes presented by some authors: Coen, 1994; Natterson, 2003; Novick & Novick, 2000), patients generally do not appear to have any difficulty becoming angry with me, absent some inhibition that needs to be addressed.

My friend and colleague Jimmy Fisher (personal communication, October 30, 2010) took me to task for not discussing or raising my loving feelings for patients with them. In reconsidering the question, I would now say that I would not now absolutely rule it out. However, I would see it as a rare event that would take place late in a therapy for specific and individual reasons; I have not, as of this writing, found occasion for doing so. Like him, I view and experience the therapeutic situation as a dialectic of one-person and two-person psychologies, of the autocentric and allocentric. I would see loving feelings as mostly being considered in the one-person mode.

So why not discuss them with our patients? Contrary to what we are taught, most of us know that some things in an analysis are best left inexplicit; I believe loving feelings are among them. The act of naming a thing has textual significance of its own that can take a narrative in unexpected and unwished for directions of meaning. In this case, an analyst's naming his loving feelings can easily produce iatrogenic transference reactions in a patient, both positive and negative, that would not have developed if the analyst had not brought them up in the first place. This, then, becomes an unanticipated expression of power that is at once problematic. Expressing loving feelings (as opposed to simply having them), in addition to the possibility of overstimulating a patient, also may make it more difficult and potentially guilt inducing for her to experience or voice the range of negative feelings that must come up in any successful therapy; anger, rage, hatred, disappointment, and fear, to name a few.

A further point must be mentioned here. I have posited throughout this book that much of what takes place in the therapeutic situation takes place outside of awareness or involves unconscious communication between patient and therapist. If the same is true for the analyst's loving feelings, and I believe it must be, then the patient knows about them already. In that case, someone might object, why not talk about it? The answer as addressed above is that knowing is not naming and does not carry with it the additional meanings or sequelae that the naming of a thing involves.

I applaud the Novicks (Novick & Novick, 2000) positing that the analyst's mature, loving feelings are not a part of transference/countertransference. However, the technical and theoretical space they create for them seems to be more of a place to talk about them than a therapeutic space that they populate. They see their loving feelings as a part of the therapeutic alliance and are rightly critical of the sharp distinctions between transference, working alliance, and real relationship that Greenson (1967) writes of.

I have taken these criticisms much further. These three categories are constructs, useful ones (they were particularly useful when all that the analytic literature described was transference), but still only constructs. Their separation is a matter of convention *not* of reality. They are three interreferential ways of viewing and describing all the events that take place in the therapeutic situation in which the analyst's loving feelings are somehow involved. As we have seen, there is also considerable disagreement about where the therapist's loving feelings fit into this arrangement. Two different theoretical perspectives may be able to cast more light on this somewhat strange state of affairs: one is complexity and systems theory and the other is the phenomenology of space.

Complexity and Systems Theory

The therapeutic situation is a complex, holistic system consisting of patient, therapist, the therapist's office (or the telephone or video link between them), and all that is going on mentally–physically within and between them (Leffert, 2010a). It is a member of a class of complex systems that we might call experience and communication systems; they include roughly what is going on in the participants' heads, what is going into them, and what is coming out of them, partly through their mouths and partly in other ways. If we consider three of the things that can characterize what goes on in the therapeutic system—transference/countertransference, therapeutic alliance, and real relationships—from a postmodern perspective, we find that we are dealing with groups of discursive practices that can never be completely separate from one another. Experience can modify these practices in ways that influence future experience.

Neurocognitively, we encounter much the same state of affairs. Here, we are dealing with memory, both narrative memory and perceptual memory, conceptual priming, and perception. All of these always interact, albeit to greater or lesser extents that determine experience.

They are also modified by that experience in ways that effect subsequent experiences.

Although the temptation exists to draw three circles with some overlap and label them transference/countertransference, therapeutic alliance, and real relationship, it is important to try not to think of the therapeutic system in spatial terms. (The functional neuroanatomy of the brain is only a partial exception that has certain functions concentrated in but not limited to, certain anatomical areas.) Laszlo (1972/1996) would describe them as atomic elements whose separation is arbitrary and lacks ontological standing. Love, in holistic systems theory, is either present or absent in the therapeutic system. If present, it has more or less, sometimes a great deal more or less, to do with each of these atomic elements. The same state of affairs exists in the more usual relationships outside of analysis.

I believe this provides a more accurate picture of the actual distinctions that the Novicks (Novick & Novick, 2000) are talking about. There is a significant degree of commonality between the therapeutic alliance and the real relationship. One would expect therapeutic love of the open and reality-based variety they describe to involve both of these areas. This is *not* to say that because it involves the real relationship between patient and therapist it is like any love relationship outside of therapy. Rather it involves who the therapeutic partners are *within the frame* of the therapeutic situation.

The Phenomenology of the Therapeutic Space

There has been a tendency to conflate the literal and psychological spaces in which a therapy takes place (Leffert, 2003), with the former often largely ignored. The office and waiting room are constructed by the analyst with various possible motivations, some more conducive to a robust therapeutic process than others. Some analysts favor a barren office, as empty as possible, out of a mistaken pursuit of neutrality. These offices aren't neutral, they're just barren or empty. Others include Freud-like objects, figurines and oriental rugs (I confess to having some of these, although my tastes tend towards the Chalcolithic and Far Eastern rather than the Egyptian). The office is richly evocative to both parties and, regardless of choice, communicates a great deal about the analyst. How often do we consider the notion that the office, first, should be a *comfortable* space for our patients and ourselves? We spend much of our lives in our offices and patients need the *opportunity* to feel relaxed and safe there, even if their thoughts take them elsewhere. As I have described it (Leffert, 2010a):

> The analytic office is not experienced in isolation but rather is inseparably embedded in a social and historical matrix. Gaston Bachelard evocatively describes in *The Poetics of Space* (1958/1994) the way occupied spaces—the house, a chest, a nest—are imbued and encrusted with meaning and emotion, not just for the individual but as social and historical signifiers. His phenomenological discussion applies to the analyst and patient situated in the analytic space. The office and waiting room can, for example, evoke elements of sanctuary, the confessional, the analytic office of popular culture, or the medical office. The office is almost always experienced as inhabited by the analyst, rarely as empty. This image is usually a comforting one. It serves to always locate the analyst and make him or her seem the keeper of a vigil. Bachelard evokes the image of an anchorite whose presence in a small cabin in a dark forest at night is signified by the presence of the lamp in the window.
>
> (p. 49)

The analyst's experience of his office varies (as does the patient's). I am unaware of mine much of the time, but can sometimes glance at an object or painting I'm fond of or, more relevantly to this discussion, think of the patient as comfortably settled there.

Descriptions of the psychological space in which the analysis takes place are probably most fully realized in the intersubjective literature (e.g., Stolorow & Atwood, 1992; Stolorow, Atwood, & Brandchaft, 1994) and in Ogden's (1997, 2003) concept of the analytic third. They talk in different ways about private space (analyst's and patient's) and shared overlapping therapeutic space. I view my loving feelings as residing in my private space, but must also assume that they have some presence, even if it is implicit, in the shared space. I will offer clinical material from two cases, a man and a woman, to illustrate what my experience of loving feelings for patients looks like to me. I make no claims that they appear the same to other analysts, nor that there is a "right" or "correct" form of experience.

Clinical Illustrations

Case One: John

John, a successful, well-dressed vice-president at Honeywell, sought analysis years ago for a variety of obsessive concerns, anxiety about his work, and an unhappy marriage (although he could not at first name it as such) within which he lived an emotionally separate life of 16-hour days at the office. He was desperately concerned lest his employers find out about his therapy and initially asked for a modification in how I would bill his insurance company. I had to refuse; he told me he would have to think about this, but called back within a few minutes to tell me he wanted to proceed. I understood, but I didn't like this inauspicious beginning. The child of superficial, narcissistic parents, he described a difficult childhood, filled with anxiety, in which he was teased and bullied at school and found pleasure only in eating. His wife was coolly distant, the perfect antidote to his seductive mother. His long hours at work made him a weekend dad to his teenage son and daughter.

Transference/countertransference developed quickly, manifesting itself in competitive struggles for control; he was successful on more than one occasion in drawing me into these. During these months, I didn't like him very much, but this feeling in myself was blunted by a degree of forbearance and an appreciation of how difficult his life was and had been for him. It emerged in due course that in battling with me he was working out anger at and disappointment in his father, who had been physically frightening and preoccupied with himself. I observed this to him, but only *after* he had fully experienced it with me. As this work progressed, his anxiety became much diminished and he could bring himself to take the higher-level position at Honeywell that had been on offer to him for some time.

My feelings for John appeared very gradually. I began to realize that I could like him and later that I liked him a lot. I felt that if he were not a patient, he could have been a close friend, but I also knew that he wasn't. We had a number of common interests and I recognized how hard he had struggled over the years to try to overcome his inhibitions and fears of living up to his potential. I came to admire how he became able to deal with people at all levels of his work, remaining remarkably even-tempered as he pursued his goals of helping them to deal with each other and the work at hand realistically rather than angrily or narcissistically.

That this new ability grew out of the analysis was clear. How this happened was not clear at all. I had to acknowledge somewhat ruefully (to myself) that he was much better at this than I was and found myself learning something from him about dealing with people effectively in difficult organizational situations. I never said anything to John about my feelings for him, reserving them for my own reflection. At the same time, I have no doubt that something of them was conveyed by the warmth with which I greeted him and the interest I showed in him and his life (although I did not see any substantial difference between these attitudes and those I experienced in my dealings with other patients). I believe I conveyed an appreciation of the work he was doing in the analysis.

Coen (1994) writes of enjoying his passionate feelings for his patients; I can't say that I have experienced my own in that way. This could easily be the result of the very inhibitions and constraints against such feelings that come with the psychoanalytic education that Coen is writing about. It may also be that, in this area, individual therapists are just different. I have to say that at this point I simply don't know. In the context of a debate over the merits of talking explicitly with patients about sexual feelings for them, Gabbard (1994a) expresses his concerns about a slippery slope that can develop from boundary crossings to frank boundary violations. I have not had any such experiences, nor have I felt any impulses, rationalized or otherwise, to loosen my technique; I would stress at the same time that what I am writing about and experiencing are loving feelings without a sexual component. As I've written, I have recognized that I should put a great deal more thought into this area to better understand these feelings for patients. I think we all should.[81]

As the analysis progressed, John was able to achieve a rapprochement with both of his parents that involved telling them how they had made him feel over the years and accepting their significant limitations. He found that his father, although limited, had more to offer him emotionally than he had thought. A major theme appeared in his guilt and mourning over the fact that he had done little better than his own father in being emotionally present for his children. This he *could* change and found his now young adult children were initially angry but later receptive.

Through all of this, he found his wife largely unreceptive to his attempts at increasing their intimacy. He spent a considerable amount of his time late in the analysis considering divorce, and ultimately decided against it. John had been married for 25 years. He felt that he got many things from the marriage, including an increasing degree of companionship that he found meaningful, if less than he might have wanted. Approaching retirement age, he had adapted to the relationship and did not want to try to start over. As this issue played out, termination was in the air. His relationship with me was not one that he could

81 A reader might well ask, "What makes you think you're so interesting?" I would answer that I don't, what I think is interesting is the struggle to grasp and make sense of this area of feeling and that more of us need to undertake that struggle. As I've said, I also believe that most of the writing in this area tends to suffer from excessive and unwarranted certainty.

adapt to and continue forever, he told me, as much as he might want to. We set a termination date and, as it approached, I felt a growing sense of loss, intense at times. I dreamt on one occasion of an empty office and an empty couch. My feelings, I think, were more intense than his; he explained to me that he felt he was taking part of me with him as a kind of presence or part of himself. As far as I or any of us can know, I conveyed little of this to John and none of it explicitly. It did not feel like a shared reaction; the loving feelings and the loss had to do with me, not with him or his reaction to me.

Case Two: Karen

Karen, a nephrologist in her mid-40s with two teenage daughters, sought treatment when her husband of 20 years told her he had been having an affair and wanted a divorce. Theirs had been an unhappy marriage punctuated by his lack of interest in working at all, much less up to the level of his two graduate degrees. In spite of this, Karen responded to the announcement with the feeling that she had been "hit by a truck." She came in traumatized, experiencing overwhelming periods of grief, insomnia, and some flashbacks to the moment he told her he was leaving her. Over the years, I had seen a number of women who presented with a picture of Post Traumatic Stress Disorder (PTSD) in similar situations.

We began meeting twice a week in psychotherapy that focused on the reality of her situation. In spite of its limitations, she very much wanted to reconstitute her marriage, even as her husband filed for divorce and sought spousal support. Beyond being sympathetic about her situation, I experienced no particular liking for her. As the divorce proceeded, I found myself feeling the outrage at her husband's behavior that she herself could not yet feel. My telling her this marked a turning point in this phase of her treatment; she found herself beginning to feel angry and started sleeping through the night.

Karen came from an intact family. Her father was an internist on the full-time faculty of a medical school and her mother was a successful corporate attorney whose income exceeded her father's academic salary. The father showed considerable warmth to his two daughters (Karen was the eldest by a year), while her mother was an aggressive, no-nonsense sort of person who cared for her children but was not much interested in their concerns. She interrupted her career when Karen was born, and did not return to work until her sister entered nursery school. This was the happiest time of Karen's childhood. In retrospect, her mother seemed to feel that she had finished with most of her mothering and her daughters should be more able to take care of themselves.

The loss to Karen was overwhelming and at best poorly understood before she began therapy. Her character incorporated identifications with both parents. She chose a sub-specialty of her father's profession, but went into private practice instead. Like her mother, she went about her life in a businesslike fashion, adeptly juggling her many commitments. Unlike her parents, she worked 30-hour weeks; her daughters were the center of her life. Her marriage had been a disappointment to her. Beneath the surface, she had felt contempt for what she saw as her husband's laziness; she had never considered the role that her focus on her daughters at his expense had in bringing this about.

Karen's psychological crisis abated over the next few months as the divorce machinery ground on. She began to recognize that outside of her relationship with her daughters, she had always felt dissatisfied and unhappy with her life. I suggested analysis and she readily agreed. I found that I had come to admire her and wanted very much to help free her to make the most of her life. A very close friend of mine, also a nephrologist, had died young and under unhappy circumstances. Rescuing her would have been a way of magically rescuing him. This, as I came to know it, I understood as countertransference; when I worked through its early roots I was left with what I would call a positive disposition towards her. This was not much different from what I experience with most patients. I did not discuss these feelings or their genetic roots with Karen as Natterson (2003) did with his patient.

A negative paternal transference soon developed in which she raged at me for the combination of her father's warmth and his unavailability. The warmth that *I* felt for her could easily have been communicated implicitly and formed the basis for her transference response. At the same time, she began to enjoy her contempt for her husband. In the face of these kinds of negative affect, I am generally able to keep listening, but feel a degree of constriction and pulling back. With Karen, I did not feel that, I felt I was rooting for her and enjoyed the torrent. I was particularly careful to keep this to myself lest I undercut her feelings; I also realized that what I was experiencing was my genuine affection for her.

This feeling grew into what I have difficulty putting into words, a form of love. That is not to say that it was very much in my thoughts or awareness; I knew of it and became aware of it from time to time, often, but not always, in the context of positive transference. I enjoyed working with Karen. However, I did not experience any of the feelings, heady gratification during Karen's hours, missing her, or daydreaming about her, that the Novicks (Novick & Novick, 2000) identify, correctly, I believe, as hallmarks of a positive countertransference with a sadomasochistic base.

As maternal material began to appear in the analysis, themes of loss accompanied by anxiety also began to appear. My vacations, which previously had aroused little affect in Karen, were now met with anxiety. Having come to an understanding of her mother's role in giving rise to these feelings, Karen asked me, quite reasonably I thought, how I could leave her if I knew just how hard it was for her. Was I really there with her if I could just leave her? These are not, in my experience, unusual questions if the therapeutic atmosphere is one in which a patient feels free to voice them. I responded over time that, while she was in one sense certainly correct, what was also true was that I was present much of the time and *could* offer reliability and predictability. She could safely have every expectation that I would return and that our relationship would continue as it had before I left.

What I offered her was a dichotomy in her relationship with me, a distinction between a transference relationship with a representative of her mother and a new relationship with a new object. I believe that every analysis hangs on such a choice, on reaching the point where a patient is in a position to make it. I remain uncertain as to whether the therapist's loving feelings are an essential part of that process *even if he or she remains unaware of them.*

After negotiating this transition, Karen began to date. She found herself exploring just what she wanted in a relationship, something she had probably never done before. She did not reach any immediate conclusions beyond the fact that her parents were irrelevant to her decision.

Karen's issues with both her parents of course played out in her termination. Angry and anxious transferences reappeared stormily, but did not take hold. She also talked about missing me as the person I had become over the course of our work together. This was a shared feeling; I would miss her and I told her so.

What I find most interesting as I read over these vignettes is not what is unusual about them, but what is not. Without the sidebar narrative of my feelings, they sound pretty much like analytic cases that demonstrate at least good enough work. This I think is the point. It addresses the potential criticism: Do loving feelings on our part interfere with a normative, mutative analytic process? These illustrations certainly suggest that they do not.

In neither of these cases did I begin with any particular liking or affectionate feelings. (With John I started out not liking him very much.) I usually begin feeling well-disposed towards the people I see. I have found that if I begin with an intense feeling of attraction or a fantasy of wanting to take care of a patient, it is a countertransference response to a preformed, hungry, needy transference. These feelings do not last beyond the first two or three sessions. *Very* rarely, I encounter a patient that I at once dislike. I can easily identify realistic reasons for my dislike, although I can also identify the same factors in patients toward whom I have no such response or trouble working with. I refer them on to other therapists in the hope that they will be able to work with them, just as I have been able to work with some patients with the same traits or manner.

I am left, after offering these vignettes, with the sense that we are ill-equipped clinically or theoretically to deal with our feelings for our patients if they are not countertransference. Countertransference, as Lacan (2006b) dryly observes, is a "conceptual impropriety" (p. 585). To address the problem, it is necessary to again move beyond psychoanalysis and see what the postmoderns and the neuroscientists have to say on the subject.

Love, Sex, and Desire

What makes experiencing, let alone talking and writing about loving feelings for our patients so difficult is that as fourth-generation analysts and therapists we have been inculcated with the *dispositif* of libido theory and the pathologizing of loving feelings in numerous social contexts, including psychoanalysis. Libido theory is a terrible muddle at cross-purposes with itself. It attempts to present itself as an integrated package combining love and sex in the service of psychic energy and development. The culprits, I believe, are the *Three Essays on the Theory of Sexuality* (Freud, 1905/1953c), although they have accomplices. Required reading in the first-year curricula of all APsaA institutes, the *Three Essays* constitute a frame, more of a Procrustean bed really, that establishes constraints to our thinking in these areas and our feelings about our patients.[82]

82 Freud was probably aware of this when he attempted to offer an addenda to his views on love in the posthumous *Outline of Psychoanalysis* (1940 [1938]/1964c).

What Freud and subsequent psychoanalytic authors failed to do was to make an explicit distinction between love and desire, and to explicitly describe what these terms signify. Instead, we are left to make do with the variously defined (or not defined) *Eros* and libido. Freud's major interest was in postulating the existence of an engine that would drive the psychic apparatus. He did not deal much with desire. He chooses *Wunsch*, meaning wish or desire, rather than Hegel's meatier *Begierde*, meaning desire, longing, and appetite, and does not deploy the term in the *Three Essays*. Strachey's translation of the former as "wish" pretty much kills the subject of desire for the American reader. Contemporary American theorists have largely abandoned the problem. Mitchell (2002) is an exception, writing about romantic love and desire, while authors writing about the analyst's love are seeking the very distinction between love, the romantic, and the erotic that he does not make.

Lacan and the French school are the exceptions. Lacan (1978/1991a, 1973/1991b, 1966/2006a, 2006b) had a considerable interest in desire which, following Hegel (1807/1969), he conceived of as a lack that could not be fulfilled. He contrasted it with need, and demand, the verbal expression of a need. There is a literature beginning to appear in American psychoanalytic journals on desire (e.g., Bernstein, 2006; Kirshner, 2005).

In addition to Hegel (1807/1969), there is a philosophical literature on desire going back to Plato's (2006) *Symposium*. Plato too wrote of desire as a lack. A more recent postmodern literature has been described as the philosophy of desire (see, for example, Deleuze & Guattari, 1972/2009; Deleuze & Parnet, 1977/2007; Goodchild, 1996; Lyotard, 1974/1993). They see desire as present in the subject and creating its objects anew. They weave this view into a strong critique of the determinism of orthodox psychoanalysis. What is important *here* is that by distinguishing between love and desire as separate things, questions about the loving feelings of the analyst for his patient that appear over the normative course of a therapy become easier to address as free of sexual components. Bion's (1970) recommendation that the analyst approach a patient with a "suspension of memory [and] desire" (p. 43) is well known. However, he (1965) also observes that "in analytic practice it is generally agreed that love or hate between analyst and patient should not obtrude" (p. 70). What desire I did experience with John and Karen had to do with a well-modulated hope for our being able to achieve successful therapeutic outcomes. Neuroscience and developmental neuropsychology have a great deal to say about love and the differences between love and desire.

The Developmental Psychology and Neuropsychology of Love

It should at once be obvious that the neuropsychology of love is at the very least a textbook-length subject far beyond the scope of a section of a specialized chapter concerning love on the part of therapists for their patients. In turning to the subject now, I am seeking answers to three questions that have been both implicit and troubling in the discussions of these feelings. The first question is, from a neuroscience perspective, how justified is the separation between the love one might feel for a patient in the normal course of therapy from romantic, erotic, or sexual love? The second is if that separation is in fact valid, what does such love entail? Where does it come from in the normal schema of emotions and their development? And finally, is this love an important, even a necessary, part of therapeutic action in therapy or analysis?

Therapeutic Love as Distinct from Erotic/Romantic Love

It turns out that there is considerable evidence for such a distinction in the burgeoning field of affective[83] neuroscience. In that field, the work of Jaak Panksepp (1998, 2008, 2009) is central to our interests. He has described (2009) what he calls primary process emotions "that are initially unconditioned, 'objectless' neuroevolutionary, affect-laden response tendencies arising from [phylogenetically] very ancient lower regions of the brain, whereas all human cognitions are thoroughly conditioned by life experiences and language processes located within higher neocortical brain regions" (p. 2). It is then necessary to distinguish between cortical cognitions and subcortical emotions. Of particular interest is Panksepp's view that social constructivist and emotional perspectives can coexist, within the complex systems of brain, body, mind, and diverse social networks.

Panksepp (2009) goes on to assert that "it is scientific fact, *and not just conjecture*, that a series of cross-mammalian emotional systems has been revealed through animal brain research" (p. 7). These systems are

83 It is necessary to say something about the universal, but at-times sloppy, distinction drawn between affect and emotion. Fredrickson and Cohn (2008) describe affect as an overarching term that includes all feeling states, among them emotions, moods, and singular feelings such as pleasure or pain. Emotions differ from moods in that they are about something, some circumstance, and can subsume feelings. A definition of emotion is beginning to emerge across disciplines as the multicomponent responses of what I have defined as the holistic self (Leffert, 2010a) and will discuss later. Panksepp (2008) considers them aspects of core consciousness.

concentrated in medial brain structures ranging from the midbrain to the medial forebrain, among them the orbitofrontal cortex (see Schore, 2003a, 2003b for a discussion of the role and functions of the right orbitofrontal cortex). He enumerates seven such systems, "SEEKING, FEAR, RAGE, LUST, CARE, PANIC, and PLAYfulness" (p. 8). Three separate lines of evidence confirm the existence of these systems. Ethological evidence demonstrates their existence across mammalian species. Functional evidence for the existence of the seven systems is derived from subcortical electrical (ESB) or chemical (CSB) stimulation of specific neural areas of the brain. Finally, these systems are neither informationally encapsulated modules nor mere behavioral output systems. Primary emotional responses exist and have been preserved phylogenetically because they provide tools for immediate assessment of the environment and the attainment of specific goals (Schore, 2009). These are powerful concepts, vastly more sophisticated than the classical psychoanalytic hypothesis that all emotions derive from the mother–infant dyad and *differentiate* out of states of pleasure and unpleasure.

Emotions, cognitions, and memory become intimately bound up with each other as development proceeds from infancy to adulthood and beyond. There is, of course, also a constant interplay among different emotional systems that produce a particular cognitive/emotional/psychophysiological state in the total self.[84] Regardless of that interplay, Panksepp's (2009) synthetic work on these basic emotional systems points to the conclusion that loving or caring for one's patients and experiencing (countertransference) or acting (sexual boundary violations) on erotic feelings for them trace their lineage to two different emotional systems, CARING and LUST. There is, then, in the field of affective neuroscience, an ontological basis for considering these feelings—the analyst's caring, and erotic/romantic experience—as two different sorts of things that do not run together or carry a risk of doing so.

Please understand that this argument does not presuppose that a therapist's caring for his patients cannot constitute a countertransference as, for example, when CARE serves as a defense against rageful or helpless feelings directed towards a frustrating or attacking patient. This argument leaves room for all kinds of countertransferences arising in the analyst, first out of his own psychopathology and then in response

84 I am going to use the term *total self* as a sort of temporary placeholder for the definition of self that I will argue for in chapter 4 as a system that comprises all the physical and mental elements that make up a particular person.

to the patient's transference. What I am arguing for is that it is not *necessarily* so and that there is no basis for consigning caring feelings directly to the countertransference without careful consideration of their origins[85] and roles. It is reasonable to start from the assumption that this is not the case, that these caring feelings *are* genuine and only then question whether they are not.

From Whence Does Caring[86] or Loving Arise?

If we are to accept that such feelings for our patients do exist, not as manifestations of psychopathology but as significant parts of our relationships with them, then what are they about and where, in our repertoire of emotional behaviors, do they arise? I would posit that they are derived from our nurturant and attachment behaviors, from normative social bonding and that, in the therapeutic situation (to which they have been applied hardly at all), they reside in the areas of the relationship that have been referred to as the therapeutic alliance and real relationship. In practice, nurturance, attachment, and bonding overlap each other to a considerable extent and have to be treated that way. As Bowlby (1979 [1977]/1984) put it, "What for convenience I am terming attachment theory is a way of conceptualizing *the propensity of human beings to make strong affectional bonds to particular others*" (p. 127, italics added).

Panksepp (1998) writes about love and social bonding across mammalian species (*he* doesn't have a problem with the *L*-word). Humans are rare among animal species in that both females and males can develop nurturant behaviors. They represent highly differentiated social behaviors that develop out of primitive emotional systems shared with other mammals. "We are finally deciphering the ancient neurosymbolic processes that first led to nurturance and social attachments in the mammalian brain. This work has important implications for the biological sources of friendship and love" (p. 246). Social bonding is controlled by neuropeptides such as oxytocin, prolactin, and endogenous opiates or endorphins. They produce feelings of acceptance, warmth, nurturance, and solidarity. Transference/countertransference

85 An example of such a countertransference could arise in the analyst out of his being required in childhood to care for an ailing parent.

86 I am using caring here in its usual sense of a feeling state, not as one of the primary emotional systems of the mind/brain.

is only *one* of the socio-cognitive expressions of basic emotional states occurring in the therapeutic situation; social bonding with its attendant nurturing/nurturant and attachment behaviors is another quite different dimension of relating. The concept that such processes might be at work in psychotherapy, quite separate from transference/countertransference, has hardly been considered at all.

A growing number of authors (e.g., Panksepp, 1998, 2009; Schore, 2002, 2009) have commented on the linkages between attachment outcomes, their effects on the developing brain, and its neurobiology. If social bonding occurs in the therapeutic situation, and I believe it does, the question then becomes how it manifests itself in the behaviors of therapists and their patients. In recent years, we have witnessed a great flowering of interest in a rapprochement between psychoanalysis and attachment theory. Authors from both sides of the aisle, that is attachment theorists and psychoanalysts with an interest in development, have written on the integration of psychoanalytic theory with attachment theory and the treatment of adult and child attachment pathology in psychotherapy and psychoanalysis (e.g., Dozier & Tyrrell, 1997; Eagle, 2003; Fonagy, 1999b; Parish & Eagle, 2003; Schore & Schore, 2007; Shane & Shane, 2001; Wallin, 2007). These papers deal with attachment experiences if not behaviors on the part of the patient, with the analyst serving as an attachment figure, a secure base, or a new object. To what extent this flowering has moved beyond the psychoanalytic literature and into widespread clinical usage so far remains uncertain. Meanwhile, the concept that patient and therapist, like mother and infant, constitute an attachment pair and that this relationship leads to feelings within the therapist for his patient existing outside the transference/countertransference has been little considered.

I have found only a very few authors who address the therapist's attachment feelings for his patients. Grotstein (1990) looks at the mother–infant and analyst–patient relationships in attachment terms and describes the latter as "Siamese-twinships" in which they attach to each other in a variety of different ways. He places this twinship in the therapeutic alliance. Grotstein frames it in the light of Kohut's (1971, 1984) concepts of the idealizing transference, the mirror transference and the corresponding gleam in the mother/analyst's eye. The characterization of twinship seems to have more to do with a variety of Kohutian transference, the alter-ego transference, than it does with attachment. He does not go on to consider specific attachment behaviors and experiences on the part of the analyst or their connection to affection.

Aronson (2001), in his work with his adolescent patient R, describes a change in his own sense of self as a result of his attachment to him. He describes the process as "imbued with components ... undeniably connecting [Aronson] to him" (pp. 439–440). Slade (1999), as part of a review of the implications of attachment theory and research for adult psychotherapy, describes the therapist's caring for patients as being parts of a caregiving system analogous to mother and child. It "implies an emotional connection that flows from therapist to patient as well as from patient to therapist" (p. 589). Slade also observes that in the secure therapist the capacity for such feelings contributes to a successful outcome, while the insecure therapist is as vulnerable to distortion as is the insecure patient.

We are left with the question of whether caring and affection for our patients is a normative or perhaps even a necessary component of therapeutic action. Before addressing this problem, it is necessary to acknowledge that this brief review of the neurobiology of caring, nurturance, and bonding necessitates a change in the premise of this chapter; if love for our patients is a part of the therapeutic relationship, it is also on some level interactive or aims at becoming so; it does not exist in an isolated therapist. This change in no way makes the interaction either romantic or sexual. It does not require anything of the patient and, while it may be conscious, it certainly need not be. It does not make angry or hostile feelings impossible for the patient to experience. People who experience or are the recipients of loving feelings seem quite able to get angry at whoever offers them; there are even anecdotal reports of angry feelings occurring in intimate relationships.

The fact that these loving feelings are interactive does not mean that the analyst cannot reserve them for her personal reflection. It also does not mean that it is necessary or therapeutically appropriate for the analyst to verbalize them or that verbalizing them wouldn't alter the feelings or potentially traumatize a patient. What it does mean is that these loving feelings *are* ontologically interactive.

Schore (2009) believes that a paradigm shift has or is in the process of taking place in clinical disciplines from a focus on cognitive approaches to a focus on emotional and motivational processes. (Like Schore, I believe that the current research warrants such a shift; in the present era of dialogic interpretations and cognitive behavior therapy, I would see us in only the beginning phases of it.) I have elsewhere argued (Leffert, 2010a), as he states here so cogently: "In contrast to the prevailing privileged status of verbal, conscious cognition [the] emotional communications between therapist and patient lie at the psychobiological core of the therapeutic alliance and that right-brain to right-brain emotional processes are essential to development, psychopathology, and psychotherapy" (p. 113). The more therapists facilitate the experience and expression of emotion in therapy, the more effective the therapy. Although the right-brain has been shown, with some controversy, to be active in the processing of unconscious negative affect (Sato & Aoki, 2006), the processing and interplay of positive emotions such as love has not yet been studied. Communication of loving feelings must also be taking place on this unconscious, right-brain to right-brain level.

Attachment takes place in the first 18 months of life (Bowlby, 1969). The mother synchronizes herself to her infant's affective states and modulates them. Resonance is achieved through play; tolerable failures of maternal synchrony are followed by periods of repair (Ainsworth, Bell, & Stayton, 1974). This homeostatic regulation between members of a dyad remains an aspect of intimate relationships throughout the lifecycle. The mother may fail at both attachment and repair functions. The infant responds to such relational traumas with hyperarousal (mediated by the sympathetic nervous system) or dissociation (the parasympathetic nervous system) (Schore, 2009). A similar process can take place in a therapy or analysis that provides an opportunity for synchronization and modulation when these developmental achievements were not possible in the mother–infant dyad. The older psychoanalytic concept of containment, introduced by the British Middle School, prefigures this clinical approach.

Panksepp (1998) observes that when children are well nurtured (securely attached), they develop a secure base (Bowlby, 1988) and a particular make-up of brain neuropeptides; things feel safe and all right. When they are not well nurtured, they develop a different pattern of brain chemicals and experience resentment and distress. In the rat, different patterns of oxytocin-sensitive cells that communicate with each other directly or across gaps appear in each case. There is considerable overlap between the circuits for maternal behavior and social bonding that exist in males and females. The brain opioid system inhibits social distress, if it has developed in the context of a relationship with an emotionally competent mother who provides a secure base. The research in these areas (Panksepp; Schore, 2009) offers new ways of understanding social attachments. Positive social interactions provide pleasure through the release of brain opioids.

Schore (2009) posits that all forms of therapy now view Affect Dysregulation as a fundamental condition of psychiatric disorder (I am not as certain as Schore that contemporary psychotherapists award it anywhere near such standing, however much it may be merited). As Schore puts it, "interdisciplinary data and updated clinical models lead me to conclude that the right hemisphere is dominant in treatment and that *psychotherapy is not a 'talking cure'*" (p. 128, italics added).[87] We would also have to believe that the right orbitofrontal cortex in general and the mirror neuron systems (MNS) of both patient and therapist play central roles in the therapeutic process. Treatment must attend to the patient's early-formed dissociation and reliance on pathological methods of autoregulation. If this dissociation is not therapeutically addressed, less favorable outcomes ensue.

If the therapist is able to modulate the patient's experience of Affect Dysregulation (as the mother was not), the therapeutic situation becomes a safe place where trust can build and the patient can begin to forgo dissociation and pathological autoregulation in favor of first relying on and then internalizing the therapist's psychobiological interactive regulation. The process draws upon "the clinician's psychobiological interactive regulation-repair of dysregulated, especially unconscious (dissociated) bodily based affective states [as] an essential therapeutic mechanism" (Schore, 2009, p. 137). If the therapist is *not* able to provide either a safe space in the manner described by Bachelard (1958/1994; Leffert, 2010a) or interactive regulation, then a pathological repetition of early maternal trauma occurs instead. Schore cites Tutte's (2004) observation that this process requires the deepest of emotional commitments on the part of the therapist working with his patients. Panksepp (2008) puts it this way. "Affect encourages people to dig deeply into their biological 'souls'—to find empathy, to communicate their major concerns sincerely, and to hope that their depth of feeling is reciprocated" (p. 47). The development of my loving feelings for a patient is at least contemporaneous with that of psychobiological attunement and the accompanying therapeutic repair of affect dysregulation. This ought to be true for other therapists as well. It seems possible, even probable, that those loving feelings are a part of that process, *whether or not* they are identified by the therapist.

So where are we left at the end of this somewhat groping and difficult chapter? I have posited that therapists can and do love their patients and

87 In view of the relevance of dysfunctional discursive practices to psychopathology and as one focus of therapeutic action that was discussed in the last chapter, I would have to argue that Schore is only partly correct here. I would also argue that addressing a patient's discursive practices verbally leads to enhancing the right-brain to right-brain communications that Schore is rightly arguing are so important a part of the therapeutic process.

that this love or affection or caring lies outside of the transference/countertransference. The cases that I described convey, most of all, a sense that an analysis looks pretty much the same whether one *considers* loving feelings or not. Most authors of the sparse literature on the subject want to place these feelings in the therapeutic alliance, which strikes me as an unnecessary localization. I attempted to maintain that these loving feelings could exist independently of the patient, a formulation already resting on dubious grounds from a postmodern perspective that the neuropsychology forced me to finally abandon.

It is also reasonable and consistent with social experience to conclude that these feelings need not stand in the way of their opposites, sometimes appearing in either patient or therapist over the course of a treatment.

The neuroscience as of September 2010 actually seems to require the presence of loving feelings for a therapy to be maximally effective. As we come to understand more about emotion and the emotional connections between two individuals, through continued work in the affective neurosciences, it is likely that these feelings will be seen as even more necessary. As psychoanalysts, we have been trained to seek quite the opposite, to label loving feelings as countertransference and to beware the threat of boundary violations. It might even be asked whether psychoanalysts are temperamentally suited to dealing with these feelings. I believe that we do and we are.

I have observed elsewhere (Leffert, 2010a) as have others (e.g., Gill, 1976; Klein, 1969/1976a) that, as analysts and psychotherapists, we have had no difficulty at all in asserting some theoretical position while blithely going about our business as clinicians as if we believed something entirely different to be the case. Things *are* more complex when love is involved, as Coen (1994) also observed, when we have to confront not only our prohibitions but also our own ego ideal. I have allowed my own struggles to remain in the chapter for the very purpose of illustrating this point. Schore's (2009) observation that feelings of this kind are mostly unconscious[88] suggests their presence even in good enough analysts struggling to maintain therapeutic "neutrality."

One place to look for caring that doesn't involve these dilemmas is the doctor–patient relationship in general medicine.[89] The doctor–patient

88 The term *unconscious* is being used descriptively rather than dynamically (I have, for that matter, argued elsewhere, Leffert, 2010a, that a dynamic unconscious does not exist).

89 I am, unfortunately, speaking here mostly in the past tense, before the days of medical service providers, HMOs, ten-minute appointments, and changing doctors as one changes insurance companies.

relationship provides a model in which it is okay to care about your patients. Adler (2002) describes it in terms of the "sociophysiology of caring" (p. 683), where caring is manifest in responsive listening to the patient. The physician experiences what the patient feels as he tells his story and, in situations that are emotionally intense, demonstrates the same physiological responses. Adler characterizes such experiences as based on three components: 1) Empathy is an essential ingredient of caring relationships, 2) these relationships are mutual and involve reciprocal engagements, and 3) empathy has social and physiologic components. Adler describes the relationship itself as a curative factor. It involves an interaction between "the patient's emotional vulnerability and the doctor's emotional availability" (p. 886). He reaches back to quote Peabody (1927), "the secret of the care of the patient is in caring for the patient" (p. 886). I would suggest that, regardless of our professional backgrounds, the doctor–patient relationship offers a foundation and a kind of permission to experience, examine, employ, and perhaps even enjoy our feelings for our patients in our work.

Different theoretical schools of psychoanalysis inevitably tie their theories of therapeutic action to aspects of psychic structure that they also define. However, these various structures (the ego, the bipolar self, etc.) are in fact only constructs, they are arbitrary and, given the controversy that surrounds them, obviously unstable. If we are to think of the therapeutic process, one aspect of which we have been discussing, as acting on some *thing (chose)*, then it should be a thing that is not a construct but rather something that has a more fundamental claim on existence. The self, depending on how it is defined, having properties, rather than being a thing of constructs, is the only thing that makes sense as an object of psychoanalysis. We will turn to it now.

4

The Self, the Self-Representation, the Psychical Self, and Their Social Network

Introduction

When psychoanalysts talk or write about the self, it is always necessary to question what exactly it is they are talking about because the term is used in so many, often idiosyncratic, ways. We need to begin by looking at this unintentional conundrum and then move on to more fertile ground: what allied disciplines—neuroscience, postmodernism, and attachment theory among them—have added to our understanding of the concept of self that makes it so much more useful and interesting. This is not a theoretical exercise. The self, the real one, is becoming clinically relevant in ways that have yet to be considered in the psychoanalytic literature. Perhaps the most important one is that if we conceptualize the psychoanalytic process as acting on the self, then it is for once acting on something that actually exists, not some construct. The topic of the self's relations with the social matrix in which it finds itself, similarly undervalued over the years, has also recently become more interesting as it has taken a new and complex turn.

Two sorts of problem areas have arisen in connection with attempts to conceptualize and locate the self. These exist in psychoanalysis as well as in other disciplines such as philosophy and neuroscience. One sort of problem has to do with the muddle of self, body, and self-representation. A lack of interest in the self has exacerbated the ensuing lack of clarity. Much of what interest psychoanalysts do have in it has to do with its relation to other concepts, as in self-analysis, self-object, self psychology or false self. The other dilemma has to do with consciousness. Most authors either consider consciousness an important property of the self, an essential part of its definition, or its equivalent. This latter difficulty first led me (Leffert, 2010a especially chapter 6) to consider the self in the context of talking about consciousness.

The relations of the self with the holistic social network in which it is embedded has also been mostly ignored. Authors who wish to critique postmodernism and its application to psychoanalysis like to describe postmodern authors as uniformly deconstructing the self to the point of its collapse into the social matrix. These critiques (e.g., Chessick, 1996, 2007; Eagle, 2003, 2009; Frie & Orange, 2009) often treat postmodernism as a unified neo-pragmatism.[90] However, a focused discussion of the social matrix is implicit in considerations of the mother–infant dyad, the Oedipus complex, and object relations theory. (Most authors appear not to recognize this connection.) Hartmann's (1939/1958) work on the state of adaptive readiness in the child that allows for a response to the demands of the social environment and the development of ego structures of secondary autonomy offered a theory of social responsiveness and network science within the tenets of classical ego psychology. Erik Erikson's (1950/1963) more radical ego psychology offers a process theory of mode epigenesis, and the interdigitation of generations that mediates the social influences that prepare an individual for life in a particular society. Erikson offers a theory of development that integrates network science with the biological and psychological development of the young child and the early infant–mother relationship. Unfortunately, beyond his contributions to psychosexual development and identity, Erikson's work in this area has been poorly understood and largely passed over.

In recent years, the field of Network Studies (e.g., Barabási, 2010; Christakis & Fowler, 2009) has offered a novel approach to the social matrix that had formerly been understood in terms of holistic systems theory (Laszlo, 1972/1996; von Bertalanffy, 1968). Network Studies have not yet been informed by postmodern ideas or complexity and are more concerned with the network itself than with the individual selves that constitute its nodes.

Psychoanalytic Theories of the Self

The self got off to a rocky start in psychoanalysis. For Freud, it was very much an elastic term (Sandler, 1983) subsequently lost in translation.

90 A discussion of these critiques and a response to them can be found in chapters 1 and 2 of Leffert (2010a).

Freud chose *Ich* to designate the self as opposed to *Selbst*. Following Bettelheim (1983), I believe he made the choice because in German, *me* exists only in a very limited way, as the pronoun *mir* in the dative case that functions as an indirect object or the object of certain prepositions. In English, beginning in the 16th century, *me* has replaced *I* in most cases except when *I* precedes a verb. For instance, we can say "It's me," a phrase that has no precise equivalent in German. Instead, *Ich* carries with it a certain *me*-ness that *I* does not and fills out the idea of a self in vernacular German.

In English, this has hardly mattered at all since Strachey translated *self* with the Latin *ego* that conveys nothing of the vernacular self and colloquially makes us think of excessive narcissism.[91] Freud's only definition of the self is to be found in the *Project for a Scientific Psychology* (1950 [1895]/1966d). Here it consists of a group of neurones [sic] that are constantly invested with psychic energy. "Thus the ego [sic] is to be defined as the totality of cathexes, at the given time, in which a permanent component is distinguished from a changing one" (p. 323). This is a process not a structural concept. He does not anywhere speak of a self-representation, but he does identify a function or capacity for self-observation that he locates in the superego (Freud, 1933 [1932]/1964b). Without altering the meaning of self, Freud (1923/1961a) appended *Ich* to refer to that part of the id that developed specialized functions through its interaction with the environment. Self hardly reappeared in Anglophone psychoanalysis for three decades.

The distinction between self and self-representation has, it is true, been made, perhaps beginning with the now often forgotten works of Jacobson (1964) and Hartmann (1950/1964a). Hartmann notes that "Freud also refers to it [libidinal and narcissistic cathexis of the ego] as the cathexis of one's own person, of the body or of the self. In analysis, *a clear distinction between the terms ego, self and personality is not always made*" (p. 127, italics added). He refers to the self as one's own person in opposition to the object. Jacobson credits him erroneously in a footnote as the first to define the self, but then goes on herself to refer to "a person's 'body self' or his 'psychical self' or his 'psychophysiological self' or his 'mental self' or his 'psychic self' "(p. 6).

91 I have tried to think or say *Ich* or *me*, but it just doesn't work. Three English-speaking generations of psychoanalysts have been imprinted on and are pretty much stuck with ego. It is an equal loss that *das Es* in all its monstrous genderlessness, a sort of golem in 1923, has been lost to the id. *Self* and *it* are much more descriptive, more experience-near than ego and id. Although their separation *is* arbitrary and unstable, they symbolize *things* rather than the identity categories of ego psychology.

Jacobson also names a self-representation, but does not say what it is. She seems oblivious to the problem she has thus created, a psychical self and a psychical self-representation that are related—*how*? They can only be positioned facing each other, like the mirrors on the walls of an old-fashioned barbershop. Her book, *The Self and the Object World* (1964), has little to do with the self beyond its being the necessary subject of an object relations theory built around the vicissitudes of the cathexes of object with psychic energy.

Unlike Hartmann and Jacobson, Rapaport ([1957]/1967) is acutely aware of the difficulties attendant on the concepts of self and self-representation. He sees the self as a murky concept, tied up somehow with identity, narcissistic cathexes, and superego formation. Its relation to self-representation is troubling:

> The self in subjective experience is something which can observe itself. [The problem is that] The self will have to be so defined in the psychological apparatus that it is observable by an ego function which is at the same time defined as a subsidiary organization within the self. [Yet] *The self cannot simply be re-defined. It is a concept that has been with man for a long time.* Its major characteristic is that it is capable of observing itself. [Instead] the self will have to be so formulated within the psychological apparatus that it is amenable to observation, though not necessarily to full inspection, because many parts of it may be, like Erikson's identity, unconscious.
>
> (p. 689, italics added)

Rapaport, unlike most psychoanalytic authors who actually take up the problem of defining the self, gets nearly all of it right. However, he does not consider the possibility of a self that is not located within the psychic apparatus and what follows from any such change in location. Much of this chapter is about just this point.

Following Rapaport, but offering a more focused conception of the self, George Klein (1976b) dispenses with the self-representation as he does with conscious or unconscious thoughts. It is the self that is the single central psychic apparatus of control, "the focus of which is either an integration experienced in terms of a sense of continuity, coherence, and integrity, or *its impairment, as cleavage or dissonance*" (p. 8, italics added). It is, or is not, conscious of itself as it chooses to be or is compelled by circumstances to be.

In mid to late 20th century psychoanalysis, the two psychoanalytic authors most associated with the concept of the self are D. W. Winnicott (1952/1975b, 1945/1975c, 1971/1989) and Heinz Kohut (1971, 1977). Although Winnicott was accepted early on in Britain, both authors were, in their times, considered heretical by American psychoanalytic audiences. Winnicott is known for his developmental construction that, in the face of a hostile (maternal) environment, a true self remains a potential while a false self emerges in adaptation to deal with the environment and sequester the true self in safety. However, Winnicott does have some less well-known things to say about the self that are unrelated to the concepts of true and false selves. He makes the developmental observation that "the basis of a self forms on the fact of the body which, being alive, not only has shape, but which [sic] also functions" (1971/1989, p. 270).

As for a definition of the self, Winnicott (1971/1989) is clearly dissatisfied with his efforts, observing "there is much uncertainty even in my own mind about my own meaning . . . For me the self, which is not the ego, is the person who is me, who is only me, who has a totality based on the operation of the maturational process" (p. 271). He places the self within the body, so, presumably, it is a psychic structure, but it can become dissociated from the body. Winnicott (1952/1975b) posits that the self begins not as an individual but as an *individual–environmental matrix* from which it differentiates. Although this has become the classical position adopted on both sides of the Atlantic, attachment theorists (e.g., Ainsworth et al., 1974; Bowlby, 1979 [1977]/1984, 1991) have given us strong reasons to question it.

Kohut (1971, 1977) is, like Winnicott, better known for a compound noun, in this case two such nouns—self psychology and self-object—rather than for the self, although it is the latter that appears in the titles of his books. He is particularly concerned about damage to or fragmentation of the self both developmentally or iatrogenically (Kohut, 1979) in psychotherapy or analysis. He is the first to locate the self at the center of the psyche and to relate diagnosis, treatment, and cure to it rather than other psychic structures or developmental issues. He too is perplexed by its definition. In the introduction to *The Analysis of the Self* (1971), he offers a definition of an intrapsychic self:

> The self, however, emerges in the psychoanalytic situation and is conceptualized, in the mode of a comparatively low-level, i.e., comparatively experience-near, psychoanalytic abstraction, as a content of the mental apparatus. While it is thus not an agency of the mind, it is a structure within the mind since (a) it is cathected with intellectual energy and (b) it has continuity in time, i.e., it is enduring. Being a psychic structure, the self has, furthermore, also a psychic location. To be more specific, various—and frequently inconsistent—self representations are present not only in the id, the ego and the superego, but also within a single agency of the mind.
>
> (p. xv)

Yet, curiously, at the opposite end of his work, the epilogue to *The Restoration of the Self* (1977), he recants:

> The self, whether conceived within the framework of the psychology of the self in the narrow sense of the term, or within the framework of the psychology of the self in the broad sense of the term, as *the center of the individual's psychological universe*, is, like all reality—physical reality (the data about the world perceived via introspection and empathy)—*not knowable in its essence.* (pp. 310–311, italics added)

What ultimately becomes important to Kohut in the context of his present definitions (he has another that is quite different) are the issues of subjective centrality and limits of knowability. He is, as Teicholz (1999) has observed, at the beginnings of dealing with the postmodern concerns of knowability and subjectivity that I have discussed elsewhere (Leffert, 2010a).

The relational school has little to say about the self. Mitchell (1988) refers briefly to Winnicott and Kohut as their work pertains to the development of a self and speaks of a "sense of self" that, by implication, has to do with perception and awareness. He does not seem to feel that definitions are required and, in any event, devotes little space to them.

Most psychotherapists and psychoanalysts take the self for granted and pay it scant attention. Perhaps it is a disparagement of such a low-level structure, as Kohut (1971) first defines it. There is little place for it in either clinical or theoretical writing. If one considers that concepts like the self and questions concerning self-representation and self-awareness *do* require definition, it becomes clear that such terms, often found in common usage, are indeed very difficult to define. Rapaport and Kohut are more aware than most of the difficulties. There are two epistemological circumstances in which there is no need to define a term, neither of which apply here. One is to treat it as elastic (Sandler, 1983), purposefully allowing the meaning to slide around. But the self is rooted in its own ontology; it requires some sort of location. The other is to declare that a term is a primitive, that there is nothing that can be added to its meaning beyond its utterance. But in seeking out the meaning of self, there are yes or no questions to be answered, so there is more to be said; the self is not a primitive. So what is it?

The Self as Holism

I have previously quoted Freeman's (1995a) description of what he calls the biology of meaning in arguing for a holistic view of memory as comprising a single complex system. I believe it is a good place to start in seeking a definition of the self:

> The biology of meaning includes the entire brain and body, with the history built by experience into bones, muscles, endocrine glands, and neural connections. A meaningful state is an activity pattern of the nervous system and body that has a particular focus in the state space of the organism, *not* in the physical space of the brain.
>
> (p. 121, italics added)

The meaningful state that Freeman is talking about *is a meaningful state of the self*. To put it quite simply, the self is everything, in all its inseparable aspects,[92] both physical and psychological. It is a holistic system manifesting complexity. That is to say, it can only be divided into subsystems for heuristic purposes and that the properties of the whole are different and greater than the sum of its parts. The definition is not very different from James' (1893/2007) early, even more expansive, definition of the conscious, empirical self as "*the sum total of all that* [a man] CAN *call his*, not only his body and his psychic powers, but his clothes and his house, his wife and children, his ancestors and friends, his reputation and works, his lands and horses, and yacht and bank account" (p. 291).[93]

For psychoanalysts, the temptation to locate the self in the psyche, something that can, in its entirety, be directly communicated with, is overwhelming. The experience of the self, about which I will have a lot more to say, is twofold. One part is the experience of everything (my arm is a part of me, a part of myself); however the other part of the experience is different. It is a *locus of awareness* that experientially sits behind the eyes, its position certainly related to the preeminence of vision among the senses.

The self *is* a record of its experience, manifest in what it and its parts have become, but offering as well a retrievable historical record. That is to say, the self manifests memory holistically, not just as some system of the hippocampus and the cerebral cortex. I have a sutured scar on my left index finger that curls around to the right for perhaps three quarters of an inch, starting at the last joint. I recall that I got the cut in July of

92 I choose "aspects" to avoid suggesting any sort of ontological dichotomy between the physical and the psychological. I have discussed elsewhere (Leffert, 2010a, chapter 6) at some length the *aporia* of the mind–body problem and reached the conclusion that the problem exists in its formulation, not its referents.

93 James, shockingly for the times, has said that the self is in its essence a social creature, inseparable in definition from its social matrix.

1968 at the Marine Biological Institute in Woods Hole, Massachusetts, where late one afternoon I rushed to heat and bend a piece of glass tubing for a laboratory apparatus only to have it break in my hand and lacerate my finger. I remember all of the events surrounding the injury, but I remember more: the quality of light in the room I used as a lab and the view and color of the ocean outside the window.

Tulving and associates (Tulving et al., 1994) have posited that the right prefrontal cortex is involved in memory retrieval and it has long been known that although the hippocampus does not store memory, it is central to its organization. For the cluster of memories I have described, still bright and shiny after over 40 years, my scar has functioned in their maintenance and as a part of my memory retrieval system. I have another small scar, about 20 years old, that has mostly vanished now. I *can* still remember the circumstances in which I got it, but these memories are vague and dimmer; like the scar, maintenance has suffered. My index finger, then, among its more usual and obvious functions, is also a part of my episodic memory.

Memory is one property of the self. There are many others that relate to mind and body. *All* the properties of the self, including the "psychical" ones, are physical in nature, even if their physicalism is not in a form that we are currently able to observe or measure.[94]

The self manifests a considerable degree of unknowability. One reason is the above; many, even most of its properties have physical attributes beyond our current abilities to observe or measure. Another is that complexity makes the behavior of any system unpredictable and its possible antecedents so innumerable as to be indeterminable.[95] Still a third are the postmodern postulates of subjectivity and interreferentiality that we bring to any observations of self, our own or others. Postmodern critics—wrongly, I believe—may dismiss the latter reason, but that still leaves the first two.

The Polyvagal Theory as Evidence for a Holistic Self

An anatomical structure that offers remarkable insight into the self's holism and interreferentiality is the X cranial nerve, named the wanderer

94 Consciousness, for example, is a physical property; the fact that we do not yet know how to measure it in no way detracts from that physicality. For a discussion of physicalism, consciousness, and panpsychicism see Freeman (2006) and Leffert (2010a).

95 For a discussion of this aspect of complexity see Buchanan (2000) and Leffert (2008, 2010a).

or the vagus in Latin. The longest of the cranial nerves, it contains efferent fibers of the parasympathetic nervous system that enervate the heart and the smooth muscle of much of the gastrointestinal tract and afferent sensory fibers that communicate the state of these organs to the brain.[96]

Porges (1998, 2009) has developed in a series of papers what he calls a Polyvagal Theory of reciprocal influence between brain and body. It describes an evolving vagus nerve and its role over the course of vertebrate phylogeny that begins in the lower classes of vertebrates with regulation of the heart and gastrointestinal tract and is co-opted in mammals, the order of primates, and then humans for social purposes. The oldest vagal system consists of slow, unmyelinated neurons that promote digestion and can slow the heart to depress metabolic activity. It is associated with inhibitory behaviors on the part of the organism and is active in response to situations involving fear and avoidance.[97]

The second to appear is the sympathetic nervous system; its actions interact with but are not a part of the vagus nerve. It shuts down digestion and increases heart rate and metabolic activity, functioning to prepare the individual to carry out flight or fight behaviors. The third stage in the phylogeny of the vagus is seen only in mammals. It consists of fast myelinated neurons that can rapidly control heart rate and motor neurons that, along with other cranial nerves, control facial expression and speech.

In mammals, primates, and humans, the evolving cerebral cortex parallels these developments by growing in size and complexity. The vagus, the central nervous system, and the facial muscles constitute a brain–face–heart circuit active in social interactions and the generation of emotion. The mammalian vagus is neuro-anatomically connected, both in the brain stem and peripherally, to the cranial nerves that mediate social engagement through speech and facial expression.

Porges (1998, 2009) posits that the Polyvagal Theory offers evidence of two forms of intimacy, courtship and the formation of enduring

96 The vagus is involved in diverse functions that include the maintenance of heart rate, peristalsis, and sweating. In addition, it enervates muscles of the mouth and larynx that are involved in speech and keeping the larynx open to maintain an airway.

97 Porges (1998, 2009) hypothesizes with limited evidence that this system serves two purposes. The first is to protect the individual, of whatever class, from discovery in time of great danger. The second, and this is the problematic one, is to allow the individual, when all is lost, to die in peace with dignity. This just *might* serve as a phylogenetic basis for Freud's (1920/1955a) theory of a death instinct that has proved such a hard sell to psychoanalysts low these 90 years.

relations, being mediated by the mammalian vagus and the brain–heart–vagus circuit (BHVC).[98] Courting is a form of social engagement that depends on the latter. (Think also of mother–infant engagement that is also mediated by the BHVC, and its unmyelinated neurons.) The establishment of long-term relationships is more interesting. Beginning with mammals and becoming progressively more differentiated in primates and humans, the unmyelinated visceral vagus—whose function in lower vertebrates was limited to lowering metabolic rate and producing immobilization in situations giving rise to fear and avoidance—is co-opted by the BHVC and undergoes a change of function. Its original function continues to be available, but it is superseded; the slowing of metabolism and the heart is now associated with feelings of safety and trust. External stimuli that would, in the absence of this vagal activity, trigger an aggressive response exert much less of an effect.

Panksepp (1998) has observed that such changes in function are not at all unusual over the course of evolution. In effect, it is "easier" to tinker with an existing system than to evolve an entirely new one unless there are overwhelming advantages in doing so. The change in function is paralleled by another change in the BHVC. The mammalian hormones oxytocin and vasopressin, synthesized by the hypothalamus, influence the source nuclei of the visceral vagus in the brain stem to facilitate sexuality and the development of lasting relationships. Through it, they trigger the parasympathetic responses that lead to feelings of safety and trust in the absence of external stimuli that trigger fear and avoidance. It is also known (Freeman, 1995a; Panksepp, 1998) that oxytocin, released post-coitally, influences the cerebral cortex in ways that facilitate bonding. Specifically, learning functions like priming (Schacter, 2001) that determine our beliefs, feelings, and perceptions are loosened and re-form around new, mutually determined, shared content.[99]

However, Porges (2009)[100] critiques those affective neuroscientists who:

> Embrace a science of parallelism that links either observable emotional expressions or subjective experiences with a "neural" specificity that is

98 It is perhaps unnecessary to stress that although such sub-systems do demonstrate specialized functions, this does not mean they are discrete; there is no point at which a boundary can be drawn between them and the rest of the interreferential self.

99 In keeping with this, numerous anecdotal reports suggest that a foreign language is best learned in bed.

100 I have made a similar argument (Leffert, 2010a, chapters 3 and 4) and do so here in connection with this all-inclusive definition of the self.

> concretized and assumed to be validated either by imaging studies that identify activation of brain areas or blockade studies that interfere with appropriate functioning of these circuits.
>
> (p. 31)

These neuroscientists essentially take the position that emotion resides only in the brain. They miss the necessary contributions of both central nervous system motor autonomic outputs and somatic and autonomic sensory inputs to affective state. Together, these constitute a feedback loop that cannot be ignored. The final participant is the body that is acted upon and manifests responses. I would argue further that affect cannot be understood absent the study of the responses of the total self.

Where do emotions fit, given the fact that they are much related to the functions we have been discussing? Greater affective differentiation and complexity would certainly be expected in the evolutionary steps to mammal, primate, and human. In Freeman's (1995a) language, emotions, including love, constitute a meaningful self-state present in the state-space of the entire organism, *not* the state-space of the brain. *Emotions then are emergent properties of the self*, not the brain. It is the self who feels, just as George Klein observed, that it is the self who is conscious (1966, 1970).

The Importance of the Self in Theory and Practice

What is being offered here is a definition of the self that is very much at odds with all of psychoanalytic thought that defines the self as residing in the psyche. The psyche is assumed to make its home in the brain (that behind-the-eyes feeling). I have argued that the self is no such thing, that the brain does not contain the self; it is rather that the brain is a complex anatomical structure anatomically embedded within the self. Although I have not explicitly made the case, it must follow that the psyche is also not confined to the brain-space but is a property of the self, albeit a somewhat ill-defined one.

This concept of a total self requires a reformulation of significant parts of psychoanalytic psychology, particularly those related to constructs of psychic structure. This would obviously be required of self psychology, but it need not be its undoing. At the same time, this self offers a holistic way of viewing psychosomatic disorders whose absence has been sorely felt. Like the body they affect, psychosomatic conditions have been separated off from the rest of psychoanalysis; one hears and reads little about them in contemporary times. The artificial separation of physical and psychological causes would similarly cease to exist.

However, the major change that would result in acknowledging this total self is that psychoanalysis, both its theory and practice, would be centered on something that actually exists. Literally billions of them are running around the planet. They have properties we can observe and measure, as well as some we can't. This highlights a problem that most psychoanalysts either do not admit exists, or, if they do admit it, they prefer not to think about. The problem is that all of psychoanalytic theory, its various competing metapsychologies, and the clinical practice that follows from them, rest on a shifting sea of constructs.

Constructs are, well, constructs. They exist as arbitrary, crafted abstractions. They are artificial and, if deconstructed, they collapse. The self is real. If one deconstructs it to understand it better, it is still standing in front of you after you're done. Foremost among these constructs in the psychoanalysis of the APsaA are the ego, the id, and the superego of *con*structural theory. Early on, Anna Freud (1936/1966) made the telling if seldom honored observation that, except in the presence of psychic conflict, these structures were not discernible. If we are speaking theory, they can easily be separated and precisely (not accurately) defined. Speaking clinically, they offer arbitrary perspectives that the clinician can choose to apply to a piece of process material. For a majority of the roughly 3000 members of the APsaA, they represent the gold standard of Freudian psychoanalytic theory and they are embraced as such. How much use is actually made of them in clinical practice is unknowable.

However, as Kirsner (2009) has noted, there are now approximately 20,000 therapists in the United States who describe themselves as psychoanalysts. They too view structural theory as the gold standard of Freudian psychoanalytic theory. For that reason, some majority of them wants nothing to do with it. One can speculate about the relative goodness or badness of this fact, but there it is.

Self psychology has a significant following inside and outside of the APsaA. Since it is a clinically based theory, experience-near, it is safe to say that its adherents keep it at hand in the therapeutic situation. Kohut's (1971, 1977) two definitions of the self discussed earlier offer a base of sorts for this theory. However, he advances still a third definition of the self, qualitatively different from the other two. He describes it as possessing two poles, an archaic self reflecting its own greatness and a mirrored self, merged with an idealized parent, connected to each other by tension arcs of skills and talents; it looks for all the world like a dumbbell floating in space. It is a thing of abstraction and mixed metaphors, an entirely new structural construct. I mean no disrespect here, but it simply won't do.

Kohut developed an invaluable clinical theory of narcissistic pathology and its treatment through transmuting internalization in the tradition of the *clinical* theories of Gill (1976; Gill & Holtzman, 1976) and Klein (1969/1976a). He also noted, and made no friends as a result, that psychoanalysts have been plagued by their own narcissistic pathology and how ineffective training analyses have been in ameliorating it. Kohut doesn't need the dumbbell, his other definitions are more complex, more interesting.

The self as I am defining it is the one reliable starting point for observation, measurement, and treatment that we have. Various elements of our disparate clinical theories can be applied to it and can be thought about in both physical and psychological terms. Others cannot. For example, (Melanie) Kleinian metapsychology has a great deal to say about the self in the first year of life. As it happens, neuropsychobiology also has a great deal to say about the developing self in the first year of life. What it has to say is measurable and observable. It says that the central nervous system of an infant simply does not have the functional capacities or the hardware to support the experiential or cognitive activity that Kleinian theory would attribute to it and would claim to be able to access via verbal interpretation.

Self-Perception, Self-Representation, and Cohesion of Self

Psychoanalytic writing and theory-building of whatever ilk have attached considerable appropriate importance to what are essentially three self-related functions: how the self represents itself, how it experiences or perceives itself, and its degree of cohesion or fragmentation. These functions are also experience-near and are in popular usage beyond the world of psychoanalysis. Any theory of the self as an exclusively psychical entity soon leads to *aporiai* when it is considered in the light of these functions. How the self is psychically *represented* is by no means a simple or clear-cut issue. If the self were thought to be psychical, we would have these two psychical things sort of staring at each other with a corresponding homunculus of each other inside of themselves. Having the physical body lie outside of the self or having separate physical and psychical selves are equally problematic and lead directly back to the conundrums of all mind–body dichotomies. What makes sense is that it is the total self who either chooses to be aware of aspects of itself or has that awareness thrust upon it *through its perceptions or its thoughts.*

Self-Perception

So it is the self that chooses with varying degrees of success to be aware (or not aware) of aspects or parts of itself. The self is thus the subject of its own inquiries. These perceptions take place when we are not active, or as will be discussed shortly when we are in a default state. When involved in carrying out some activity, these perceptions are inhibited. What we mostly tend to be aware of are things about our bodies, when we see or choose to look at ourselves or focus on bodily sensations. These sensations can originate on the skin surface or internally.

With practice, we can learn to perceive a great deal more about ourselves. We can notice *how* we see or hear, instead of just *what* we see or hear. We can observe how sensations reach us; stub a toe and touch and pressure sensations reach us immediately, while pain comes after a 2- or 3-second pause. If we know something about the peripheral nervous system, we realize this is because touch comes by way of fast myelinated nerve fibers while pain is transmitted via slow unmyelinated fibers that conduct impulses at a rate of only about 1–2 meters per second. We can also learn to observe how we think, how our minds work in addition to merely taking the contents of our mental processes as they come to us. A highly advanced form of this reflection is self-analysis. In addition to perceiving what is there, we can learn to perceive the blanks, the spaces in our thoughts where something is lost. The latter can be highly dysphoric and, like failures in word-finding, can thrust themselves upon us. They can also be subtle and require great attention if they are to be perceived.

Self-perception can fail in ways that are easily noticed. However, in the case of large or small distortions, delusions, and disordered thinking, these failures can be invisible and denied. Self-perceptions are, by definition, conscious. Although we are constantly receiving a stream of unconscious sensory information about ourselves and are acting upon them automatically as the need arises, these are not self-perceptions.

In addition to these perceptions, another kind of self-perception can take place. What is being perceived or reflected on here is the self as object; it is not the subject as the self is the subject of self-perception. The object that is being reflected on is a representation of the self.[101]

Self-Representation

This representation is psychical, but it is anchored as well in the physical; the scar on my index finger anchors a self-representation to a particular event-memory. As the choice of the indefinite article indicates, there is no single self-representation; there are a number of *possible* self-representations. A unique self-representation is usually but not always very similar to preceding or succeeding ones, is brought into consciousness with each act of reflection.[102] It is a distributed property of a neural network (Rumelhart & McClelland, 1986), concentrated, as we will see, in certain areas of the brain, but state-dependent on far-reaching connections to the holistic brain–body–self.

Another property of self-representations is that our consciousness of them is fragmentary. A moment's scrutiny reveals that what at first seems to us like an integrated whole is but a chosen fragment of self that is represented and then, at its margins, vanishes out of consciousness. A holistic representation of the self *must* exist, but it is constantly being updated, and only some single aspect of it or a rough schema of the whole can be brought into consciousness at a given time. Self-representations are not veridical and their parts are not proportionate to the real aspects of self that they portray; they are approximate but close enough. They can be updated as what they represent (i.e., the self) changes, often in small ways. The updating also is not veridical; it is subjective and emphasizes particular aspects or changes for subjective reasons. Much of the time we are not conscious of any self-representation at all; we become aware of it volitionally when a series of thoughts lead us to it or when external perceptions thrust it upon us in some fashion. Self-representations constantly serve as fundamental reference points, while we are conscious of them or while we are not.

The problem with this discussion until now is that it describes a series of schemata that, although they change over time, are individually static

101 Authors writing about the self and consciousness (e.g., Damasio, 2010) sometimes confuse self-representation with self in an attempt to construct a purely psychical self. As I have argued, a psychical self does not stand up ontologically where a psychical self-representation does.

102 We have all had the experience of having some event radically change a self-representation for good or ill.

representations. This terminology does not convey representations of the past, and a potential for change or action in the future is always a part of both how we see ourselves and how we unconsciously function. When we do choose a term, representation, image, schema, or something else entirely, we are also moving away from the immediate experience we are trying to represent; *we are creating a construct.* Such creations are dubious at best and are always subject to deconstruction; all we can do is make sure as best we are able that the construct closely represents all of the properties we want it to convey and remember that it is still a construct, not a property.

Such a construct has already been employed by another discipline for several decades. The concept of an internal working model (IWM) has been adapted by attachment theorists, beginning with John Bowlby (1973). It descends from an oft-quoted paragraph of a slim volume, *The Nature of Explanation* by Kenneth Craik (1943/1952), whose untimely death in 1945 at the age of 31 precluded his further work on it:

> Thus there are instances of symbolization in nature; we use such instances as an aid to thinking; there is evidence of similar mechanisms at work in our own sensory and central nervous systems and the function of such symbolization is plain [this was in 1943!]. If the organism carries a "small-scale model" of external reality and of its own possible actions within its head, it is able to try out various alternatives, conclude which is the best of them, react to future situations before they arise, utilize the knowledge of past events in dealing with the present and future, and in every way to react in a much fuller, safer, and more competent manner to the emergencies which face it.
>
> (pp. 60–61)

Internal working models bring with them the ability for carrying out trial actions, a property that static concepts such as representation, image, or schema do not possess. Bowlby (1973) was interested in IWMs for this reason; they were consistent with a systems theory approach to development, an epigenetic approach that replaced standard psychoanalytic developmental theory that captures a sequential series of static schemata.

We all build and maintain IWMs of the world and of the self. Bowlby's interest was in the models of an individual's attachment figures, the self in relation to them and the nature of that relation. They developed systemically out of the feedback loops of innumerable infant/child–caregiver interactions, *social* interactions. Bowlby used these models to explain how the attachment process was carried forward by the individual. Failures on the part of caregivers led to the development of faulty IWMs of self, attachment figures, and their relationship. These models were distorted; they were not based on accurate representations but rather on coping strategies for accommodating a caregiver manifesting severe failings. Bowlby believed that these models were capable of being updated, but treated them, as did subsequent researchers (e.g., Ainsworth et al., 1974; Main, 1991; Main, Kaplan, & Cassidy, 1985) as metastable and resistant to change. Recent models of therapeutic action (Holmes, 2010; Wallin, 2007) have been based on addressing distorted or damaged attachment and its attendant IWMs through the therapeutic relationship.

Attachment theorists had co-opted the concept of internal working models to such a degree that it has come to exclusively signify attachment models (of self, caregivers, and their relationship). This is quite similar to what Kohut (1971, 1977, 1984) did with the self in self psychology. Much is lost in this narrowing of the IWM concept.

Craik (1943/1952) had in mind something more far-reaching; he had taken the first steps in a radical theory of cognition. In a not so well-known or well-cited paragraph, he observes:

> By a model we thus mean any physical or chemical system which has a similar relation-structure to that of the process it imitates. By "relation-structure" I do not mean some obscure non-physical entity which attends the model, but the fact that it is a physical working model which works in the same way as the process it parallels, in the aspects under consideration at any moment. Thus, *the model need not resemble the real object* pictorially . . . but it works in the same way in . . . essential respects.
>
> (p. 51, italics added)

This is what I mean by an IWM of the self; an encompassing model that includes many kinds of working and is regularly updated to parallel changes in the self. The model is constructed in part through conscious experience and in part through the unconscious processing of cognition and perception. It contains the experience of relationships but also includes the wider experience of the world. Main (1991) describes metacognition as a singular property of IWMs that involves knowledge and control of cognition. "The regulation of cognition, or metacognitive monitoring, includes planning activities monitoring them and checking outcomes" (p. 134). However, IWMs are not, as she would seem to imply, structures. There is no hardwired part of the brain that they reside in. They are in fact *process models*, constantly reforming distributed networks. The presence of strange attractors does account for the metastable appearance of certain features (both normative and pathological) of these models across time. Craik was almost there in 1943 and would surely have gotten there had he lived.

The assumption so far has been that although not veridical, these models are roughly accurate. Sadly, this is not the case. Distortions can be, and to a greater or lesser extent usually are, introduced into the model as a result of perceptual errors or psychopathology. They can occur in the way either the self or its capacity for action (the working part) is represented. IWMs, then, can represent symptoms or distortions irrespective of and across competing metapsychologies.[103] A particular kind of distortion resulting from the formation of multiple simultaneous IWMs will be discussed below.

Although IWMs are constantly modified and updated, these distortions are relatively stable. They can be modified under two circumstances; the impact of major life events or that of psychotherapy and analysis. Both complexity theory and postmodernism offer insights into their metacognitive stability. IWMs are complex phenomena that manifest what are usual properties of complex systems, the presence of strange attractors, and attractor basins. These account for the resistance to change in elements such as symptoms and distortions that were formed as attractors to cope with experiences that seem overwhelming and at one time were. Without qualitative change producing a phase shift, attractor basins revert to their original architectures after some period of time. We have all observed the temporary disappearance of symptoms followed by their reappearance if no fundamental changes in the self have been brought about through the therapy. In addition to IWMs being inherently subjective and interreferential, they and the self come with their own archaeologies and genealogies. Symptoms and distortions represent the persistence of rules of knowledge from an individual's prior developmental epistemes.

My work with Roberta, a college senior, illustrates how a loss raised psychodynamic, conflict-based issues, but also caused problems that could only relate to an internal working model suddenly becoming obsolete and non-functional. Roberta was in twice weekly psychotherapy when her beloved father announced that he was leaving the family. It soon emerged that he had been having an affair with a colleague for some time. Roberta had felt herself to be the apple of his eye and the term "princess" emerged on more than one occasion. She was initially "in shock" and felt enraged at what he had "done to her mother." Months of work, including a joint session with her father, were needed to reach

103 Metapsychologies of whatever sort depict internal working models of psychopathology in which various elements, self, objects, and relationships are distorted in the service of coping with what is experienced as a dangerous environment. While they can succeed as local knowledges, they fail ontologically to support the wide application and validity their proponents claim for them.

an understanding that, although Roberta was certainly responding to the traumatic loss that his leaving had brought on the family, on a deeper level she could not understand why *she* wasn't enough for him.

With this behind her, Roberta guardedly resumed irregular contact with her father, but told me one day that she just didn't know how to have a relationship with him, with this different father. (The above analytic work had offered no help with *this* problem.) She did not know what to expect him to do or how she should act with him, what her part of the relationship should consist of. Coming after the good therapeutic work we had already done, it struck me that her internal working model of herself, which included her relationship with him, was hopelessly out of date and in need of reformulation (let me be clear that, although I kept this formulation in mind during this work, I did not offer it to her directly). A number of months of trial and error followed, as she struggled to develop ways of understanding and dealing with this newly perceived narcissistic and rather shallow man. Her attempts were at times accompanied by angry frustration, but not by jealousy or feelings of betrayal. She eventually reached a new sense of who she was with him, who he was, and how their relationship worked.

The fact that the concepts of internal working model and self-representation are theoretical constructs derived from psychoanalytic and attachment research is cause for ontological concern. Is there any *outside* corroborative evidence available to support what would otherwise be just usage? A neuroscience literature (e.g., Molnar-Szakacs & Arzy, 2009; Spreng, Mar, & Kim, 2008; Uddin, Iacoboni, Lange, & Keenan, 2007) on the functional neuroanatomy of self-representation has been appearing over the last decade. Molnar-Szakacs and Arzy, in a significant review article on self-representation, note that it has been well-established that there is a "default mode" for brain function that includes awareness of self-representation and is suspended during goal-directed behavior. One is, in effect, either self-aware or engaged in action, not both.

A quantitative meta-analysis of neuroimaging studies (Spreng et al., 2008) demonstrated the existence of a core set of cortical midline structures (CMS) that comprise a default network involved in high-level functions such as autobiographical memory, mental time travel (MTT), prospection, and empathy.[104] The study looked at four separate

104 It cannot be restated often enough that such areas of specialization should not be taken to indicate isolated autonomous function. The brain/self is a holistic organism; areas of specialization are disautonomous and subject to distant influences. Put another way, that scar on my right index finger is very much involved with the activities of these cortical midline structures.

domains—autobiographical memory, navigation,[105] theory of mind, and default mode—and found a high level of correspondence across them. Autobiographical memory and theory of mind, although studied as distinct, appeared to demonstrate extensive functional overlap.

The mirror neuron system (MNS) has been shown to be active when either an action is performed or someone else is observed performing an action (Iacoboni, 2007; Iacoboni et al., 1999). It provides a bridge between self and other. Uddin and colleagues (2007) posit that there are thus two separate large-scale neural networks that represent self and other. One is the MNS, which processes motor activity and facial expression in both self and other, producing either mirror action or simulation. The other is comprised of the CMS, the default network that processes higher-level information about self and other. Right cerebral hemisphere function has been shown to be of great importance in supporting the self.

Uddin et al. (2007) also observe "the neural systems of midline structures and mirror neurons show that self and other are two sides of the same coin, whether their physical interactions or their most internal mental processes are examined" (p. 153). Or, as Molnar-Szakacs and Arzy (2009) put it, "The MNS together with the 'default network' have been hypothesized to represent abstract and concrete aspects of the self, respectively, and interact to give rise to a unified representation of the self as a social being" (p. 369). Whereas self-representations are, or are capable of becoming, conscious, the neural hardware, the MNS and the CMS, operates outside of consciousness.

The most embodied aspect of self-representation is self-face recognition (Uddin et al., 2007). Only our species is capable of achieving it. This distinction would suggest a uniqueness of self-representation and self-awareness as compared to other primates or mammals. When presented with an image of one's face, the right frontoparietal neural networks become active. Such activation includes the self-body and the self-voice, the latter indicating that this is not solely a visual phenomenon.

This network also overlaps the mirror neuron system (MNS). Right frontoparietal damage results in a condition called mirror sign, in which patients misidentify their own face while retaining the ability to identify the faces of others. Transcranial magnetic stimulation (TMS) of the right inferior parietal cortex similarly interferes with self-face

105 Navigation refers to the ability to maintain topographical orientation by imagining where one is, where one's destination is, and how to get from one to the other.

recognition, while TMS of the left parietal cortex has no effect. To the extent that self-face recognition can be considered a singular marker of physical self-representation, it too leads us to the MNS and, indirectly, to the CMS and its lateral extensions.

Self-representation "emerges as an integration of representations across the domains of time, space, physical embodiment and social cognition" (Molnar-Szakacs & Arzy, 2009, p. 365). Integration is accomplished through simulation, a term taken from cognitive psychology that corresponds to the "workings" of the IWM. It involves the use of existing self-representations to predict representations going forward in novel situations. The core network of CMS projecting laterally into the temporal, parietal, and occipital lobes is responsible for two central synthetic functions of the self that figure prominently in the recent neuroscience literature (Spreng et al., 2008). One is self-projection, the ability to place oneself in simulations of different times (future, present, or past), places, and/or perspectives. The other is scene construction, the ability to construct or imagine fictitious scenes or experiences. Hassabis and Maguire (2007) argue for the pre-eminence of the latter and its links to episodic memory without considering the implicit presence of a self-representation in its functions. In the absence of a telling argument, it seems best to treat self-projection and scene construction as meta-functions of equal importance.

Theory of Mind (ToM)[106] is an equally important synthetic function of the internal working model of the self and its relations with others. Gallagher and Frith (2003) argue that it is the "one aspect of social cognition [that] sets us apart from other primates. It underpins our ability to deceive, empathize, cooperate, and to read others' body language" (p. 77). It allows us to see things from another's perspective and to predict the actions of others. It requires the ability to recognize other people as agents who are capable of thinking and acting differently from us. Autism is a physically based condition whose symptomatology would seem to be characterized by a *selective* impairment of those functions that constitute ToM. Autism research (Baron-Cohen, Leslie, & Frith, 1985) confirms this supposition. This form of

106 Theory of Mind is another borrowed term, co-opted from philosophy and going back at least to Descartes. There it refers much more generally to any theories *about* mind held by expert observers who attempt to explain mind, consciousness, mentalization, and the relations of mind and body. The ToM described here and formulated by cognitive neuroscientists refers to a particular mental capacity normally present in humans to reflect on the nature of their own mentalizations and those of others.

mentalization requires the ability to construct scenes that are imagined and understood to be separate from reality, as well as the shared processing of experiences of self and other. In other words, the two large-scale neural networks of self-representation, the MNS represented by the medial pre-frontal cortex, and the core network of CMS with its lateral projections, are required to allow an individual to formulate a theory of mind.

Conditions other than autism can render ToM dysfunctional without any impairment of the neural hardware involved in its function. It is entirely reasonable to suppose that, like any other systems of the brain that involve emotion and perception, intact hardware requires good enough development to become fully functional. The most obvious psychological conditions where this is lacking in ToM development lie in the spectrum of narcissistic disturbances. My work with Tanya will illustrate such a psychologically-based failure in ToM development.

Tanya is an attractive, 38-year-old physics professor at the local university. She sought analysis for low self-esteem and a reluctant awareness that her arrogant outbursts caused problems at work and ruined every relationship she had ever attempted. Much of her analysis focused on her narcissistic fragility for which her arrogance provided a dysfunctional compensation. Tanya's mother had viewed her as competition from the start. We learned gradually how she neglected her infant daughter and later competed with her, delighting in pulling the rug out from under her when the opportunity presented itself.

It did not occur to Tanya that other people had feelings; they were instead rather two-dimensional, like photographic cutouts who were either on stage or disappeared from her awareness when not around. Tanya lacked a theory of mind. She was shocked when I observed to her in the third year of her analysis that her colleagues who were less gifted than she felt injured and angry when she critiqued their work from a position of superiority. She had to first learn that other people felt the same things she did before she could go on to learn that they could also feel differently than she did. This came alive in the transference when I first "became" a person like her who didn't like it if she didn't appear for a session and then, more scarily, when it struck her that I could feel differently than she did. Tanya clearly had had the *capacity* for a theory of mind. However, I would posit that it had never become operational because of failures in her early childhood relationship with an impaired mother; she needed the experience of a good enough therapeutic relationship to make them functional.

This fairly brief review has only scratched the surface of the burgeoning neuroscience literature, most of it having appeared in the last three or four years, on self-representation and its function. For our purposes, two points stand out. One is that these authors are talking almost entirely about *self-representation*, not self. They largely avoid a putative psychical self and none of their data are applicable to it. The second is that the self-representation and its properties that we have discussed describe an internal working model or models as posited by Craik (1943/1952) and refined in the attachment literature (e.g., Ainsworth et al., 1974; Bowlby, 1969, 1973, 1979 [1977]/1984; Main, 1991; Main et al., 1985).

Cohesion and Fragmentation of the Self: Metaphor or Reality?

Even before the advent of self psychology, psychoanalysts have been much concerned diagnostically and therapeutically with fragmentation of the self. Their concern has ultimately foundered on the absence of a definition of self (Kohut is, again, an exception of sorts)[107] and a default implication that it is an intrapsychic structure. The very term *schizophrenia*, coined by Bleuler a century ago, refers to splitting or fragmenting of the mind/self. Tausk (1933), in his classic paper "On the Origin of the 'Influencing Machine' in Schizophrenia," describes psychosis as a multiphasic process in which there is first a disorganization and then a reorganization along psychotic lines, but a reorganization nonetheless. Although schizophrenia has come to be recognized as an organic illness usually in the domain of neurobiology and psychopharmacology rather than psychoanalysis, Tausk's observations remain valid as a description of a psychological process occurring in the context of a neurochemical catastrophe.

A major concern among those authors writing about theory of technique in the psychotherapy and psychoanalysis of more seriously disturbed patients has been the danger that probing too deeply into a fragile personality might precipitate a fragmentation of a psychical self or

107 Although card-carrying self psychologists accept Kohut's definition of a bipolar self, more eclectic psychotherapists and analysts may prize his discussions of normal and pathological narcissism without accepting it. Self-objects are a different matter and are widely accepted. The discovery of the MNS as a shared processing system of self and other (e.g., Iacoboni, 2007; Iacoboni et al., 1999) raises the interesting possibility of a neural basis for the existence of self-objects and a potentially fruitful path for future inquiry.

a psychotic episode. Kohut (1979) ostensibly broke off the second analysis of Mr. Z for this reason and Kernberg (1968) recommended that therapists almost entirely eschew interpretations of the genetic past in the treatment of borderline patients. Many therapists treat such recommendations as revealed truth. Although seemingly reasonable, there is little evidence that a psychotic episode is all that easy to produce and considerable evidence that it is not. Kleinian psychoanalysts in fact have made deep genetic interpretations, often from the first session, for many decades. Without rendering any judgment concerning the therapeutic efficacy of this technique, there have been no reports concerning the appearance of widespread iatrogenic psychoses in their patients. Similarly, Winnicott (1975a) believed that the only way to produce a reunion of true and false self was to induce a profound regression in these manifestly disturbed patients to a point prior to the split in an environment of therapeutic containment. This clinical theory has, if anything, been more widely applied by the British Middle School since his death. Again, putting questions of efficacy aside, there has been no evidence of significant psychotic decompensations in these patients. Concerns about fragmentations of self-perceptions or self-representations in the therapeutic situation occurring as a result of either technical errors or failings in theory of technique would appear to be overstated. (Although only anecdotal, I have never observed such fragmentation over 40 years of working with patients and conducting supervision.)

Psychotic decompensation does occur in *life* and brings with it many possible impairments of the neurocognitive elements of the holistic self, some of which we are accustomed to thinking about in ego-psychological language, while others, such as a delusional failure of the MNS, we are not. Defects can be subtle or gross, affecting mental function in highly variable and often reversible ways.

Clinicians are accustomed to dealing with various sorts of defects of self-representation, both of the physical body and of cognitive function, many of which have been discussed in the previous section. These defects can appear in the somatic delusions of schizophrenia, like the idea that one's teeth are equipped with radio transmitters, or the grandiosity of a bipolar patient in the manic phase. Anorexia nervosa (Bruch, 1962) diagnostically brings with it frankly psychotic distortions of body image. Highly dysphoric failures in integration can occur in the *experience* of the image of the physical body or the self-representation, a kind of holistic failure. Lesser failures of self-representation are common, if not normative, readily accessible and responsive to therapeutic exploration and interpretation.

The neuroscience we have been discussing points to the importance of the MNS and the CMS in the maintenance of internal working models and the processing of self-perceptions. At this point, the literature in these areas is just too new to be applied systematically to clinical problems and the study of psychopathology.[108]

The now mature attachment literature has considered developmental failures that give rise to pathological attachment styles in both the young child and the adult and to problems constructing IWMs. Attachment modeling of developmental psychology in children and adults has been well known for some time. The development of faulty IWMs (Bowlby, 1969, 1973) has been used to explain the appearance of pathological attachment styles such as anxious or avoidant attachment. Disorganized attachment is a different matter, for which different origins are posited.

Main (1991) observes that "the internal working model is expected to contain a rough-and-ready sketch of the environment and the self which can be mentally manipulated prior to undertaking possible future action" (p. 131). The IWM must contain multiple representations that include experiences with the attachment figure and representations of the self that are derived from these experiences. If this can be accomplished within a developmental trajectory, then the IWM exists as a single, coherent, metacognitive model.[109] We can take a wider view of the IWM that goes beyond the attachment paradigm to include other functions and ways of relating. Main posits that we can come to know an

108 A challenge to the mirror neuron hypothesis has been mounted in the neuroscience literature (e.g., Hickok, 2008; Hickok & Hauser, 2010) and from within psychoanalysis (e.g., Pulver, 2003; Vivona, 2009) since I discussed it in 2010. Although beyond the scope of a chapter section, it must at least be briefly mentioned. The neuroscience challenge alleges limited applicability of the monkey neuroscience, a shortage of human data, and the observation that the MNS is not the sole means by which the brain processes action observation. The psychoanalytic challenge essentially cites these complaints, questions the rigorousness of the neuroscience, and cautions against premature applications to psychoanalysis. In the face of the neuroscience critiques, there is an ever-growing body of human mirror neuron research (e.g., Bråten, 2007a; Bråten, 2007b; Bråten & Trevarthen, 2007; Ferrari & Gallese, 2007), and the notion that other ways of processing action observation exist is indeed to be expected in a non-modular brain. With respect to the psychoanalytic critiques, it is of course early in the game and information from related disciplines should never be used as psychoanalytic plug-ins. With respect to rigor, there are two points to be made. The data *are* becoming increasingly relevant and accurate (e.g., Hari, 2007). However, the more serious issue is that psychoanalytic critics who question the rigor of data obtained from outside our field ignore just how lousy and unrigorous our own data still remain after more than a century.

109 Main (1991) defines *metacognition* as cognition about the domain of cognition. Cognition is the *subject* of metacognition. In the neurocognitive language of 2010, the kind of cognition Main is talking about is that which is related to Theory of Mind (ToM) and it involves the participation of cortical midline structures (CMS) and the mirror neuron system (MNS).

individual's IWM through its "representational artifacts" (p. 132) that are elicited in the Adult Attachment Interview. In Foucault's (1969 & 1971/1972, 1966/1994) terms, these artifacts can be thought of as constituting *archaeologies and genealogies of attachment*. Insecure children and adults manifest a lack of coherence and integration in their attachment landscape. They cannot be spoken of as having a single IWM. Bowlby (1973) introduced the idea of multiple models to explain a situation in which incompatible or contradictory experiences with attachment figures or incompatible self-representations (and for our purposes, with wider experiences as well) could not reside within the same model. This would result in a situation in which a number of contradictory working models would exist at the same time. Multiple models would also serve the purpose of preserving models containing prized experiences, ways of functioning, and perceptions of self and objects from other destabilizing ones. This is a more powerful explanation of the phenomenon of vertical splitting than psychoanalysis has been able to come up with on its own.

Main (1991) also offers a way of conceptualizing the relationship of attachment IWMs to other more general IWMs of self-representation that had, until now, caused us some difficulty. We have been struggling to transform the concept of IWM developed by attachment theorists into a wider more generalized concept of internal working models of the self, its relationships, and the functioning of both. Main notes in passing various embeddings and hierarchies of mental models as *normal* aspects of mental life. These may include "models of diverse aspects of reality, as well as models of [the self] and [other] possible realities ... some models are contained within or contain others ... [and] hierarchies of varying degrees of abstraction [also] exist" (p. 132). In looking for the most general working model of the self we would, then, be looking at a hierarchical arrangement of models constituting a complex system only parts of which could be grasped at a given time.

Main (1991) is talking about a phenomenon quite different from Bowlby (1973) in his discussion of multiple models. He is referring to *contradictory and incompatible* models of the same aspects of reality at the same level of abstraction. These multiple models might, for example, preserve and protect the model of the young child being nurtured by an at-times warm, caring mother from that same mother being depressed and unavailable or sadistic; those experiences and the child's responses would comprise a separate IWM. The result of *this* multiple modeling, Main (1991) also tells us, is metacognitive incoherence. This incoherence is manifested in a lack of singularity and cohesiveness of the self and of its supra-ordinate working model or representation.

The self is a fundamentally social creature. It remains for us to discuss its relations beyond infancy and early childhood with the social system in which it is embedded.

The Disautonomous Self, Its Social Network, and Social Network Theory

The disautonomy of the self has been a topic of little interest for many psychoanalysts who have incorrectly equated it with neo-pragmatist critiques of the self as an arbitrary and unstable identity category that is subject to collapse on deconstruction. They have similarly rejected both the irreducibility of subjectivity and the limits of knowability of the self that follow from a centrist postmodernism, complexity theory, and a close reading of the attachment literature. Although contemporary psychoanalytic authors (e.g., Hoffman, 1996; Stern, 1997; Stolorow, 2011; Stolorow & Atwood, 1992; Stolorow et al., 1994; Stolorow, Orange, & Atwood, 2002) embrace subjectivity, they do not deal with postmodern and neurobiologically based critiques of knowability. I have already discussed these issues elsewhere in this book, as well as in a previous volume (Leffert, 2010a) where I made the case for both disautonomy and the interreferentiality of social embedding coexisting with an ontologically stable self. Perhaps it is less obvious than it should be that to say that the self cannot be separated from its social matrix is not the same as saying it doesn't exist. The comparatively new discipline of Network Studies brings to the table the ability to quantify and document social relationships between individuals across multiple relational dimensions. Psychoanalysts and psychotherapists ought to be most interested in three different social networks: the wider network in which each individual is embedded and the two-person networks of infant–mother and patient–therapist, all of which we encounter clinically whether we realize it or not. To state their relationship in a controversial way, we are (mostly) prisoners of our networks, our mothers (mostly) get us into them, and our analysts (sometimes) loosen our ties to them.

Social Network Theory

The self is a disautonomous entity embedded in its own unique and changing social matrix. Unlike so many of the named, purely psychical constructions of psychoanalysis, the self is not a construct but a more or less stable being who depends on its relations with that matrix or network for its stability. Its autonomy or disautonomy is represented psychically with varying degrees of accuracy. Until recently, we have had no tools with which to understand or quantify its disautonomy. Enter Network Studies, a field taken up with the way in which individuals are embedded in their networks, but more particularly with the behavior of social networks themselves.

Network Studies is a burgeoning field in its early stages of development. It currently exists within the disciplines of physics, biology, computer science, mathematics, biology, and the social sciences. Although some papers on the subject have been cited over a 1000 times in the past five years, it is still a highly compartmentalized field, as yet lacking a common voice (Barabási, 2005c). As with any discipline, new or established, there is considerable disagreement and, at times, acrimony between its researchers. Network Studies focuses on the way in which individual members of a network (called "nodes" in its at-times arcane language) are connected to, influence, and transmit information to and from each other. If these individuals are people, they make up a social network, but they can also be molecules, neurons, or automobiles. The World Wide Web is a frequently studied social network. A comprehensive discussion of the field is beyond the scope of the present chapter. I am going to confine my discussion to the work being done at two major research laboratories in the United States: Albert-László Barabási's (2005a, 2005b, 2005c, 2010; Barabási & Bonabeau, 2003; Palla, Barabási, & Vicsek, 2007; Ravasz & Barabási, 2003) at Notre Dame and Nicholas Christakis' (Arbesman & Christakis, 2010; Cacioppo, Christakis, & Fowler, 2009; Christakis, 2004; Christakis & Fowler, 2007, 2008, 2009; Mednick, Christakis, & Fowler, 2010; Rosenquist, Murabito, Fowler, & Christakis, 2010) at Harvard. I will also discuss critiques of both Christakis and Fowler and Barabási that have recently appeared in the Network Studies literature. After looking at their work, we will go on to consider its relevance to clinical psychoanalysis.

Each author looks at different aspects of networks. Barabási studies network properties on a more macro level, while Christakis is more focused on the properties of individual social networks. Both describe properties that are likely to make therapists, who are dedicated to the autonomy and freedom of the individual, uncomfortable and will require additions and modifications to current theories of therapeutic action and outcome. Their work leads to the conclusion that our thoughts, feelings, and actions are significantly determined by the social networks in which we are embedded and most if not all of this influence takes place outside of our awareness. To be useful to us we need to find ways to access network influences in the therapeutic situation and then to address them in therapeutic action.

Christakis and Fowler

Nicholas Christakis and James Fowler (2009) describe social networks as "superorganisms" whose properties are different from and greater than those of the individuals that comprise them. They are implicitly making a case that networks manifest complexity. They go on to posit that linking the study of individuals to the study of groups can explain a great deal about human experience. Or, to put it differently, "to know who we are we must understand how we are connected" (p. xiii).

The language of Network Studies is both strange and familiar to us. We are certainly aware of the social networks of which we are a part. People configure themselves into networks. The members are *nodes* (Christakis & Fowler, 2007) with different numbers of connections that can be *mutual* or *unidirectional.* Behaviors and information pass through these connections and are referred to as *contagion.* Contagion is *not* a conscious process; it operates unconsciously. Connections and contagion characterize networks. A particular individual whose behavior is being studied is referred to as an *ego* and a person connected to the ego who may influence her behavior is an *alter.* Christakis and Fowler describe a number of principles that characterize our behavior in our social networks. These principles are *not* hypotheses; they are characteristics common to networks that Christakis and Fowler have identified through their research.

1) "We shape our network" (Christakis & Fowler, 2009, p. 17). We shape and re-shape our networks based on *homophily*, in order to associate with people who resemble us. We choose whom we want to be connected to, how densely interconnected we want to be, and how central we want to be to our network.[110] We decide whether we will introduce people we know to others or invite them to a gathering. A telephone tree in which each person calls two others to quickly pass information on to a large group with a minimum of calls is an example of a simple network we shape or are shaped into.

110 If we are to include considerations of power relations issues, it is also a question of what choices we are *allowed* to make (see Lukes, 2005).

Networks can be organized or organic; they demonstrate the beauty of complex structures. We know lots of people, but are close to only a few of them. We average four close social contacts; there is a 52% chance of any two of them knowing each other (Christakis & Fowler, 2009). The networks around us are interconnected in ways we do not know. Our networks in turn affect every aspect of our lives. "How we feel, what we know, whom we marry, whether we fall ill, how much money we make, and whether we vote all depend on the ties that bind us" (p. 7). Our networks determine what we think is cool. It is indeed reasonable to ask how we can possibly conduct a psychotherapy or an analysis *without* acquiring systematic knowledge of our patients' social networks.

2) "Our networks shape *us*" (Christakis & Fowler, 2009, p. 20). Someone with few social connections (friends) will have a life that is very different from someone with many. A simple example of network influence will suffice. Christakis and Fowler describe Kristensen and Bjerkedal's (2007) study of IQ in Norwegian military conscripts. First-borns score a few points higher than second-borns, who in turn score a few points higher than third-borns. However, if a second-born son's older brother dies while he is in childhood, his IQ will come to resemble that of first-borns. Taken still further, the data show that if a third-born loses one of his older siblings, his IQ will increase and resemble that of a second-born and, if he loses both older siblings, it will resemble that of a first-born.

3) "Our friends affect us" (Christakis & Fowler, 2009, p. 21). The map of a network's connections tells only part of the story. What flows across these connections, the network's contagions, is at least as important. People tend to influence and copy each other. The appearance and spread of bulimia in networks of college women seems to have begun in the 1970s. We are accustomed to taking family histories of our patients with eating disorders, but we do not routinely inquire about friends with the same disorder in any systematic fashion.

4) "Our friends' friends' friends affect us" (Christakis & Fowler, 2009, p. 22). Up until now, these characteristics must have seemed somewhat interesting, but hardly game changers for us or our work with patients. This characteristic is different. Christakis and Fowler (2007) have used data from the well-known Framingham Heart Study and the Framingham Offspring Study (children of the original Framingham participants) to study different aspects of network behavior. The offspring study of 5124 egos used data originally collected by the Framingham researchers (not Christakis and Fowler) for seven 3-year periods between 1971 and 2003. Data about each subject had been

hand-recorded on tracking sheets; they included medical histories and listed family and friends. The social data had not previously been studied.

Christakis and Fowler (2007) were able to use the data to plot this rather large social network as it existed at each three-year study point (p. 374). In all, 45% of the egos were connected by friendship to at least one other person also in the network. They found that the risk of obesity among people (alters) who were connected to an obese ego (one degree of separation) was about 45% higher in the observed network than would be expected in some purely random network. They also found that the incidence of obesity in friends' friends of an obese ego (two degrees of separation) was 20% higher than in the random network and that the incidence in friends' friends' friends (three degrees of separation) was 10% higher. (Beyond three degrees of separation, there is no excess effect.) What was surprising and counter-intuitive about these findings was that this 20% increased incidence obesity in the friends of friends of an obese ego occurred *regardless of whether the friends of the obese ego were themselves obese.* In other words, the contagion of obesity could spread from person to person without its necessarily being expressed in each link. Our patients, it is reasonable to conclude, are subject to all kinds of contagions interacting in all kinds of ways. It would be foolish to imagine that they do not interact with the therapeutic process (neutrally, or for good or ill) either specifically, based on the particular contagion, or quantitatively. Through contagion patients can also unconsciously pass on the properties of their social networks to us as we can pass on the properties of our networks to them.

In this study (Christakis & Fowler, 2007), the network contagion has to do with obesity. Since contagion spreads beyond the first degree of separation, it is referred to as *hyperdyadic spread.* We do not know exactly *what* the transmission consists of. The neuroscience of social networks has not as yet been studied. We do know that in humans and other primates the MNS comprises a shared processing system for affective communications between self and other (e.g., Iacoboni, 2007; Iacoboni et al., 1999) and that it is somehow defective in conditions such as autism (Baron-Cohen et al., 1985). The MNS would have to have a central role in connecting us to our social networks. Since these connections also involve perceptual information and verbal and written communications, more than the MNS must be involved.

Humans have two different problem-solving systems a slow, small, conscious, serial system and a large, very fast, unconscious parallel distributed system (Baars, 1993/2003). Problem solving results in action or thought outputs. It seems probable (this has not been studied) that inputs from a social network would impinge on this large parallel distributed processing (PDP) system and produce disparate unconscious effects. The way some new fashion or device (e.g., an iPad) suddenly seems *right* would constitute an example of this. Lower vertebrates also form themselves into social networks; we marvel at the way flocks of birds and schools of fish can move almost synchronously. However, the phylogeny of social networks or the MNS have also not been studied.

5) "The network has a life of its own" (Christakis & Fowler, 2009, p. 24). Network properties need not be understood, perceived, or controlled by members of the network. To understand them you have to study the network, not the individuals in it. This is another way of saying that social networks represent complex systems and the properties of such systems are not equal to the sum of the properties of its parts. It will trouble us even more when network scientists tell us that network properties are best studied if its members are treated as zero-intelligence units. An example of network behavior can be found in the "human waves" that occur among the spectators of large sporting events. The waves always advance clockwise (one would think that the unknown reason for this is the same reason that clockwise *is* clockwise) and advance at a rate of twenty seats per second. These network events, including the gyrations of schools of fish or flocks of birds just mentioned, can be studied using mathematical models of excitable media that flip one way or the other; studying the behavior of individuals reveals nothing. Another way of describing these phenomena is to say that *social networks have emergent properties.*

Christakis and Fowler (2009) flesh out their description of social network properties and behavior with a number of points. Although everyone is connected by no more than six degrees of separation, three degrees of separation mark the frontier of social influence where contagion peters out. In a now classic paper, Dunbar (1993) studied brain size and group size across primates and came up with a human cohesive group size of 150, now called Dunbar's number, determined by the information processing limits of our large neocortex. He traced this number as far back as 6500 BC in Mesopotamia as the size of bands or villages. Language is used to maintain group cohesion; we spend 42% of our time employing it.

A social network manifests both positional and situational inequalities reflected in the degree to which some members affect others. These inequalities serve to express power relations hierarchies within networks. Networks outlive their members and heal gaps in themselves by shrinking or adding new members. Christakis and Fowler (2009) have taken the additional step of referring to social networks as superorganisms. Although this seems warranted, the implications are staggering and have not yet been explored. Networks have lives of their own. They perform actions of which its members are unaware.

As members of networks, we are deeply influenced by people we don't even know. For example, an analyst attends a clinical seminar. As a result, his behavior with a patient the next day may change; he may or may not be aware of this change; his patient may be affected by it, but is unaware of the change. The self is impinged upon by events in its network that it doesn't know happened, and which are manifestations of the network's complexity and unknowability.

Barabási and His Colleagues

Albert-Lázló Barabási and his colleagues (Barabási, 2003, 2005a, 2005b, 2005c, 2010; Barabási & Bonabeau, 2003; Palla et al., 2007; Ravasz & Barabási, 2003) study the behavior of networks, not confined to social groups, at multiple levels of organization. They have focused on two particular areas: the way that events occur over time in individuals and networks and the way in which networks are organized. These networks can be made up of human beings (in Christakis & Fowler's 2007 study they were the offspring of the subjects in the original Framingham Heart Study) or other sorts of nodes, such as neurons in the brain.

The incidence of human activity and social patterns over time used to be forecast by using equations that model regular distributions of events with relatively short waiting times between them (Barabási, 2005b). This is called a Poisson distribution after the much-celebrated 19th century French mathematician who first used it to predict the probability of jury error in differently designed jury systems. This distribution has since been used to model things like traffic flow and call-center volumes. However, increasing numbers of measurements of human activity indicate that distributions frequently deviate from the Poisson predictions. (Hence traffic jams and dropped calls.) What we see instead are bursts of activity with very short waiting times that then taper off into very long periods of inactivity between events. This pattern is ubiquitous in biological and human functioning, be it at the level of single cells, individual organisms, or large social networks. It is a kind of heavy-tailed, slowly decaying distribution named after Vilfredo Pareto, a

19th century economist who used it to model the presence of a few, extremely wealthy individuals in populations at a rate beyond what would be predicted by a normal distribution. This property of burstiness is a generic feature of human dynamics; activities like emailing and texting follow this pattern. Verbal activity of analysts or patients is presumably bursty as well. In recent years, sophisticated statistical tools have become available that could, in fact, be used to model therapeutic discourse and confirm its burstiness.

Barabási (2005b) posits that the burstiness of human behavior is a result of queuing; when someone is confronted with a series of tasks, the tasks are ranked in some fashion, not simply done on a first-come, first-served basis as seen in service tasks. Queues can be handled in one of three ways. The first is first-in, first-out in the order in which they entered the queue. Or, they can be handled through random selection, regardless of time spent in the queue or the importance of the task. They also can be handled through human choice; those tasks given the highest priority are done first, regardless of when they enter the queue. Humans handle tasks by setting up queues based on *perceived* priorities; the process is not conscious. This always seems to result in some tasks being done very quickly in a burst, followed by tasks then being done singly with longer and longer waiting times between them. In other words, when we look at how humans perform groups of tasks, we find a Pareto distribution.

Until fairly recently, scientists treated the organization of complex biological or communication networks as consisting of groups of nodes with randomly placed links between them (Erdos & Rényi, 1959). The nodes of such democratic networks would all have approximately the same number of links and would follow a Poisson distribution. For example, Barabási and colleagues (Albert, Jeong, & Barabási, 1999) studied the topology of the World Wide Web, where they expected to find a random network. They thought that the sheer size of the web and the unique interests of people setting up their web pages (the nodes of the network) would result in a random distribution of connections. Instead, they found (Barabási & Bonabeau, 2003) that 80% of the pages they mapped had fewer than four links and a very small percentage (0.01%) had more than a thousand. This would be like standing at a street corner measuring the height of passers-by and rarely finding an individual who was 100 feet tall. Different classes of networks or their elements demonstrate massive variations in size. Because of these large variations, they are referred to as being *scale-free*. The scale-free network of the World Wide Web was being held together by a relatively small number of highly connected web pages (hubs). Social networks manifest the same property; groups of people tend to be held together by a few well-connected individuals.

In addition to being scale-free, social and biological networks manifest a high degree of clustering (Barabási & Bonabeau, 2003). Randomness would predict neither property. These properties taken together lead to a hierarchical organization that would not be observed in a network demonstrating either property in isolation. These hierarchical organizations are often modular; densely connected groups of nodes have relatively few connections to the outside. This is not the "plug-and-play" modularity that has often been erroneously advanced by neuroscience (e.g., Doidge, 2007; Schacter et al., 2000) as the underlying structure and connectivity of the brain, but is rather an organization of subsystems. Scale-free networks are blind to modular considerations and "care" only about the degree of separation among their nodes.

Barabási is uncertain about whether scale-free networks do indeed exist in the brain. However, Freeman (2005, 2007) has identified them as underlying patterns of organization in the neocortex by examining high spatiotemporal resolution rabbit electroencephalograms, and demonstrating the existence of virtually instantaneous scale-free, self-organizing phase transitions of independent domains ranging in size from a few hypercolumns of cerebral cortex to an entire hemisphere.

Scale-free networks tend to be robust in the face of individual hub failure and are virtually unaffected by the loss of nodes having low connectivity. If multiple hubs fail, a smaller intact network will remain. This is an important property of biological systems that helps to maintain them in the face of damage.[111] The more important a hub is, the more vulnerable a network is to its removal. Targeting hubs becomes a useful way of mediating change in biological networks. Large groups can persist only if they are dynamic and capable of changing their membership; small groups are relatively more fragile and persist only if their membership remains unchanged. The time commitment of individuals to a group is related to its lifetime. As the Facebook community has expanded and thrived, membership in the MySpace community has declined by half; it seems probable that by the time you read this it will have ceased to exist. If members of an organization devote less time to it, hubs will fail and the organization will first shrink and then disappear.

111 This self-healing property could explain the return of function following a stroke or the appearance of a neurotic symptom following the appearance of an external stressor.

There are some properties of social networks that have not yet been studied. For reasons of experimental simplicity, studies have focused on single contagion networks. For example, Christakis and colleagues (Cacioppo et al., 2009; Christakis & Fowler, 2007, 2008; Mednick et al., 2010; Rosenquist et al., 2010) have studied the individual spread (induction) of obesity, sleep loss, alcohol consumption, loneliness, and smoking in social networks. In real life, we can be parts of more than one social network and each network has multiple contagions. These contagions must interact, but it is not yet known how or whether their interactions can be deciphered or predicted.

Social networks are complex systems. Another way of studying them is to model their topology, their arrays of nodes, as landscapes of *attractor basins*. Attractors attract.[112] They exist in complex systems where they can be open, resulting in massive and nearly instantaneous phase transitions, or closed organizations exerting local effects. They are organized in groups or basins that I believe also model the behavior of clusters in networks. Freeman and colleagues (Freeman, 1995a, 1995b; Freeman & Barrie, 2001; Freeman et al., 1997) have looked at the role of attractors in the functioning of groups of neurons. They discovered that densely packed arrays of neurons were stabilized by the electrical noise common to brain function. Stabilization may well be achieved in dense social networks in a similar noisy fashion. Multiple contagions could create just such a stable, noisy network environment, affecting different clusters of nodes and moving on through the network over time.

Another property of attractor basins is that they resist change and, if displaced in some fashion, tend to return to their original orientation after the displacement passes. However, displacement beyond some threshold results in a permanent phase transition to a different level of organization. If we recognize that the self is a complex network, then, as therapists, we mostly seek change incrementally and, much less frequently, through much prized phase transitions of the self (Leffert, 2008).

Critiques

Criticisms of both Christakis and Fowler's and Barabási's work have appeared in the recent Network Studies literature. Members of social

112 For a discussion of attractors and their relevance to psychoanalysis, see Leffert (2010a, especially chapter 4).

networks relate to each other in three different ways. One is homophily: Individuals choose to connect to others who are like or resemble them. The second involves external environmental factors that sometimes act to form individuals into social groups. The last is contagion: the [mostly] unconscious spread of information across a group. Critiques fall into two major categories: the statistical and the secular. Three authors—Lyons (2011), Noel and Nyhan (2011), and Shalizi and Thomas (2011)—all criticize Christakis & Fowler's (e.g., 2007) statistical methods, which they find flawed and unable to substantiate the existence of contagion. Both Noel and Nyhan and Shalizi and Thomas also address a secular problem; they argue that homophily confounds contagion to such a degree that the latter cannot be independently validated.

Barabási's (e.g., 2005b) work has also been criticized on statistical grounds. Malmgren and colleagues (Malmgren, Stouffer, Motter, & Amaral, 2008) have argued that the heavy tailed distributions that Barabási describes as evidence of a Pareto distribution in fact represents a non-homogenous Poisson distribution characterized by different statistics. This is a methodological rather than a secular criticism.

Although social networks form for reasons of homophily or environmental factors (think athletic clubs or college class sections), the cross-network transmission of unconscious information not necessarily related to the reasons for a network forming must still be explained. In other words, networks do manifest contagion. If Christakis & Fowler's (2007) methodology is flawed (the fact that they designate a network, i.e., obese individuals in the Framingham Study, by the very condition whose contagion they endeavor to prove suggests that it might be), that does not disprove their hypotheses. However, they would require re-study of their original data, perhaps by looking at multiple contagions in order to avoid the confounding effects of homophily relating to only one of them.

Network Studies and Clinical Psychoanalysis

Given that Network Studies is certainly an interesting field, what does it have to offer us as psychoanalysts and psychotherapists? I have suggested a number of possibilities over the course of the previous discussion. If what we are about clinically is changing the self (never mind for the moment how), then network considerations become relevant on two levels. They involve remembering that the self is a biological network and that, in order to alter it, we must consider it in network terms alongside the psychological terms (of whatever ilk) that we are accustomed to employing. It is also important to remember that we and our patients are members of different social networks connected to each other by at least this one tie between us.[113]

These networks extend far beyond the family figures we are accustomed to thinking about in relation to our clinical work and they manifest a constant transmission of information that we are unaware of. They can act implicitly and unknowingly to advance or retard the therapeutic process. Psychoanalysis and psychotherapy prioritize the individual. In these days of managed care, this priority is, if anything, even more important. In thinking about network effects, we have to make the difficult shift to also thinking about our patients as parts of systems in which their individuality is irrelevant and find ways of addressing this irrelevance clinically.

With some notable exceptions, it is very difficult to identify network effects, let alone be able to inquire specifically about them. Clinically, what we in effect attempt to do is to study with our patients a select group of relationships in their lives occurring in different time frames. This group generally is limited to parents, siblings, spouses or significant others, and occasionally friends, bosses, mentors, or mentees. Analysts and psychotherapists then usually go on to consider these relationships from whatever object relational, developmental, or structural metapsychologies appeal to them as individuals. Should treatment not progress in some area, we then tend to look for obstacles in the patient (I do not personally use the term *resistance* because of its power-relations connotations), ourselves, or our relationship. We then act, often interpretively, to try to change the therapeutic situation.

I would suggest instead that, parallel to this usual approach, we also try to think generally about the situation in network terms and extend it beyond the few, intimate objects. Admittedly, this is difficult to do because what is happening in someone's social network is mostly out of awareness. I'm not suggesting that we should translate our language into network language; this would be pointless (let alone that the languages are not at all interchangeable). What I am suggesting is that if some movement is not occurring, perhaps nothing is wrong in the therapeutic situation. Perhaps, out of any awareness, the patient is being held in

113 Some years ago, I noted that, as a training analyst, all of the patients in my practice were connected to each other either directly or through other single individuals (one or two degrees of separation). I naively understood that this observation had some effect on their respective treatments, but at the time lacked any tools for thinking about what this effect might consist of.

place by her network. This would be a non-specific effect in that it is not due to some explicit or implicit response by someone in the patient's social network, but is simply some result of the flux of contagions the patient is exposed to. (We are of course aware that specific responses by significant others can easily occur; we cast them in the familiar language of psychoanalysis and deal with them interpretively or not as seems most appropriate to us.) An analyst informed by network theory might choose to do nothing differently in such a situation and simply watch or, alternatively, cast her net a bit wider among a patient's network connections.

Specific network effects can also be observed and folded into a treatment. In the fall of 2008, I began seeing Lisa and Sandra, two slim, attractive college sophomores suffering from Bulimia Nervosa, non-purging type. They both also struggled with depression. The women attended different colleges and were unknown to each other; age of onset was 14 for Sandra and 17 for Lisa. Both were unhappy with their current body mass; Lisa was a size 2 but looked back fondly to having been a size 0 two years earlier, while Sandra, currently a 0, had been a 00 (I had had no idea that these sizes even existed). I saw both in twice-weekly psychotherapy.

For our purposes, the important difference between these two women was that while Lisa lived off campus with her boyfriend, Sandra lived in a dorm suite with three other women and was immersed in what I will call her college's eating disorder network (such undergraduate cultures are widespread, I believe, if only one cares to observe them). Two of Sandra's roommates and some of her friends had varying degrees of bulimia. She told me that eating disorders were widespread throughout the college. The school was concerned about the problem; there was an annual eating disorder awareness week, weekly weigh-ins and counseling were available, and seniors who were in recovery were visible and available to students on a confidential basis. The effectiveness of any of these laudable measures was unclear to me; I have since come to think that it is even possible that, by strengthening the connections of this de facto network, they made the problem worse.

Sandra was acutely aware of the eating behaviors of the women around her. She would look for signs of someone being out of control and comment to me about which women acknowledged their struggle with food and who denied it, who purged (Sandra had, but no longer did) and who didn't. All found the disorders deeply shameful.

I felt that I had evidence for the existence of an eating disorder network at this college based on what Sandra had told me. All of the material I had read about social networks also suggested that this network would influence the behavior around food of its members and that it was influencing Sandra. Indeed, although I went about my tasks as a therapist in my usual manner, Sandra's bulimia had not much improved after a year of therapy.

Since networks exist and exert their influence outside of awareness (which is not to say they are repressed), offering an interpretation would be valueless. I recalled Christakis and Fowler's (2009) observation that networks were best studied if their nodes were treated as zero intelligence units. I wondered if the converse were also true; if one could make them into intelligent units, would network effects then be lessened? I decided to test out this hypothesis with Sandra by trying to make her "more intelligent" about her network. Whenever she gave me an opening, I would talk to her about her friends' eating disorders, events relating to them at school, and her thoughts and feelings about the subject. My goal was not to interpret anything, but rather to make her as aware as I could of the content we explored. I said nothing about why I was doing this; there was no need to do so. Presumably, Sandra thought that, since she had an eating disorder, it was appropriate to talk about it in her therapy.

I stopped focusing on the personal and internal aspects of the problem: what and how she ate, what precipitated binges, how she felt about them. After about six months of this, the binges tapered off and disappeared; they have not reappeared in the three years since. I am not offering this as proof of anything, or as a suggestion that we should dispense with our usual therapeutic practices. However, it is a promising observation, there seems little risk of harm (if there *was* such a concern, one could simply demur), and I would repeat the practice in the future if another clinical opportunity came my way.

When I saw her, Lisa did not seem to be a part of an eating disorder network. She was not immersed in any sort of network at school. She had had a difficult childhood with her borderline mother abandoning the family when she was five. Lisa had been inconsolable and sleepless for a year. Her bingeing decreased over the course of a fairly standard sort of analytic psychotherapy in which I tended to seek out meaning and focus on relationships, the therapeutic relationship among them. At some point, it became clear that the few remaining bulimic episodes always occurred in the context of Lisa being lonely, or being left alone. Connecting them to the maternal loss, and a compensatory maternal identification, over several months of therapy led to their cessation and an amelioration of the depression.

I would suggest that as clinicians we routinely, albeit naively, make use of network dynamics with our patients. In considering a patient's relationships with those around them (alters), usually parents, siblings, spouses, and occasionally friends, we identify pathological network ties, often looking back in time to do so. The content of the ties may be destructive and they may be unidirectional, from the alter to the ego, when they should become bilateral. Implicitly we look to break up these ties or restructure them.

In the complex system focused on the social network of our patient and ourselves, the tie between us is mutual; whether we acknowledge it or not, the connection passes contagions back and forth between us, beyond our awareness. If we think in terms of attractor basins, the relationship hopefully acts to push the patient into a phase transition that is a permanent realignment rather than a temporary effect (e.g., a transference cure) that settles back into equilibrium after the therapeutic relationship is no longer present.

I do not mean to suggest that there is any value per se in translating what we usually do into network terminology, a criticism on occasion appropriately leveled against how psychoanalytic imports are employed in our discipline. My goal in discussing clinical applications has been twofold: to show that we are already familiar with network concepts although we call them by different names, and to encourage thinking about social networks as novel sources of information about the therapeutic situation.

This chapter and the three preceding ones have looked at clinical and theoretical concepts at the edge of psychoanalytic thought. Researching and writing about them has moved me clinically into a phase transition, and I hope for a similar effect in my readers. At this point, it is reasonable to look back and to ask whether there is still a place for Freud, somewhere in all of this. Most contemporary theoreticians and clinicians, voting with their feet, have largely turned away from him, in name if not in deed. Perhaps surprisingly, I would insist that Freud does have a place, but that it must be different from the one we have been taught or, all too often, still teach our student-heirs. I would posit that what I am about to consider is not especially new but simply takes up things about the corpus of Freud's work and the *Standard Edition* that have not been brought together before. It will turn out that some of those things have already been discussed and lend themselves as tools in this next inquiry.

5

Reading (or Not Reading) Freud in the 21st Century

Introduction

The case for reading Freud in the 21st century rests largely on who will be doing the reading and why they will be doing it. Is it to be students, teachers, or graduate therapists reading on their own? Is Freud to be read in the academy? Are the readers to be affiliated with the mostly Freudian psychoanalytic institutes of the APsaA, or those trained and practicing under the aegis of the contemporary institutes grounded in relational or intersubjective theories, or still others grounded in other named metapsychologies? Each of these groups has evolved its own responses to and relative involvement in Freud's work. Since it is hoped that the unfolding intellectual life of a psychoanalyst or psychotherapist is a dynamic rather than a static thing, these responses and involvements may well change over time. As our lives change, our professional world is also changing; it offers ideas and challenges to Freud's work that did not exist a half-century ago.

Kirsner (2009) observes that there are approximately 20,000 practitioners in the United States who identify themselves as psychoanalysts or psychoanalytically oriented, of which approximately 3000 are members of the APsaA. The remaining majority is associated with psychoanalytic institutes directly accredited by the International Psychoanalytic Association (IPA) or with freestanding institutes. It is clear from the numbers that the APsaA is no longer the dominant psychoanalytic player in the United States it once was but still imagines itself to be.

No studies have assessed the views of *any* of the 20,000 psychoanalysts regarding how they assess the current importance of Freud's work; any attempt to do so here must be purely speculative. That said, it is probably safe to say that significant numbers of the members of the above-named psychoanalytic associations view his work as having at least some importance, and it is equally likely that significant numbers of the remaining psychoanalysts do not. Trying to assess the actual position that psychoanalysts and psychotherapists take on Freud's work is further complicated by the fact that, whatever their ilk, psychoanalysts are adept at "speaking in tongues." That is to say, they can talk, write, or supervise in some particular meta-psychological language, while, *at the same time*, doing something quite different in their offices with their own patients. Taking all of this into account, it is probably safe to assume that many psychoanalysts have relatively little use for, or interest in, Freud as they go about their clinical work. For them, Freud lacks resonance with that work or with their identity as analysts and therapists. In this chapter I will offer a critique of how Freud is read or not read, address the issues of relevance and resonance, and suggest a very different approach to his work.

One problem with reading (or not reading) Freud is that, practically speaking, the reading is inseparable from appraising Freud the person. Psychoanalysis is similarly inseparable from him. This is not to say that Freud's theories and writings dominate psychoanalysis today or that psychoanalysis is a monolith that can be dominated by anything. What it means is that if you are an analyst, a psychotherapist, or even simply a reader of psychoanalytic writings, then you also have some fairly strong and often conflicted opinions of Freud that influence your approach to his work.

Particularly for those of us who trained professionally some decades ago, our experience of Freud is colored by idealizations and transferences, both positive and negative, that interdigitate with those of our personal analytic experiences. In the triad of postmodern textual analysis consisting of text, reader, and author, it is often possible to make a case for dispensing with the author, allowing the text to stand on its own, and taking up the subjectivity of the reader. With authors like Freud, geniuses (I think when all is said and done, one does have to credit Freud with genius, albeit normatively flawed genius) or charismatic figures, this is simply not possible; who you think Freud was and how you feel about him are always on the table when you read him. Equally germane is the fact that Freud's writings often had a political or power relations component that reflected his need to banish dissent and expel dissenters from the psychoanalytic movement.[114] In the United States, his work was later used for similar purposes.[115]

It seems remarkable that contemporary analysts often remain oblivious to the interreferentiality of the scientific and power components of Freud's work and that of other named leaders of competing metapsychological schools. The solution to the problem is twofold: to learn the psychoanalytic history and then to deconstruct the power components from the text. Thus freed, it is much easier to read for meaning and ideas, allowing the power relations to remain present in the background. Any discussion of reading Freud must include an analysis of these power issues.

A prerequisite for reading Freud requires a consideration of the stumbling blocks that confront a 21st century Anglophone trying to understand what Freud actually said and wrote in 19th century Vienna. Although these considerations have been described in abstract form from time to time in the psychoanalytic literature (I have alluded to them in earlier chapters), they have never been applied to the actual task of reading Freud for understanding.

An additional issue that comes from the relatively new field of Science Studies (Latour, 1991/1993, 1999) is that it is impossible to separate the social from the scientific, a separation that most disciplines, including psychoanalysis, have taken for granted. Scientific knowledge is inseparable from the social and temporal circumstances in which it is created and subsequently employed. Consistent with this premise, Latour and Woolgar (1986), in their work *Laboratory Life in the Construction of Scientific Facts*, describe the dynamic concept of science-in-action. Briefly, one can construct a nonlinear timeline on which a series of scientific events related to some area of inquiry can be positioned.[116] These events become closed "packages" that are treated as fact, but must be reopened if new science-in-action calls them into question. However, as new events unfold, earlier packages move into the ever more distant

114 A footnote to Freud's case history of "The Rat Man" (Freud, 1909/1955e) begins, "Dr. Alfred Adler *who was formerly an analyst. . .*" (p. 160, italics added). One at the beginning of "The Wolf Man" (Freud, 1918 [1914]/1955b) states, "At the time I was still under the impression of the *twisted re-interpretations* which C. G. Jung and Alfred Adler were endeavouring to give to the findings of psychoanalysis" (p. 7, italics added). These footnotes could not be any plainer in their indictment of dissenters.

115 In 1941 the power elites of the NYPI first branded Karen Horney a heretic, then demoted her, and finally forced her to resign (Hale Jr., 1995).

116 Elsewhere, I constructed such a timeline of neuroimaging beginning with Golgi's staining procedures of 1873 and ending with the use of fMRIs in 2003 (Leffert, 2010a).

past, and at some point undergo qualitative change; they cease to be packages of science and, instead, become packages of history.

I am *not* suggesting that this is true of all of Freud's work, but it is true of a significant part of it. I would expect little disagreement that this is true of chapter 1 of *Die Traumdeutung* (Freud, 1900).[117] What for the first and, possibly, the second decade of the 20th century was an interesting and useful review of the literature has become, at this point, a powerful treatment for insomnia for most of us. I would expect placing chapter 7 in the same category, as a historical curiosity, would engender more disagreement. For example, in a recent paper, Levy (2009) described chapter 7 as offering an adequate discussion of the topographic model and assumes that it is universally taught. Questions relating to its teaching would then be confined to the choice of pedagogic strategies.

Similarly, the telescopic topography of 1900 is an early curiosity, comprehensively replaced 15 years later by the dynamic unconscious of the metapsychology papers (e.g., Freud, 1915/1957e). To study different kinds of thought and feeling is to struggle with these papers with Klein (1970, 1976b) and Fisher (1954) at hand, along with an appropriate selection of readings drawn from neuroscience to provide contemporary context. Levy posits that the middle chapters of *Die Traumdeutung* contain a wealth of data on what it means to work with dreams. I would argue instead that it is simply a comfortable and familiar way to talk about dreams, as we were taught to talk about them in our analytic education decades ago.

What these chapters do offer, as Schorske (1980) so cogently demonstrates, is a fascinating window into Freud's self-analysis for those who are interested in it. (Schorske is not currently taught alongside Freud.) Freud's ideas about the formation and analysis of dreams, if they are taught, must be taught side by side with the alternative psychoanalytic theories on the subject (i.e., *not* taught in isolation in the first year with alternative views relegated to later years). Our current understanding of the neuropsychology of dreaming that both expands and imposes constraints on Freud's views must be taught *simultaneously*.

As a colleague recently remarked to me, 1905 was an interesting year. In psychoanalysis, it saw the publication of Freud's *Three Essays* and the case history of "Dora," while in physics Einstein's paper on the theory of relativity was published. All are considered to have been revolutionary.

117 In his correspondence with Fliess, Freud (1985c, 1985d) himself made it clear that, even then, he considered this material tiresome.

Einstein's paper was metabolized by the discipline of physics over a number of decades, after which the field moved on without reference to the original paper. The *Three Essays* partially enjoyed a similar fate, shaping the work of perhaps two generations of psychoanalysts but only to linger on as a kind of undigested relic of libido theory in institute curricula instead of teaching it in the context of where psychoanalysis has gone.

"Dora," alas, is another matter. The case history contains a bizarrely formulated description of the Oedipus complex, further obfuscated by Freud's complex agenda, as well as his analytic connection to her father (his former patient). He lectures Dora (Freud, 1905 [1901]/1953a) about her psychopathology and dreams, and is furious when she walks out on him. Until Erikson (1962) rescued her reputation, so to speak, she was demeaned and ridiculed by other analysts such as Deutsch (1957), who gloats as he catalogues her subsequent misfortunes. Let me be blunt: This is disgusting. It would seem a rather squalid and best-forgotten episode in psychoanalytic history. But no. Generations of students of orthodox psychoanalysis have had to struggle with "Dora" in an "emperor's-new-clothes" fashion, casting a blind eye on its theoretical distortions, social context, and Freud's "therapeutic" technique. Dora, at 16, is supposed to succumb to the dubious charms of *Herr* K to compensate him for Dora's father, Freud's patient, having his way with *Frau* K. Freud's hostile superiority towards his young patient and her refusal to see things his way, although it virtually jumps off the page, is to be similarly ignored. *Please.* Instead, the students are to direct their attention only to Freud's "brave" admission of a therapeutic error, his "discovery" of the transference, and the interpretation of her dreams—but not his technique of analyzing them.[118]

The foregoing should not be considered a contemptuous dismissal of Freud's work; nothing would be further from my position. However, I have no patience for the hagiography that Freud sought and which continues to be bestowed upon him in some circles even now. This tendency towards idealization must be addressed in the teaching of Freud to students of psychoanalysis; this is acknowledged by some psychoanalytic educators (e.g., Fogel & Glick, 1991; Levy,

118 Freud did not comment on the *countertransference* and the role of self-analysis in dealing with it until 1910 (1910/1957c), when he observed that "Anyone who fails to produce results in a self-analysis ... may at once give up any idea of being able to treat patients by analysis" (p. 145). He did not, at least in print, ever make reference to "Dora" or his feelings about her in this context.

2009). The body of Freud's contributions to psychoanalysis is of great importance.

Graduate analysts who reread Freud do so for diverse reasons and contexts, often related to the teaching of Freud to students of psychoanalysis. Fogel and Glick (1991) describe a study group they participated in after graduation. They sought to consolidate further their identities as psychoanalysts and educators, and to address their "powerful individual and institutional resistances to fully working through the wishful, rageful, and fearful distortions that [might have been] embedded in [their] early analytic identifications" (pp. 396–397). They also sought to further work through unresolved transferences to training analysts, supervisors, teachers, and founding fathers. These are laudatory goals that we should all seek to reach by whatever path or paths seem most useful to us.[119]

Fogel and Glick's study group chose as their path the rereading of the *Standard Edition* from beginning to end, which is problematic. Although a reconsideration of Freud from a (hopefully) more mature perspective is doubtless of value, the use of such an emersion in isolation as a foundation for reformulating one's analytic identity cannot help but result in an identity that claims continued privileged standing for both Freud and his work. To offer any single founding father, or mother, or psychoanalytic "school" such privilege and to adopt it as a self-signifier is a serious mistake that inevitably constrains both one's identity and one's work as a psychoanalyst. However, the selective rereading of Freud, absent this context, is a useful and necessary part of any graduate analyst's personal reading program.

Understanding Freud: A Matter of Epistemes and Translations

Attempting to understand what Freud meant to say and write presents two sorts of problems. The first has to do with positioning his work in the contemporary cultural episteme of American psychoanalysis given that it comes from an entirely different time and place. An episteme is frequently misunderstood as referring to the *Zeitgeist* of some particular era. It actually refers to the rules governing the formulation and

119 My own analytic identity was reformulated on at least two occasions, once around a reanalysis and becoming a training analyst, and again, as a result of a self-analysis and my study of postmodernism that led, among other things, to my becoming a psychoanalytic author and a sculptor.

interpretation of knowledge in a particular time or place. Clearly, there is dissonance between the epistemes of *fin-de-siècle* Vienna[120] and 21st century America. The result of this dissonance is that, for many contemporary psychoanalysts and psychotherapists, Freud lacks *epistemic resonance* and is explicitly or implicitly discarded before, during, or after post-graduate training in psychoanalytic theory or practice.

If this situation were not already complex enough, psychoanalysis also manifests a particular kind of temporal dualism. There is at once a kind of paradox about Freud and his work. Freud was and remained a man of the late 19th century whose work was shaped by its epistemology, its scholarship, and the influence of classical culture.[121] However, psychoanalysis, his creation, was a creature of the 20th century, not the 19th. It had a profound impact on developing 20th century thought; psychoanalysis, ignored and unknown in the 19th century, was first idealized, and then reviled, in the 20th.

Epistemes can also be conceptualized in terms of systems theory (e.g., Laszlo, 1972/1996) and Network Studies (e.g., Barabási, 2003; Christakis & Fowler, 2009). As rules of knowledge, they are both explicit and implicit and can reflect the properties of both very large and small social networks that were discussed in the last chapter. The intellectual community in which Freud lived and worked can be treated as a social network[122] in which the key players would easily have totaled fewer than Dunbar's number (150), the optimum size of a functional social group. Information, called contagion by social network theorists, can move through a network resulting in thoughts or behaviors that are not so much subjectively experienced by individuals as they are implicitly influenced by it. The reception of ideas takes place in such groups; ideas

120 Grasping this Viennese episteme in a comprehensive way is easily the work of a career; we can only sketch out some of its broad themes here.

121 Confirmatory evidence for this observation comes from an unexpected source. Most psychoanalysts have a general sense of what Freud's office looked like: the numerous antiquities, books, and Persian carpets. Days before the Freuds and their possessions were to leave Vienna for Britain in May of 1938, a then young photographer, Edmund Engelman, was asked by August Aichhorn to photograph Freud's offices and the adjoining apartment in which the Freuds lived. *Bergasse 19 Sigmund Freud's Home and Offices* (Engelman, 1976) was the result. What is striking about the 54 exhaustive photographs that Engelman took that day and eventually published is that *there is nothing of the 20th century to be found in any of them*. They record a space (Bachelard, 1958/1994) of the 1890s. No furniture or appliances of the first four decades of the 20th century intrude. There are personal photographs, 19th century prints on classical themes, and the hundreds of antiquities of course. But the impressionists of the 19th century and the expressionists of the 20th do not exist within these walls. Freud simply never got there.

122 Timms (1986/1989, p. 8) offers a diagram of the overlapping social networks of intellectual *fin de siècle* Vienna.

that had a place in the Vienna of 100 years ago are often rejected by the much larger social network of 21st century mental health professionals.

The second and not unrelated problem for the Anglophone audience arises out of the necessity of having to read Freud in translation. A number of authors (e.g., Bettelheim, 1983; Grubrich-Simitis, 1993/1996; Mahony, 1987; Ornston, 1992a) have discussed the problem and have been variously critical of the *Standard Edition*. To my knowledge, translation problems have, at most, been mentioned rather than discussed as a part of institute curricula. Beyond detailing the existence of these issues (at a level of scholarship sometimes surpassing that of the *Standard Edition*), this literature does not suggest how knowledge of them can be used to inform an ongoing study of Freud's texts.

I hope that I have been successful in arguing that reading and teaching Freud involve actively engaging complex issues that go far beyond the level of asking theory-based questions concerning whether or not Freud should be read and reread. It is impossible to separate his texts from the social, political, and philosophical issues present in the milieu of the Vienna of a century ago where they were born. Nor can they be separated from the contemporaneous 21st century issues of analytic identity formation, the embedding of the analytic self in the social matrix of psychoanalysis, and the role of power relations in this matrix. (In my experience, the decision to read or not to read has all too often boiled down to this last point: considerations of power within and between analytic organizations.) To pretend otherwise is to sacrifice much of our ability to truly study Freud's texts and to allow epistemological contexts to inform our thinking (Leffert, 2007a, 2007b).

Then, of course, there is the additional complication of translation and the various agendas of the translators. And, finally, however much we might wish to cling to the "objective" texts, each reading or discussion of readings remains a unique event that has never occurred before and will never be repeated.

Epistemic Problems

It is not possible to offer a cultural history of Vienna, however fascinating such an undertaking might prove to be. Beyond representing a career-sized task, it is one that strays from our purpose—to consider how culture in its very broadest sense comes to be represented in the ways of knowing that make up the Viennese episteme.

Viewed at a superficial level from a distance of over a century (Janik & Toulmin, 1973/1996), *fin-de-siècle* Vienna at first appears to be a place of café society: brilliant intellectuals, grand public architecture, all-night civic balls, quaint uniforms, Strauss *Waltzer*, and *Schlag* that suggests nothing so much as a glorious empire at the height of its powers. It was the City of Dreams. Although in reality it represented a society on the brink of dissolution, this fact alone in no way tells us of its dark, gritty strangeness or how that strangeness affected Freud and found its way into his work. (Ironically, the Hapsburg Empire did represent a true 1000-year Reich, crumbling in the last decades of the 19th century, that would die in the final spasm of the First World War.) As psychoanalysts, years of repeated study of Freud's texts have only served to obfuscate matters for us; we no longer even notice what strikes new readers as arcane and *old*. Unfortunately, the English translations available today are of little help to us here.

In his introduction to *Freud's Discovery of the Unconscious: The Politics of Psychoanalysis*, McGrath (1986) immediately brings together a series of epistemic concepts concerning the origins of Freud's work that he centers on *Die Traumdeutung*. In the letter to Fliess (Freud, 1985d) in which Freud announces his intention to finally complete and publish this work, he ironically links it to the recurrent political crises that the Austro-Hungarian Empire was undergoing, and the at-times apocalyptic, satiric writings of Karl Kraus (Janik & Toulmin, 1973/1996; Timms, 1986/1989)[123] about the last days of Austria. "So the dream[124] will be" (1985d, p. 353), Freud tells Fliess. If "this Austria is supposed to perish in the next two weeks . . . why should the dream perish with it" (p. 353). In an earlier letter (1985c), Freud observes about himself that

123 Kraus was a biting satirist who brilliantly critiqued all aspects of Austrian society at the brink (among them Freud's theories) through his bimonthly journal *Die Fackel* (*The Torch*), which he founded in 1899, edited, and wrote until his death in 1936. To give some sense of the man, in *Die Fackel*'s first quarterly report, he included the following personal information:

Anonymous reviling letters	236
Anonymous threatening letters	83
Assaults	1

(Janik & Toulmin, 1973/1996, p. 69)

124 Freud frequently refers to *Die Traumdeutung* in correspondence as simply *der Traum* (the dream). Although this has been interpreted as an otherwise incomprehensible abbreviation, Freud may have meant, as he usually did, just what he said, albeit at times with some ambiguity. In other words, he identified this book as unlike any other: "No other work of mine has been so completely my own, my own dung heap, my seedling and a *nova species mihi* [roughly, a new language] on top of it" (1985d, p. 353). It *was* his dream, his "finest and probably [his] only lasting discovery" (p. 353), the source from which all his subsequent work would spring.

"one always remains a child of his age, even in what one deems one's very own" (p. 275). McGrath tells us that he has crafted his own title to locate Freud's work as a discovery of human nature rather than a theory or invention and his subtitle as a link to the political aspects of the episteme of *fin-de-siècle* Vienna. Perhaps. What we reference today with the term *psychoanalytic politics* is quite different (Leffert, 2010a) and obscures this earlier meaning just as "the dream" highlights translational obscurities.

The European revolutions of 1848, the Springtime of the Peoples, ushered in a period of hope and increasing social freedoms. The following 30 years (Gay, 1988), corresponding to Freud's early life, found a liberalized Austria repealing virtually all its anti-Semitic laws. Their return in spirit in the 1880s and 1890s, along with a waning of liberalism, led to Freud's feeling crushed, socially and professionally. Although a significant part of the intellectual and medical communities of Austria were Jewish or of Jewish decent, barriers existed to their joining or advancing in government, or university and medical faculties. The government of what had been the Austro-Hungarian Empire had become a fragmented absurdity comprising the Austrian Empire and the Kingdom of Hungary. Its organization was so arcane that its elements were described by the adjectives *kaiserlich* (imperial) and *königlich* (royal). They were usually abbreviated as "*k* & *k*" because, if they were to be written out, it required great care to determine which term, royal or imperial, should come first in a particular instance.

Freud struggled for his entire life with the sociopolitical reality of Vienna as a scientist-Jew. He was, and felt himself to be, an unrecognized outsider even as he went on to worldwide fame. In addition to the usual theoretical importance given to *Die Traumdeutung*, Schorske (1980) also saw it in the context of Freud's search for recognition. Like Freud, he viewed it as his most important work, the cornerstone of a new science and a source of renewal from the academic banishment of the 1890s. I would see its publication in terms of power relations and of Freud's struggle to best the Viennese elites who excluded him. (*Die Traumdeutung*'s initial failure to achieve recognition had to have been crushing.) Anyone who doubts this agenda need only look at the title page from which Freud hurls his challenge to the world in the form of the then well-known quote from Virgil's *Aeneid: Flectere si nequeo superos, Acheronta movebo* (Freud, 1900/1953b, front piece).[125] *Der*

125 "If I cannot bend the higher powers, I shall stir up hell" (Schorske, 1980, p. 200). The reference here is to the river Acheron, the river of pain that was for Virgil the source of the Styx, the river that had to be crossed to reach the underworld or the unconscious.

Traum was a scientific and literary treatise with a biographical subplot contained in the ongoing narrative of its author's dreams. It reaches upwards to metapsychology and rarified power and draws downward from Freud's unconscious. Such a construction, as we will see, could only have come from a student of Franz Brentano.

In the educated world of *fin-de-siècle* Vienna, *everyone* discussed philosophy and all things were culturally interreferential (Janik & Toulmin, 1973/1996). The Viennese intellectual community viewed the central issues of post-Kantian thought as relevant to their own individual concerns, be they art, science, law, or politics. Everyone worked in this wider literary and cultural milieu and was in turn influenced by it. This was a culture steeped in the discussion of ideas. Johnston (1972), in his influential study, *The Austrian Mind: An Intellectual and Social History 1848–1938*, begins by observing that "it was in Austria and its successor states that many, perhaps even most, of the seminal thinkers of the twentieth century emerged" (p. 1). Seventy of these mostly men lived and worked in Vienna, the City of Dreams, for at least parts of their lives. Austria witnessed the creative combination of the *fin-de-siècle* worldview known as Viennese Impressionism, which prized ephemerality, aestheticism, and nostalgia, side by side with positivistic science. I would describe this interreferentiality today in terms of postmodernism with its sheaves of *différance* (Derrida, 1972/1982) and Science Studies (Latour, 1991/1993; Leffert, 2010a). Impressionism and its referents are major elements of the Viennese episteme.[126] Freud, like many of his contemporaries drawn from a range of intellectual disciplines (Buber, Mach, and Wittgenstein notably among them), was first drawn to this path during his undergraduate years at the University of Vienna by the work and teaching of Franz Brentano (Jacquette, 2004a; McGrath, 1986).

Beginning with the publication of *Psychology from an Empirical Standpoint* (1874/1995), Brentano sought to offer an epistemology of psychology as a science. Where the study of the natural sciences involved the study of the laws and properties governing the ontology and behavior of physical bodies, Brentano saw the study of psychology as involving the laws and properties of the soul. He sought to combine the study of the anatomical (ontology) and the physiological (behavior) with the

126 *Die Traumdeutung* is written epistemically as just such an interweaving of these multiple elements, so much a part of 1900 Vienna and so largely unnoticed by contemporary psychoanalytic readers. Much analytic writing has continued to be organized along these lines, again unnoticed for what it is by its authors or readers.

personal psychological observation of the inner self in the service of formulating theories of psychology. Brentano separated perception as an inevitably flawed process from reality, a separation that he dealt with by moving back and forth as necessary between the subjective and the objective.[127] The Vienna of 1900 was at once a place, perhaps the only place, where such organization and process made intellectual sense; it serves to further define the episteme of that time and place.

The most important of Brentano's hypotheses was his concept of the intentionality of mind (Jacquette, 2004b), for which he drew upon Aristotle and the medieval scholastics. Mental processes are always *about* something; they have both a referent and a meaning. He believed that *all* psychological events and *only* psychological events are intentional. As Jacquette observes, the intentionality thesis offers the possibility of understanding the nature of thought. It also would require that all thought has meaning, meaning that can be discovered. It is because of this premise, implicit in Brentano's work of 1874, that the process that would come to be called psychoanalysis would make sense. This aspect of the Viennese episteme would continue to power the explosive growth of mental health services through the post-World War II years. However, with the appearance of alternative modes of therapy, pharmacotherapy among them, and third party payment for services in the 1970s, 1980s, and beyond, the meaning and nature of thought ceased to have epistemic resonance for the majority of mental health professionals beyond the shrinking numbers of psychoanalysts and psychoanalytically oriented psychotherapists.

We know from Freud's correspondence with his friend Eduard Silberstein (McGrath, 1986) that he was much taken with Brentano's ideas. In addition to reading his work, Freud enrolled in five of his courses and studied zoology and physiology as well as philosophy. The result was that Freud thought from the start that he was involved in a science, a science informed by philosophy. *Die Traumdeutung* would embody Brentano's dualism of a psychology derived from the study of the objective and the subjective, although the postmodern tools necessary to truly understand it as a creature of *autres* were lacking. Schorske's (1980) description of it as a scientific treatise with a biographical subplot also had its roots in Brentano. This epistemic structure with its intimations of heaven and hell had much in common with the fiction being turned out by the circle of Viennese authors then referred to as *Jung Wien*.

127 Although unrecognized as such, this formulation encompasses rudimentary elements of what would become postmodernism (Leffert, 2010a) and Science Studies.

Another aspect of the Viennese episteme (Schorske, 1980) much embraced by Freud was the love of science (albeit a hybrid sort of science) coupled with the belief that *anything* could be explained scientifically. This love joined that of classical Greek and Roman culture shared by all Viennese of Freud's generation with an admiration for Joachim Winkelmann, the 18th century founder of scientific archaeology. Classical culture was an important component of all forms of *Wissen* (knowing or knowledge). For Freud, his science was linked to power and became his weapon against the politics of anti-Semitism that made him wait 17 years for the professorship he should have had in eight. It was at the heart of the 19th century liberal slogan *Wissen macht Frei!* (knowledge produces or leads to freedom). This epigram became the basis of Freud's theory of therapeutic action. For therapists of diverse theoretical orientations, the therapeutic goal of personal freedom from the constraints of internalized politics and power continues to have epistemic relevance and is easily grasped in the 21st century.

In his writings and particularly in his theory-building, Freud made use of dialectical analysis in the form of thesis, antithesis, and synthesis.[128] He seems to have positioned himself somewhere between post-Kantian nominalism and Newtonian positivism. However, there were and are problems with substituting a rhetorical device for science, however the latter might be defined. I would take a postmodern position that such a construction is unstable, epistemologically limiting, and subject to deconstruction. A replacement with greater standing would be thesis, antithesis, and *différance*, which is quite in keeping with the "constructive deconstruction" of late 20th century Science Studies (Latour, 1987, 1991/1993).

A similar problem arose for Freud from his decision to tie what was, in essence, a structural psychology to the episteme of 19th century physical science, specifically a motive force of psychical energy modeled on the first and second laws of thermodynamics and Claude Bernard's principle of homeostasis. A debate concerning the existence and relevance of the concept of psychic energy raged in American psychoanalysis during the 1970s (see Rosenblatt & Thickstun, 1970, 1977a, 1977b). It resulted, if one is an optimist, in the concept's abandonment, or if one is a pessimist, in the silence of its proponents, and its epistemic

128 This triad originated in the German Enlightenment and constituted a means of understanding and knowing prominent in *fin-de-siècle* Vienna. It has been much attributed to Hegel, but, according to Kaufmann (1966/1988), was first developed and used extensively by the earlier Neo-Kantian philosopher, Johann Fichte.

replacement by modern (equally quantitative) motivational theory. Unfortunately, psychic energy is still another example of a 19th century concept that contemporary Freudian psychoanalysts reading or rereading Freud are used to and ignore, while non-Freudian analysts, eclectic psychotherapists, psychiatrists, and cognitive neuroscientists find it both antique and arcane and are led in the direction of largely dismissing Freud's work as being without contemporary relevance.

In this necessarily brief discussion of, if you will, the intellectual ontology of *fin-de-siècle* Vienna, we come finally to the perplexing *Beyond the Pleasure Principle* (1920/1955a). Freud's formulation of the existence of a death instinct as a complement to the pleasure principle did not sit well with the majority of his growing international psychoanalytic audience. Even at the heights of Freudian psychoanalytic orthodoxy that ruled the United States during the two decades following World War II, the great majority of American psychoanalysts followed him as far as the beginnings of the essay and the concept of the repetition compulsion but no further. An aggressive drive was acknowledged instead, but was not pursued in the literature.

Freud's biographers have taken this work seriously and have attributed it to Freud's grief over the loss of his beloved daughter Sophie Halberstadt and the devastation and death of the First World War. Max Schur (1972), who was Freud's personal physician before training as a psychoanalyst, wrote about his preoccupations with death and the year he would eventually die. Gay (1988) dismisses the two explanations,[129] mistakenly elides the death instinct with the concept of an aggressive drive, and attempts to treat the concepts on their own as Freud's creation. It is embarrassing to have to say it, but none of these explanations has merit. Freud's views of death and his expression of them are inexorably linked to what Johnston (1972) calls Austria's fascination with death, a fascination that contains elements of a love affair.

In the early 1970s, a young colleague of mine (who wasn't young in the 1970s?) was able to wangle a trip to Vienna and there, as sometimes happens, he became much enamored of a young woman. As a token of his affection, he brought her flowers (it being Vienna, they could only have been long stemmed roses). After expressing her pleasure, she brought out a large long box and opened it, revealing it to be filled with dried roses. In response to his surprise, she explained that all Viennese

129 Gay (1988) duly cites Fritz Wittels (1924), Freud's first biographer, as making the claim about Sophie's death, but goes on to say that Freud himself denied it, saying he had had a complete manuscript of *Beyond the Pleasure Principle* in hand in 1919, before her death.

women of a certain class kept the flowers they had been given throughout their lives in this fashion, in order that they could be placed in their graves at the time of their burials. I never sought confirmation of this anecdote, but had no particular reason to doubt it. What it tells us is that Vienna, Freud's Vienna, was a place where love, life, beauty, and death were at once woven together.

Aestheticism, impressionism, and therapeutic nihilism[130] all revealed the Austrian attitude towards death (Johnston, 1972); "Austrians cultivated a Baroque vision of death as the fulfillment of life" (p. 165). The author Hermann Bahr (1863–1934, a spokesman for *Jung Wien*) viewed death not as a savior but as a consummator. Stefan Zweig (1943/1964), who along with his wife committed suicide after fleeing Austria and reaching physical safety in Brazil in 1942, saw the Viennese custom of elaborate funerals staged with a beautiful corpse as a symptom of aestheticism. Mourning could prompt a histrionic fatigue that sounded much like a form of neurasthenia.

Fin-de-siècle literati wrote of life as ephemeral and death as evanescent (Johnston, 1972). This fit under the rubric of impressionism, here defined as the changeable, ephemeral, nervous fluctuations of Viennese city life. Bahr posited (Johnston, 1972) the existence of at-times dark latent contents beneath a changing surface. For the unemployed youth of the middle and upper classes, death was a remedy for the weariness and ennui of life and suicide the envied means of achieving it. Young authors, inside and outside the *Jung Wien* set, many Jewish, some also openly anti-Semitic (an existential combination consistent with a warm and positive view of death that strikes us today as bizarre) shared this position. Johnston calls them "poets of death" (p. 171), the most celebrated of whom was the Viennese-born Arthur Schnitzler.

Schnitzler, a Jewish doctor and doctor's son turned playwright, portrayed death as comforting and "assuaging the wounds of the living" (Johnston, 1972, p. 171). His characters are involved in illicit sex for whom "the meaninglessness of sex reflected the identity crisis of the individual" (Janik & Toulmin, 1973/1996, p. 63). Death brings them a reckoning and an awakening, a liberation very much in the manner of psychoanalysis. As Johnston observes, "nothing illustrates so well Freud's symbiosis with Viennese culture as the resemblance between his insights and those reached independently by Arthur Schnitzler" (p. 241). In two

130 Therapeutic nihilism was a mid-19th century attitude towards medicine that cures did little good or even harm and that it was best to leave the body to heal itself through its own devices.

letters to Schnitzler, Freud (1960/1992b, 1960/1992c)[131] describes him as his *Doppelgänger* (double) who reached, through his creativity, the same insights that Freud had reached through painstaking investigation. Freud refers specifically to *Beyond the Pleasure Principle* (Freud, 1920/1955a) in which he describes *Eros* and the death instinct as "the motivating powers whose interplay dominates all the riddles of life" (p. 339) and equates them with Schnitzler's interweaving of love and death.

Both Johnston (1972) and Janik and Toulmin (1973/1996) comment on the high suicide rate among Austrian intellectuals in the decades before and after 1900. Although chronic illness and the Nazi *Anschluss* no doubt contributed to these numbers, these suicides often had to do with intellectuals or their work not being appreciated or, worse, being ridiculed. The most notorious among them was that of Prince Rudolph at Myerling in 1889, involving a suicide pact and feelings of humiliation. Often the suicides were men and women unable to live in the shadow of their parents' greatness, a fate mirroring that of the empire during this period. Suicide appears to have been accepted as a matter of course in Austria, similar perhaps to any infectious epidemic. (Contagion in this Austrian social network should not be overlooked as a causal factor.) A culture that esteemed death may well have invited suicide, making it seem attractive and even natural. Regardless, the pattern fit with the culture's therapeutic nihilism that so contrasted with its surface gaiety, at least prior to 1914. A conviction that death healed the living all but sealed the bargain.

Freud in Translation

Reading Freud's texts cannot be discussed without addressing problems of translation. As I review the comments I made concerning this issue in the short piece (Leffert, 2010b) on which this chapter is based, I find myself less optimistic than I was then about the possibility of making Freud's deeper meaning, his *Deutung*, more accessible to his Anglophone readers. Although there is a thoughtful literature on translating Freud (e.g., Grubrich-Simitis, 1993/1996; Kirsner, 2007; Mahony, 1987; Ornston, 1985a, 1992a; Steiner, 1987), it is a fairly small one for what

131 These two letters are part of a collection (Freud, 1960/1992a) selected and edited by Freud's son Ernst to portray Freud the man. They should not be considered a complete record of the Freud–Schnitzler correspondence.

seems like an important subject. It reflects two bursts of interest: one when the *Standard Edition* was coming out in the 1960s and a second one situated around 1990. That interest has not continued. Although it is possible to offer an overview of the problems in a few pages, deciding what to do about them is another matter.

The *Standard Edition* has many flaws; they fall into three broad categories. The first two involve the translation of specific terms that Strachey called scientific and Freud did not, and the broader issue of how Freud's prose is handled and translated. The third, and by far the most serious issue, involves the charge leveled against him by a number of writers (e.g., Ornston, 1985b) that Strachey introduced major conceptual errors in his translations. Strachey took complex and distinct terms present across Freud's work, translated them into a single scientific *sounding* term, and then stuck with it throughout (Holder, 1992; Kirsner, 2000; Ornston, 1982, 1985a, 1985b). *Cathexis* is perhaps the most notorious example of this problem.

This criticism has undoubtedly become shopworn over time, but Ornston's (1985a) discussion of the politics and power relations inherent in the term, the meaning of *Besetzung*, and the many compound nouns that Freud constructed with it (Ornston counts 13), are anything but. A not well-known example concerns the German *Verdrängung*, which Strachey translates as the oh-so-familiar "repression." However, the *Duden* (*Duden: Deutsches Universalwörterbuch 6 auflage*, 2007), the most authoritative German dictionary currently in print, defines it roughly as to be pushed out, to be crowded out, to be pushed from one's place (p. 1799).[132] *Verdrängung* illustrates the complex ambiguities of Freud's German as contrasted with Strachey's "scientific" precision. (It cannot be said often enough that precision should not be confused with accuracy.)

Freud also considered the processes of repression and regression to be intimately caught up in one another; they could only be torn apart in the service of constructing sequential models (Ornston, 1982) at the cost of lost meaning. *Rückbildung* is a compound noun constructed of the German words *rück* meaning to jerk or pull back and *Bildung* which means a loss of culture or education. Together, they have the biological

132 A second contemporary psychological definition involving roughly pressuring experience from the conscious into the unconscious (*Duden: Deutsches Universalwörterbuch 6 auflage*, 2007, p. 1799) is included, but is irrelevant in that there were no psychological definitions in German in Freud's time; he used words as he found them.

meaning of atrophy.[133] Strachey singled out *regression* as the single scientific way to translate it, a word that Freud by the end of his life had little use for (Freud, 1940 [1938]/1964c). Freud also used *Rückläufig*, moving back, recoiling, or receding, *Rückgreifen*, meaning grasping or gripping back, and *Rückkehr* meaning simply return. If Freud used them all (Ornston, 1982), why did he do so? If he didn't like regression, why not stick with *Rückbildung*?

Ornston (1985b) tells us the answer culled from *Die Traumdeutung* in its original German. Freud disliked jargon and thought the repetition of the same word sounded ugly. More importantly, his usage reflected a kind of scientific strategy that he called his "describing psychology" (Freud, 1900/1991c, p. 531).[134] "Freud thought that it was essential to describe a concept in *as many different and detailed ways as possible*. Therefore, he varied his descriptions of the most useful psychoanalytic ideas" (Ornston, 1985b, p. 395, italics added). This is the most important single key to Freud's original prose: the how and why of what he said. Strachey never grasped this aspect of Freud's writing; the old man was not just being sloppy,[135] he had reasons for both what he said and how he chose to say it. And, because Strachey didn't get it, we don't get it either.

Three-quarters of a century later, without mentioning Strachey's translation, Sandler (1983) argued strongly against his false precision:

> Elastic concepts play a very important role in holding psychoanalytic theory together. As psychoanalysis is made up of formulations at varying levels of abstraction, and of part-theories which do not integrate well with one another, the existence of pliable, context-dependent concepts allows an overall framework of psychoanalytic theory to be assembled ... The elastic and flexible concepts take up the strain of theoretical exchange, absorbing it while more organized newer theories or part-theories can develop.
>
> (p. 36)

He could just as easily have been talking about Freud and the way he used imprecision and elasticity to keep his options open for 40 years.

A second and related problem is that Freud wrote in the vernacular, subtly weaving together many levels of meaning that he alluded to in his

133 Ornston translates it as reverse development, which, although certainly neater, is less evocative.

134 Freud initially borrowed the concept from Wilhelm Dilthey's (1894/2010) eponymous monograph "Ideas for a Descriptive and Analytic Psychology" that has only recently become available in this reliable English translation.

135 Strachey (1961) in effect makes just such a suggestion in his Appendix A to *The Ego and the Id.*

choice of language. Freud used his prose to convey ambiguity, uncertainty, and approximation. He wrote in layers encrusted with fluidly interacting meaning. In other words, strange as it may seem, he was something of a postmodern (Leffert, 2007a, 2007b). Who knew? Ornston (1982) describes his writing as "stubbornly descriptive" (p. 410) and this is apt on many levels. Freud does not want to be drawn into the mechanically scientific and, when we encounter it in the *Standard Edition*, we can be reasonably sure that we are reading Strachey and not Freud. This is how Freud saw the "state of the art" of psychoanalysis at the start of his analytic career and at its end; even a moment's thought reveals that we are not in so different a position today.

Freud had other reasons for staying with a vernacular redolent of uncertainty, restatement, and ambiguity. It was his great respect for unconscious mental process. On the one hand, he tells us repeatedly that the concepts he is trying to describe vanish into it. But on the other hand, he is trying to present things in a way that we can intuitively grasp them, not reason them out. Terminology, he tells us (Freud, 1915/1957d), is convention, but convention, he rushes to tell us, must not be arbitrary. He expected terminology to be elastic and unstable, evolving with understanding. He wanted to bring our unconscious process into play; he wanted to place before us, his readers, "relations that we seem to sense before we can recognize and demonstrate them" (p. 117). You can't do this with Strachey.[136]

The most serious difficulty of all involves the question of whether Strachey, in his translation, tampered with any of Freud's broad concepts. We must remember that, in 1953 when the first volumes began to appear, the *Standard Edition* was welcomed with great enthusiasm by English-speaking psychoanalysts. Many purchased it by advance subscription, defraying expenses and making publication possible.[137] It at once made Freud accessible beyond the *Collected Papers* and *The Interpretation of Dreams*. Strachey was viewed as the expert in whose hands we could safely place ourselves. Not so fast. Little is known of Strachey, even today.

As Ornston (1985a) tells us, Strachey came from money. He had tried law, medicine, and writing book reviews, but none was able to retain his

136 I remember spending hours with institute classmates trying to puzzle out what Freud meant by "unconscious affects" (Freud, 1915/1957e). We failed, but the problem was that we thought we were trying to understand Freud when it was only Strachey we were struggling with.

137 In much the same way, subscriptions to *Psychoanalytic Electronic Publishing*, the compendium of psychoanalytic literature, were sold years in advance of the appearance of the first set of discs.

interest. He married Alix. He consulted Jones in 1920 about an analysis, hoping to be seen by Freud. He could pay in British pounds. Jones sent him on to Freud with the suggestion that Strachey could help with translation. Jones wrote that Strachey was " 'I think a good fellow, but weak and perhaps lacking in tenacity' " Freud read this letter aloud to Strachey in one of their first sessions" (p. 391). In 1920, Strachey and Alix duly arrived in Vienna. After two weeks of "analysis," Freud assigned them the translation of "A Child is Being Beaten." They were off and running and continued two years of "analysis" and translation. The obvious question that was never asked is: What were two people with no particular credentials or knowledge of German doing translating a major oeuvre? That was just the point. Power and translation were inextricably wound up with one another and a weak and malleable person was just the thing. Freud simply bound James and Alix to him with positive transference and, in 1920, must have known he was doing so. Strachey, it must be acknowledged, grew into the job and consolidated his identity around it.

Despite the happy reception of the *Standard Edition*, all was not well. Lewis Brandt (1961, 1965, 1966, 1968) began to raise serious questions about it in the 1960s, questions that, in the psychoanalytic literature, were largely ignored. The first of these papers raises what have now become usual questions about Strachey's choices for translating Freud's terminology, among them id, ego, and superego for *Es*, *Ich*, and *Berich*. Noting that Freud had won the Goethe prize for literary merit (his only award) and, presumably, was capable of saying what he meant, Brandt (1961) goes on to quote Jones[138] on the subject of "the advantages of the classical nomenclature," to wit, "that there is no other way of securing terms free from the numerous accessory connotations and associations inevitable in a spoken language, and hence of escaping possibilities of misunderstanding" (pp. 331–332). In other words, he chose to substitute his voice and Strachey's for Freud's with the results we have been discussing. Indeed, the "numerous accessory connotations and associations" were *precisely* what Freud wanted.

The following three papers (Brandt, 1961, 1965, 1966) constitute an indictment of structural theory and ego psychology. He found that "Freud's English translators have rather consistently replaced affect-laden German terms with neutral English words and dynamic, active constructions with passive ones" (p. 50). He posited that what Freud

138 The bibliography of this 1961 paper lacks sufficient information to track down the quote.

had described as a process became in Strachey and Jones' hands a structure, a term that Freud used very sparingly. He is particularly critical of the translation of Freud's dictum *Wo Es war, soll Ich werden* into the familiar "where id was, there shall ego be" instead of "where *it* was, *I* should become." His point is that psychoanalysis is a process of becoming that never ends, not an exchange of structure. When one says "my ego," one can always distance oneself; when one says "I," no distance is possible.

Ornston (1985b) takes up the argument when he asks, with a certain disingenuous naiveté, "if Strachey had actually changed Freud's theory, surely we would have been told—wouldn't we?" (p. 380). Strachey (1966b) claimed that Freud was offering an "anatomical structure of the mind." Freud suggested no such thing; his expository diagram in *The Ego and the Id* was just that, an explanatory *sketch*, rather than an anatomical drawing. Freud never abandoned the premise that accessibility to consciousness was the observational starting point for psychoanalysis, never defined psychic structure, and never offered any concise or complete account of metapsychology, despite what Strachey claimed for the *Standard Edition*. In *The Ego and the Id*, what Freud had in mind was more of his *beschreibende Psychologie*. It is safe to say that neither structural theory nor its more virulent American cousin, ego psychology, existed until they were created after his death. When all is said and done, they have served us rather poorly, isolating us clinically from our patients and theoretically from other disciplines.

If there was a guiding hand behind the group responsible for the preparation of the *Standard Edition*, it was certainly that of Ernest Jones; he sought both an international trademark[139] (Ornston, 1985a; Steiner, 1987) and something worthy of both definitions of "standard," that which is usual and that to which all others are compared. The result was a work that inserted a mid-20th century pseudo-scientific British episteme between Freud's texts and the contemporary American reader. Strachey (1966a), with surprising naiveté, gives the game away in his general preface to the *Standard Edition* when he observes, "The imaginary model which I have always kept before me is of the writings of some English man of science of wide education born in the middle of the nineteenth century. And I should like, in an explanatory and not patriotic spirit, to emphasize the word 'English' " (p. xix). That may have

139 After the Second World War and the holocaust, a German language brand would have been decidedly short on cachet.

worked for Strachey and Jones, but as the prior discussion of the Viennese episteme should make clear, Freud was not an Englishman and didn't write that way.

There have been a number of new developments on the translation scene, so perhaps help is on the way. New translations of Freud's seminal works have recently been brought out by Penguin Books (Freud, 1914, 1914, 1920, 1923, 1926/2003; Freud, 1917/2005a; Freud, 1911, 1915, 1915, 1915, 1925, 1927, 1940/2005b; Freud, 1899/2006) under the general editorship of Adam Phillips. Unfortunately, the foot soldiers in the faculties of the APsaA's institutes seem largely unaware of them and hence that they could be read side by side with, or in place of, the Strachey translation. As of this writing, The Penguin *Interpreting Dreams* (Freud, 1899/2006) is not yet available in the United States and must be ordered from Britain. This markedly superior, vernacular translation is worth the effort. Kirsner (2007), in his "Fresh Freud: No Longer Lost in Translation," discusses the orthodoxy of the *Standard Edition* and compares it to the *New Penguin Freud*. The latter is planned to eventually reach 16 volumes, compared to the *Standard Edition*'s 24 and the *Gesammelte Werke*'s 18. He finds them, as I do, a livelier, fresher read beside which Strachey's translations seem stilted. He takes as an example, "Mourning and Melancholia" (Freud, 1917/1957a, 1917/2005a) which, in the original, is a paper of speculation, hypothesis, and play, very much in the tradition of Freud's *beschreibende Psychologie*. If we read the two translations side by side and paragraph by paragraph, not all that much emerges. As has already been observed, Strachey adds a word here and there that sounds more scientific (for example, in the second paragraph, Strachey makes "causes" into "exciting causes"), removes occasional words, and completely changes some sentences around (as Strachey does at the beginning of the ninth paragraph). On the face of it, this does not seem to be something to get excited about and perhaps it is not. However, if each translation is read through on its own, something does emerge. Although the Strachey translation does talk about uncertainty and speculation, at the end of the Whiteside translation, the feeling emerges that one has read something the author (that is, Freud) thinks is a lot *more* speculative and descriptive and a lot *less* scientific.

Let's take a look at Freud's vernacular in translation, using the sentence about descriptive psychology from *Die Traumdeutung* as an example. Here's the sentence in the original German:

> *Die beschreibende Psychologie lehrt uns ja, daß die Hauptbedingung der Traumbildung der Schlafzustand der Seele ist; wir könnten nun die Erklärung*

> *hinzufügen: der Schlafzustand ermöglicht die Traumbildung, indem er die endopsychische Zensur herabsetzt.*
>
> (1900/1991a, p. 531)

Now, here's Strachey's translation:

> Descriptive psychology tells us that the principal *sine qua non* for the formation of dreams is that the mind shall be in a state of sleep; and we are now able to explain this fact: *the state of sleep makes the formation of dreams possible because it reduces the power of the endopsychic censor.*
>
> (1900/1953b, p. 526, as written)

Finally, here's a vernacular translation of my own, but even this is a bit less vernacular than Freud's:

> *The* descriptive psychology teaches us truly that the required condition for the creation of dreams is that the *soul* is deeply asleep; we can now add the explanation: Deep sleep makes possible the creation of dreams by lessening the endopsychic censorship.

This gives something of the flavor of Freud's prose, although the cumulative effect over the course of a complete work is qualitatively greater. It is serious writing—notice the term "endopsychic"—but it is not pretentiously scientific. "The descriptive psychology" is specific and declarative, but there is also "teaches us truly" and, of course, the *soul.* Its, well, *heimisch.*

Adam Phillips, the general editor of the Penguin series, chose translators with broad experience in literature and philosophy, but without particular exposure or training in psychoanalysis. There are pluses and minuses to this decision that, to a degree, share some overlap. He wanted and got fresh translations of Freud's language approached without baggage or psychoanalytic expectations (this advantage was partially lost by Phillips' translators reading Strachey). What is also lost is any awareness or attention to issues of theory or practice that would be of concern to a professional readership. We see few of the multiple describings of the original Freud (this in the service of readability), and little guidance or awareness of conceptual drift. Some of the Penguin series do offer Freud's vernacular; I particularly like Underwood's *Interpreting Dreams* (Freud, 1899/2006) in this respect. These could be provided in annotations and translation footnotes (on the page, not as endnotes!), but that would require psychoanalytic scholarship beyond what can be offered by Phillips' staff.

Continuing with what is available in the present, *Psychoanalytic Electronic Publishing* (*PEP*) has offered a searchable *Standard Edition* for some time. Its most recent release also offers the *Gesammelte Werke*. As of this writing, there is an indexing feature: At the bottom of each page is a red number that, if clicked, will take the reader to the corresponding page in the other work. (There appears to be some question concerning whether this capability will continue to be available, and *Die Traumdeutung* so far lacks this feature.) This allows readers to spot-check translation questions, dictionary in hand, regardless of their knowledge of German. It would be of interest to know how much these texts are in use, who the editors of *PEP* expected would use them, and what their purposes might be.

Moving on from the real to the hypothetical, we come to the Second Edition of the *Standard Edition*. Ornston (1992b) stated that the British Institute of Psycho-Analysis was planning to "preserve its entire Standard Edition [sic] as 'a second edition'" (p. 100). It would include translations of papers currently available only in the *Gesammelte Werke*, and correct errors or misprints, but only those noted by Strachey or Angela Harris. In widened margins a limited number of words in Freud's German would be noted and the reader would be referred to a new "preferred glossary," which would include those of Strachey's choices that have drawn the most criticism. At that time, they planned not to alter Strachey's translation in any other way because they considered it to be iconic. Since then, Mark Solms became the general editor of this *Revised Standard Edition* with the date of publication advancing in more or less two-year steps, last forecast to be 2009 (Kirsner, 2007). For this writing, I queried Solms via email about the current state of these plans and received a prompt response (P. Barkay, personal communication, April 8, 2011) that the *Revised Standard Edition* was now in "proof stage" at the publishers and would be ready next year (2012). So there you have it, for the moment at least.

We will have to wait and see whether this edition will be what the British Institute said it would be in 1992, or whether Solms has in the intervening years come to offer us something more substantive. At some point Solms apparently commented that he had found the Strachey translation less problematic than might have been imagined, not on the face of it a promising observation.

None of these new offerings shows any signs of being able to fully capture the meanings contained in Freud's vernacular style and poetic repetition of ideas and concepts. This remains then a side of Freud not readily accessible to students or scholars of psychoanalysis who are not fluent in German. A translation that encompasses this material could maintain the readability of the Penguin series but would add heavy footnoting to include the additional material. It seems unlikely that, with two new translations, one out and one apparently coming out, such an effort is on the horizon. We are left then with only a possibility that a cottage industry could arise around the teaching of psychoanalysis that would develop annotations to existing translations. This is not as farfetched as it might at first seem if psychoanalysts and academics were to be made more aware of the problem.

No discussion of translating Freud, or of the Viennese episteme for that matter, would be complete without considering two questions: Does anyone care? And does it matter? Unfortunately, the answers to both are to a degree equivocal and unknowable. Kirsner (2007) says that "we need to ask: Are we reading Freud? Or are we reading Strachey and what lay behind him?" (p. 659). He thinks the latter, as do I, but how many of "us" actually ask these sorts of questions? When Fogel and Glick (1991) decided, roughly ten years post-grad, to read through the *Standard Edition* for the purposes of growth and consolidation of their analytic identities, they did not, at least in print, consider the translation's reliability. Analysts who consider themselves Freudians, if aware of the problems with Strachey's translation, operationally treat Strachey as Freud. (This does not mean that, if the *Standard Edition 2* were to address these problems, analysts and psychotherapists wouldn't be interested in it.) It is probably safe to say that those analysts, certainly a majority of Kirsner's (2007) 20,000, who have either turned away from or never approached Freud, would have little or no interest in translating his texts from the German. I'm afraid that the answer to the first question would seem, operationally at least, to be: not particularly.

The question if it really matters if there are major inaccuracies in the *"Standard" Edition* is harder to answer. To the extent that a psychoanalyst or a psychotherapist considers herself to be a scholar as well as a clinician, it obviously does. But again (and again, I must be vague) for some probable majority of clinicians, it does not. We have discovered that there is much reason to doubt ego psychology as such, or the putative shift to it from topographic psychology. But most analysts have long been aware of (and made use of) non-conflict based models[140] in their clinical work. To the extent that clinicians cleave rigidly to the *Standard Edition*, I might expect these discrepancies to cause considerable

140 Freud himself was certainly moving in that direction with "Analysis Terminable and Interminable" (1937/1964a).

difficulties, but then I would also expect (not without stirring up controversy) that the clinical work of any analyst who hews rigidly to *any* theoretical orthodoxy would encounter difficulties, noticed or otherwise.

A different way of saying this would be to suggest that an analyst who approaches his work in a "polyphony of . . . style, [including] ambiguities, uncertainties, and imaginative ponderings" (Holder, 1992, p. 85) is likely not to encounter difficulty. And this is really what allows us to answer the second question with an equivocal "yes," because Holder is talking here about Freud (not Strachey–Freud). If we could use *this* Freud to teach such an approach to patients and to theory, it would be of great didactic importance. Unfortunately, it is not something that can be found anywhere in Strachey–Freud.

But Is It Science?

During the 1980s an at-times bitter, take-no-prisoners debate raged between Marshall Edelson (e.g., 1984) and Adolph Grünbaum (e.g., 1984) over the question of whether psychoanalysis was a science or an exercise in hermeneutics. Let me at once reassure you that I am not about to re-open that miscast debate, but rather to raise instead the question of just what sort of science psychoanalysis in general and Freud's work in particular might be. If we *are* to consider his work as science, then certain rules must be applicable to it. However, the days when science could be conceptualized in positivist terms using models drawn from 17th century Newtonian physics are now long gone.

The relatively new field of Science Studies (Latour, 1987, 1991/1993, 1999; Latour & Woolgar, 1986) developed as a result of a number of postmodern critiques leveled at modernist science. They include the impossibility of separating the social from the scientific, the inevitability of subjective observation, and the interreferentiality of most phenomena that results in uncertainty and renders measurement in isolation impossible (Leffert, 2010a, especially chapters 1 and 2). Attempts to separate science from these factors by processes termed by Latour (1991/1993) as purification and translation yield at best arbitrary and unstable local knowledges.

An example of this would be attempting to treat the outcome of a research study that purported to show the efficacy of a new antidepressant medication in isolation from attendant social and statistical factors. Science Studies would preserve all of these factors *and their connections* as a branched hybrid comprised of social and scientific elements. In this simple example, social elements would include things like funding: Was the study supported by a "grant" from the pharmaceutical house that makes it, and did the investigators profit financially from the study or its outcome? Did the study compare the drug with other therapies of known efficacy? Other "scientific" elements of the hybrid would include other studies of the new medication and their results. They would include information about whether they were published or suppressed because findings differed from the current study. The major social factor addressed in this hybrid is the effect of human motivation on outcome and the inseparability of the two.

In the case of Freud's oeuvre, the resulting hybrid is more complex and nuanced. We have already discussed how he was enmeshed in the social network and the episteme of *fin-de-siècle* Vienna. Many of his theoretical ideas, such as the concept of an unconscious that contained roiling, unknowable depths, were widely subscribed to and discussed in intellectual circles[141] before and coincident with Freud's writings on the subject. If he was not accepted by the Viennese medical establishment, he was interreferentially connected with the city's authors, poets, and philosophers.

Freud's writing contained neurobiological and psychological hypotheses as parts of hybrids that included the social (his case reports) and the subjective (the analysis of his own dreams and the latent self-analysis that was at times just beneath the surface). Although the psychoanalytic literature, as well as Freud's later writings, was much less self-disclosing, he had established the ground rules for much of the writing that was to appear in psychoanalytic journals. There seems to have been little recognition of the fact that psychoanalysis was a hybrid and could claim epistemological standing as such.

A final point that seems obvious outside of psychoanalysis is that science is a dynamic entity that progresses over time (Latour, 1987; Latour & Woolgar, 1986). It is a vast branched hybrid in which individual chunks of it are arrayed in nonlinear fashion. Time adds more chunks and, on occasion, changes the existing structure of the hybrid and its branches. Some new event, the advent of the mirror neuron hypothesis on the psychoanalytic scene, for example, may render some of its old connections untenable. But it is in the very nature of chunks that they change over time. A chunk may begin its life as an experiment.

141 As Ellenberger (1970) observes, Nietzsche began playing with a concept of the unconscious and its role in dreaming after 1885.

If the results are confirmed (by other chunks) over time, the experiment becomes instead a procedure (I described elsewhere, Leffert, 2010a, the way fMRI began as an experiment and became a standard procedure for measuring brain activity). As still more new chunks appear, some old ones may become obsolete, demonstrating a falloff in knowledge yield and dropping away.

Changes in psychoanalytic theory and technique happen in this way; Loewald's (1960) famous paper on therapeutic action midwifed such a change. As time goes on, the experiment/procedure becomes of interest only for its current uses, where it came from being of little interest. It has become a black box that performs a specific task. But as time passes, the chunk undergoes further change. What it measures may no longer be of interest, or better ways of measuring may have subsequently appeared. The chunk may still be interesting, but in different ways. The chunk still exists, but it is no longer science; it has become history.[142]

This is all by way of saying that *Die Traumdeutung* has become a fascinating piece of history. However, its theories of the neuropsychology of the dream process and its technical recommendations have been supplanted and, although we can still see elements of it in contemporary dream analysis, technique has broadened and changed since then (the concept of self-state dreams being just one such change). Nevertheless, what it, along with the Fliess correspondence (Freud, 1985a), tells us about the history of psychoanalysis, its birth in Vienna, and Freud's self-analysis (Johnston, 1972; Schorske, 1980) remains fascinating. This does not mean that it belongs in a theory or clinical course taught in a psychoanalytic institute; indeed trying to teach it to candidates as such does them a disservice (more about this later). But there are excerpts from it that should be taught because they illuminate larger issues concerning Freud's writing and theory-building.

There are other papers and monographs by Freud that, ontologically, also constitute history, but unlike *Die Traumdeutung* do not appear to merit contemporary study. For some, this constitutes merely belling the cat while, for others, it is a matter of some controversy. The needs of those readers involved in learning psychoanalysis and those involved in its teaching are very different from the needs of graduate therapists or academics reading to enhance their own understanding or as part of

142 The process is nonlinear. Antibiotics remain black boxes for at most a few decades, while steam engines have been with us for centuries. The anesthetics ether and chloroform lie somewhere in between, but are now mostly history.

scholarly research. It does not seem to have occurred to anyone that these different readers might benefit most from reading different things. The task is then to pull together the fruits of these disparate lines of inquiry into a hybrid conceptual space and there to craft new lines of approach to different parts of the vast canvas of Freud's work.

Teaching Freud

It is hard to imagine less redeeming ways of teaching Freud than how he is treated in psychoanalytic curricula, regardless of the theoretical orientation of the psychoanalytic institute teaching it. The overriding pedagogical principle seems to be to chronologically ladle out pure Freud in the first year of study. The size of the ladle depends on the theoretical orientation of the particular institute involved. If big enough, Freud overflows the first year and runs into the second and perhaps the third. In psychoanalytic institutes of Freudian orientation, much time is spent on his theories, which are treated as having contemporaneous clinical and theoretical relevance. In more relational institutes (using smaller ladles), Freud is usually confined to parts of the first year and taught historically, as a way of acquainting the beginning student with the origins of psychoanalysis. In the latter instance, assuming that both students and faculty are satisfied, there is nothing more to be said. However, if an institute wants to teach something about Freud's theories from the vantage point of 21st century psychoanalysis and its students are interested in learning about them, it is hard to imagine a worse way of going about it.

The fact that Freud over his professional life filled 18 volumes in German and 24 volumes in English does *not* mean that one has to read all, or even most of it, during one's psychoanalytic education. Nor is it necessary to do so as a graduate analyst, despite whatever laudable comments are made about undertaking such an enterprise. (I am happy to admit that although I believe I have demonstrated considerable interest in his work, I have not read the *Standard Edition* in its entirety.) These observations suggest the possibility of approaching a Freud curriculum in a new way as opposed to trying to race through much or most of the *Standard Edition* over two or three years of study.

What might such a new curriculum look like, and how would it function? It would begin with an introductory course of ten sessions, give or take, called something like "Who was Freud and How Does He Mean?" (If something more romantic were desired, "Freud and the City of

Dreams" would do nicely.) It would consist of much of the material and many of the references discussed in this chapter. Certainly, it would contain Schorske's (1980) chapter on Freud. A selection of Freud's shorter papers and some excerpts from others would be included, not at this point to teach theory, but as specimens of Freud's work. The papers would be read side by side with alternative translations (in later courses, alternative translations might be read in place of the *Standard Edition*). Again, these would be specimen readings illustrating translation issues. This would be the only course to be organized historically[143] and the only one in which Freud would be read in isolation from other more recent psychoanalytic or neurobiological authors. I think the course would find a place in most any institute's curriculum regardless of how much of the rest of Freud was present.

Carefully chosen papers would be included in the reading lists of theoretical and clinical courses throughout the curriculum where relevant.[144] "Analysis Terminable and Interminable" (Freud, 1937/1964a), for example, would find a place in a theoretical course introducing non-conflict based models, or in a clinical course on intractable therapeutic problems. "On Narcissism: An Introduction" (Freud, 1914/1957b) should appear in a course on self psychology as might "Mourning and Melancholia" (Freud, 1917/1957a *and* 1917/2005a). The goal would generally be to keep page numbers down and intensity of reading up.

Like any other author, Freud can be engaged at three different levels: the macro level, the mid-level, and the micro level. At the mid-level, papers or monographs can be read to understand the subject, usually contained in the title of the work. So "On Narcissism" would be read to understand narcissism, "Mourning and Melancholia" to understand what Freud had to say about depression, and so on. This is how these works are often studied, usually with the original date of publication included for purposes of orientation. I would suggest that this is perhaps the least useful way to approach Freud, particularly for the student. What he had to say about diagnostic entities, psychopathology, or named psychic structures has not stood the test of time (as nothing

143 Any of us who trained as psychoanalysts or psychotherapists even as recently as two decades ago have been so indoctrinated in a historical approach and have read his more important papers so many times that we can, and on occasion do, teach Freud historically in our sleep. The result scarcely provides a worthwhile educational experience, but to break out of that mold asks a lot of an instructor.

144 Recognizing that the statement I'm about to make is controversial, I would not include anything beyond excerpts of pre-1900 Freud, unless a course on the history of psychoanalysis is planned.

80+ years old should be expected to do). The following chapter will offer some alternatives to it. Although we treat this terminology as second nature and often do not question it, for those outside the field, it is both arcane and alienating. Date of publication is potentially as disorienting as it might be orienting because it relies on bibliographical context rather than letting the texts stand on their own beside those of later theoreticians.

I believe that the macro and micro levels of Freud's texts offer the student of psychoanalysis as well as the graduate analyst or psychotherapist greater and, ultimately, richer, more satisfying rewards. Focusing on the macro level enables the reader to engage broad ideas. Studying regression offers an example of reading Freud at the macro level. As currently taught, candidates are trained to separate out several different kinds of regression—topographic, telescopic, structural, temporal, formal, and so on. If the curriculum includes written examinations, candidates will be asked to first list and then discuss them separately. Freud described these concepts as *properties* of regression; he did not define them as separate *kinds* of regression. As we have seen, he shied away from reification, using several different terms to signify what Strachey translated with a single one. Freud did not use these terms to signify one property or another; they appear and disappear throughout his work and, in the original German, carry subtle vernacular shifts in meaning that are context related. He considered regression and repression to be linked concepts; this is hard to know from the Strachey translation and the two have not, to my knowledge, been much taught in that way.

Unconsciousness also lends itself best to a macro approach. It is mostly taught with the metapsychology paper (Freud, 1915/1957e) of 1915, this in spite of the fact that Freud preferred "A Note on the Unconscious in Psycho-analysis" (1912/1958b) that was *originally written* in English. Then *The Ego and the Id* (Freud, 1923/1961a) is taught, usually alongside of Arlow and Brenner (1964) to demolish the concept of a systemic unconscious and its importance.[145] The curriculum then usually moves on to mostly American ego psychology. A macro approach questions this disposal and examines the property of unconsciousness and the concept of a systemic (that is to say a structural) unconscious across Freud's writings in the light of contemporary

145 Freud's observation, correctly translated by Strachey at the end of the first section on the unconscious in *The Ego and the Id*, that "the property of being conscious or not is in the last resort our *one beacon-light* in the darkness of depth-psychology" (1923/1961a, p. 18, italics added) is usually missed or ignored.

neuroscience (e.g., Schore, 2011). It would also explore later psychoanalytic contributions to these questions, such as those found in the work of George Klein (e.g., 1970, 1976b). Lastly, it would consider the utility of process rather than structural models.

A micro approach would involve the close processing of the text of a single paper, seeking out meaning on a paragraph by paragraph basis rather than information about the stated topic of the paper. "Mourning and Melancholia" (Freud, 1917/1957a) is but one of many papers suitable for this level of study. No more than one paper should be considered in a class session. For the micro approach to be meaningful, translation becomes of key importance; if the Strachey translation muddles it, alternatives must be discussed or this kind of reading becomes pointless.

To teach on macro and micro levels calls for a high level of scholarship and a degree of course preparation that may not be routinely present in institute faculties. An instructor needs to be conversant with the literature on translating Freud, to have read alternate translations where they are available, and to check translations of key terms against the *Gesammelte Werke* (Freud, 1991b). All of these are more easily accomplished with shorter papers; they are well worth the effort.

Freud and Power

A final problem in reading Freud has to do with the necessity of deconstructing issues of power relations from his texts and how they are used. I have written about power earlier in this volume as well as in a previous work (Leffert, 2010a, chapter 7). There are two additional areas of power manifest in Freud's texts and in their teaching that are relevant to reading him.

Freud's writing has been inseparable from its author and his original attempts to control the psychoanalytic movement. It is equally inseparable from the highly ambivalent idealization of which he was and still is the object. It is well known that Freud did not tolerate dissent and regularly expelled dissidents. He refused to compete in the marketplace of ideas and viewed disagreement as heresy requiring banishment. This practice readily found a home in American psychoanalysis, ironically, given Freud's (1926/1959b) position to the contrary, first in its hostility towards "non-medical" analysts. There is a vast interdisciplinary literature on power, unknown to the majority of psychoanalysts. Most relevant here are Foucault's views on power and its relation to knowledge (2000) and Lukes' (2005) groundbreaking discussions of power and the behavior of groups who wield it. Foucault posits that the creation of knowledge and its subsequent use are inseparable from issues of power relations and Lukes describes the social tools utilized in the formation and maintenance of dominance of groups by elites.

There is a long history of Freud's work being used in the service of power considerations that, although it has significantly moderated in some quarters, still exists in others. However, Freud's theories offer still another power tool, the ability to psychopathologize and hence to discredit dissent and the standing of the dissenter. Freud (1925 [1924]/1961b) himself pioneered this tradition when he labeled social disagreement with the theories of psychoanalysis as resistance. Such thinking can become so ingrained and ego-syntonic that its practitioners are not only unaware of it, but go so far as to hotly deny it when confronted. It is important that the teaching of Freud and the responses of individual students to his work not be used for these purposes; it is a much more difficult task to avoid using Freudian orthodoxy, or, for that matter, its repudiation in the service of power goals on the institutional level. "Historically, then, it has been a hallmark of much psychoanalytic education for mystification to transform illegitimate power into irrational authority" (Kirsner, 2009, p. 236).

In psychoanalytic institutes wedded to a particular theoretical orientation, a rare confluence of events confronts beginning candidates with a kind of perfect power storm in their first year of study. This has the potential to create difficulties that will later limit their therapeutic effectiveness. It is particularly true for the more orthodox Freudian curricula that offer little initial exposure to alternative points of view.

For first year candidates, three things are happening at once, all of which exert a regressive pull. Most candidates begin their coursework relatively early in their personal analyses. As a result, they are in a state of some clinical[146] regression and experience rampant transference distortions that are easily, perhaps inevitably, displaced from the person of the analyst to the persons of the faculty and from the therapeutic situation to the didactic one. The personal analysis, which is shielded *to a degree*[147] from institute power relations, is elided into faculty relationships that do directly affect the candidate's academic and at-times

146 I hesitate to use the term *therapeutic* here because *iatrogenic* might well apply instead. The question of whether or not these regressions are in fact therapeutic has not been given the scrutiny it deserves. I have my doubts.

147 If, for example, a candidate is in analysis with the dean of his institute, how can this not be an analytic issue, regardless of how scrupulous or careful the latter might be in her behavior?

economic success.[148] It is also Freud, the ambivalently held father, who is usually the transference focus of some major part of the first year.

The result of all this is that whatever is studied at this time will exert a deep and lasting influence on a candidate's developing analytic identity, an influence that will be potentially greater if it is Freud that is studied and greater still if a didactic regression as well as a therapeutic one is encouraged. If power goals are pursued by institutes, even if they go unrecognized by otherwise well-meaning faculty and institute officers, the result is that candidates are effectively indoctrinated in the particular belief system of their institute, a belief system that, by definition, is offered without epistemological validation.

If an institute is honestly aware of these issues, steps can be taken to minimize them. Something can be said by institute administrative officers or in the student manual (assuming an institute actually *has* a student manual; mine does not) about some of the pitfalls encountered in the first year. Instructors can make deliberate efforts to minimize the transference potential and the power relations aspects of coursework. While staying within the usual guidelines of dosage, tact, and timing, the personal analyst can comment briefly on these problems and facilitate their analysis. The very fact that the unspeakable is spoken can meaningfully alter both power relations and the tendency towards destructive idealizations.

I have suggested, when all is said and done, that there are better ways of reading Freud. A guiding principle is that, initially at least, Freud's oeuvre should be enjoyed and digested in small portions. He can continue to be read in the context of contemporary theories with which his original writing resonates to an at-times surprising degree. We have already seen how the irreducibility of unknowability and subjectivity that Freud repeatedly acknowledges demonstrates an early appearance of the postmodern turn that *fin-de-siècle* Vienna would morph into as the new century progressed.

It is not necessary to be a Freud scholar or to have read the great majority of his work in order to become a psychoanalyst or psychotherapist conversant with his theories. For those who are involved in the teaching of Freud and his ideas, a higher level of scholarship *is* required. The days when all one needed to know as an analyst could be found between the

148 Referrals of patients to candidates and the referrals of candidates for analysis with particular training analysts have sometimes been distributed as rewards for theoretical orthodoxy or political support.

covers of the *Standard Edition* are long since past (I last heard this in 1975 from a senior training analyst). Understandably, many of Freud's ideas have not stood the century-long test of time. These largely involve the mid-level concepts. *Die Traumdeutung* (Freud, 1900/1953b) is probably the most prominent example still taught in most of APsaA's institutes, but even it has useful concepts to be found and studied in the form of shorter excerpts. Its broader historical significance has not been much taught and certainly could be.

It has been my hope in this chapter to re-establish at least some of the resonance that Freud's work has had and largely lost in the contemporary world of psychoanalysis and to correctly reposition Freud in *his* world, *fin-de-siècle* Vienna. In my view, Freud offers a profound beginning; some of his concepts remain relevant today, even if they are not as all-encompassing as they were once thought to be. They offer a useful counterpoint that can illuminate contemporary psychoanalytic thought and, obviously, play an important role in the ideas discussed in this book and the previous volume (Leffert, 2010a). These ideas deserve the same critical reading as do other, contemporary psychoanalytic concepts. Their relevance will come up at various points in the following chapter on therapeutic action.

6

Some Particular Issues Concerning Therapeutic Action

Introduction

Implicitly, and at times explicitly, much of this book has been concerned with therapeutic action and the clinical circumstances that foster or impede it. The chapter following this one will serve to weave these various discussions together into a sheave, at times a sheave of *différance*. In the meantime, there remain some specific points to be covered before moving on to those discussions. A great deal has been written about therapeutic action in recent years; we will examine that literature here in some novel ways. The very term *therapeutic action* came to prominence out of a desire to describe in process terms more than change and less than cure. I have written on particular aspects of the subject on several occasions (Leffert, 2003, 2007a, 2008, 2010a) and do not propose to restate this material here. What I *am* offering is an exclusively experience-near clinical theory, one of the two psychoanalytic theories posited by Gill (1976, 1994). Perhaps more dangerously, I am proposing to go a step beyond Gill and a step beyond the positions I have taken in the past, to posit that the second theory, metapsychology, has no ontological basis at all and that clinical theory, or theory of therapeutic action, is best formulated in its absence.

I will begin by attempting to understand the well-known observation that more or less the same degree of clinical success is achieved by therapists and analysts regardless of their stated theoretical orientations. This will lead into a discussion of differing levels of inquiry into therapeutic action. A corollary to this discussion is that all psychotherapy and psychoanalysis are relational (small *r*); to *be* in the relationship is allocentric (Schachtel, 1959), while to think *about* it is autocentric. The pieces that need to be thought about here that go beyond the relationship are what comprises the something more than the relationship that goes into a therapy, transference, conflict, and hermeneutics.

In an unusual study of therapeutic action, Tessman (2003) interviewed graduate psychoanalysts in the Boston area concerning their own analytic experiences. Thirty-four analysts, who between them had had 64 analyses, participated in the study. The interviews consisted of spontaneous narratives and responses to 13 open-ended questions. They lasted for 2 to 8 hours, depending on how much each participant chose to say. Based on the resulting narratives, Tessman placed each analysis into one of three groups according to the degree of satisfaction experienced by the analysands. Descriptively, these then were the three categories: deeply satisfying, moderately satisfying, and unsatisfying.[149]

What was most striking about the results of the study was what the participants described as being therapeutic about their analyses. They did not report that the theoretical orientation of their analysts or the various theoretical or clinical constructs employed by them had anything to do with their subjective assessment of outcome. Instead, each related their levels of satisfaction to the nature of the emotional bond that was established between them and their analysts. The degree of emotional engagement was crucial for all. Of central importance to the participants was how they felt their analysts emotionally experienced them. Implicit in these concerns was how this other, to whom they had presumably presented their worst, as well as their best, selves felt about them. In a somewhat confirmatory way, those participants who had had unsatisfying analyses identified these same qualities, absent in their own analyses, as essential components of a satisfying analysis.

Another way of describing the results is that, of the 64 analyses, 25 were judged very good, 25 as somewhat good, and 14 as, well, bad. (This is either a good thing or a not so good a thing, depending on one's perspective, and does not consider the question of whether analysts choose better analysts for themselves and, as a result, have more very good analyses than non-analysts seeking treatment.) It also turned out that the good analyses were more concentrated in recent decades

149 Tessman does not say how she came to choose these particular categories. Unfortunately, Tessman begs two important questions. She does not claim for her subjects and for patients generally the singular importance and validity of their subjective experience (i.e., degree of satisfaction) of their therapy as a measure of therapeutic success, nor does she discuss the problems that would be inherent in defining such success in terms of some metapsychological formation.

(1975–1985 and 1985–1995) and that some of the subjects of analyses that took place in earlier decades had some difficulty with the concept of a satisfying analysis.

In Tessman's (2003) discussion of the results of the study, two other issues were not included that I will take up here. The first is to actually pose the question: What does it mean that the analysts' theoretical orientation and choice of clinical constructs proved irrelevant to therapeutic outcome? I think we have all encountered this question at some time or another, but have chosen to elide it in a number of ways. One is to take some comfort in the notion that our own particular theoretical orientation is best, and to ascribe to colleagues of differing ilks the good fortune of inadvertent success. Another is to counter the question with the argument, "You are reducing analysis to an aesthetic experience." This is then taken to be an absurd statement that ends the conversation. Putting aside for the moment any suggestion that the statement is perhaps not so absurd (it hinges on the rather complex question of what exactly comprises aesthetics), it still begs the question. A third alternative is to simply allow the question to go unanswered. Instead of these options, I will attempt to answer it here.

In the previous chapter and in other writing (Leffert, 2010a), I have suggested the utility of examining any phenomenon conceptually on three different levels: the macro, the mid, and the micro. I have not much encountered this approach in our literature, but have found it to have particular applicability to the various areas of psychoanalytic theory, practice, and thought. I will posit that most clinical writing and nearly all of that concerned with therapeutic action has been on the mid- and micro levels and, on those rare occasions when macro concepts *are* considered, they are implicitly positioned and confused with these narrower perspectives. I plan to offer a number of macro-level hypotheses as a way of answering the question posed above and to offer a preliminary theory of therapeutic action that accounts for the participants' view of a satisfying analysis.

A hallmark of psychoanalysis as a clinical discipline is that the vitality of its practice is dependent on continued thought and study, whatever venues may be chosen for their pursuit. For most of us, they include the psychoanalytic literature in current journals and the past literature made more accessible for the past two decades by *PEP*. I plan to consider the clinical literature of the past 50 years on a macro and, to a much lesser degree, on a mid-level using two novel techniques. Both will take advantage of *PEP* as a survey tool and one will make use of the Network Studies perspective described in chapter 4. Through them, we can get a sense of what has been happening clinically in psychoanalysis that goes beyond the discussion of schools of psychoanalytic thought or controversies between them that are approached by following a single conceptual trail, paper by paper.

A Historical Survey of the Literature over the Past 50 Years

Over the past 20 or 25 years, a sea change from one-person to two-person relational psychologies has occurred in writing about clinical psychoanalysis. The usual way of researching such a statement is to do a subject search of the literature and look at the citations in the papers one finds. This is without doubt a powerful tool and can lead to the development of a nonlinear timeline such as can be constructed with tools developed in the field of Science Studies (Latour, 1987; Latour & Woolgar, 1986). It is both the power and the drawback of this approach that it explores the past of those things that are important in the present. Put another way, it opens a window into the archaeologies and genealogies (Foucault, 1969 & 1971/1972, 1966/1994) of what is viewed contemporarily as knowledge.

What this approach fails to do is to look more broadly at the psychoanalytic literature at various points in time to see what constituted psychoanalytic knowledge, or knowledges really, at those times. This literature still exists in its entirety and is fully accessible in the searchable *PEP* database. I was in search of a sense of what psychoanalysis actually looked and felt like on the ground, across theories, at various points in time. I came up with the idea of sampling one issue of two journals, once every ten years, choosing the first issue of each volume number. (More frequent samplings would have yielded more information, but would also have been beyond the scope of a chapter section.) What is offered here is a kind of hyper-macro view of the clinical literature of the past 50 years.

Without in any way proposing that this kind of search can reveal more than local knowledges (Foucault, 1980), a *surveillance* of the *Journal of the American Psychoanalytic Association (JAPA)* from the psychoanalytic right and *Contemporary Psychoanalysis (CP)* from the psychoanalytic left does reveal significant trends.[150]

150 I somewhat arbitrarily chose to begin with 1957 and 5(1) of *JAPA*. This gave me six decades, a very respectable interval, to look at. *JAPA* opened for business in 1953 and I wanted to give them a few years to get the bugs out before looking in. *CP* has had the longest run of the contemporary journals, currently approaching 50 years. This is why I chose it over *Psychoanalytic Inquiry* (est. 1981) and *Psychoanalytic Dialogues* (est. 1991). It started up in 1964; when I sampled 4(1) (1967), I found that some startup issues unfortunately still remained, but decided not to introduce the artifact of purposefully changing years.

Journal of the American Psychoanalytic Association

With occasional exceptions (e.g., Loewald, 1960; Strachey, 1934),[151] mid-century clinical writing first tended to offer descriptions of analytic patients demonstrating unusual symptoms and the author's understanding of them. The information was conveyed in a declarative style, presented with an air of completeness and certainty. Volume *5*(1) of *JAPA* includes several of these papers (Fox, 1957; Gifford, 1957; Grinstein, 1957; Jacobson, 1957; Sperling, 1957).

The 1950s represented the postwar heyday of American psychoanalysis. Physicians and psychiatrists home from the war[152] and convinced of the efficacy of psychoanalytically oriented therapies in the treatment of what was then called combat fatigue (and is now called post-traumatic stress disorder) sought analytic training in droves. Meanwhile, the American public, fascinated by psychoanalysis since Freud's visit to the United States, sought therapeutic analyses in increasing numbers. With significant psychopharmacological challenges still a decade away, it was truly a golden age for the medical analysts of the APsaA. The focus of their writing was on the direct application of metapsychology to clinical material; whether this had again to do with the recent war(s), a desire to demonstrate applicability, a consolidation, or all of the above,[153] we have no way of knowing. With the exception of Jacobson's (1957) paper, "Denial and Repression," which has been referenced 70 times over the decades, these papers have not been much cited.

Ten years later, *JAPA 15*(1) had become a different journal. Clinical-theoretical contributions of the type seen in 1957 had become much less frequent; instead, we find papers on metapsychology (mostly ego psychology and libido theory) authored by well-known Freudian theorists with the odd clinical illustration thrown in. This trend continued ten years later in *25*(1). It appears that from the admittedly limited perspective of our survey, not much was being published about therapeutic change or action in *JAPA* during those years.

151 The Strachey paper appears to be the first psychoanalytic publication to use the term *therapeutic action*. A search for the term in *PEP* returned nine "hits" prior to 1990 as opposed to 2616 from 1990 through 2010, confirming the idea of a qualitative change in writing on clinical theory and technique.

152 Leo Rosten (1961), in *Captain Newman, M.D.*, a now mostly forgotten book, offered a fictionalized account of the wartime experiences of one such returning physician, the psychoanalyst Ralph Greenson.

153 Indeed Franz Alexander (1948) had already opined that much of psychoanalytic theory had already been worked out.

A number of things stand out about these decades. They were a major, perhaps *the* major, period of theory building for American ego psychology. Melanie Klein and the British Middle School were not much in evidence in the literature on this side of the Atlantic. Developments in ego psychology took place across the entire ideological spectrum of psychoanalysis from the conservatism of Arlow and Brenner (1964) to the radicalism of George Klein (1970, 1976b). Our survey of *15*(1) missed by a year the theoretical birth of what would become self psychology (Kohut, 1966) in *JAPA*. However, two things did *not* appear in *JAPA* that were already beginning to challenge classical psychoanalysis as a treatment modality. With the social upheaval of the 1960s came a desire for shorter therapeutic approaches that were, for lack of better terms, more personal and relational. In addition, the 1960s saw a range of antidepressants and minor tranquilizers appear on the scene that addressed some of the same symptoms that had brought patients to the offices (and couches) of psychoanalysts and psychotherapists. *JAPA* took no notice.[154]

An interesting panel report appeared in 1979 when I mistakenly clicked on *27*(1) rather than *25*(1) of *JAPA*. Titled "Conceptualizing the Nature of the Therapeutic Action of Psychoanalytic Psychotherapy" (Wallerstein & Nemetz, 1979), it treated the process as differentiable from and of less depth than psychoanalysis, but otherwise described many of the features we find today in relational psychotherapy *and* psychoanalysis. However, implicit to the panel was the notion that these features involved dilutions and "parameters" that resulted in something less than analysis, necessary perhaps, but definitely not the real thing, at least not in 1979.

I had formed an expectation prior to this search (that I now see was derived from reading as a candidate and beginning instructor) that the technical literature from this period largely consisted of case reports in which limited therapeutic progress had been made. Examination of the case material led to some new theoretical understanding that was then applied to a patient or two, resulting in analytic success. These case illustrations were presented as having evidential value. I had this expectation based on the individual readings I had been introduced to, not on what

154 I do not think that the senior psychoanalysts whose writing *JAPA* showcased believed that either of these developments had anything to do with them or with psychoanalysis. These analysts were at the top of the practice pyramid; it would take at least until the 1980s for the effects of these changes to be felt in their practices and even more time for them to be acknowledged.

was actually going on in the literature as a whole. I suspect this view is widespread in analysts and psychotherapists trained in the 1960s and 1970s. However, it was not borne out; these papers existed, to be sure, but had been selected from the much larger numbers of technical papers coming to press during those years.

Stuart Asch's (1976) paper on the negative therapeutic reaction is an example of such a paper that was frequently read at the time and appeared to convey important knowledge.[155] Since then, what is seen as constituting knowledge about the therapeutic situation has changed. If a therapy is not progressing, therapists tend now to look first at their failure to understand a particular patient and the reasons behind that failure (as opposed to global shortcomings in clinical knowledge that the 1950s authors were describing) or a problem in the therapeutic relationship.

With the appearance of *JAPA 35*(1) (1987), clinical papers are again much in evidence and often describe two people in the therapeutic space interacting with each other interreferentially. Our search happened to snag Arnold Cooper's (1987) important paper on here-and-now transference interpretation, which I recall reading when it was published and have since found to stand the test of time. Cooper expands on Gill's (1982) analysis of the here-and-now transference by describing its interactive, interpersonal, and intersubjective nature and the role of the therapeutic space in its successful analysis. Although he calls this perspective "modernist," what he is actually describing are postmodern ideas.

In another paper, Pulver (1987) describes the analysis of the manifest dream as an interactive and relational enterprise. Williams (1987) offers

155 Rereading the paper (Asch, 1976) today, one is struck by the focus on the interpretation of conflict within an ego-psychological framework. The failure to progress is laid entirely at the patient's feet. There is no mention of Asch's *behavior*, how he *was* with his patients; no insight into his on-the-ground thinking, and no way of knowing if, as many of us observe today, failures in empathy (growing out of approaching patients with a Procrustean bed of narrow conflict-based theoretical understanding) led to these negative reactions. Asch's paper was cited a very respectable 45 times in the psychoanalytic literature from 1980 through 2010. I looked at five of these papers and found the citations to constitute brief and pro-forma referencing of the classical literature on negativism or masochism. In other words, it was not cited for conceptual reasons. Three of them (Coen, 2003; Kohler, 1984; Levy & Inderbitzin, 1989) located the problem of negativism not in a negative therapeutic reaction but in a (dysfunctional) transference/countertransference (enactment). The Asch paper, like the papers I randomly found from this period, does not seem to be much read today. The epistemology, the definitions of knowledge about the therapeutic situation, has changed over the intervening years; therapists have moved on to conceptualizing therapeutic impasses in other, usually two-person, terms.

a 1950s-style clinical paper about a patient who had a failed prior analysis but had a successful one with her when she offered a reconstruction of a traumatic childhood sexual seduction. What is new about this paper, and in keeping with the 1980s, was its latent message that sexual seductions can really happen; they need not be the stuff of fantasy.

Lastly, a paper by Lichtenberg and Galler (1987) further illustrates the dual positions on therapeutic action presented by *JAPA* in 1987. In surveying how analysts presented the fundamental rule to their patients at the start of treatment, the authors discerned two broad patterns: a classical, one-person, these are the rules-of-the-game approach, as opposed to a two-person overture that stressed the mutuality and [interpersonal] nature of the work.

JAPA 45(1) begins with a plenary address by Lawrence Friedman (1997) describing a psychoanalysis then in a state of ferment and a therapeutic situation rich in the analyst's inquiry into his own feelings. Each analysis is a kind of ongoing experiment; the certainties of the 1950s are now long gone. The three remaining clinical papers in this issue of *JAPA* (Bucci, 1997; Freedman & Lavender, 1997; Kantrowitz, 1997) all focus on the relational aspects of the therapeutic situation, with an emphasis in two of them on what is going on within the analyst. By 1997, the sea change has definitely taken place for *JAPA*.

I was not consciously aware when I began sampling a series of decades ending in seven that I would eventually come to one of my own papers (Leffert, 2007a), "A Contemporary Integration of Modern and Postmodern Trends in Psychoanalysis" in *JAPA 55*(1). The paper directly applies an integration of modern and postmodern thought to clinical psychoanalysis and is not dependent on the processing of those ideas through the Relational and Intersubjective schools. It is situated on the radical edge of clinical theory. It positions analyst and patient on a very level playing field and stresses the existence of irreducible limitations of the analyst's knowledge of himself or his patient. There are other edgy papers in this issue. They explore the role of coercion in the therapeutic situation (Ginsburg & Cohn, 2007), self-disclosure and self-revelation on the part of the analyst (Levine, 2007), and validation as an essential component of therapeutic action (Schecter, 2007).

55(1) also contains the first paper on applied neuroscience (Gallese, Eagle, & Migone, 2007) to appear in our survey. The authors discuss recent findings on the MNS and their clinical importance. The MNS would be central to the psychological processes of mirroring, empathy, and attunement. It could provide a neurological basis for such aspects of the therapeutic situation as unconscious communication and projective identification. It is the preeminent organ of any two-person psychology.

Contemporary Psychoanalysis

Contemporary Psychoanalysis did not exist in 1957; its first issue appeared in 1964. To follow the schedule established in surveying *JAPA*, we will begin our survey with volume *4*(1) (1967, 1968). This short issue of 82 pages is of historical rather than clinical interest. I was surprised to find that five of its six articles were authored by physicians in contrast to the more current situation at *CP* where medical authors are scarce.[156] I do not know if its publisher, the William Alanson White Institute of Psychiatry, Psychoanalysis, and Psychology, was then mostly a medical shop as its name might imply, or whether, as seems quite possible, there simply was still a scarcity of "non-medical" analysts in 1967. It does appear that *CP* got off to a rocky start; volumes contained two issues and sometimes required two years to complete.

There are no papers about clinical theory or theory of technique in *4*(1), although two papers (Chrzanowski, 1967; Rubins, 1967) offer phenomenological descriptions of clinical material. The journal happens to include a brief encomium/memoir by Hannah Green (1967) of her experience as a patient of Frieda Fromm-Reichmann[157] that is of interest on a number of levels, including what can be inferred from it concerning Fromm-Reichmann's theories of therapeutic action. Her decidedly relational approach to her patient differed sharply from the classical psychoanalytic stance of the 1940s and 1950s.

From an editorial perspective and irrespective of subject matter, the writing of these papers is not of good quality. One is struck by their having some of the characteristics of early drafts: They are not tightly reasoned and the prose does not hold together particularly well. Again, irrespective of subject matter, the papers in *JAPA 15*(1) of the same year are better written. (This should not be taken to imply that *JAPA* constitutes any sort of standard.) These issues could reflect the newness

156 This and what follows are simply observations about what I found. I did check other issues and found that this authorship pattern was typical of those years.

157 Hannah Green, a pseudonym for Joanne Greenberg, is the author of *I Never Promised You a Rose Garden*, a memoir of her successful treatment for a psychosis at Chestnut Lodge that included her work with Frieda Fromm-Reichmann.

of the journal as manifested in its editorial policies or in the quality of the manuscripts it was then receiving.

A decade later, *13*(1)[158] bears out some of these suppositions. Over the intervening years, *CP* became an established journal, publishing four issues annually. The authorship is now fairly evenly divided between physicians and psychologists. (Again, it is unclear what this change represents and it still differs from the current situation.) The overall quality of the writing that was unexpectedly low in 1967 is now at a higher level, indistinguishable from that of *JAPA* and other journals.

Unlike *JAPA 25*(1), this issue of *CP* has many papers pertaining to clinical psychoanalysis. Three are descriptive studies (Chrzanowski, 1977; Moulton, 1977; Schimel, 1977) of multiple cases manifesting a common clinical pattern or problem. There are a number of thoughtful papers (Feiner, 1977a, 1977b; Issacharoff, 1977; Wolstein, 1977c) on countertransference and transference that appear to be a focus of this issue. They prefigure relational and intersubjective concepts that we know, from the history of psychoanalysis, will appear in the coming decade.

Of particular interest is one of two papers by Benjamin Wolstein, "Psychology, Metapsychology, and the Evolving American School" (1977a), that appeared in the net of *13*(1). Wolstein was a prodigious psychoanalytic scholar who authored 113 publications (Shapiro, 2000). His work moved psychoanalysis and therapeutic action forward and, while he abandoned what he called libidinal psychoanalysis, he retained Freud's later works in which he saw social and interpersonal themes. A passage towards the end of the paper aptly characterizes his work:

> The therapeutic inquiry of psychoanalysis is, in sum, a continuous and cumulative analysis of the human psyche. Its structure of inquiry, both in range and in depth, is therefore devised with a commitment to the primacy of direct, irreducible, psychic connectedness, and sustained by openness to the generative, self-moving sources of unique, active, first-personal spontaneity within the psychic connection of psychoanalyst and patient. That, in fact, arises within a shared, two-way field of experience and inquiry.
>
> (p. 152)

Much of what has been written since about therapeutic action in a postmodern, relational, or intersubjective vein could easily be derived from the ideas contained in this seminal paragraph.

158 Due to the early publishing irregularities of *CP*, the volume number doesn't correlate with the decade.

It turned out that *CP 23*(1) (1987) was largely devoted to two symposia: A discussion of Stern's *The Interpersonal World of the Infant* (1985) and one of Langs' paper, "Clinical Issues Arising from a New Model of the Mind" (1986). What Langs proposed (Simon, 1987) was a new topographic model that encoded and passed on emotional information and would account for all clinical data. Central to it was a "message-analyzing center" referred to as "MAC," a kind of switching station for emotional "data." Simon describes the system as a series of analogue computers and defines a number of areas of interest to be pursued within it.

The MAC and the arguments connected to it seem dated and arcane from today's perspective. It is a restatement of the topographic model derived in the manner of a bygone era of psychoanalytic theory-building in which theory was formulated metaphorically around the newest machines: In Freud's time the steam engine, and here the computer. This is typical of a class of theoretical papers, appearing in the 1980s, that have since passed from view. This conclusion is supported by the record of subsequent citations of the papers presented in the symposium. With the exception of Langs' (1987) rejoinder to the discussion that Langs alone subsequently cited (six times), none of the papers (Dorpat, 1987; Goodheart, 1987; Simon, 1987) has ever been cited in the literature. Apprehension of the actual apparatus, the self, its subsystem the central nervous system, and their relevance to psychoanalysis is still years away.

I also saw on *PEP* that our survey just missed *23*(2), an issue that contained Wittenberg's "Clinical Innovations and Theoretical Controversy" (1987) and a discussion including a paper by Hoffman on "The Value of Uncertainty in Psychoanalytic Practice" (1987). Taken together, these papers argue the question (although they do not use the terms) of whether the failures of theory represent a modernist failure or whether they serve to formulate a postmodern critique of certainty and knowability. Given that Mitchell's *Relational Concepts in Psychoanalysis* (1988) would appear the following year, this discussion was relevant and *au courant*.

With the exception of its book reviews, all but one of the papers in *33*(1) (1997) of *CP* are clinical and relational.[159] (To be sure this was not a sampling error, I looked at *33*(2) and found it to be much the same.)

159 I will be using the term *relational* with a small *r* in the usual dictionary sense of the term to denote all clinical theory and theories of therapeutic action that conceive of the therapeutic encounter as an interreferential, two-person psychology. This is in distinction to "Relational," which signifies one of these schools.

Although the subjects of these clinical papers differ significantly, they have a number of refrains of clinical theory in common. The authors all position themselves on the psychoanalytic left. Descriptions of patients and clinical situations are in the service of various subjects that manifest relational threads drawn from the Intersubjective, Relational, and Self-Psychological schools and eschew, for lack of a better term, Modern American Ego Psychology. They show some linkage between Self-Psychological and Intersubjective ideas. Some authors include more than one of these schools and some are closer to the psychoanalytic center, wishing to preserve concepts such as surface-to-depth psychoanalytic technique.

This is a curious group of papers. For the 1997 reader who was thoroughly familiar with the psychoanalytic literature and who did not read with a theoretical axe to grind, there is nothing here that goes much beyond a restatement of then prevalent psychoanalytic ideas. I do not mean this to be a criticism of the papers or their authors. I would rather hypothesize that in 1995–1996, when these papers must have been written, there was a kind of pause or consolidation in theory building during which there was not much in the way of new ideas to be had.[160] The absence of theoretical papers from *33*(1) might suggest confirmatory evidence for this hypothesis. A number of integrative books that would take things forward to a new level were being written but would not be released until the millennial period (e.g., Fairfield, Layton, & Stack, 2002; Hoffman, 1998; Ogden, 1997; Stern, 1997; Stolorow et al., 2002; Teicholz, 1999). The ideas and debates put forward in these texts and others like them would carry the psychoanalytic left through the next decade.

43(1) (2007) of *CP* is unusual in that it, in effect, offers two mini-seminars: one consisting of two papers and a discussion (Crastnopol, 2007; Goldman, 2007; Grand, 2007) and the other of a paper, a discussion, and a response (Aron, 2007; Cushman, 2007a, 2007b). The content of the two seminars is as different as can be, and yet on a process level they are powerfully linked, a linkage that would not be apparent unless *43*(1) was looked at as a whole. Both seminars are hermeneutic discourses *about* hermeneutics, the original religious kind and the psychoanalytic kind. I can do no more here than allude to these two complex sets of papers. The first involves multiplicities of self, self-worth, and a critique of the dichotomies of truth/falsity or fake/real. The second takes up the hermeneutics of the Jewish midrashic tradition. Both carry the latent

160 I will posit below that we are in a similar interval today.

message that psychoanalysis is a hermeneutic discipline devoted to multiple levels of interpretation.

A single clinical paper (Tintner, 2007) remains in *43*(1) that stands in sharp contrast to these discussions. In this short paper, Tintner describes bariatric surgery and two overweight patients who chose to undergo it. She likens the surgery to Freud's well-known observation that to treat a phobia one must first induce the patient to challenge it in order to involve him in the treatment and get its meaning to surface.[161] What is interesting here is that this approach (with which I have no problem) is anti-hermeneutic in that it depends, for its success, on something from *outside of the analysis*.

Thus, there is in *43*(1) an unremarked upon tension between these two positions that speak to the very ontology of psychoanalysis. By its organization, it seems to posit that those analysts and psychotherapists who would hold to the position of the mini-seminars—that psychoanalysis is exclusively hermeneutic—must deal with or reject out of hand the increasing intrusions from an ever-expanding world that includes other disciplines. There will be more to say about this. Arguably, this latent conflict represents the most relevant issue for psychoanalysis in the coming decade.

What can be gotten from this flying survey of a half-century of psychoanalytic literature? I expect many to dismiss it as superficial. However, it does demonstrate a number of things about our subject, a history of writing on therapeutic action, that simply could not have been better gotten at in any other way. There *are* differences between *Contemporary Psychoanalysis* and the *Journal of the American Psychoanalytic Association*. The papers *read* differently. As they get into relational and interpersonal theories of technique, change, and therapeutic action, the papers in *CP* seem to mine the material of the authors' experience at a greater depth. Often, such self-exploration is completely absent in otherwise comparable *JAPA* papers. The authors in *JAPA* talk more about theory and transference/countertransference interplay. Both journals succeed, in their own ways, in getting to two-person psychologies. *JAPA* has, of course, a good deal of ego psychology that is absent from *CP* and, for many, of little consequence today. However, none of this is surprising or all that interesting. What is interesting is

161 This is the only use of direct suggestion officially countenanced in the early psychoanalytic literature, although it is well known that Freud made broad use of suggestion in his early days as a hypnotherapist and alluded to it in his later writings (e.g., 1912/1958a).

that both journals do get the job done. They both present a similar clinical history of the last 50 years, a history of a clinical revolution, and mostly offer contemporaneous accounts of it. The differences between them were expectable; the similarities less so.

The Social Network of the Psychoanalytic Literature

There is another way to survey the literature on therapeutic action. In chapter 4, we turned to the relatively new field of Network Studies to better understand the way in which the disautonomous self is embedded in the complex system of its social network. Network theory applies widely to organizations of individuals; people, cells, and traffic, are but a few examples. In particular, Barabási and colleagues (Albert et al., 1999; Barabási, 2003; Barabási & Bonabeau, 2003) have used it to study the World Wide Web. Network theory can also be used to study the psychoanalytic literature, and, for our purposes, the sub-system of the literature on therapeutic action. In this case, individual papers (or books) are the hubs, and citations are the connections between them. The network connections are all unidirectional; citations only go one way. The properties of *our* network are similar to those of the Web. The literature network, we'll call it the LN for convenience, is a scale-free network. There are very few papers that have been cited hundreds of times and very many that have been cited rarely, if at all.

This information was unavailable before the appearance of *PEP* and a ranking of *all* papers in order of their frequencies of citation has only appeared in its most recent release (*Psychoanalytic Electronic Publishing*, 2010). Rank order is determined by the number of times a paper has been cited in the past five years; data for ten years, twenty years, and cumulatively since 1871 are also included. Not all citations are created equal; the meaning, the reasons for citing, and the nature of the information that a citation carries differ. In Network Studies language, there are different *contagions*.[162] The only way to learn the contagion is to read the paper and see why individual citations were made. Similarly, trying

162 References can be cited to demonstrate scholarship, to trace history, sometimes to reference ideas that have been abandoned, or for power-relations reasons to claim standing, to claim kinship, or to please another author. Sometimes an author cites another paper in order to disagree with it or its conclusions. Citations of papers that are also discussed in depth or quoted by an author are less frequent. There is a branch of Science Studies (Latour, 1987; Latour & Woolgar, 1986) that studies citations and why they are made.

to analyze how patterns of citation change over time is hard to do. Information about contagions is thus much harder to come by, but we can easily find out if a paper is being cited, in other words, if it is alive. If we were looking at a network of papers on a given subject, like therapeutic action, we would expect them to have some references in common and that those references would be likely to be significant.

Using *PEP* to look at the 20 most-cited articles, we find that six of them deal explicitly with therapeutic action. Another three, dealing with the therapeutic relationship, however conceived, might be said to be roughly situated on the border of dealing with therapeutic action. (This is either a little or a lot, depending on one's point of view.)

The most-cited article in the psychoanalytic literature as of 2010 happens to be "Non-Interpretive Mechanisms in Psychoanalytic Therapy: The 'Something More' than Interpretation" (Stern et al., 1998). It has been cited 167 times in the past five years and 339 times since it appeared, well on its way to becoming the most cited paper ever, surpassing Loewald's (1960) classic paper on therapeutic action, also in the top 20, at 78 and 538 respectively. The Stern et al. paper is pretty much what it says it is; drawing on developmental and neuroscience concepts, it posits that the therapeutic relationship (small *r*) is an essential component of therapeutic action. It does so rather well indeed and anyone writing on these subjects today pretty much has to cite it (see, I just did).

Loewald (1960) advances the now well-known concept that the analyst as a new object (as opposed to an old, transference object) plays a major role in therapeutic action. Strachey (1934), also in the top 20 at 64 and 526, appears to have coined the term *therapeutic action*. For Strachey, the analyst is also a new object, but one that the patient discovers a little bit at a time, mediated by "mutative" interpretations that operate on the superego. There is, perhaps not surprisingly, more than a little Melanie Klein in Strachey's approach. Stern et al. (1998) appears to be adding citations at a rapid clip, while Strachey and perhaps Loewald are becoming relatively less cited.

What have I just done here? These are complex, interesting papers. I do not pretend to have discussed them. In effect, I have written out place cards for them as major hubs in our virtual diagram of the social network of the psychoanalytic literature on therapeutic action.[163] There

163 The other three papers on therapeutic action in the top 20 are Ogden (1994) at 89 in the past five years and 247 cumulatively, Renik (1993) at 75 and 341, and Gabbard and Westen (2003) at 53 and 65.

are a number of other things that we can and can't say about this network. Consistent with what Barabási and colleagues (Albert et al., 1999; Barabási & Bonabeau, 2003) have written about scale-free networks, the number of citations falls off fairly rapidly as we go down the list. Stern et al. (1998) is 167 and 339, while Gabbard and Westen (2003), number 19 on the list, has 53 and 65.[164] In other words, very few papers are cited much of the time. The network is being held together by a comparatively small number of hubs. The roughly 1500 hundred citations accumulated by Stern et al., Loewald, and Strachey probably define much of the network of the literature on therapeutic action.[165] Many of these citations are duplicates; an author who cited one of these papers was quite likely to cite two or three of them.

There is much that we *don't* know about this network. The contagions, the reasons for citation, vary widely. More importantly, the network is a living thing; as just mentioned, it changes over time. We are studying a picture of it taken by *PEP* in 2010; it will already have changed by the time you read this. The ages of the three hubs that we have been discussing are different. Loewald (1960) had 50 years to accumulate 538 citations, while Stern et al. (1998) has already accumulated 339 in 12 years. It seems likely that Stern et al. will continue to accumulate citations for some years to come and will surpass Loewald. In other words, this living network is growing all the time and parts of it are dying. Citations are permanent, but papers drop out of the network.

In the survey of the *Journal of the American Psychoanalytic Association* and *Contemporary Psychoanalysis*, we turned up some papers that haven't been looked at for a very long time or haven't been looked at *at all* since they were published. We have not talked about papers being read,[166] as this is very hard to measure or interpret, but "citations over the past five years" is a good measure of a paper's still being alive. Just as papers can fall out of the network, they can also be "discovered" a few years after publication and then begin to be cited.

In this discussion of our network, I have not said anything about scholarship. Like a network scientist, I have treated its nodes as "zero intelligence units." Stern et al. (1998) has the most citations for the past five years. That of course does not make it the best paper or the most

164 If we go down the list, past the top 20, we find many more papers with numbers similar to Gabbard and Westen's.

165 This approximate observation and those that follow were obtained from sampling rather large searches for citations of these hub papers and of the topic "therapeutic action."

166 A colleague recently remarked that getting published is *easy*, it's getting read that is hard.

important paper, or the paper with the "best" scholarship. (Indeed, Stern et al. focuses on a serious subject, but manifests major flaws in its scholarship and methodology.) The paper does say some new things and some old things in new ways that are of considerable current interest. Networks are ruled by trends and at times fads. The psychoanalytic literature often tends to work over topics for a decade or so and then move on. This can be so because a subject gets pretty well figured out, the work that needs to be done on it is done, or simply because people get bored with it and want to write and read about the next big thing. Sometimes a topic can reach a point of urgency for reasons external to psychoanalysis; contemporary developments occurring in neuroscience are examples of such circumstances.

Taken together, these two approaches to the literature, a chronological survey and the network study, offer a very different kind of information than can be had from a close reading of a few "good" papers on any psychoanalytic subject. They offer a phenomenological view of what has gone on and what is going on in psychoanalysis rather than a subjective view of what a small number of authors thought was going on. If one is building a paper, looking at the network offers a new place to start.

This discussion of the "science" of psychoanalytic publications inevitably brushes up against issues of politics and power relations. Relatively small groups of individuals, the journal editors, and their reviewers, determine what even *gets* published. Decisions made ostensibly about science are replete with issues of power and politics (Leffert, 2010a). It would be impossible to study this effect systematically, but anecdotal descriptions of acceptances and rejections of papers abound. *PEP* has served as something of an equalizer here, offering a more level playing field. In the past, one would usually subscribe to and store a small number of journals; it was logistically impractical to get any real picture of what was available in the others. As a result, papers published in lesser-known journals or journals of lesser prestige were seldom read. Articles from these journals now appear in author or subject searches and can easily be read.

I believe, without the benefit of statistics in support of this view, that a majority of psychotherapists and psychoanalysts are multifaceted clinicians who do not restrict themselves to a single school of analytic thought. For them, this dual perspective of the literature as a whole must have considerable value as a way of more firmly situating what they do and where and when their ideas originated. Is it possible to say something more about this group beyond defining them in terms of what they are not? Going back to the goal of this chapter, is it possible to explain the startling irrelevance of theoretical commitment to therapeutic outcome (Tessman, 2003)? How do we frame what *is* clinically relevant and where do we place it in a general analytic scheme of things? I'm going to make a preliminary attempt at a restatement of clinical theory in the absence of metapsychology (much as chapter 3 involved another preliminary attempt).

This is not new, although perhaps stating it so baldly is. The radical critics of ego psychology in the 1960s and 1970s did much the same thing without completely leaving behind the classical terminology. Gill (1976; Gill & Holtzman, 1976) unpacked classical metapsychology and found two theories: a clinical and a metapsychological one. He indicated that he did not have much use for the latter. Gill went on (1982, 1994) to posit the importance of working in what he called the here-and-now transference rather than the genetic transference, two-person psychologies, and the inevitable subjectivity of the therapeutic relationship. George Klein (1970, 1976b) abandoned classical ego psychology for the concept of a supra-ordinate self, a stepping-off place for much of what I have done in chapter 4. In offering a restatement of clinical theory I will strive to remain as phenomenological and processual (rather than structural) and as experience-near as possible.

Levels of Inquiry

Events in a discourse can be examined on different levels of inquiry. To ignore this fact results in a Babel of conversations going past each other, failing to engage or losing engagement. This is particularly true for explorations of therapeutic action. Although different levels can be defined in different ways, it makes sense here to describe three levels of discourse, the macro, the mid-level, and the micro.

Conducted at a micro level, an inquiry into therapeutic action would consist of examining a therapeutic discourse between patient and therapist line by line and sentence by sentence. Such examinations can be an important part of clinical writing. Authors write at this level regardless of their theoretical orientation, although *what* they describe and reflect on about the therapeutic conversation differs greatly. A question that must be asked, but mostly goes unasked and unanswered, is how accurately does what is written down reflect what was actually *said*? This point is rarely taken up and as anyone who has ever listened to recordings of sessions knows, what you hear are not the nice neat sentences you read; nobody actually talks like that outside of speeches and theater.

It is probably fair to say that what we read at best captures the gist of what was said, with the big caveat that it is filtered through the author's inevitable subjectivity.

It could be argued that this brings us up against the limits of knowability, but it could also be argued that the inevitable subjective filter results in a better picture of what went on than would be gotten from a very lengthy verbatim transcript. Both arguments are, maddeningly, to a degree both true and false.[167]

Mid-level discourse on therapeutic action takes place on the level of clinical theory, which for nearly all authors seems to blur into the metapsychology of the various schools of psychoanalytic thought. Much of this discourse occurs within these schools and is more or less collegial, whereas discourse *between* schools can be conducted in a spirit of ecumenism (e.g., Dunn, 2003) or factional strife (e.g., Clement, 2010; Jacobs, 2010; Ringstrom, 2010). I have elsewhere (Leffert, 2010a) argued the shortcomings of either strategy. If ecumenism is pursued for the purpose of arguing that competing theories are more alike than different, then it reduces otherness in a way that sacrifices meaning. If conflicts between competing theories are pursued in search of claims of unique standing, these efforts must also fail as the protagonists can never prove more than the status of local knowledge. The greatest knowledge yield at this level comes from treating these different schools as *autres* and their multiple dialectical relationships as objects of study. Distinctions always remain and the many great battles fought within psychoanalysis, as much for power-relations reasons as for theoretical ones, have never been won or lost;[168] at most, they are subsequently reformulated and refought.

This leaves macro level concepts of therapeutic action. These concepts are not accountable to any theoretical school and are applicable across them. The purpose of formulating clinical ideas at this level is *not* to posit a lessening of differences, of *différance* really, between these schools. It is rather to suggest that their differences are not necessarily as

167 I have not here taken up the unavoidable postmodern problem that, even beginning with "facts," relating them by written or spoken word involves the construction of a narrative requiring choices that subjectively shape the text.

168 This statement would appear to fly in the face of conventional wisdom. Mitchell (1992a), for example, observed that "the battle against [psychoanalytic] orthodoxy has been largely won" (p. 443). He is positing just that, that a battle has been won. But this is not true. Orthodoxy did not disappear; it continues to exist until this day. What has happened is that people of particular differing (*différance*) theoretical persuasions have, for the present, lost interest in fighting about it.

important as their proponents believe them to be when formulating clinical theory. It is, I think, fair to say that an analyst or therapist claiming allegiance to some school goes about her business in a way that is somewhat characteristic and different from an analyst belonging to another school. However, if one is concerned about therapeutic outcome, the critical question is not one of which school she belongs to, but rather if her work is *good enough*. The Tessman (2003) study would seem to tell us that often it is; sometimes it isn't. It is the good enough part that takes us to the macro level.

Macro level concepts have a number of things in common. Although they have usually arisen in the context of some metapsychology, they are, or can be successfully deployed, independently of theory. They sometimes involve concepts drawn from outside of psychoanalysis and require ontological justification for their inclusion. They are experience-near; to move too far from clinical conversation increases instability. This is not really much different from Freud's "*beschreibende Psychologie*" (1900/1991c, p. 531), where it all started, so to speak. It should be possible to describe a case on a micro level with reference to macro concepts and without reference to mid-level ones.[169] Macro level concepts implicitly subject mid-level concepts to deconstruction. I do not pretend that I will be offering anything like a complete list of macro concepts and am not certain that such a list could exist.

Macro Level Concepts: A Preliminary Restatement of Clinical Theory and Therapeutic Action

Immanent to the discussions that follow are the postmodern positions I have developed over the course of a number of papers and a book (Leffert, 2007a, 2007b, 2010a, particularly chapters 1 and 2), of which only the briefest of overviews can be given here. I view external and internal reality as only partially knowable in the face of the observer's irreducible subjectivity.[170] The knowability of an account, or a text, is inseparable from the unique instance of the subject's reading of it; if it is a verbal accounting, that account is also unique. The subject as an agent of discourse is embedded in her social and historical matrix and, as

169 This is, of necessity, a learned art. A psychoanalytic education explicitly or implicitly requires the student to link clinical facts to metapsychological theories. Not all graduates are up to the challenge of separating the two and freeing one from the other.

170 In addition, many functions of the self operate outside of awareness.

such, is radically disautonomous. Although deployed to increase understanding, metanarrative, for our purposes metapsychology, inevitably disenfranchises other knowledges and must be viewed with a high index of suspicion. Postmodern discourse privileges deconstruction as a clinical technique for addressing epistemologically unstable elements in a patient's discourse (and our own via self-reflection) and celebrates irreducible *différance*, as it is variously manifest in the therapeutic situation. A psychoanalysis informed by postmodernism treats evolving personal narrative, irreducibly subjective as it must be, as a necessary component of therapeutic action. Finally, following Latour (1991/1993), attempts to separate the social from the scientific inevitably founder; we must think in terms of these seemingly polar ways of knowing as always connected to each other as parts of larger hybrid knowledges.

All Psychoanalyses Are Relational

I do not mean to assert here that psychoanalysis is relational simply because it involves two people in a room who have some kind of relationship. What I do mean, in a modification of that very convenient shorthand of Stern and colleagues (Stern et al., 1998), is that the analytic couple is connected by something more than the content and process of association and interpretation. That connection resides in their relationship and it has to be good enough if a highly satisfying or mildly satisfying (Tessman, 2003) therapeutic outcome is to result.

To stay with common usage and differentiate this macro level concept from the Relational School (upper case *R*), some definitions are in order. The *Shorter Oxford English Dictionary* (Trumble, 2007) defines *relationship* as "the state or fact of being related; a connection, an association, an *emotional association* between two people" (p. 2519, italics added). *Relational*, the adjective, for our purposes signifies those aspects of the therapeutic situation that pertain to implicit or explicit expressions of the relationship (or discourse about it) that take place between the two participants. These two elements, if employed with tact and attention to dosage and timing on the part of the analyst, constitute major forces of therapeutic action. Much depends on these qualifiers; as we know from experience, therapeutic relationships can be good or bad, novel or repetitious, healing or retraumatizing.

It is easy to forget that, prior to Freud, patients suffering from nervous or emotional conditions were hardly treated as people. What kindness the more seriously ill of them received was the kindness of a sort similar to that afforded lepers. It is only necessary to remember Charcot and his public demonstrations of hysteria at the Salpêtrière to situate this attitude documented by Foucault (1961/2006a) in his monumental *History of Madness*.[171] In spite of his critiques of psychoanalysis, Foucault comments here:

> It is in that respect that all the psychiatry of the nineteenth century really does converge on Freud, who was the first to accept the seriousness of the *reality of the doctor–patient couple*, and who consented never to avert his gaze and his research from this link, and who sought not to mask it in a psychiatric theory merely attempting to keep in harmony with the rest of medical knowledge.
> (p. 510, italics added)

Freud's way of working with his patients, as documented in their memoirs (e.g., Blanton, 1971; Kardiner, 1977) of their analyses, supports this view. With the rather stark exception of "Dora" (Freud, 1905 [1901]/1953a), his case writing also supports it.

If consistent with the work of the Relational or Intersubjective analyst, how can a relational approach also be consistent with that of those who have been variously referred to as orthodox Freudian analysts, modern classical analysts (Dunn, 2003), or modern American ego psychologists? These descriptors conjure up concepts like defense, resistance, and transference analysis occurring in a "neutral," "abstinent," largely silent analytic environment in which the analyst holds to the process as a one-person psychology (while the patient sometimes lapses into an iatrogenic regression). Can the work of these analysts be termed relational? More specifically, can the work of an analyst or psychotherapist who sees that work as focused on the elicitation and analysis of transference, itself a relational distortion, be considered relational?

Examining clinical process material from an analyst working from this general point of view would be a way of making a beginning in answering these questions. Should we be able to offer a relational "take" on the material, *not* as a replacement but rather as an important supplement to the more classically oriented approach offered by the analyst, we would be well on our way to an answer.[172] In search of such clinical material, I

171 It is worth noting that in the world of inpatient psychiatry these attitudes persist, albeit in a somewhat attenuated form, into the present.

172 Approaching this question from the opposite direction, Spezzano (1998), in a paper titled "Listening and Interpreting—How Relational Analysts Kill Time Between Disclosures and Enactments: Commentary on Papers by Bromberg and by Greenberg," concluded that they pretty much go about conducting a psychoanalysis in the usual, dare I say "classical-ish" or not-so-orthodox Freudian, manner.

thought a likely place to look would be the work of Paul Gray who, among others, has built a clinical theory around the close processing of the patient's contributions to the analytic hour. Gray works at the micro level of therapeutic action against a backdrop of mid-level concepts that do not appear in his therapeutic discourse. I easily found a paper (Gray, 1990) with the promising title "The Nature of Therapeutic Action in Psychoanalysis" that turns out to serve our purpose.[173] In treating the paper as a text subject to deconstruction, I will take what Gray says about how he works, his clinical formulations of his patient, and his record of the analytic discourse between him and his patient as a phenomenological representation of this case and what happened in it. We are, of course, free to reach our own conclusions about the case material.

In his abstract, Gray (1990) tells us three things of considerable importance in understanding his approach. The first is that therapeutic action varies with each patient's predilection for making use of particular opportunities for change and with the opportunities presented by his analyst. Somewhat surprisingly, this theory of therapeutic action would appear to have some elements in common with Bacal's (2006) Specificity Theory. The second is that Gray's narrow focus on clinical material to bring about therapeutic action is aimed at minimizing the use of suggestion and what he refers to as internalizing processes. (Gray critiques both.) Finally, "the therapeutic actions arise from analyst and patient sharing observations of the patient's intrapsychic activities of resistance to drive derivatives the patient briefly allowed into consciousness, and represent processes of ego maturation set in motion by intellectually gained experientially exercised insights" (p. 1083).

Gray (1990) goes on to say that he adheres to a conflict based model, that he becomes active only when resistance appears, and that he analyzes the transference that he conceptualizes as the re-externalization of early authority figures resident in the superego much in the manner of Strachey (1934). Gray interprets only those issues that appear in the patient's associations or their redirection manifested by what he calls a "breaking point" or a "change of voice." His work is experience-near. He avoids interpretation based on the analyst's intuition of material (at a depth not immediately observable by the patient) that calls on suggestion to carry the day. I will have more to say about this last point later.

173 I exercised considerable care in choosing an article so as not to offer an argument based on a straw man. In addition to my reading of Gray's (1990) paper, I also found in *PEP* that it has been cited 51 times, further evidence of its legitimacy for our purposes.

For illustrative purposes, Gray (1990) provides a vignette of his work with a patient that I am excerpting here.

> He [the patient] spoke briefly of wanting to know more about me than I revealed during our work together; he had long avoided any active curiosity in this direction. He paused briefly, almost imperceptively, and his tone took on a different quality—a moment of "change in voice." He now spoke of the day he had first telephoned me (he has displaced to the past), and continued, "When I heard you saying, 'I can see you . . . Will next week be all right, *or is it more urgent*?' I was so moved that tears came to my eyes" (in the displacement the conflicted active curiosity has given way to a more passive, dependent mode). At this point his feeling could be clearly heard. He paused very briefly and continued—now without the emotion (another "change of voice")—"It was a time when I was staying with my sister (a sibling with whom he was very close) . . . it was in the country, but I was so depressed, and something about your willingness to see me . . ."
>
> (pp. 1089–1090, italics added)

Gray understands this material as the patient's experiencing some freeing up of his active curiosity about him. This becomes too dangerous and he switches to a passive receptive experience in the past. This receptive passive-dependent stance becomes dangerous too and the patient switches again, still in the past, to living at the time with his sister that is rendered with an absence of affect. It is this last switch, the most recent *defense*, that Gray calls to the patient's attention.

> I drew his attention to what had just taken place. I pointed out that what he had spoken last was said rather differently—with less feeling—than he had permitted himself when he first began to recall the telephone conversation and to think about me. I showed him, further, that when he had run into difficulties with those feelings about me, a familiar solution occurred; it was to reach—ever so briefly, but it was there—for a thought about a gratifying woman. He was able to attend to this, to think back and review for himself what he had just done involuntarily.
>
> (p. 1090)

As the session goes on, Gray (1990) tells us that the patient had tried to avoid the felt discomfort at the surfacing drive derivative. The patient tells Gray that if he didn't defend himself he would always want to be with him and he can't allow that. What Gray describes is entirely consistent with his described theory of technique. He does not interpret the longing in the homosexual drive derivative and refrains from doing so as a matter of technical policy, not for reasons of tact or timing.

Perhaps surprisingly, I have no problem with Gray's (1990) obviously very thoughtful work with his patient. It differs to some degree with how I would work with this patient (I would need to know more about him in order to know how much), but that is neither here nor there. I believe we all accept that there are many potential paths a successful analysis may take that are all capable of reaching at least a similar therapeutic outcome.

However, I also think, as will be obvious to many readers, that there is more going on in this brief communication than Gray (1990) chooses to comment on or work with. What I am talking about is the patient's relating to Gray that he was moved to tears by their first contact, x years (?) before, when Gray asked him if his difficulties were too urgent to wait a week to see him. Again, without critiquing Gray's formulation, the patient is also telling Gray how moved he was by his initial offer. Implicit in that offer is the fact that Gray believes he has help to offer, no small thing, and that he will responsively offer it sooner rather than later based on the patient's own assessment of his needs. As the patient heard it, this is a deeply powerful communication of caring made to someone Gray had never spoken to before. But there is more to be learned here. In speaking of that first encounter years ago now, in the present, the patient is implicitly telling us that Gray has done nothing to disabuse him of that first impression and, at least in a general way, has acted to foster it.

In my experience, it is not unusual for a patient, months or years into a therapy, to comment for the first time about some aspect of the initial contact with me that moved them deeply, usually but not always in a positive way. These communications are always important. A patient told me years after the fact that it had meant a lot to him that I returned his initial call within the hour and that another analyst (to whom I did not even know he had been referred) had waited two weeks to call him back. Another patient told me later that she had felt rebuffed when I did not use her initial phone contact to ask her in some detail about why she was coming to see me. If one accepts the notion that whenever the patient turns something towards the therapist he has to turn other things away in order to say it, then a decision must be made. For Gray's patient, it seems equally possible that his curiosity about Gray[174] was the introduction to the first contact material rather than the first contact sentence representing a manifestation of defense. I would think that at

174 If an analyst does not as a matter of policy answer questions, patients usually adapt and stop asking them in order to avoid the narcissistic injury. Everyone is then more comfortable. Unfortunately, the patient's feelings are then lost to the treatment and the analyst's conviction that not answering questions is best remains.

least an acknowledgement of the importance of the *content* of the communication and my interest in it was called for, but was it necessary? The hypothesis of different possible paths makes the answer uncertain.

If we agree, and some may not, that Gray's (1990) initial query was a relational sort of comment that contained "something more" than the scheduling of an appointment, what did he think he was doing? The query could have been explicitly, implicitly, or inadvertently relational. It seems unlikely that Gray set out to say something relational to put the patient at ease and it is equally unlikely that his question was merely a scheduling one. (It is equally unlikely that the "most" relational among us would ever set out to say something relational let alone that such a course would not be a contradiction in terms.) In the same way, we see Gray communicating to the patient via the *manner* in which he works how interested he is in the patient and how important he thinks every word or phrase the patient utters is. Somehow, one gets a sense that Gray likes his patient; it is clear from what the patient is able to say that he feels safe with him. One can contrast this with a cool and distant analyst whose comments (there are no queries) are always neutral or another analyst bent on exploring a patient's feelings for him and who occasionally comments on his own feelings. Gray gives us no sense of being affected in any way by his patient's communications and makes no reference to his own inner process; clearly, his is a one-person psychology.

Another curative aspect of Gray's technique is his refusal to use his authority, mediated by the transference and suggestion to drive the patient to accept interpretations he cannot feel. I can't tell from the text whether he is aware of the neutral power relations position implicit in his technical stance. When interpretative strategies do fail, as they not infrequently do, therapists may resort to the use of their power over a patient in order to drive them to seemingly accept such an interpretation. Patients are by no means oblivious to this and frequently tell a subsequent therapist their feelings about it.

If we agree there is something more to this vignette, that it demonstrates evidence of a relational element in Gray's work, is it necessary to unpack these elements in the treatment as a Relational or Intersubjective analyst would do? The answer *appears* to be not necessarily or, more intriguingly, not necessarily for Gray but necessarily for an analyst who organizes his work and analytic identity Relationally or Intersubjectively. As Gray's work cannot succeed if it is cold or distant and uninvolved, the work of the latter will be equally unsuccessful if the analyst fills too much of the space (Bachelard, 1958/1994) of the analysis with a discussion of the relationship or the analyst's ideas about it.

I believe that this case discussion offers a partial response to the challenge posed by Tessman's (2003) findings about what led to satisfying analytic results, but there is still more to say; perhaps context is a good term for it.

Something More than the Relationship: Emotion, Meaning, and Narrative

For an analysis to be effective, to be satisfying, it cannot just be about what a good guy the analyst is or how much he likes and respects his patient, warts and all. Indeed, in these relational times one hears from time to time of just such analytic failures. A successful analysis or psychotherapy has to also involve deep emotion and pursue the expansion of meaning and personal narrative for the patient. Indeed, some of those feelings, both the patient's *and* the analyst's need to be negative at least some small part of the time. Without this freedom from constraint, something has to be wrong with the therapeutic situation.[175] Gray's (1990) "intellectual understanding" is also probably not enough. In offering this as a macro level concept, I am not suggesting anything that would be considered profound. It does, however, involve some interesting corollaries. The analyst's commitment to and pursuit of goals or material in these areas, and her success in helping the patient to realize them, is a part of what makes the patient's experience of his analyst good enough and his analysis satisfying. To put it a bit differently, successfully (or unsuccessfully) going about the work of analysis is also relational; it is a part of the relationship.

I would posit that this kind of psychoanalytic work accompanied by implicit relational elements much as we saw in Gray's (1990) paper offers an adequate explanation for some successful outcomes, some satisfying analyses. This hypothesis applies to analyses that pre-date any systematic awareness of the relational point of view as well as to contemporary analyses conducted in this manner.

What is also of interest here is the absence of any reference to metapsychologies of either contemporary or more classical ilks. Macro level concepts of therapeutic action stay on the experience-near level of *beschreibende Psychologie*. However, they draw on ideas developed

175 Patients can leave such an analysis with an emperor's-new-clothes idealization of both analysis and analyst and only later, sometimes years later, begin to realize what went wrong.

over the long history of psychoanalysis by clinicians (patients have *always* been a part of it) who often signify themselves with the names of various theoretical schools. In the literature, metapsychology resides in mid-level concepts that I would suggest have more to do with packaging than with fact. At best, they can attain the status of local knowledges. One does not need to be a Freudian to talk about a patient's ambivalent attraction to his mother, a Self Psychologist to talk about another's grandiosity and need to idealize important figures, or a Kleinian to talk about projection. These concepts can be, and I suspect mostly are, employed phenomenologically by a majority of contemporary clinicians.

Although the more jargon-free an analysis is the better, some of the analyst's theoretical orientation, or orientations, inevitably finds its way into the language of the analytic discourse. I don't know if patients actually find their analyst's chosen metapsychology to be of any great importance. (Prominent exceptions here are mental health professionals who brand themselves, sometimes to a degree approaching religious fervor, and demand an analyst who does likewise.) Analytic patients by virtue of being (one hopes) analyzable are very adaptable and can adopt the particular theoretical vocabulary of their analysts within the range of good enough. It becomes the language that the patient learns and then uses to understand his deepest self. The language is maybe not so important after all, just as an analysis in German or French is still about the same deep meaning. Unless there is a real mismatch between the patient's psychopathology and their analyst's theoretical orientation,[176] the patient is able to internalize and make use of whatever theoretical language is offered, *so long as it is not presented as a substitute for any of the macro level elements of therapeutic action.*

The shared pursuit of meaning and the development of personal narrative out of what can at times feel like a quagmire of experience to patient and therapist alike does not require special language. They do require that the analyst hold meaning and narrative for a patient and give or return it to him as an appropriate awareness of dosage, timing, and tact dictates. These too are atheoretical macro level elements of therapeutic action.

A corollary to these arguments as a plea for such atheoretical macro level psychoanalysis is that much of the therapeutic communication

176 A narcissistic patient with a Kleinian analyst might represent an example of such a therapeutic situation.

takes place between the unconscious parts of the selves (see Leffert, 2010a, chapter 5, for a discussion of unconsciousness) of patient and analyst. Although some of this does come into consciousness, much of it does not. Partly it may not need to but, more importantly, much of it is unable to come into consciousness because it involves neurocognitive processes like priming, the operations of the MNS, or construction of perceptions out of sensory inputs (Gregory, 1997; von Senden, 1932/1960) that are *incapable* of becoming conscious. Another way of saying this is to note somewhat controversially that an analysis or a psychotherapy goes far beyond the exchange of verbal material that Gray (1990) and others write about. Beginning with Freud ("it is a very remarkable thing that the *Ucs.* of one human being can react upon that of another, without passing through the *Cs*"; 1915/1957e, p. 194), one occasionally sees this mentioned without amplification in the literature; I will try to say something more about it.

Unconscious communication between the participants figures in therapeutic process via different pathways: unconscious to conscious to conscious to unconscious, unconscious to conscious to unconscious, and unconscious to unconscious. These communication patterns are bidirectional, interchanges that are not really separable, and can be thought of as originating in either of the therapeutic partners. The single role difference between the two is that it is the therapist who holds (if he realizes it) the knowledge that there is more going on than either partner is aware of. The relations between conscious and unconscious parts of an analysis can be thought of as a kind of mutual pump priming that can only occur when the therapeutic discourse is on track and experienced as significant by both parties. It takes place when the partners mutually engage and pursue emotion, meaning, and narrative development. This view of unconscious communication posits powerful limits to knowability in the therapeutic situation.

If we look at the neuroscience of this unconscious encounter, some features stand out. We are talking about cognition in the right-brain, although any attempt to separate out one hemisphere as discrete from the other is in the end arbitrary and cannot succeed. However, if we treat the separation as a heuristic device, then it can be said that unconscious communication represents right hemisphere to right hemisphere communication. So far, there is not much clinical relevance here. But wait. We have known for a long time that both hemispheres are capable of self-elaborating cognition in isolation (e.g., Galin, 1974; Risse & Gazzaniga, 1978). One aspect of therapeutic action is to invite the right hemispheres of the participants into the dialogue by staying with relevant discourse. I think many of us implicitly do this.

A significant feature of any interaction between two people is the way in which the two hemispheres act on or process the encounter. While cognition in the left, "conscious hemisphere" (see Leffert, 2010a, for a discussion of this usage and the problem of consciousness and the bilateral brain) is linear and takes place at the rate of seconds or at best fractions of a second, right-brain processing takes place nonlinearly and is accomplished in *2 msec* (Schore, 1994, 2003a, 2003b). This means that whatever might be going on verbally in the therapeutic situation, it is hopelessly behind *what has already taken place* in the right-brains of patient and therapist. The unconscious can never be dealt out of the game of therapeutic process; it can only be willfully ignored.

The Trouble with Transference

The hallmark of psychoanalysis has always been a theory of therapeutic action that privileges the analysis of transference, especially its ancient origins. However, there are a number of largely overlooked secular problems connected with both the term and the technique of working with it that must be considered.

The first is one of definition. In their personal definitions of transference, most analysts and psychotherapists seem to include displacement and inappropriateness. Forty years ago Laplanche and Pontalis (1967/1973) had already recognized that a formal definition was difficult because "for many authors the notion has taken on a very broad extension, even coming to connote *all the phenomena which constitute the patient's relationship with the psycho-analyst*" (p. 456, italics added). They opt for a definition that includes the "actualization of unconscious wishes" and a situation in which "infantile prototypes re-emerge and are experienced with a strong sensation of immediacy" (p. 455). They refer to Freud's view of transference as a mode of displacement for which he used the term *Übertragung*, which translates *now* as transference but in Freud's time, more literally, as carryover. Object relations begin with infantile objects which lay down an individual's first cognitive and affective patterns of relating that become a form of conceptual priming (Schacter, 1996). Subsequent relationships are, by definition, *descendants* of these original relationships, incorporating to a greater or lesser extent the ever-growing world of personal experience and a variable degree of carryover.[177] Transfer and displace do not reflect this state of affairs; carryover and the re-emergence of infantile prototypes do. In agreement with Laplanche and Pontalis' reservations, I would opt for a very elastic definition and consider the possibility that, in transference, we are dealing with a primitive that begs a complete definition and can only be a subject of discourse.

Another problem is that any separation of carryover from the other elements of a relationship is artificial, arbitrary, and inherently unstable. Even deploying such a separation for heuristic purposes founders on the impossibility of knowing where to draw the line. Sticking with Laplanche and Pontalis' (1967/1973) "all the phenomena" (p. 456) is probably, all in all, the safest bet.[178]

One *could* dismiss these points as quibbles if one wishes, but that still leaves a more serious problem in clinical theory, that of therapeutic regression, the process that is seen as bringing transference to the fore. I believe again that analysts and psychotherapists have a multiplicity of views on the subject, ranging from seeing therapeutic regression simply as a process that happens in an intensive therapy, to something that the analyst, in keeping with his theory of technique, consciously acts to bring about. The problem with this end of the spectrum is that in fostering a regression unbeknownst to the patient, the analyst is manipulating him (can you think of a better term?) in the service of *lessening his connection to adulthood and reality.*

To be sure, in acting thus, the analyst believes he is acting in his patient's best interest. However, that does not mean that his belief is warranted. Such behavior has an unavoidable power relations element that involves, in the language of Bachrach and Baratz (1970) and Lukes (2005), the analyst's assuming an elite role and dominating the patient. The fact that the analyst's conduct is never addressed, let alone acknowledged, further justifies this interpretation. Therapist behaviors that fall into this category include but are not limited to silence, particularly in response to questions or requests, attempting to at all times purge one's

177 Gill (1982, 1994) posited a wider definition that included the analysis of the here-and-now transference in the therapeutic situation. He saw its absence from contemporaneous psychoanalytic technique as widespread and problematic. He had, in effect, mounted a radical critique in which he considered the majority of analyses then being conducted to be of poor quality. I believe Gill's ideas were subsequently incorporated into modern relational thinking. A correspondence between Philip Bromberg and Merton Gill consisting of five letters written between 1979 and 1984 has recently become known (Bromberg, 2011). It offers clues about how this process, an integration of Gill's views and interpersonal psychoanalysis, began.

178 These arguments apply equally to countertransference.

speech of emotion, and failing, in the words of Ella Sharpe (1950 [1930]/1968) to "be guided by the tact and courtesy we should extend to a formal guest" (p. 30).[179]

The way to avoid injecting power components into the therapeutic setting is to *at all times* act to respect the patient's autonomy. Whatever regression and endowment of the analyst with power that does occur can then be treated as arising in the patient; they can be understood as being about the patient and the power can be returned to him via interpretation at the clinically appropriate moment.

A final problem that has been discussed in other contexts is that even if definable, most of the transference, the countertransference, and the interplay between them takes place beyond the awareness of patient or therapist.

Resistance

I take the position that, in a normatively progressing therapy or analysis what might be described as resistance is present only on rare occasions where resistance can be defined as a patient's decision or wish at a given moment not to participate in the therapy. This would include situations in which a patient has explicit reasons for not wanting to participate in therapy, which, arguably, is then not therapy at all. I would define *resistance* as consisting of an iatrogenic response on the part of a patient to the therapist's countertransference, deficient knowledge of the therapeutic situation, or some ignorance of appropriate technique. In these situations the patient is resisting the analyst because, arguably, he needs to do so.

The problem with the term resistance is that it is a power term (Foucault, 2000; Lukes, 2005; chapter 1 of this volume); someone is resisting because they are being forced to do something or being verbally beaten up. As the term has come into analytic usage, it refers only to the first part, the patient as subject of resistance. It ignores the fact that it is a response and becomes an instance of dominance and submission or resistance and the party doing the forcing, the dominant subject, is the therapist. To put it differently, the problem is the therapist's ignorance,

179 Although Sharpe (1950 [1930]/1968) prefaces this recommendation with the qualification that it applies only to situations when the patient is off the couch, in the subsequent text she makes it clear that she treats patients in precisely the same way whether they are on or off it.

sadism, or temporary submission to his own countertransference.[180] This is no small point and should not be considered an issue of terminology.

Patients, it is true, are sometimes, even frequently, unable to face things or avoid things out of anxiety and are often unaware that they are doing so. I would prefer the term self-palliation as the most accurate description of this process, but, given its strangeness, would settle for the psychoanalytic "defense." Defense itself is a rather poor representation of Freud's choice of *Widerstand* (literally to stand against), a gentler term than the militaristic *Abwehr*. Attempting to address defenses head on is doomed to fail and ignores the fact that something important is going on. A therapeutic technique based on allowing the patient to talk and when they stop or lose the thread to act in some way so as to "interpret *the* resistance" only serves to enhance the power relations problem. Some patients will be undone by it, but most will, as they do with other shortcomings in their therapists, simply adapt to the procedure and get on with the analysis. Such "success" is ultimately bought at the price of a diminished analytic result.

Instead, if in the normal progression of a therapeutic discourse it becomes clear that something is missing or does not make sense, I might (or might not if circumstances did not recommend it) simply call the patient's attention to it or offer a thought identified as my own. To the response on someone's part that this is how he deals therapeutically with resistance, I would raise no objection but still suggest that they consider their personal use of the term.

Whither Conflict?

If therapeutic action is to be approached without metapsychology, where does that leave conflict? At first glance, the two would seem to be inseparable; conflict has to be between psychological elements with at least structural characteristics, in other words, metapsychology. Or does it? The major attempts to situate conflict on the part of Freudian theoreticians have involved topography and ego psychology. Conflict has, at the same time, played a definitional role in both of these

180 I do not believe that conceptualizing resistance and its management in terms of a therapist's ironic authority (e.g., Hoffman, 1996, 1998), freely bestowed by the patient, works if it is used for the express purpose of rationalizing a power relations issue. This is not to say that the concept isn't useful in describing the playful passing of authority, not power, back and forth as part of a healthy therapeutic process.

metapsychological points of view that has only muddled the picture in an inevitably circular fashion. Kohut (1984) attempted to minimize the importance of conflict by positing a shift from "conflicted man" to "tragic man." This created a number of possibilities. Some analysts continue to prioritize conflict as Gray (1990) does, while some others have undoubtedly followed Kohut. Relational authors do not write much about conflict, but, as Spezzano (1998) observes, this does not mean that they don't think about it or use it in their work. That leaves, I think, a majority who employ both conflict and non-conflict based models to understand psychopathology (that of dysfunction as well as that of everyday life).

Demonstrably, conflict exists. It is experience-near. However, if it does not involve models of the mind, what does it involve, what is it between? Ontologically, it is the self that is in conflict with itself. Not the self as some psychological construct, one out of so many that it is impossible to choose, but the self as described in chapter 4. That self does not necessarily know that it is in conflict or that, in the end, it either chooses or does not and is subject to inhibition. The latter result is often intensely dysphoric.

In terms of the argument I have been developing over the course of this book (particularly in chapters 2 and 5), conflict is also between epistemes. Specifically, it is between persistent childhood epistemes from an individual's archive of knowledge (Flynn, 2003; Foucault, 1969 & 1971/1972) and the present-day episteme, the rules governing knowledge in the world we all must navigate. This affects the choices we make or are inhibited from making in our individual necessarily subjective worlds. The archive contains the past epistemes of childhood, including experiences, memories, and the rules of knowledge that governed life in the nuclear family. We are familiar with some of these concepts under different names: developmental psychopathology, regression, and fixation, to name a few. Transference consists of combinations of these.

Why bother with all this? The terminology that we use is familiar and when employed we seem to understand what is meant. Unfortunately, the familiar terminology is also corrupt. By this I mean that it cannot stand up to scrutiny. If we look for definitions we find instability and definitional elements that some of us are always unwilling to accept. (We saw this problem with the definition of transference.) Instead, we have a knowledge-based[181] definition of conflict; childhood epistemes still

181 Knowledge includes emotion as well as cognition.

dominate elements of present-day discourse. This is experience-near and discursive. It is free of metapsychology, that is, free of experience-distant constructions and is epistemologically stable. It is a macro level concept.

Problems with Hermeneutics

Texts have been devoted to hermeneutics, the art or science of interpretation, that are beyond the scope of what can be considered here. For our purposes, hermeneutics in the therapeutic situation conceptualizes a closed circle of discourse in which interpretation follows on interpretation without reference to what lies outside of the circle and depends on previous understanding for coherence. No knowledge, other than that of the interaction of patient and therapist, however the latter is defined, is seen as relevant to the therapeutic enterprise. In contemporary times this position has been embraced by some members of the Relational (e.g., Hoffman, 1998; Stern, 1997, 2002) and Intersubjectivist (e.g., Stolorow, 2011) Schools. I believe that the extreme position grows out of either a neo-pragmatist reading of postmodernism that rests on the work of Richard Rorty (1979, 1982), or the writings of Heidegger (1928/2008) and Gadamer (1975/2004).

Others have adopted a much less extreme positioning of hermeneutic discourse that sets it in parallel with other kinds of knowledge. Mitchell (1992b), for example, refers to a contemporary hermeneutic/constructivist perspective, not to banish external science from the therapeutic encounter but simply to argue against any "single, correct, and complete understanding of human experience" (p. 280). He (1998) observes elsewhere that "whether the kinds of knowledge generated by historians and psychoanalysts are best termed science, social science, or hermeneutics is much less important than an appreciation of *the nature of this knowledge and its legitimacy*" (p. 8, italics added). Similarly, Coburn (2002) includes hermeneutics simply as one of several philosophical underpinnings of intersubjective systems theory and goes on to describe other sorts of underpinnings. My problems lie not with this moderate, even phenomenological view of hermeneutics in psychoanalysis (which I embrace myself), but rather with its extreme cousin.

Looking back, a spirited if somewhat misconstrued debate had occurred between Adolf Grünbaum (1984) and Marshall Edelson (1984) on the subject of whether psychoanalysis was a science or a hermeneutic discipline. Remembering that debate as it occurred in the 1980s, it strikes me that, at the time, it had more emotional than pragmatic significance. As a psychoanalyst, I felt then that of course psychoanalysis must be a science: After all, even Freud had said it was. But at the time it didn't matter all that much because, whichever side you came down on, you weren't going to do things in the office any differently. For some of us that would change.

A critique of the extreme hermeneutic view of psychoanalysis could be mounted from any of a number of directions, including the philosophical and the pragmatic. In the interests of staying experience-near and maintaining clinical relevance, I will take the latter approach and introduce arguments in three areas: Social Network Theory, neuroscience, and psychopharmacology.

Social Network Theory, a refinement of social systems theory, has already been discussed in chapter 4. For our purposes here, it posits that when therapist and patient encounter each other, they do so as members of their own social networks. These networks influence their behavior in ways they are sometimes aware of, but also in ways that are beyond their awareness. Therapists' networks include colleagues, ongoing personal analyses, and exposure to information like clinical theory. In network terms, the latter represent contagion, only a part of which can be known. Therapist networks include other patients as well. What happens in an hour with a patient in the morning may influence what a therapist does with another patient in the afternoon. Both participants' networks include the usual emotional and social connections that exert ongoing and changing influences, also in part beyond awareness. An extreme version of Network influence occurs when a case is in supervision. All these properties are quite consistent with a post-Cartesian worldview. However, they all repeatedly break any claimed closed circle of hermeneutic discourse. Although Social Network Theory appeared on the scene fairly recently, its ancestor systems theory has been with us for over half a century (von Bertalanffy, 1968). Neither has been much applied to the way the psychoanalytic situation is influenced by social networks existing *outside* of the therapeutic space.

Although neuroscience has existed under a variety of names for well over a century and was thought of by Freud as an eventual replacement for psychoanalysis, it did not begin to show signs of a *potential* to impact it until Kandel and colleagues' work (Kandel & Tauc, 1965; Kupfermann & Kandel, 1969) on synaptic facilitation through learning in the 1960s. It was not until Rumelhart and colleagues' (Engel et al., 1994) development of functional magnetic resonance imaging (fMRI) that this potential could be actualized. This precise technique made it possible to study the normal brain in action as opposed to the shortcomings of a surgically or traumatically ablated brain. It also became possible to study development in new ways and to identify heretofore-unimagined sub-systems[182] of the brain, such as the right prefrontal cortex and the MNS. Each impacted psychoanalysis.

Neurocognitive studies of development revealed that the infant brain was essentially an unmyelinated right cerebral hemisphere in contact with the mother until myelination; left hemisphere activity demonstrated with fMRI data and the father did not make an appearance until two to four years of age (Leffert, 2010a; Schore, 1994, 2003a, 2003b). These findings demonstrated that any clinical theory based on accessing the first two years of life via verbal interpretation could not be sustained. Schore (2002, 2009) went on to apply developmental neuroscience to attachment theory, trauma, and psychotherapy.

Schore (1994, 2003a, 2003b) also identified the right prefrontal cortex as a center for extremely fast (2 msec) affective-cognitive processing outside of awareness that far outpaced the action of the logical left and meant that conscious cognitive processing of the therapeutic encounter by either participant occurred long after immediate unconscious conclusions had been reached by both.

The MNS is one of several shared processing systems active in the brain (Ferrari & Gallese, 2007; Gallese et al., 2007; Iacoboni, 2007; Iacoboni et al., 1999). Mirror neurons are found in the prefrontal motor, visual, and somatosensory areas of the cerebral cortex. They become active when another person acts or moves in a particular way and we act in the same (mirroring) way or think about acting in the same way. Activity in the MNS is the same in either case; this means that it is not involved in the choice of initiating action. It represents an innate capacity for intersubjective exchange (Bråten, 2007b) that is activated, not created, by nurturance in the first months of life. I have argued elsewhere (Leffert, 2010a) that use of the couch in effect turns the MNS off and this has consequences for the therapeutic situation.

At the very least, the MNS hypothesis explains the mechanism by which breaking eye contact frees *both* patient and therapist to experience their verbal and affective associations without immediate reference to each other. Alternatively, when patient and therapist face each other,

182 I have elsewhere (Leffert 2010a) critiqued the equating of such subsystems with separable, stand-alone brain modules and do not mean to endorse such absolute separations here.

more unconscious information is conveyed, at least some of which has therapeutic implications. One would expect, for example, that the positive view that Tessman's (2003) subjects experienced coming from their analysts in satisfying analyses was conveyed at least partly in this manner, even if this part were limited to the face to face contacts at the beginning and end of sessions.

It must be remembered that the direct application of the findings of cognitive and functional neuroscience to the clinical situation is still in its early days. Even so, they already provide information from outside the hermeneutic circle that, although it can be ignored, nonetheless offers an additional epistemological footing for psychoanalytic treatment.

A controversial epistemology that is more difficult to ignore is that of psychopharmacology. Perhaps the best place to begin here is by saying that I do not plan to make a detailed case for the merits of pharmacotherapy or to offer a blanket endorsement of it as a treatment modality. I am prepared to stipulate in advance that psychotropic drugs are often misused for reasons growing out of greed, power, or incompetence, that they are particularly misused on young children, and that the companies that produce these drugs act to bring to publication research findings favorable to their products and withhold research information unfavorable to them. These activities lead to what has come to be referred to as publication bias. They also wine and dine clinicians and pay them to give presentations to other clinicians in order to influence them to prescribe the most expensive drugs that are still under patent as opposed to much cheaper generic alternatives. All of these points have been made and made well in two articles by Marcia Angell, a past editor of the *New England Journal of Medicine*, appearing in the *New York Review of Books* (Angell, 2011a, 2011b): "The Epidemic of Mental Illness: Why?" and "The Illusions of Psychiatry."

However, in spite of all of this, when the smoke clears, the drugs do sometimes work and are an essential part of some treatment plans. Thorazine, beginning with its introduction in the 1950s, did much to empty state hospital wards and return patients suffering from schizophrenia to society. Tricyclic anti-depressants appearing in the early 1960s did much for what was then called involutional melancholia, replacing routine treatments with ECT that were not always effective and sometimes damaged memory and intellectual functioning. None of the authors (Angell, 2011a, 2011b; Carlat, 2010; Whitaker, 2010), who raise serious and appropriate concerns about contemporary psychopharmacology, describe what patients were like on these wards half a lifetime ago; it was beyond their experience.

The use of psychotropic agents is more complex and limited in an outpatient setting that includes general psychiatry, psychotherapy, and analysis. Drugs don't work all of the time. Sometimes a successful outcome occurs as a result of luck rather than the uncommon competence of the prescribing psychiatrist. Often, they do not work as well *without* accompanying psychotherapy as *with* it. It is often forgotten that many patients choose a pill prescribed by a primary care physician and either want nothing to do with therapy, can't afford it, or can't make use of it. In such circumstances, therapeutic results are limited.

Why, then, should one consider medication in a psychotherapeutic or psychoanalytic setting in the context of the more severe affective disorders? The first reason is that severe depression and bipolar illness have significant mortality rates and ethical questions exist concerning withholding even a trial of medication. If untreated, depressed or psychotic patients can also be unable to participate cognitively in a therapeutic encounter. They may have thought disorders that interfere with understanding the therapy. Severe depression usually is accompanied by cognitive slowing; the patient is literally unable to think about the therapy or what the therapist is saying. Such effects on the bilateral brain may well be asymmetrical. On the other hand, anti-depressants and anti-psychotics can act on some patients *to make therapy or analysis possible*. Finally, medication can act to relieve emotional pain. Some of us feel this is a good thing. Some of us, to the contrary, still believe the idea left over from the early days of psychoanalysis—that the pain is necessary for a patient to work in treatment, that without it nothing happens. I have never seen this myself, but if one chooses to go down this particular path, there are issues of informed consent and medical liability that cannot be avoided. At the very least, the patient must be told that there is a significant possibility that medication will relieve their symptoms. I am uncertain how often this responsibility is actually honored.

If we open the door in our work to patients receiving adjunctive psychopharmacological treatment, the circle of extreme hermeneutics is again broken. We are instead approaching our patients with multiple knowledges and it is hard to see how this could be a bad thing. Referring the patient for a medication consultation does not really get it out of the therapeutic space. One can explore the meaning of it with a patient, but the pill is truly an external element introduced into the therapeutic situation. Finally, part of that meaning—the knowledge of how the changes in mental functioning, the changes really in the functioning of the self—is to a degree unknowable.

In place of a restrictive hermeneutic view of clinical psychoanalysis, I am again offering a post-structural hybrid (Latour, 1991/1993) comprised of all the social and scientific elements we have been discussing. They are connected to each other in multiple ways that embody specific elements drawn from both modern and postmodern thought (see Leffert, 2010a, for a discussion of this point).

This chapter must strike the reader as a somewhat odd or unusual effort. I have not chosen to take aim at the subject directly by offering another discrete theory of therapeutic action. From everything I can tell (after a very creative period of 20+ years), that kind of study of therapeutic action has entered a period of potentially useful stock-taking and consolidation. Intersubjectivity theory seems, for better or worse, to be in the process of evolving the higher levels of abstraction that sometimes go along with the development of a metapsychology. Stolorow (2011), for example, continues to develop connections between intersubjectivity and postmodern thought, particularly that of Heidegger. The Relational School continues, experience-near, to trace out its roots (Bromberg, 2011; Harris, 2011) and to seek out interesting and beguiling things to say about some of the same good ideas it has already been involved with over the course of this period. Whether these schools will, in the process, find themselves becoming more "metapsychologized" remains to be seen.

I have offered instead some novel ways of viewing what has been transpiring *clinically* in our field for the past 50 years. I have stayed with the concept that outside influences, postmodernism, complexity theory and Network Studies, and neuroscience research are of crucial importance in keeping psychoanalysis clinically relevant, and have suggested how they can inform our heterogeneous discipline. I have become less concerned about the different theoretical schools and the theories of their proponents than in trying to think about what analysts actually *do*.

Stolorow (2011) has made the interesting suggestion that if you treat a patient in the manner of a particular theoretical school, the writings of that school then "come alive." Combining this view with Tessman's (2003) findings would suggest that these orientations are perhaps not so important. Many will not care for this position. I have instead offered a theory of therapeutic action based on macro rather than mid-level concepts. It represents an attempt to search for the essential in what we do, not a search for commonality as it might, on first reading, appear to be. It is certainly a preliminary effort that, hopefully, will lend itself to further refinement.

In the final chapter I will try to offer both some stock-taking of where we have gotten to and some thoughts about where we might be going, including relatively brief sketches of ideas, new to psychoanalysis, that I believe will become increasingly important in the years ahead. I expect to pursue them further in a future volume.

7

A View from the Edge

Introduction

The title *The Therapeutic Situation in the 21st Century* (*TS21*) is not just a conveniently catchy phrase. We have begun a new century that brings with it new ways of formulating what we do clinically. If the second half of the 20th century is any source of comparison, it is hard to imagine how we will be talking to patients in 2050, or, for that matter, whether we will be talking to them at all.

Perhaps optimistically, I am assuming that we will be, that pharmacotherapy, gene therapy, and information processing technologies, while becoming more essential to what we do as psychoanalysts and psychotherapists, will not replace the talking cure. (The latter has, I have posited, already morphed into therapeutic discourse.)

This book has offered a radical reformulation of how we think about our work and the theories that underlie it. It has deconstructed and freed up our ways of psychoanalytic knowing, many of which are over a century old, comprising at times arcane psychoanalytic epistemologies and metapsychologies. In doing so, I have broken the logically impossible circle of psychoanalytic theorizing in which theory is first developed out of clinical process (the origins of both topography and ego psychology are but two examples known to most of us) and then given standing to describe and theorize about *the same clinical process.* Our thinking must have at least some basis drawn from both inside and outside of psychoanalysis. This led to the critique of pure psychoanalytic hermeneutics that was mounted in the last chapter.

I have sought that outside confirmation among the usual suspects drawn from *Contemporary Psychoanalytic Foundations (CPF)* (Leffert, 2010a): postmodernism, neuroscience, and a collection of information processing techniques that include systems theory, complexity theory, Network Studies, and distributed processing models. With the exception of Network Studies, no systematic account of these disciplines has been offered here. This has asked a lot of those readers with little background in these areas who have persevered to this point; I did not feel that it was necessary to suggest *CPF* as a prequel, but I did frequently reference its various chapters.

CPF (2010a) laid out the material in most of these disciplines more or less as I found it, and I used it to demonstrate that psychoanalysis had grown into a group of theoretical towers, towers of unstable hierarchies that I hypothesized could no longer sustain their own weight. In it, I offered two things: a series of radical critiques of established psychoanalytic concepts—consciousness, unconscious, memory, and psychic determinism among them—and new foundations to replace them. The writing was very much in the tradition of the radical psychoanalytic criticism that came before it. I built on and cited the works of Erikson (1950/1963), Gill (1982, 1994), George Klein (1970, 1976b), Rapaport (1956; Rapaport & Gill, 1959), Hoffman (1998), Mitchell (1988), and Stern (1997), to name but a few. I am grateful to them for their ideas.

TS21 has not been that sort of book. I have identified topics for its long chapters that have not been much discussed in connection with the therapeutic situation. Some, like the first two, "Power Relations in the Office" and "Archaeology, Genealogy, and Memory," have not, to my knowledge, *ever* been considered in this context before. While I have cited psychoanalytic authors, many of the same ones, I have referenced rather than built on their work. Although it is true that chapter 5 is all about Freud and his oeuvre, it offers a radically new reading of him. The chapters all address essential aspects of psychoanalysis, aspects that already existed in latent or implicit form. They were not invented here. Things like power, archives, and love all existed already, and analysts did inevitably act in ways based on them for good or ill, whether or not they were aware of doing so. The only choice, really, is whether or not to explicitly address them.

At about the same point in *CPF* (2010a), I made the observation that "The goal of all of this has been to describe a path for psychoanalysis from its present hierarchical and structural instability to a creative [horizontal] instability characterized by growth and expanding knowledge" (p. 241). Once again, I am after a creative instability rather than a series of new rules. On a number of occasions, I have labeled ideas as preliminary; it is my hope that others will both critique them and further them.

What is not preliminary is a shift in the general way the therapeutic process is conceptualized. Characterizing the therapist or analyst as a participant-observer no longer has particular utility in describing what is taking place in the therapeutic situation. The therapist can listen to the patient and, in doing so, be either participating *or* observing. Although it can be more difficult to bring off, it is also possible to participate or observe while speaking. Schachtel (1959), in a now seminal work, offered instead the distinction between the allocentric and the autocentric modes of being. In the allocentric mode, the analyst is fully involved in the moment of the situation, in participation with the patient (whether or not the patient is similarly involved) and has temporarily lost any discrete awareness of self. In the autocentric mode, the therapist is discretely self-aware, reflecting on the patient-as-object (of reflection). Although seldom commented upon, it must be remembered that the patient is similarly capable of both modes of being in the therapeutic situation.

Therapeutic Discourse

Although we have long-used the term *analytic listening* to characterize just what it is that we do, and while it is true that some analysts spend nearly all of their time with their patients in this mode, it misses Schachtel's (1959) distinction and only tells us for sure whether or not the therapist is speaking. Unfortunately, both ways of thinking focus on what the analyst is doing (being allocentric or autocentric) and don't draw our attention to where it should be: on the therapy as a two-person psychology, disautonomously embedded in a number of wider social networks.

The best term to describe the entirety of what takes place in the therapeutic situation that the preceding chapters have been aiming towards is *therapeutic discourse.* I mean this in its widest possible meaning rather than the narrow one of therapeutic *dialogue.*[183]

Signifying what takes place in the therapeutic encounter as discursive does not carry with it a guarantee of success. Although we remain hopeful, individual analyses do not always have happy endings. Sometimes they are not as successful as we might wish; sometimes they even fail. As

183 Labov and Fanshel (1977) first used the term *therapeutic discourse* as the title of a book in which they sought to analyze the therapeutic conversation and its language as a way of seeking out the sub-lingual meta-communications between the therapeutic participants.

analysis is a shared endeavor, there is also shared responsibility for its outcome. However, as the identified and sought-out expert, more of that responsibility falls on the therapist's shoulders than it does on the patient's. Discourses can be constructive or destructive, respectful of the freedom of the participants or mere exercises in power relations, expansive of mutual knowledge or stagnant. Each chapter of this book has offered a particular discursive challenge to be faced by the participants in a therapeutic situation that leads to one or another of each of these descriptive pairings. The result is a sought-after creative instability capable, from the perspective of complexity theory (e.g., Bird, 2003), of continued post-termination phase shifts or the maladaptive creation (or reinforcement) of closed strange attractors.

In *CPF* I took up the shift in understanding of discourse as one moves along the spectrum from modern to postmodern thought. As a starting point let me briefly reprise that discussion. Goldner (2002) sees postmodernism as arising in an interdisciplinary culture and, in the therapeutic situation, involving a series of shifts in the epistemology of meaning. First, there is a shift in the attention of the analyst from what the patient needs or wants to what she, the analyst, knows and how she knows it. This is a shift in interest from patient as object to therapist as subject. The second shift is from the analyst as "subject who theorizes to the relational context through which any form of knowing is created and meaning performed" (p. 160). This involves a change from a one-person to a two-person psychology and from subject–object to subject–subject interaction (Benjamin, 1988). Goldner's third shift, which is of particular interest to us, is from "the dialogic to the discursive, from the intersubjective cocreation of meaning to the discourses and cultural narratives that set the terms for what the dialogic partners can think and know" (p. 160). She goes on to note (as would I) that relational analysts have largely engaged the second but not the third shift.

Since writing this, I have come to take a much wider view of what constitutes discursive practice and therapeutic discourse. Goldner (2002) is right to assert that cultural and social narratives shape discourse for the participants and determine what therapists can know or even think about. The mechanics of power relations and dominance (Lukes, 2005) in training analyses is just one example of such effects. These discursive practices exist in society and time.

I have gone on to posit that sets of personal discursive practices also exist for the individual and time. Each member of the analytic couple brings to the relationship their own set of practices. Their essence is not that they are subjective, but that they set forth, mostly unconsciously, the underlying positions and rules that formulate subjectivity. This subjectivity of knowing determines what an individual is capable of knowing or thinking about, distinct from what members of a given society are capable of knowing. Practice, located at some given time in someone's life, is derived from the sum of discourses up until that time and from the defined bodies of statements about some particular thing (*chose*) (Foucault, 1966/1994). Just as there is an archaeology and genealogy of knowledge (Foucault, 1969 & 1971/1972), there is also an archaeology and genealogy of practice. Conflictual inhibition can shape the discursive practices of a patient, what he can know or think about, while the term *neurosis* offers the therapist a sum of one group of societal practices. We have seen that the sum of these discourses and practices constitutes the personal archive.

Discourse goes beyond dialogue and beyond awareness; it is comprised of both conscious and unconscious elements. The latter is not much talked about, but it takes the concept beyond what Goldner (2002) and Benjamin (1988) are describing. However, things are even more complex. Discourse is not confined to the verbal and not confined to language; it includes emotion.

As therapeutic discourse is a process engaged in by the self, it becomes necessary to talk about the neurobiology of that discourse. Biology is an aspect of discourse. Conceptual priming (Schacter, 1996) is the neurocognitive function that shapes discursive practice. It has been known to involve the temporal lobes, but more recent work (Doya, 2000) suggests that the cerebellum is also involved. Like other forms of priming, it is not capable of becoming conscious. The mirror neuron system has come up on a number of occasions. It is a dual-processing system that, among its functions, conveys information between two people usually looking at each other. It too is unconscious. This communication between therapist and patient can constrain or free discursive practice and limit or expand what may be talked about.

There are also neuroendocrine influences on discursive practice. We have already discussed how the hormone oxytocin loosens conceptual priming. Oxytocin administered nasally to normal subjects has been shown to increase feelings of trust (Kosfeld, Heinrichs, Zac, Fischbacher, & Fehr, 2005). Discourse taking place in the presence of higher circulating levels of this hormone must be qualitatively different than that taking place in its absence. Plasma oxytocin levels have been shown to be decreased in schizophrenics (Goldman, Marlow-O'Connor, Torres, & Carter, 2008) and nasally administered oxytocin has been shown to increase emotion recognition in schizophrenics (Averbeck, Bobin,

Evans, & Shergill, 2011). Human oxytocin levels are known to be regulated through the neuroendocrine link between the thalamus and the pituitary. This is only one example of a pathway by which the neuroendocrine system, like speech, emotion, and perception, participates in discourse. The thalamus can act on the pituitary in either discursive partner to secrete or stay hormones that add emotion to the ongoing therapeutic conversation.

Therapeutic discourse is the most meaningful description of what takes place in a therapeutic encounter. It encompasses multiple channels of communication. It is worth noting that the concept of discourse is entirely descriptive and experience-near; it doesn't and need not include any metapsychology.

Power

The therapeutic situation, discursive or otherwise, is inevitably a creature of power relations. Surprisingly, this has been little acknowledged in the psychoanalytic literature. One individual in emotional pain, a degree of functional impairment, usually possessing limited knowledge and designated as a patient or client, seeks out another—societally identified as an expert and designated as a therapist, psychologist, or physician—for relief and a return of lost function. The situation speaks for itself and we don't need Foucault (2000) to tell us, however well he does so, that the creation and deployment of knowledge is inseparable from the wielding of power. What we can do is monitor the situation carefully to prevent that power being employed to implicitly create a situation of dominance and submission. This is not as simple as it might at first appear.

Therapists are capable of engaging in a spectrum of dominating behaviors ranging from the overt and despicable to the implicit and, at times, naive. At the overt end are therapists and analysts who knowingly exploit patients for financial or sexual gain (Gabbard, 1994b; Gabbard & Peltz, 2001; Leffert, 2011b; Wohlberg, 1997). These are predators regardless of which of these aims may be pursued. Moving away from this end of the spectrum we come to those analysts whose unshakeable clinical and theoretical conviction at times makes it impossible for them to listen to their patients. Following Freud (1925 [1924]/1961b), any disagreement is at once pathologized, labeled as resistance, and subject to interpretation or silence. Iatrogenic regressions, sometimes labeled as "therapeutic," often occur in such therapeutic settings. These therapists adhere to a one-person psychology in which an objectified patient is acted upon. At this level of interaction, when countertransference appeared on the scene, it was treated as an infrequent event in which the therapist had slipped into psychopathology or a more frequent event (e.g., Schafer, 1997) in which the therapist was seen as the victim of the patient's projections.

The majority of contemporary analysts and psychotherapists do not fall into any of the above categories. Instead, they are generally aware of these abuses of power, although they lack any systematic theory of dominance, submission, and power relations, or even an awareness that such theories exist.[184] They successfully eschew these expressions of power, sometimes label authority as "ironic" (Hoffman, 1996), and mostly view the therapeutic situation at least partly in terms of two-person psychologies. It is not so simple.

Regrettably, power relations theory is not taught in psychoanalytic institute or psychology graduate school curricula. As a result, most therapists are not equipped to recognize when power inequalities (as opposed to expressions of transference or countertransference) are intruding on the therapeutic situation. Psychoanalytic therapy, although it needs to have its lighter moments, is serious business, sometimes deadly serious business. By its very nature, the therapist is in a position of power that routinely risks dominance.

There are technical ways of dealing with these inevitable power differentials and the risks of dominance. Some have already been discussed in chapter 1. One can, following Gray (1990), limit one's observations to what is, for the patient, experience-near. One can refrain from interpreting what is far from experience. Such an interpretive stance undermines the *patient's* authority by emphasizing that the therapist is the authority. Even if factually correct, these interpretations leave the patient to grapple intellectually with their content when interpretations, in order to be useful, must also be *felt*. Suggestion is a direct expression of power and dominance. As such, it is best to avoid it, whether used inadvertently or designed to convince, even though Freud (1912/1958a) expressly recommended its use. When the context for doing so arises, it is appropriate to reflect and comment on the realistic power inequalities of the therapeutic situation. This serves

184 An issue of *Psychoanalytic Inquiry* (Lichtenberg, 2004) was devoted to the subject of power in psychoanalytic institutions. However, none of the contributors either cited or seemed in any way aware of the interdisciplinary literature on power.

as a way of returning power to the patient and speaking to her authority.[185]

A Plea for Uncertainty

Although less prominent today than it was a half century ago, much analytic writing, clinical as well as theoretical, is presented with an air of certainty that seems unwarranted by what is known or knowable about the material presented.[186] Battles between advocates of one or another theoretical school similarly manifest complete certainty on the part of the combatants about the rightness of their respective causes. Conferences organized around case material have become more civil in recent years, but still involve a degree of certainty among diverse participants that their particular take on a patient is correct, a certainty that has in no way been lessened by their never having seen the patient being described. A certainty that is of more concern is that which is contained in what psychoanalysts and psychotherapists sometimes say to their patients, although we must be uncertain about how common this form of certainty is. As I have thought about these things over the years, they led me to ask myself a question: How do I know that what I have decided to say to a patient isn't a mistake?

What each of these activities has in common is that they all involve a decision on the analyst's part to act, but to act with incomplete information. A term of art for such actions is that these decisions are said to be taking place "under uncertainty" (Kahneman, Slovic, & Tversky, 1982); a problem faced by many disciplines besides our own. What seems like a fairly simple, straightforward process of organizing our thoughts as we listen to a patient and forming them into an interpretation becomes at once complex if we ask ourselves: What if we're wrong?[187] It is curious how infrequently that question gets asked unless something subsequently *goes* wrong.

I want to touch on three areas in this necessarily brief discussion. The first is to consider the diverse literature on uncertainty both inside and

185 The fact that the patient is presumably there by choice does not, as some might imagine, lessen the power relations problem. Foucault (2000) argues to the contrary that it is *only* in situations where there *is* freedom to choose that a situation of true dominance and submission can play out (a slave in chains is incapable of submission).

186 See chapters 2 and 6 for discussions of this point.

187 By this I do not mean "OMG, what if I'm wrong!" Rather I simply mean, "What if my conclusions about this moment of the therapy are false?"

outside of psychoanalysis and wonder why we are so unfamiliar with it. Then, if analytic certainty is so dubious, why do we cling to it so? Lastly, how can we let uncertainty enter our work and are there different ways of viewing it?

An easy place to start is the *Uncertainty Principle* published by Werner Heisenberg in 1927 (Wheeler & Zurek, 1983). Briefly, it is a principle of quantum mechanics that the position of one particle cannot be measured in relation to another because any act of measurement involves putting energy into the system that changes its location. This is not a measurement error; it is *inherent in this act* of measuring. The Uncertainty Principle is of more than metaphorical interest to psychoanalysts. When we gather information in the psychoanalytic situation we must act on it in ways that change it, our actions affect our ability to know, and change the very thing we are trying to know.[188]

A less easy path begins with Paul Meehl's (1954) now classic study of predictions made by expert clinicians as opposed to those made actuarially. Despite a high degree of certainty evinced by the clinicians, it turned out that the actuarial predictions were the more reliable. Or, as Gilovich and Griffin (2002) put it, "the juxtaposition of modest performance and robust confidence inspired research on faulty processes of reasoning that yield compelling but mistaken inferences" (p. 2). When presented with these findings the clinicians *still believed that their judgment was superior to the actuarial results*. At this point, one might begin to feel a degree of discomfort concerning how one goes about deciding among possible clinical interventions.

From this and other work it became clear that real world intuitive judgments, what we do in the office, resulted in less than optimal outcomes. Simon (1956) suggested that models based on actuarial rationality imposed unrealistic standards on human judgment and coined the phrase "bounded rationality" to describe a lesser standard that humans, that is us, ought to be capable of. This still left the problem of biased real-world decision-making described by Meehl (1954).

Enter Kahneman and Tversky (1982). In a now classic series of papers (that eventually led to Kahneman's receiving the Nobel Prize in 2002;

188 This argument should in no way be thought of as a replacement for the postmodern critique of certainty and knowability in the face of irreducible subjectivity that I have offered elsewhere (Leffert, 2010a) and touched on throughout this book. However, in keeping with its post-structural roots, that critique should not be taken as an argument that the therapeutic situation lacks any objective reality, but only that there are stark limits to the knowability of that reality.

Tversky died in 1996 and the Nobel is not awarded posthumously) they began to explore their own take on bounded rationality. They concluded that intuitive judgments made under uncertainty were not only the result of a simpler process than that of rational-decision making, but that they resulted from an entirely different *kind* of process. It is also a process that often works quite well. They "described three general-purpose heuristics—availability, representativeness, and anchoring and adjustment—that underlie many intuitive judgments made under uncertainty" (Gilovich & Griffin, 2002, p. 3). These techniques are both simple and powerful because they rely on the very neurocognitive procedures that the self-brain has evolved over time to carry out. Availability of information has to do with memory retrieval systems that offer up prior examples of the point under consideration (I started Paul on an SSRI last week). Representativeness involves pattern matching procedures: Are two things alike or different, and how (Paul is like three other patients that I treated in the same way)? Anchoring and adjustment refer to how an uninformative piece of information nevertheless affects subsequent decisions; they involve the priming function in memory (20% of Americans take some form of psychotropic medication).

Kahneman and Tversky (1982) initially found that even when they broke judgment under uncertainty into its individual heuristics, subjects still got it wrong too much of the time. They had to account for the presence of a set of biases associated with each heuristic, deviations from the normative expectations of what one would discover with each. Bias in the availability heuristic can result from all too common biases in memory retrieval of prior examples (I wrote Paul's prescription recently). Biases in the representativeness heuristic can result from already "knowing" what we're looking for (I just know Paul is depressed). Biases in the anchoring heuristic can result from where we got our data from (I determined base rates from the article I read in yesterday's *Wall Street Journal* that said 20% of Americans are taking psychotropic medications). We tend to recall unusual events more often than usual ones. Most of the biases Kahneman and Tversky found were based on simple variations in the laws of probability. The model they developed for judgments rendered under uncertainty became Heuristics and Biases.[189]

189 It would be of great interest (and relatively easy) to study what goes into the way psychoanalysts and therapists formulate what they say or, if they speak spontaneously, what they make of what they've said afterwards.

Heuristics and Biases (H&B) manifest several characteristics. Although the use of heuristics results in patterns of biased judgment, they are based on quite reasonable estimation procedures. They yield what Gilovich and Savitsky (2002) term "quick and dirty" results, but do so based on highly sophisticated neurocognitive processes. Heuristics are not processes that are rarely used to solve complex problems; they instead characterize regular everyday decision-making.

H&B offers useful solutions to two different sorts of problems. It describes an efficient way of obtaining subjectively compelling and usable solutions to problems.[190] However, these results are not always as accurate as one might wish. H&B provides ways of describing those situations when intuitive judgments depart from the rules of probability, that is, when they become biased. Kahneman and Tversky (1982) had observed that errors in intuitive judgment had to do with failure to take into account regression towards the mean, adequate sample size, and/or making full use of base rates in making predictions. These errors referred back to the three heuristics.

In a sort of prequel to Heuristics and Biases, Tversky and Kahneman (1971/1982) wrote a paper that they called "Belief in the Law of Small Numbers" in which they examine biases related to representativeness in the study of small samples. Researchers (or clinicians) tend to expect small samples of subjects or events drawn from a large population to be more similar to each other and to the population than sampling theory would predict. Indeed, they would expect the incidence of some events to be the same across the board, regardless of sample size. For example, assume that the incidence of red-headedness in the population of California is 5%. The law of large numbers (*which exists*) guarantees that very large samples drawn from this population will be highly representative of that population and will have very close to if not exactly 5% redheads. People's intuition about random sampling, regardless of sample size, is that *these* samples will also have 5% redheads. They demonstrate what Tversky and Kahneman call the law of small numbers (which exists only in the eye of the beholder), a *belief* that the law of large numbers applies to small numbers as well.

A corollary to the law of small numbers is called the gambler's fallacy. Assume the mean IQ of eighth graders is known to be 100 (Tversky & Kahneman, 1971/1982). You are going to draw a sample of 50 students

190 Heuristics should not be thought of as deliberative strategies. They are employed rapidly and automatically in cognitive psychology language; we would also say that they, for the most part, operate outside of consciousness.

and the first one you draw has an IQ of 150. What will be the mean IQ of the sample? The answer is 101. A large number of people believe that it is still 100. Their thinking is based on the belief that if you draw a student with an IQ of 150 subsequent draws will be lower, still resulting in a mean of 100 for your sample. People intuit (falsely) a self-corrective property to probability. It is called the gambler's fallacy after the belief that if dice are thrown and three times running they come up craps (two, three, or twelve), then the next toss is more likely to come up seven. It isn't; the likelihood is just one in six as usual. If the gambler's fallacy were in fact true, then the law of small numbers would also be true.

What this means (and why it is relevant to us) is that a researcher who studies small effects with small samples is likely to come up with results that cannot be distinguished from noise in the system. Clinicians are researchers and our sample, the number of patients we have treated or are treating, is also quite small. This means we run a great risk of the conclusions we draw clinically—which intuitively seem so right to us, so certain—being false. I would suggest that the areas in which this risk should be of most concern lie in our individual theories of therapeutic action and the way we understand out patients.

All this actually does have a lot to do with clinical psychoanalysis. Imagine having said something to a patient about their high level of anxiety in some context, and finding that the remark led nowhere. Employing Kahneman and Tversky's (1982) method, one could consider if there had been episodes of lesser intensity before or since (regression towards the mean), was it a sample limited to one anxiety episode (inadequate sample size), and how likely is such an experience to produce anxiety (the base rate)? Depending on the results, you might conclude that you simply made a mistake, a biased judgment. This must all seem rather odd. However, it is useful; how often do we actually even consider that we might have made a mistake? If we go on from this relatively simple example of interpreting a therapeutic event to developing a clinical process based on the therapist's crafting theory-based interpretations, we are one step further removed from experience, from objectively collecting information. The probabilities of getting it wrong must rise as a result of autocentrically stepping back into theory. The anchoring or adjustment heuristic confirms this concern, reminding us that we have a natural tendency to allow entirely extraneous information to get woven into our narratives and influence our judgments.

Less easy still is Tannert and colleagues' (Tannert, Elvers, & Jandrig, 2007) work on the ethics of uncertainty. They recognize that we encounter uncertainty in most aspects of life and that it routinely turns up in disciplines involving risk and probability. They offer a classification of uncertainty dividing it first into objective and subjective uncertainty. The former is again divided into epistemological uncertainty involving knowledge-guided decisions and ontological uncertainty requiring quasi-rational decisions. Subjective uncertainty is divided into moral uncertainty requiring rule-guided decisions, and rule uncertainty requiring intuition-guided decisions. They posit that in the presence of a risk of uncertainty with the potential for a dangerous outcome, we have an ethical duty to lessen our uncertainty and to do "research" to bring that about. Research involves collecting information that lessens biases. It should be clear that this has a lot to do with the process of psychoanalysis. We encounter all or some of these four situations in every moment of the clinical encounter, each of which involves a different kind of decision-making. We are not at all accustomed to thinking of it clinically in this way. We also have the opportunity, and this we are accustomed to, to do research *in* the therapeutic situation, to listen more and to interact more with our patients to lessen a part of our now-acknowledged uncertainty before acting.

There are, perhaps surprisingly, old arguments for uncertainty coming from within psychoanalysis, from the psychoanalytic right. Eissler (1968), drawing on the work of Dilthey (1894/2010) and Hartmann (1927/1964b), argues for the existence of two psychologies: one of explanation and one of understanding. What he means by the latter is something like a holistic-intuitive grasping of the therapeutic situation from moment to moment that has much in common with the allocentric position. By explaining, Eissler means the development of theories and hypotheses that are meant to describe and explain what has been understood. Similarly, this position is roughly analogous to the autocentric mode. He posits that as long as one simply tries to understand, one's knowledge grows; once one offers an explanation, a circle is closed. Subsequent, different understandings, even if correct, cannot find a place in a picture that has been co-opted by the explanation. The longer we refrain from explaining, the more we come to know. The way out of this hermeneutic dilemma is through the eventual realization that material is building up beyond the existing area of explanation. The process can then repeat itself. What Eissler does not address is the possibility that the longer you try to only understand, the more ideas will suggest themselves without closure.

Part of the human condition, I think, is a craving for certainty that we can only try to overcome. As clinicians we feel a need to know what is going on in situations when it is impossible to know. A number of years ago, a prominent psychoanalytic author presented a case as part of a conference. He described a point in his work with a patient when the explanation he had been using no longer fit what his patient was telling him. His reaction was to stop listening and *immediately* search for a new explanation. He felt obvious and intense relief when he could choose a misunderstood term taken from astrophysics and metaphorically apply it to his patient. When our explanations, our certainties, fail, we are made afraid.

A number of authors dealing with judgment under uncertainty (Gilovich & Savitsky, 1996/2002; Nisbett & Ross, 1980) have considered its role in clinical psychoanalysis. Nisbett and Ross (1980), in their work on human inference observe, "two of the more basic ideas in this book [*Human Inference: Strategies and Shortcomings of Social Judgment*] do amount to a rediscovery of two of the most important ideas with which Freud's name and the psychoanalytic tradition are associated" (p. 242). One is that much of mental life is inaccessible to reflection; that is to say it is unconscious.[191] What this means is that *any* judgment or interpretation of those events is of necessity a judgment made under uncertainty; it must reference Heuristics and Biases.

The second of these fundamental ideas has no name in psychoanalysis. As Nisbett and Ross (1980) put it, "the cornerstone, the chief contribution, and the Achilles heel of psychoanalytic thought all are one—[is] Freud's discovery, for it was his, of the enormous importance to mental life of the representativeness Heuristic" (p. 242). The representativeness Heuristic denotes the human problem-solving strategy of pattern recognition, of matching like to like. Two of its uses are to first determine whether some instance belongs to a category of instances with which one is familiar, and second to assign causes to effects, again based on past experiences. Both patients and therapists frequently use this Heuristic, with the latter group referring to categories derived from the holism of their clinical experience and studies. The technique that we use to access the Representativeness Heuristic is none other than

191 Nisbett and Wilson (1977), in one of the most frequently cited papers in psychology, were the first to *prove* empirically that mental processes, such as preferences, biases, and choices, are not accessible to consciousness and that people's belief in their own introspective awareness (reported as introspective certainty) has no basis in fact. These are also processes that involve conceptual priming, which is similarly inaccessible to consciousness. As analysts we operate under the same limitations when we grope to understand what we are thinking and feeling about our patients. When Nisbett and Wilson asked their subjects why they had made certain decisions, they answered with conviction in ways that demonstrated that they did not have the slightest conscious idea of why they did so.

tracking free association. Representativeness is deployed with varying degrees of consciousness. As a therapeutic discourse proceeds, listening and reflection lead one or both partners to recognize a connection between what has just been said (or has happened) and a category of experience. Whether to comment on it or not then becomes an issue of dosage, tact, and timing for the therapist and of how free the patient feels to speak of the connection.

However, as Nisbett and Ross (1980) observe, the problem that has always confounded us is whether the link truly exists in the head of the patient or only in that of the analyst. They offer the same critique of psychoanalytic hermeneutics (although without using the term) as I do. In orthodox psychoanalytic theory building, the analyst's guesses about what his patient is representing are elevated to the level of causality. Once this epistemological error is committed, the guesses are used to elucidate psychoanalytic theory, which is then used to dictate subsequent guesses with subsequent patients.[192]

If the representativeness Heuristic makes sense, if we recognize it as something we employ in the therapeutic situation, then we must deal with the fact that categories are unstable, artificial, and somewhat arbitrary constructs. This is a postmodern critique, but it is entirely consistent with the Biases part of the H&B equation. It also speaks to the way pattern recognition can be impaired neurocognitively by conceptual priming.[193]

The Heuristics and Biases argument becomes a serious issue when some of us argue, with not a little certainty, that central to what we do as analysts is the intuitive connection that we and our patients develop with each other over time. Many of us would probably claim, this time *with* certainty, that our intuition trumps H&B and we do not make mistakes of this kind. This is another version of the argument that sustained empathic inquiry gets us through subjectivity to some version of truth. It is the same intuitive certainty that Meehl (1954) found in his subjects. I have previously (Leffert 2010a) critiqued this argument. I would posit at this point that we do make mistakes, more of them than I originally thought we did. The research part of the therapeutic encounter can lessen but not eliminate them.

192 The derivation of structural theory (Freud, 1923/1961a) out of the deficiencies of the topographic model on ostensible clinical grounds (e.g., the "negative therapeutic reaction") is an example of such a process. The very concept of a negative therapeutic reaction has long since been dispensed with by the great majority of therapists (see the discussion of this point in chapter 6).

193 An older, flawed version of this argument is that countertransference enters the therapeutic situation and biases how we think about and speak to a patient.

Recent studies (Bornstein & Emler, 2001; Klein, 2005) have demonstrated that, relying on the availability and representativeness heuristics, clinicians tend to focus quickly on some initial idea about a patient or a symptom he presents with. They then ask further questions that would support that idea and few or no questions that might disprove it. A similar tendency is expressed in the particular diagnostic tests that are ordered. The anchoring and adjustment heuristic then comes into play when irrelevant data seem to confirm the physician's initial guess. Kahneman (2011) has observed that while evidence-based, logical reasoning offers a solution to this problem, the mind lazily shies away from this hard work and tends to want to stay with the guess. Psychoanalysts are equally vulnerable to such pitfalls. Protected by privileging spontaneity and intuition, hunches can be shared with the patient via interpretation or reconstruction. Then adequate weight is not assigned to the data that are subsequently collected during the session or the ones that follow. The most common problem I have observed in students I have supervised or in colleagues I have listened to is this tendency to make interventions in the "fire and forget" mode, moving on without really stopping to observe what happens beyond the patient's immediate response.

If we take it as givens that some analyses or therapies are successful while others are less so, and that mistakes are present in all of them, then how do we differentiate them on the basis of mistakes? Is it the kind of mistakes we make? Some that involve a fundamental misunderstanding of the patient, versus others that do not? Are some mistakes problematic because they arise out of simple ignorance of some psychoanalytic knowledges relevant to a given patient that also lead to failures of understanding? Is the volume, the number, of mistakes important? I don't profess to be able to answer any of these questions (although a complete failure to understand a patient must be considered important), but I do know that they are amenable to clinical research.

A number of chapters have come close to but have not specifically discussed the distinction between insight and support or the privileging of the former over the latter. We can now turn more explicitly to that distinction.

Support, Palliation, and Care

Of these three terms, at least the first two carry with them a negative connotation of something different from and less than the "pure gold" of psychoanalysis. The third term, care, has not been much talked about in connection with what we do. From the earliest days of psychoanalysis, support has been contrasted with insight and psychotherapy with psychoanalysis. Once again, I can only offer the unsatisfying observation that, currently, some numbers of analysts still espouse this view, while, operationally, some lesser number actually practice that way.[194] I take the position, along with many others, that there is no sharp distinction between therapy and analysis, but rather a spectrum of treatment in which differences become more recognizable the greater the distance is between them. I would also posit that a sharp distinction between insight and support is difficult and sometimes impossible to make.

There are some things still to be said about this spectrum. A given therapy is located somewhere along it based on the nature of the therapeutic action operating within it. How then should these different locations be thought of? Must they involve a dilution of some sort? Finally, what process brings a therapy to a particular point on the spectrum? Dilution would be a return to the pure gold hypothesis, unless one were to acknowledge that there is no "best" treatment, with only some patients up to the job, and that different therapies are appropriate for different patients at different times. We could refer to them all simply as talk therapy (as long as we recognize that it involves more than just talking). The spectrum might best be thought of, somewhat unsatisfyingly it is true, in terms of how much analysis is actually going on in some particular therapy. There are some people who, for differing reasons, cannot participate in talk therapy at all and they either don't make it onto the spectrum, or they quickly fall off it.

A therapy may end up at a certain point as a result of conscious decisions made by either participant; the patient choosing to talk or not to talk about something or the therapist choosing to employ or hold back certain procedures. (This is an entirely different matter from that of moment-to-moment choices—about whether or not to comment on a particular issue.) These are less than satisfying distinctions, although some patients and therapists do elect to adhere to them. A freer and more creative way of beginning is to approach each therapy without preconception and allow it to evolve or develop, as the therapeutic situation dictates, viewing it from a phenomenological perspective.

194 This would entail an analyst or psychotherapist treating therapy and analysis as distinct procedures in which, albeit with some overlap, different sets of methodologies, tools, and techniques are employed.

Different points on the spectrum do amount to different amounts of insight in the mix; they do not require value judgments.

However, training in psychoanalysis or psychoanalytic psychotherapy privileges insight/interpretation and depreciates support or palliation as a sort of necessary evil. Such valuing or privileging has no ontological basis in fact; it amounts to no more than arbitrary practice that dates from Freud's (1919 [1918]/1955d) original comments on the subject, comments that are inconsistent with how he actually worked (Blanton, 1971; Freud, 1909/1955e; Kardiner, 1977). This bias has not been rethought in the contemporary literature in the light of relational (small *r*) ideas and the evolution in thought about therapeutic action that has taken place. Definitions of support generally hinge on helping someone, metaphorically or literally, to stand or proceed, whereas palliation is defined as providing temporary relief (*Oxford English Dictionary*, 1989). I will argue here that there is more going on therapeutically when one makes use of these terms than what is contained in their definitions.

When speaking of support, most analysts think in terms of leading to a patient's strengths and interpreting at the surface rather than depth. It is synonymous with offering less of an "analytic" experience. We overcome our distaste for the procedure by speaking of "analytic support." Palliation is only rarely spoken of (only 14 "hits" in *PEP* from 1871 to the present) and when it is mentioned, it is disparaged or even viewed as a danger.[195] Older clinical models view psychological pain as an essential motivating factor to get the patient to do the difficult work of therapy; any procedures that reduce it are viewed as counterproductive and anti-analytic.[196] The alleged problem with support and palliation is that they gratify the patient. Analytic support really means any support that is not gratifying. Concern over gratification made theoretical sense in times past, when libido theory occupied a prominent place in a clinician's armamentarium and was of singular importance in the analysis of transference. For most of us, this has not been the case for some time. A patient's libidinal wishes remain of clinical importance, but the analytic focus has shifted to their relational underpinnings, past *and* present. We are, in effect, less interested in instincts, their components and the like,

195 Cooper's (2002) observation, "palliation, the wish for the patient to feel better, to be less anxious, whatever, or the analyst's wish to be more attentive are both goal directed and have little to do with what is going on and emotionally real in the moment" (p. 110), is typical of the 14.

196 A related old idea is that the fee charged the patient should be set high enough to cause pain and motivate the patient to work harder and faster.

than we are in their subjects and objects. In keeping with this shift, gratification per se is not a useful distinction; what, after all, is so wrong with some or a little gratification that is not meant to be a regular part of the therapy? Is there any reason why a therapy should not be a process that is both gratifying and fulfilling? During and after all the hard work that has been done to bring about palpable change, shouldn't one hope that it would be?

A couple of decades ago, a patient in analysis (as much as I can know, I think the analysis turned out rather well) complained that I never said anything positive about the hard analytic work she was doing. She was not a needy or narcissistic person; what she said was accurate and descriptive of my technique at that time.[197] In retrospect she even tried to teach me, describing her own work with a patient and how she had spontaneously said "good job!" I listened to what she had to say. I did not, thankfully, interpret either neediness or resistance. At the time I had no place in my clinical thinking to put what she was telling me. I made do with telling her that I thought we had different styles of working with people. I believe that what carried the day was not this rather silly statement, but that I was a good enough analyst and she forgave me my shortcoming.

What I found was that as my thinking changed, I would occasionally praise or urge a patient on with the work when it seemed appropriate. It began to strike me as strange to imagine a relationship, that would go on for years, without either party having anything good to say about the other or about the work they were doing to ameliorate the problems of one of them that wasn't attributed to transference or countertransference acting out. (This is not to say that transference or countertransference acting out never occurs.) As far as I have been able to tell, the results of having made such comments have only been positive. I have found that responding in this way is usually spontaneous and uncalculated; mostly it takes place in the allocentric mode. I do not do this with all of my patients. Some *would* find it overstimulating and, if there were a need for distance and an avoidance of close feelings on a patient's part, then an exploration of such feelings would be more useful.

Some support is inherent to the analytic process itself or the way an analyst goes about it. Gray's (1990) asking his patient on their first

197 I would describe myself then as a non-silent, rather eclectic analyst. I had been largely educated as a Freudian and had added to that elements which I identified as originating in other theoretical schools. My thinking has come a very long way since.

telephone contact whether he could wait a week or needed to come in sooner is an example of this kind of support. The frequency of visits, compared to a 15-minute med-check every six weeks, and the analyst's interest in the patient and everything she has to say, also convey support.

Is there a way of characterizing the difference between overstimulation and the useful encouragement or gratification that has a place in a two-person psychology? The distinction that needs to be made is that whatever gratification is to be had from support or palliation should not involve *boundary violations* or *boundary crossings*. What this amounts to is that the gratification should not be for its own sake and should not be derived from or based on the desires of either analytic partner.

Paralleling the discursive shifts spoken of earlier, there is a shift in analytic attention on the part of both discursive partners (and yes, support is an aspect of discourse) from support or palliation to the person (analyst as subject) who is doing the supporting or palliating. That shift is partly conscious and partly unconscious. The latter activities offer the patient something more than interpretation and the therapist as a new object for the patient's use. That use includes, but is not limited to: changing ways of experiencing objects, the patient's expectations of them, and using the therapist as a new object of identification. For many patients, the experience of being in therapy with a good enough therapist gives them their first experience with a person who behaves in these ways, offering new possibilities for experiencing self and other.

By this time it should be clear that the terms *support* and *palliation* fit less and less well the process that I have been describing. The term that does fit this process is the one we reached at the end of chapter 3: care of the patient. Care, as a group of practices performed by a therapist or analyst for the benefit of her patient, does not appear to have been discussed in the psychoanalytic literature.[198] *Care* has a number of meanings, but the one that fits what we are after in *The Oxford English Dictionary* is "oversight with a view to protection, preservation, or guidance" (1989, p. 893). Many of us do care for our patients in this sense of the word, sometimes implicitly in the practice of psychoanalysis or psychotherapy and sometimes explicitly in what we do or say. Protection, preservation, and guidance also subsume analytic activities first conceptualized far away from care. We provide a safe space in which to work

198 Because of its multiple referents, it was difficult to perform a textual search of *PEP* for "care" in the context described here, but it did not appear in the title of any journal article appearing in the literature since 1871.

and guard the patient's confidentiality. We do not interpret in ways that would lead a patient to harm inside or outside of an analysis, and we address issues of self-harm if necessary. Finally we offer paths, metaphorically and actually, that lead to change.

In coming upon care as, I would posit, a necessary part of what analysts do, we have come to a part of therapeutic action that hasn't really been talked about before. We need to place it, to situate it in this larger whole.

Therapeutic Action: A Reconsideration

An obvious question, after the metaphor of old wine in new bottles, is whether care is just a fancy version of a corrective emotional experience. Aside from the power relations terminology (*corrective*) that has always seemed distasteful, it is not. If we drop Alexander and French's (Alexander, 1950; Alexander & French, 1946) proposal that the analyst consciously behave like a father, say, to give the patient a healthy relationship to replace a defective one with the patient's actual father, what is left is a *new* emotional experience with a person who is also the object of transference. This emotional experience can transform a patient via an ongoing process of transmuting internalization (Kohut, 1984; Strachey, 1934), a clinical concept in its own right whose evolution is independent of any theory of care. Such a new experience is one of the *practices* of care that we have been discussing.

Before going further with this argument there is something more to be said about therapeutic action. Whatever theories exist concerning it, therapeutic action takes place over the long haul, in a time scale measured in months and years. We never see immediate evidence of it in action and it is very hard to argue convincingly or with certainty that some particular thing is working (or not working). We can have personal convictions about doing A or not doing B, but conviction is not proof and we are all prone to the sense that we know best, a sense that must be regularly scrutinized. Theories *about* psychoanalysis are even further away from what we can see and are difficult if not impossible to prove. They usually seem to relate to habits of thought (the anchoring heuristic) rather than fact. What we can track on an hour by hour and sometimes a minute by minute basis is whether process is present and ongoing in the therapeutic encounter. That, we *are* very good at. We can feel a palpable sense of mutual engagement in a process, of something happening or not happening. With some patients this sense is never present and they are not involved in a psychoanalytic therapy.

It is hard to see how any quantitative psychotherapy research, however well-intentioned, could get at this. Here, I am in complete agreement with Hoffman (2009). Arguably, one *could* develop a research protocol that looked at fMRIs at various points in a treatment and compared them to those of other subjects with different psychological organizations or psychopathology. This might suggest that something in particular is happening (or needs to happen) in the brain as part of a therapy. That would be good to know, but we are still some years away from knowing where to look, what to look for, having the methodologies to do so, and possessing any idea of what to do with them if we did.

Information gleaned from other disciplines, around which this book has been organized, does offer insights into what can and should be going on in the therapeutic situation. On this point I am in complete disagreement with the hermeneutic-constructivist position of some contemporary schools of psychoanalysis (e.g., Hoffman, 1998, 2009; Stern, 1997, 2002).

We do know that in taking and periodically reviewing notes of sessions, however they are obtained, we find process literally jumping off the page at us or its not doing so. Either outcome tells us important things about what we are doing.

Schore (2009) believes that we are in the midst of a paradigm shift across therapeutic disciplines from a focus on cognitive approaches *including the privileging of content-based verbal interpretations* to a focus on emotional and motivational processes. He posits that these processes lie at the psychobiological core of therapeutic action involving direct right-brain to right-brain communication in the therapeutic encounter. I support Schore's views in this area, although bitter controversies on this point currently exist. While the sea change he describes is very much in the offing, it is not yet with us.

Secure attachment, both in the mother–infant dyad (Bowlby, 1988) and throughout the life cycle, is increasingly seen as of central importance to normal development (Panksepp, 1998, 2009; Schore, 2002, 2003a). Its absence results in an inability to regulate emotion and alterations in brain chemistry. Treating affect dysregulation through the therapeutic relationship is both practical and essential. If the therapist is able to modulate his patient's emotion where the mother was not, the patient is able to build trust and abandon pathological auto-regulation for a new allocentric regulation that can then be internalized.

In this new context, do interpretations matter at all or, if they do, are they important only as communications to a patient of how closely her therapist is attuned to her? Are they then only the analyst's ticket of admission to the game, so to speak? For myself, it is too soon to completely answer these questions. Verbal interpretation *in the absence of emotion in both participants* seems of little value. I am similarly dubious about interpretations aimed at unconscious ideas or impulses that a patient is out of touch with. I believe that there is an essential place for interpretations that speak in novel ways to personal narratives and their archaeologies, as well as the patient's sense of being. Arguably, understanding a patient and conveying that understanding to him is at the center of care *and* of therapeutic action. In order to accomplish this, we do actually have to understand the patient correctly. Conveying that understanding requires these communications, called interpretations, although their verbal content is only a part (sometimes a small part) of what is conveyed.

If even some of these hypotheses (which is what they are at this point) are true, then the question I asked near the end of chapter 3—whether care and affection for our patients is normative or necessary—must be answered in the affirmative. Care and affection are certainly part of a real relationship, not a transference one. They were, once upon a time, a part of the doctor–patient relationship that has largely fallen victim to the 21st century health care machine. If they are to continue to exist, it is only in the therapist–patient relationship that they may do so. It is almost impossible to find anyone who will talk or write about it and there will need to be some of both if it is to start to make sense to us.

Adler (2002) describes the doctor–patient relationship as involving demonstrated empathy, mutual and reciprocal emotional engagement, and social and physiological (i.e., neuropsychological) components. He is a psychiatrist writing in the *Journal of General Internal Medicine* for an audience of internists and primary care physicians. However, even Adler will not take the small additional step of applying his findings specifically to the *psychiatrist*–patient relationship.

The Self as Bio-Psychosocial Holism

A further discussion of the self is a good place to conclude, in that it emphasizes that therapeutic situation is, first and last, an encounter between selves. By naming it as such, role definitions immediately fall away. Inequalities are less apparent and it emphasizes *mutual* influence and how such influence takes place. It also encourages and virtually requires metapsychology-free thought. There are bodies as well as minds in the room (or over the telephone; Leffert, 2003) that are equally involved in the therapeutic discourse.

The two selves in the therapeutic encounter are discursively involved with each other through speech and language and, neuropsychologically, through two cortical systems. The first involves the shared processing system, the mirror neuron system (MNS) of the prefrontal cortex. It processes perceptions of motor activity and facial expression. The second is made up of cortical midline structures (CMS) (Molnar-Szakacs & Arzy, 2009), right-brain systems that operate extremely rapidly (on the order of 2 msec for a given neurocognitive event to take place). Speech is a left-brain function that takes at least seconds to formulate and utter; its time frame may be voluntarily extended to almost any length. But they are also bodies that are involved with each other through the five senses.

As I have argued, the self is not confined to the brain and certainly not the right-brain. This seems like a fairly obvious point, but nearly all authors miss it in their urgency to privilege the psychical over the physical, writing as if the two were separable. James (1893/2007) originally made this point, but is mostly forgotten for doing so. The self has representations that *partly* reside in the brain. It is unknowable in its entirety, and what is knowable of it is only knowable a smallish piece at a time. Although in normative states it is experienced cohesively, self-examination reveals a number (many?) of fragmentary representations that can contradict each other to greater or lesser extents.

Following Molnar-Szakacs and Arzy (2007), self-representations are often, probably mostly, inaccessible to conscious reflection and incapable of becoming so. It is also a process self, a self-in-motion, and that motion is even harder to know. At best, the motion involves very large numbers of events. They take place in real time, in different locations, at very different velocities, and in parallel; they can only be known one event at a time. The separation of brain from body and right-brain from left, although at times of some heuristic value, has no analogue in the reality, the functioning, or the location of the holistic self.

This is not to minimize the importance of what goes on in the right-brain and its connections to the rest of the brain and the body, nor its interest to growing numbers of researchers. As Schore (2011) observes, "a large number of interdisciplinary studies are now converging upon the centrality of ... implicit right brain motivational and emotional processes that are essential to adaptive functioning" (p. 77).[199] He

199 Schore (2011) is referring here to the much-to-be-desired rapprochement between the neurosciences and psychoanalysis; however, we have seen that this is just a small though important part of the interdisciplinary story.

comments appropriately on the growing number of regulatory functions, particularly those related to emotion and motivation, that are coming to be understood as concentrated in the right-brain. However, his wish to locate an "implicit" self in the right-brain is fraught with difficulties. Schore chooses the term apparently out of a wish to describe the self as unconscious, but not psychodynamically so. This is all well and good, but it fails to address the issues of self, self-representation, and the partial representations of self we have been discussing.

However, this is only a part of the neurocognitive story. The right-brain *is* a specialized part of the self. It does, no doubt, have its own partial self-representations. Since we have moved into neuroscience, it is more useful to think in that language and speak of schemata or distributed processing networks (McClelland & Rumelhart, 1986; Rumelhart & McClelland, 1986). The right cerebral hemisphere is involved with the rest of the brain directly though neural connections, but it is also involved indirectly with the body through a number of different highways: the spinal cord, the sympathetic and parasympathetic nervous systems, the cranial nerves (particularly the vagus, the tenth cranial nerve), and the circulatory system (as a pathway for the transmission of hormonal information). Most of these conduct two-way traffic, afferent and efferent neurons and hormonal feedback loops. The self is connected to the external world through all of these pathways.

Winnicott (1975a) offered a well-known observation to the effect that there is no such thing as a baby. What he meant by this is that a baby is not existentially separable from its mother. The self is similarly inseparable from the social matrix and the external world in which it is embedded. This is not a statement of metaphors. In the real world experiments of sensory deprivation tanks and solitary confinement, the self begins to decay. If it is left to these states, the decay worsens and becomes to a degree permanent. The self is as much a creature of its objects as it is of itself. It cannot exist or continue to exist without them. What all of this means is that the self is in constant, intimate communication with its external world and the selves that populate it. That communication takes place largely outside of awareness; much of it is also incapable of coming into awareness. Attempts at older usages where objects are defined as mental representations (of what?) do not work ontologically. It works to say that objects are in and of the world and that we can carry within us mental representations of them.

As we have said before, much of what takes place in the therapeutic situation takes place beyond awareness and is incapable of coming into awareness. This point cannot be overemphasized. Nevertheless, the self is still the object of therapeutic action. But the self is also the subject that acts on the analyst, as the analyst is the object of the patient's feelings and thoughts and the subject of therapeutic action. Therapeutic action modifies the self. That is its aim. However, we can only *direct* it at those aspects of the encounter that we are aware of. Action, therapeutic or otherwise, is constantly taking place beneath the surface.

There is a final pathway of therapeutic action that we have not yet considered. That pathway operates within the awareness of one or both participants, and can also effect change in parts of the self that are incapable of becoming conscious. Much of what we feel, think, say, or do is governed by what cognitive neuroscientists term *conceptual priming* (Leffert, 2010a; Schacter, 1996, 2001). We have considered this in chapter 2. Priming involves internalized patterns of thought, feeling, memory, and perception that exist and operate completely outside of awareness. They exist only in some sort of brain language, for lack of a better term. They act adaptively or maladaptively as the case may be and are highly tenacious. *We* act consciously to change these patterns when we grasp their operation in a patient. Often we are successful, even if we don't know of or make use of these labels (varieties of priming) to describe the damage that they are doing to a patient or how we go about approaching it.

I find, as I did before (Leffert, 2010a), that it is difficult for me to bring this book to a close. I have felt myself searching for the one last thing to say that would bring it all together. But of course there is no such thing. As the title of this chapter would suggest, we are always on the brink, there is always more to say. I will again reference Said (1994) that a text is both shaped and informed by the point at which we *choose* to enter it. However, we also shape a text by the point at which we choose to exit it (Leffert, 2011b). Having begun the chapter by speculating about what psychoanalysis would look like at mid-century, that is in 2050, it seems appropriate to leave the end of this text open. If a reader has stayed with the narrative thread and followed my arguments and accepts them, then two things will have happened. First, it will have become clear that there is not much place or need for psychoanalytic theories, aka metapsychologies, in what we do (except perhaps as a source of comfort). In their place, I have left two kinds of uncertainty: 1) that we can only know a fraction of what is going on in the therapeutic situation; and 2) that the secular uncertainty of Heuristics and Biases contributes to the postmodern concept of the limits of knowability. In this volume, I have merely scratched the proverbial surface of these two uncertainties. There will inevitably be much more to say about them in the future.

References

Abel, E., Christian, B., & Moglen, H. (Eds.). (1997). *Female subjects in black and white: Race, psychoanalysis, feminism*. Berkeley, CA: University of California Press.

Abend, S. M., Porder, M. S., & Willick, M. S. (1983). *Borderline patients: Psychoanalytic perspectives*. Madison, CT: International Universities Press.

Addis, D. R. (2008). Constructive episodic simulation: Temporal distance and detail of past and future events modulate hippocampal engagement. *Hippocampus, 18*, 227–237.

Adler, H. M. (2002). The sociophysiology of caring in the doctor–patient relationship. *Journal of General Internal Medicine, 17*, 883–890.

Ainsworth, M. D. S., Bell, S. M., & Stayton, D. J. (1974). Infant–mother attachment and social development: "Socialization" as a product of reciprocal responsiveness to signals. In M. P. M. Richards (Ed.), *The introduction of the child into a social world* (pp. 99–135) Cambridge, UK: Cambridge University Press.

Albert, R., Jeong, H., & Barabási, A.-L. (1999). Diameter of the world-wide web. *Nature, 401*, 130–131.

Alexander, F. (1948). *Fundamentals of psychoanalysis*. New York: Norton.

Alexander, F. (1950). Analysis of the therapeutic factors in psychoanalytic treatment. *Psychoanalytic Quarterly, 19*, 482–500.

Alexander, F., & French, T. M. (1946). *Psychoanalytic therapy principles and applications*. New York: The Ronald Press.

American Psychiatric Association. (1994). *Diagnostic and statistical manual of mental disorders* (4th ed.). Washington, DC: Author.

Angell, M. (2011a, June 23). The epidemic of mental illness: Why? *The New York Review of Books, 58*, 20–22.

Angell, M. (2011b, July 14). The illusions of psychiatry. *The New York Review of Books, 58*, 20–24.

Arbesman, S., & Christakis, N. A. (2010). Leadership insularity: A new measure of connectivity between central nodes in networks. *Connectivity, 30*, 4–10.

Ardila, A. (1984). Right prefrontal syndrome. In A. Ardila & F. Ostrosky-Solis (Eds.), *The right hemisphere: Neurology and neuropsychology* (pp. 171–193). New York: Gordon & Breach.

Arlow, J. A., & Brenner, C. (1964). *Psychoanalytic concepts and the structural theory*. New York: International Universities Press.

Aron, L. (1997). Are we to have a meeting of minds? A reply to the discussions of a meeting of minds. *Psychoanalytic Dialogues, 7*, 885–896.

Aron, L. (2007). "Black fire on white fire, resting on the knee of the holy and blessed one": Discussion of Philip Cushman's "A burning world, an absent God: Midrash, hermeneutics, and relational psychoanalysis." *Contemporary Psychoanalysis, 43*, 89–111.

Aronson, S. (2001). "Only connect": The mutuality of attachment in the treatment of a resilient adolescent. *Contemporary Psychoanalysis, 37*, 427–441.

Asch, S. S. (1976). Varieties of negative therapeutic reaction and problems of technique. *Journal of the American Psychoanalytic Association, 24*, 383–407.

Averbeck, B. B., Bobin, T., Evans, S., & Shergill, S. S. (2011, August 11). Emotion recognition and oxytocin in patients with schizophrenia. *Psychological Medicine*, 1–8.

Baars, B. J. (2003). How does a serial, integrated, and very limited stream of consciousness emerge from a nervous system that is mostly unconscious, distributed, parallel and of enormous capacity? In B. J. Baars, W. P. Banks, & J. B. Newman (Eds.), *Essential sources in the scientific study of consciousness* (pp. 1123–1129). Cambridge, MA: MIT Press. (Original work published in 1993).

Bacal, H. A. (2006). Specificity theory: Conceptualizing a personal and professional quest for therapeutic possibility. *International Journal of Psychoanalytic Self Psychology, 1*, 133–155.

Bachelard, G. (1994). *The poetics of space* (M. Jolas, Trans.). Boston: Beacon Press. (Original work published in 1958).

Bachrach, P., & Baratz, M. S. (1970). *Power and poverty: Theory and practice.* New York: Oxford University Press.

Balsam, R. H. (1994). Relational and irrational: Remarks on the clinical gendering of language in psychoanalysis. *Psychoanalytic Study of the Child, 49*, 145–158.

Barabási, A.-L. (2003). *Linked.* London: Plume Books.

Barabási, A.-L. (2005a). Network theory: The emergence of the creative enterprise. *Science, 308*, 639–641.

Barabási, A.-L. (2005b). The origin of bursts and heavy tails in human dynamics. *Nature, 435*, 207–211.

Barabási, A.-L. (2005c). Taming complexity. *Nature Physics, 1*, 68–70.

Barabási, A.-L. (2010). *Bursts: The hidden pattern behind everything we do.* New York: Dutton.

Barabási, A.-L., & Bonabeau, E. (2003). Scale-free networks. *Scientific American, 288*, 50–59.

Barabasz, A. F., & Barabasz, M. (2008). Hypnosis and the brain. In M. R. Nash & A. J. Barnier (Eds.), *The Oxford handbook of hypnosis: Theory, research, and practice* (pp. 337–363). Oxford, UK: Oxford University Press.

Baron-Cohen, S., Leslie, A. M., & Frith, U. (1985). Does the autistic child have a "theory of mind"? *Cognition, 21*, 37–46.

Benjamin, J. (1988). *The bonds of love.* New York: Pantheon.

Benjamin, J. (2000). Intersubjective distinctions: Subjects and persons, recognitions and breakdowns: Commentary on paper by Gerhardt, Sweetnam and Borton. *Psychoanalytic Dialogues, 10*, 43–55.

Bergmann, M. S. (1991). *The anatomy of love: The story of man's quest to know what love is.* New York: Ballantine Books. (Original work published in 1987).

Bernheim, H. (1973). *Hypnosis and suggestion in psychotherapy: A treatise on the nature and uses of hypnotism* (C. A. Herter, Trans.) (3rd ed.). New York: Jason Aronson. (Original work published in 1887).

Bernstein, J. W. (2006). Love, desire, jouissance: Two out of three ain't bad. *Psychoanalytic Dialogues, 16*, 711–724.

Bettelheim, B. (1983). *Freud and man's soul.* New York: Alfred A. Knopf.

Bion, W. J. (1965). *Transformations: Change from learning to growth.* London: Tavistock.

Bion, W. J. (1970). *Attention and interpretation: A scientific approach to insight in psychoanalysis and groups.* London: Tavistock.

Bird, R. J. (2003). *Chaos and life complexity and order in evolution and thought.* New York: Columbia University Press.

Blanton, S. (1971). *Diary of my analysis with Sigmund Freud.* New York: Hawthorne Press.

Blinder, B. J. (2007). The autobiographical self: Who we know and who we are. *Psychiatric Annals, 37*(4), 276–284.

Blos, P. (1968). Character formation in adolescence. *Psychoanalytic Study of the Child, 23*, 245–263.

Bornstein, B. H., & Emler, A. C. (2001). Rationality in medical decision making: A review of the literature on doctors' decision-making. *Journal of Evaluation in Clinical Practice, 7*, 97–107.

Bowlby, J. (1969). *Attachment and loss, volume 1: Attachment*. New York: Basic Books.

Bowlby, J. (1973). *Attachment and loss, volume 2: Separation, anxiety and anger*. New York: Basic Books.

Bowlby, J. (1984). The making and breaking of affectional bonds. In *The making and breaking of affectional bonds* (pp. 126–160). London: Tavistock. (Original work published in 1979 [1977]).

Bowlby, J. (1988). *A secure base: Parent–child attachment and healthy human development*. New York: Basic Books.

Bowlby, J. (1991). Ethological light on psychoanalytic problems. In P. Bateson (Ed.), *The development and integration of behavior: Essays in honor of Robert Hinde* (pp. 301–313). Cambridge, UK: Cambridge University Press.

Brandt, L. W. (1961). Some notes on English Freudian terminology. *Journal of the American Psychoanalytic Association, 9*, 331–339.

Brandt, L. W. (1965). Psychoanalytic concepts and the structural theory, by Jacob A. Arlow and Charles Brenner [Book review]. *Psychoanalytic Review, 52C*, 155–156.

Brandt, L. W. (1966). Process or structure? *Psychoanalytic Review, 53C*, 50–54.

Brandt, L. W. (1968). The id and the regulatory principles of mental functioning, by Max Schur. [Book review]. *Psychoanalytic Review, 55*, 151–152.

Bråten, S. (Ed.). (2007a). *On being moved: From mirror neurons to empathy*. Amsterdam: John Benjamins Publishing Company.

Bråten, S. (2007b). Altercentric infants and adults: On the origins and manifestations of participant perception of others' acts and utterances. In S. Bråten (Ed.), *On being moved: From mirror neurons to empathy* (pp. 111–136). Amsterdam: John Benjamins Publishing Company.

Bråten, S., & Trevarthen, C. (2007). Prologue: From infant intersubjectivity and participant movements to simulation and conversation in cultural common sense. In S. Bråten (Ed.), *On being moved: From mirror neurons to empathy* (pp. 21–34). Amsterdam: John Benjamins Publishing Company.

Breger, L. (2009). *A dream of undying fame: How Freud betrayed his mentor and invented psychoanalysis*. New York: Basic Books.

Brentano, F. (1995). *Psychology from an empirical standpoint* (L. L. McCalister, Trans.). London: Routledge. (Original work published in 1874).

Bromberg, P. M. (2011). The Gill/Bromberg correspondence. *Psychoanalytic Dialogues, 21*, 243–252.

Brownmiller, S. (1993). *Against our will: Men, women, and rape*. New York: Ballantine Books.

Bruch, H. (1962). Perceptual and conceptual disturbances in anorexia nervosa. *Psychosomatic Medicine, 24*, 187–194.

Bucci, W. (1997). Patterns of discourse in "good" and troubled hours: A multiple code of interpretation. *Journal of the American Psychoanalytic Association, 45*, 155–187.

Buchanan, M. (2000). *Ubiquity: Why catastrophes happen*. New York: Three Rivers Press.

Buchwald, E., Fletcher, P., & Roth, M. (Eds.). (2005). *Transforming a rape culture* (rev. ed.). Minneapolis: Milkweed Editions.

Cacioppo, J. T., Christakis, N. A., & Fowler, J. H. (2009). Alone in the crowd: The structure and spread of loneliness in a large social network. *Journal of Personality and Social Psychology, 97*, 977–991.

Carlat, D. (2010). *Unhinged: The trouble with psychiatry—A doctor's revelations about a profession in crisis*. New York: Free Press.

Cavalcanti de Albuquerque, J. D. (1993). Explicit and hidden objectives of the process of training psychoanalysts. *International Forum of Psychoanalysis, 2*, 46–48.

Ceci, S. J., & Bruck, M. (1993). Suggestibility of the child witness: A historical review and synthesis. *Psychological Bulletin, 113*, 403–439.

Ceci, S. J., & Bruck, M. (1995). *Jeopardy in the courtroom*. Washington, DC: APA Books.

Celenza, A. (2006). Sexual boundary violations in the office: When is a couch just a couch? *Psychoanalytic Dialogues, 16*, 113–128.

Celenza, A., & Gabbard, G. O. (2003). Analysts who commit sexual boundary violations: A lost cause? *Journal of the American Psychoanalytic Association, 51*, 617–636.

Chessick, R. D. (1996). The application of postmodern thought to the clinical practice of psychoanalytic psychotherapy. *Journal of the American Academy of Psychoanalysis and Dynamic Psychiatry, 24*, 385–407.

Chessick, R. D. (2007). *The future of psychoanalysis.* Albany, NY: State University of New York.

Christakis, N. A. (2004). Social networks and collateral health effects. *British Medical Journal, 329*, 184–185.

Christakis, N. A., & Fowler, J. H. (2007). The spread of obesity in a large social network over 32 years. *New England Journal of Medicine, 357*, 370–379.

Christakis, N. A., & Fowler, J. H. (2008). The collective dynamics of smoking in a large social network. *New England Journal of Medicine, 358*, 2249–2258.

Christakis, N. A., & Fowler, J. H. (2009). *Connected: The surprising power of our social networks and how they shape our lives.* New York: Little, Brown and Company

Chrzanowski, G. (1967). Symptom choice in schizophrenic manifestations. *Contemporary Psychoanalysis, 4*, 41–52.

Chrzanowski, G. (1977). The occurrence of emergencies and crisis in psychoanalytic therapy. *Contemporary Psychoanalysis, 13*, 85–93.

Clement, C. (2010). Commentary on paper by Philip A. Ringstrom. *Psychoanalytic Dialogues, 20*, 219–223.

Coburn, W. J. (2002). A world of systems: The role of systemic patterns of experience in the therapeutic process. *Psychoanalytic Inquiry, 22*, 655–677.

Coen, S. J. (1994). Barriers to love between patient and analyst. *Journal of the American Psychoanalytic Association, 42*, 1107–1135.

Coen, S. J. (2002). White and Columbia: Intersection . . . Union. *Contemporary Psychoanalysis, 38*, 205–212.

Coen, S. J. (2003). The thrall of the negative and how to analyze it. *Journal of the American Psychoanalytic Association, 51*, 465–489.

Cooper, A. M. (1987). Changes in psychoanalytic ideas: Transference interpretation. *Journal of the American Psychoanalytic Association, 35*, 77–98.

Cooper, P. (2002). Between wonder and doubt: Psychoanalysis in the goal-free zone. *Journal of the American Psychoanalytic Association, 62*, 95–118.

Corbett, K. (2001). Faggot = Loser. *Studies in Gender and Sexuality, 2*, 3–28.

Covington, C. (1995). No story, no analysis? The role of narrative in interpretation. *Journal of Analytical Psychology, 40*, 405–417.

Craik, K. (1952). *The nature of explanation*. Cambridge, UK: Cambridge University Press. (Original work published in 1943).

Crastnopol, M. (2007). The multiplicity of self-worth. *Contemporary Psychoanalysis, 43*, 1–16.

Cushman, P. (2005). Between arrogance and a dead-end: Psychoanalysis and the Heidegger–Foucault dilemma. *Contemporary Psychoanalysis, 41*, 399–417.

Cushman, P. (2007a). A burning world, an absent God: Midrash, hermeneutics, and relational psychoanalysis. *Contemporary Psychoanalysis, 43*, 47–88.

Cushman, P. (2007b). Response to Lewis Aron. *Contemporary Psychoanalysis, 43*, 113–120.

Dahl, R. A. (1957). The concept of power. *Behavioral Science, 2*, 201–215.

Dahl, R. A. (1958). A critique of the ruling elite model. *American Political Science Review, 52*, 463–469.

Damasio, A. (2010). *Self comes to mind: Constructing the conscious brain*. New York: Pantheon.

Davies, J. M. (1994). Love in the afternoon: A relational reconsideration of desire and dread in the countertransference. *Psychoanalytic Dialogues, 4*, 153–170.

Davies, J. M. (1996). Dissociation, repression, and reality testing in the countertransference: The controversy over memory and false memory in the psychoanalytic treatment of adult survivors of childhood sexual abuse. *Psychoanalytic Dialogues, 6*, 189–218.

Davies, J. M. (1998). Between the disclosure and foreclosure of the erotic transference–countertransference: Can psychoanalysis find a place for adult sexuality? *Psychoanalytic Dialogues, 8*, 747–766.

Deleuze, G., & Guattari, F. (2009). *Anti-Oedipus: Capitalism and schizophrenia* (R. Hurley, M. Seem, & H. R. Lane, Trans.). New York: Penguin Books. (Original work published in 1972).

Deleuze, G., & Parnet, C. (2007). *Dialogues II: Revised edition* (H. Tomlinson & B. Habberjam, Trans.). New York: Columbia University Press. (Original work published in 1977).

Derrida, J. (1978). *Writing and différence* (A. Bass, Trans.). Chicago: University of Chicago Press.

Derrida, J. (1982). *Margins of philosophy* (A. Bass, Trans.). Chicago: University of Chicago Press. (Original work published in 1972).

Derrida, J. (1998). *Archive fever: A Freudian impression* (E. Prenowitz, Trans.). Chicago: University of Chicago Press. (Original work published in 1995).

Deutsch, F. (1957). A footnote to Freud's 'Fragment of an analysis of a case of hysteria'. *Psychoanalytic Quarterly, 26*, 159–167.

Dilthey, W. (2010). Ideas for a descriptive and analytic psychology. In R. A. Makkreel & F. Rodi (Eds.), *Wilhelm Dilthey: Selected works* (Vol. 2, pp. 115–210). Princeton, NJ: Princeton University Press. (Original work published in 1894).

Dimen, M. (2003). *Sexuality, intimacy, power.* Hillsdale, NJ: The Analytic Press.

Dimen, M. (2011). Lapsus linguae, or a slip of the tongue? A sexual violation in an analytic treatment and its personal and theoretical aftermath. *Contemporary Psychoanalysis, 47*, 35–79.

Doidge, N. (2007). *The brain that changes itself.* New York: Viking.

Doris, J. (Ed.). (1991). *The suggestibility of children's recollections.* Washington, DC: American Psychological Association.

Dorpat, T. L. (1987). Discussion. *Contemporary Psychoanalysis, 23*, 132–144.

Doya, K. (2000). Complementary roles of basal ganglia and cerebellum in learning and motor control. *Current Opinion in Neurobiology, 10*, 732–739.

Dozier, M., & Tyrrell, C. (1997). The role of attachment in therapeutic relationships. In J. A. Simpson & W. S. Rholes (Eds.), *Attachment theory and close relationships* (pp. 221–248). New York: Guilford Press.

Duden: Deutsches Universalwörterbuch 6 auflage. (2007). Mannheim: Dudenverlag.

Dunbar, R. (1993). Coevolution of neocortex size, group size and language in humans. *Behavioral and Brain Sciences, 16*, 681–735.

Dunn, J. (2003). Have we changed our view of the unconscious in contemporary clinical work? *Journal of the American Psychoanalytic Association, 51*, 941–955.

Eagle, M. N. (2003). The postmodern turn in psychoanalysis: A critique. *Psychoanalytic Psychology, 20*, 411–424.

Eagle, M. N. (2009). Postmodern influences on contemporary psychoanalysis. In R. Frie & D. Orange (Eds.), *Beyond postmodernism: New dimensions in clinical theory and practice* (pp. 27–51). London: Routledge.

Eagle, M. N., Wolitzky, D. L., & Wakefield, J. C. (2001). The analyst's knowledge and authority: A critique of the "new view" in psychoanalysis. *Journal of the American Psychoanalytic Association, 49*, 457–488.

Edelson, M. (1984). *Hypothesis and evidence in psychoanalysis.* Chicago: University of Chicago Press.

Eisen, M. L., Quas, J., & Goodman, G. S. (Eds.). (2002). *Memory and suggestibility in the forensic interview.* Mahwah, NJ: Lawrence Erlbaum Associates.

Eissler, K. R. (1968). The relation of explaining and understanding in psychoanalysis—Demonstrated by one aspect of Freud's approach to literature. *Psychoanalytic Study of the Child, 23*, 141–177.

Ellenberger, H. F. (1970). *The discovery of the unconscious.* New York: Basic Books.

Elliott, A., & Spezzano, C. (1996). Psychoanalysis at its limits: Navigating the postmodern turn. *Psychoanalytic Quarterly, 65*, 52–83.

Engel, S. A., Rumelhart, D. E., Wandell, B. A., Lee, A. T., Glover, G. H., Chichilnisky, E.-J., et al. (1994). FMRI of the human visual cortex. *Nature, 369*, 525.

Engelman, E. (1976). *Bergasse 19, Sigmund Freud's home and offices, Vienna 1938: The photographs of Edmund Engelman*. New York: Basic Books.

Erdos, P., & Rényi, A. (1959). On random graphs, I. *Publicationes Mathematicae, 6*, 290–297.

Erickson, M. H. (1980). *The nature of hypnosis and suggestion: The collected papers of Milton H. Erickson on hypnosis, Volume I* (E. L. Rossi, Ed.). New York: Irvington Publishers Inc.

Erickson, M. H., & Rossi, E. L. (1980). The indirect forms of suggestion. In E. L. Rossi (Ed.), *The nature of hypnosis and suggestion: The collected papers of Milton H. Erickson on hypnosis* (Vol. 1, pp. 452–477). New York: Irvington Publishers Inc.

Erikson, E. H. (1962). Reality and actuality: An address. *Journal of the American Psychoanalytic Association, 10*, 451–474.

Erikson, E. (1963). *Childhood and society* (2nd ed.). New York: W. W. Norton & Co. (Original work published in 1950).

Etheredge, L. (1980). The hypnosis model of power. *Psychoanalysis and Contemporary Thought, 3*, 415–456.

Fairfield, S., Layton, L., & Stack, C. (Eds.). (2002). *Bringing the plague: Toward a postmodern psychoanalysis*. New York: Other Press.

Feiner, A. H. (1977a). Countertransference and the anxiety of influence. *Contemporary Psychoanalysis, 13*, 1–15.

Feiner, A. H. (1977b). Lowering the barriers to psychoanalysis. *Contemporary Psychoanalysis, 13*, 116–124.

Ferenczi, S. (1930). The principle of relaxation and neocatharsis. *International Journal of Psychoanalysis, 11*, 428–443.

Ferenczi, S. (1952). Technical difficulties in the analysis of a case of hysteria. In J. Rickman (Ed.), *Further contributions to the theory of technique of psychoanalysis* (pp. 189–197). New York: Basic Books. (Original work published in 1919).

Ferenczi, S. (1988). *The clinical diary of Sándor Ferenczi* (M. Balint & N. S. Jackson, Trans.). Cambridge, MA: Harvard University Press.

Ferrari, P. F., & Gallese, V. (2007). Mirror neurons and intersubjectivity. In S. Bråten (Ed.), *On being moved: From mirror neurons to empathy* (pp. 73–88). Amsterdam: John Benjamins Publishing Company.

Fisher, C. (1954). The role of preconscious primary modes of perception in dream formation. *Journal of the American Psychoanalytic Association, 2*, 389–345.

Flynn, T. (2003). Foucault's mapping of history. In G. Gutting (Ed.), *The Cambridge companion to Foucault* (2nd ed.) (pp. 29–48). Cambridge, UK: Cambridge University Press.

Fogel, G. I., & Glick, R. A. (1991). The analyst's postgraduate development: Rereading Freud working theory through. *Psychoanalytic Quarterly, 60*, 396–425.

Fonagy, P. (1999a). Memory and therapeutic action. *International Journal of Psychoanalysis, 80*, 215–224.

Fonagy, P. (1999b). Psychoanalytic theory from the viewpoint of attachment theory and research. In J. Cassidy & P. R. Shaver (Eds.), *Handbook of attachment: Theory, research, and clinical applications* (pp. 595–624). New York: Guilford Press.

Fonagy, P., & Target, M. (1996). Playing with reality: I. Theory of mind and the normal development of psychic reality. *International Journal of Psychoanalysis, 77*, 217–233.

Foucault, M. (1972). *The archeology of knowledge & The discourse on language* (A. M. S. Smith, Trans.). New York: Pantheon. (Original work published in 1969 & 1971).

Foucault, M. (1980). *Power/knowledge: Selected interviews & other writings 1972–1977* (C. Gordon, L. Marshall, & K. Soper, Trans.). New York: Pantheon Books.

Foucault, M. (1994). *The order of things: An archeology of the human sciences*. New York: Vintage Books. (Original work published in 1966).

Foucault, M. (1995). *Discipline and punish: The birth of the prison* (A. Sheridan, Trans.). New York: Vintage Books. (Original work published in 1979).
Foucault, M. (2000). *Power* (R. Hurley & others, Trans.). New York: The New Press.
Foucault, M. (2006a). *History of madness* (J. Murphy & J. Khalfa, Trans.). London: Routledge. (Original work published in 1961).
Foucault, M. (2006b). *Psychiatric power: Lectures at the College de France 1973–1974* (J. Langange, Ed., G. Burchell, Trans.). New York: Palgrave Macmillan. (Original work published in 2003).
Fox, H. M. (1957). Body image of a photographer. *Journal of the American Psychoanalytic Association, 5,* 93–107.
Fredrickson, B. L., & Cohn, M. A. (2008). Positive emotions. In M. Lewis, J. M. Haviland-Jones, & L. F. Barrett (Eds.), *Handbook of emotions* (3rd ed., pp. 777–796). New York: Guilford Press.
Freedman, N., & Lavender, J. (1997). On receiving the patient's transference: The symbolizing and desymbolizing countertransference. *Journal of the American Psychoanalytic Association, 45,* 79–103.
Freeman, A. (Ed.). (2006). *Consciousness and its place in nature: Does physicalism entail panpsychism?* Exeter, UK: Imprint Academic.
Freeman, W. J. (1995a). *How brains make up their minds.* London: Weidenfeld & Nicolson.
Freeman, W. J. (1995b). *Societies of brains: A study in the neuroscience of love and hate.* Hillsdale, NJ: Lawrence Erlbaum Associates.
Freeman, W. J. (1999). Consciousness, intentionality, and causality. *Journal of Consciousness Studies, 6,* 143–172.
Freeman, W. J. (2005). A field-theoretic approach to scale-free neocortical dynamics. *Biological Cybernetics.* doi:10.1007/s00422-005-0563-1.
Freeman, W. J. (2007). Scale-free neocortical dynamics. *Scholarpedia, 2,* 1357.
Freeman, W. J., & Barrie, J. M. (2001). Chaotic oscillations and the genesis of meaning in cerebral cortex. In W. Sulis & I. Trofimova (Eds.), *Nonlinear dynamics in the life and social sciences* (pp. 13–37). Amsterdam: IOS Press.
Freeman, W. J., Chang, H. J., Burke, B. C., Rose, P. A., & Badler, J. (1997). Taming chaos: Stabilization of aperiodic attractors by noise. *IEEE Transactions on Circuits and Systems—I: Theory and Applications, 44,* 989–996.
Freud, A. (1966). *The ego and the mechanisms of defense revised edition.* New York: International Universities Press. (Original work published in 1936).
Freud, S. (1900). *Die Traumdeutung.* Leipzig and Vienna: Franz Deuticke.
Freud, S. (1953a). Fragment of an analysis of a case of hysteria. In J. Strachey (Ed. & Trans.), *The standard edition of the complete psychological works of Sigmund Freud* (Vol. 7, pp. 3–122). London: Hogarth Press. (Original work published in 1905 [1901]).
Freud, S. (1953b). The interpretation of dreams. In J. Strachey (Ed. & Trans.), *The standard edition of the complete psychological works of Sigmund Freud* (Vols. 4 & 5). London: Hogarth Press. (Original work published in 1900).
Freud, S. (1953c). Three essays on the theory of sexuality. In J. Strachey (Ed. & Trans.), *The standard edition of the complete psychological works of Sigmund Freud* (Vol. 7, pp. 130–243). London: Hogarth Press. (Original work published in 1905).
Freud, S. (1955a). Beyond the pleasure principle. In J. Strachey (Ed. & Trans.), *The standard edition of the complete psychological works of Sigmund Freud* (Vol. 18, pp. 7–64). London: Hogarth Press. (Original work published in 1920).
Freud, S. (1955b). From the history of an infantile neurosis. In J. Strachey (Ed. & Trans.), *The standard edition of the complete psychological works of Sigmund Freud* (Vol. 17, pp. 7–122). London: Hogarth Press. (Original work published in 1918 [1914]).
Freud, S. (1955c). Group psychology and the analysis of the ego. In J. Strachey (Ed. & Trans.), *The standard edition of the complete psychological works of Sigmund Freud* (Vol. 18, pp. 69–143). London: Hogarth Press. (Original work published in 1921).
Freud, S. (1955d). Lines of advance in psycho-analytic therapy. In J. Strachey (Ed. & Trans.), *The standard edition of the complete psychological works of Sigmund Freud* (Vol. 17, pp. 157–168). London: Hogarth Press. (Original work published in 1919 [1918]).

Freud, S. (1955e). Notes upon a case of obsessional neurosis. In J. Strachey (Ed. & Trans.), *The standard edition of the complete psychological works of Sigmund Freud* (Vol. 10, pp. 155–318). London: Hogarth Press. (Original work published in 1909).

Freud, S. (1955f). Two encyclopaedia articles. In J. Strachey (Ed. & Trans.), *The standard edition of the complete psychological works of Sigmund Freud* (Vol. 18, pp. 235–259). London: Hogarth Press. (Original work published in 1923 [1922]).

Freud, S. (1957a). Mourning and melancholia. In J. Strachey (Ed. & Trans.), *The standard edition of the complete psychological works of Sigmund Freud* (Vol. 14, pp. 243–258). London: Hogarth Press. (Original work published in 1917).

Freud, S. (1957b). On narcissism: An introduction. In J. Strachey (Ed. & Trans.), *The standard edition of the complete psychological works of Sigmund Freud* (Vol. 14, pp. 73–102). London: Hogarth Press. (Original work published in 1914).

Freud, S. (1957c). The future prospects of psycho-analytic therapy. In J. Strachey (Ed. & Trans.), *The standard edition of the complete psychological works of Sigmund Freud* (Vol. 11, pp. 141–151). London: Hogarth Press. (Original work published in 1910).

Freud, S. (1957d). Instincts and their vicissitudes. In J. Strachey (Ed. & Trans.), *The standard edition of the complete psychological works of Sigmund Freud* (Vol. 14, pp. 109–140). London: Hogarth Press. (Original work published in 1915).

Freud, S. (1957e). The unconscious. In J. Strachey (Ed. & Trans.), *The standard edition of the complete psychological works of Sigmund Freud* (Vol. 14, pp. 166–215). London: Hogarth Press. (Original work published in 1915).

Freud, S. (1958a). The dynamics of transference. In J. Strachey (Ed. & Trans.), *The standard edition of the complete psychological works of Sigmund Freud* (Vol. 12, pp. 97–108). London: Hogarth Press. (Original work published in 1912).

Freud, S. (1958b). A note on the unconscious in psycho-analysis. In J. Strachey (Ed. & Trans.), *The standard edition of the complete psychological works of Sigmund Freud* (Vol. 12, pp. 260–266). London: Hogarth Press. (Original work published in 1912).

Freud, S. (1958c). Observations on transference love (Further recommendations on the technique of psycho-analysis III). In J. Strachey (Ed. & Trans.), *The standard edition of the complete psychological works of Sigmund Freud* (Vol. 12, pp. 159–171). London: Hogarth Press. (Original work published in 1915 [1914]).

Freud, S. (1958d). Remembering, repeating and working through (Further recommendations on the technique of psycho-analysis II). In J. Strachey (Ed. & Trans.), *The standard edition of the complete psychological works of Sigmund Freud* (Vol. 12, pp. 147–156). London: Hogarth Press. (Original work published in 1914).

Freud, S. (1959a). "Civilized" sexual morality and modern nervous illness. In J. Strachey (Ed. & Trans.), *The standard edition of the complete psychological works of Sigmund Freud* (Vol. 9, pp. 181–204). London: Hogarth Press. (Original work published in 1908).

Freud, S. (1959b). The question of lay analysis. In J. Strachey (Ed.), *Standard Edition* (Vol. XX, pp. 179–258). London: Hogarth Press. (Original work published in 1926).

Freud, S. (1961a). The ego and the id. In J. Strachey (Ed. & Trans.), *The standard edition of the complete psychological works of Sigmund Freud* (Vol. 19, pp. 12–66). London: Hogarth Press. (Original work published in 1923).

Freud, S. (1961b). The resistances to psycho-analysis. In J. Strachey (Ed. & Trans.), *The standard edition of the complete psychological works of Sigmund Freud* (Vol. 19, pp. 213–222). London: Hogarth Press. (Original work published in 1925 [1924]).

Freud, S. (1963). Introductory lectures on psycho-analysis (part III). In J. Strachey (Ed. & Trans.), *The standard edition of the complete psychological works of Sigmund Freud* (Vol. 16, pp. 243–463). London: Hogarth Press. (Original work published in 1916–1917).

Freud, S. (1964a). Analysis terminable and interminable. In J. Strachey (Ed. & Trans.), *The standard edition of the complete psychological works of Sigmund Freud* (Vol. 23). London: Hogarth Press. (Original work published in 1937).

Freud, S. (1964b). New introductory lectures on psycho-analysis. In J. Strachey (Ed. & Trans.), *The standard edition of the complete psychological works of Sigmund Freud* (Vol. 22, pp. 7–182). London: Hogarth Press. (Original work published in 1933 [1932]).

Freud, S. (1964c). An outline of psycho-analysis. In J. Strachey (Ed. & Trans.), *The standard edition of the complete psychological works of Sigmund Freud* (Vol. 23). London: Hogarth Press. (Original work published in 1940 [1938]).

Freud, S. (1966a). A case of successful treatment by hypnosis. In J. Strachey (Ed. & Trans.), *The standard edition of the complete psychological works of Sigmund Freud* (Vol. 1, pp. 117–128). London: Hogarth Press. (Original work published in 1892–1893).

Freud, S. (1966b). Hypnosis. In J. Strachey (Ed. & Trans.), *The standard edition of the complete psychological works of Sigmund Freud* (Vol. 1, pp. 105–114). London: Hogarth Press. (Original work published in 1891).

Freud, S. (1966c). Preface to the translation of Bernheim's *Suggestion*. In J. Strachey (Ed. & Trans.), *The standard edition of the complete psychological works of Sigmund Freud* (Vol. 1). London: Hogarth Press. (Original work published in 1888 [1888–1889]).

Freud, S. (1966d). Project for a scientific psychology. In J. Strachey (Ed. & Trans.), *The standard edition of the complete psychological works of Sigmund Freud* (Vol. 1, pp. 95–397). London: Hogarth Press. (Original work published in 1950 [1895]).

Freud, S. (1985a). *The complete letters of Sigmund Freud to Wilhelm Fliess 1887–1904* (J. M. Masson, Ed. & Trans.). Cambridge, MA: Harvard University Press.

Freud, S. (1985b). Letter, 21 September, 1897, Vienna, IX. Bergasse 19 (J. M. Masson, Trans.). In J. M. Masson (Ed.), *The complete letters of Sigmund Freud to Wilhelm Fliess 1887–1904* (pp. 264–267). Cambridge, MA: Harvard University Press.

Freud, S. (1985c). Letter, 5 November, 1897, Vienna, IX. Bergasse 19 (J. M. Masson, Trans.). In J. M. Masson (Ed.), *The complete letters of Sigmund Freud to Wilhelm Fliess 1887–1904* (pp. 277–278). Cambridge, MA: Harvard University Press.

Freud, S. (1985d). Letter, 28 May, 1899, Vienna, IX. Bergasse 19 (J. M. Masson, Trans.). In J. M. Masson (Ed.), *The complete letters of Sigmund Freud to Wilhelm Fliess 1887–1904* (pp. 352–354). Cambridge, MA: Harvard University Press.

Freud, S. (1991a). *Die Traumdeutung Gesammelte Werke* (Vol. 2/3). London: Imago. (Original work published in 1900).

Freud, S. (1991b). *Gesammelte Werke.* London: Imago.

Freud, S. (1991c). *Zur Psychologie der Traumvorgänge. Gesammelte Werke* (pp. 513–626). London: Imago. (Original work published in 1900).

Freud, S. (1992a). *Letters of Sigmund Freud: Selected and edited by Ernst L. Freud* (E. Freud, Ed., & T. Stern & J. Stern, Trans.). New York: Dover Press. (Original work published in 1960).

Freud, S. (1992b). Letter 123 to Arthur Schnitzler 8 May, 1906, Vienna, IX. Bergasse 19 (T. Stern & J. Stern, Trans.). In E. Freud (Ed.), *Letters of Sigmund Freud: Selected and edited by Ernst L. Freud* (p. 251). New York: Dover Press. (Original work published in 1960).

Freud, S. (1992c). Letter 197 to Arthur Schnitzler 14 May, 1922, Vienna, IX. Bergasse 19 (T. Stern & J. Stern, Trans.). In E. Freud (Ed.), *Letters of Sigmund Freud: Selected and edited by Ernst L. Freud* (pp. 339–340). New York: Dover Press. (Original work published in 1960).

Freud, S. (2003). *Beyond the pleasure principle and other writings* (J. Reddick, Trans.). London: Penguin Books. (Original work published in 1914, 1914, 1920, 1923, 1926).

Freud, S. (2005a). Mourning and melancholia (S. Whiteside, Trans.). In A. Phillips (Ed.), *On murder, mourning and melancholia* (pp. 203–218). London: Penguin Books. (Original work published in 1917).

Freud, S. (2005b). *The unconscious* (G. Frankland, Trans.). London: Penguin Books. (Original work published in 1911, 1915, 1915, 1915, 1925, 1927, 1940).

Freud, S. (2006). *Interpreting dreams* (J. A. Underwood, Trans.). London: Penguin Books. (Original work published in 1899).

Freud, S., & Ferenczi, S. (1996). Letter from Sándor Ferenczi to Sigmund Freud, December 19/20, 1917 (P. T. Hoffer, Trans.). In E. Falzeder & E. Brabant (Eds.), *The correspondence of Sigmund Freud and Sándor Ferenczi Volume 2, 1914–1919* (pp. 252–254). Cambridge, MA: The Belknap Press.

Freud, S., & Ferenczi, S. (2000). Letter from Sigmund Freud to Sandor Ferenczi, December 13, 1931 (P. T. Hoffer, Trans.). In E. Falzeder & E. Brabant (Eds.), *The correspondence of Sigmund Freud and Sándor Ferenczi Volume 3, 1920–1933* (pp. 421–424). Cambridge, MA: The Belknap Press.

Freud, S., & Jung, C. G. (1974). Letter 174F 13 January, 1910, Vienna, IX. Bergasse 19 (R. Manheim & R. F. C. Hull, Trans.). In W. McGuire (Ed.), *The Freud/Jung letters* (pp. 286–288). Princeton, NJ: Princeton University Press.

Frie, R., & Orange, D. (Ed.). (2009). *Beyond postmodernism: New dimensions in clinical theory and practice.* London: Routledge.

Friedman, L. (1997). Ferrum, ignis, and medicina: Return to the crucible. *Journal of the American Psychoanalytic Association, 45*, 20–36.

Friedman, L. (2005). Is there a special psychoanalytic love? *Journal of the American Psychoanalytic Association, 53*, 349–375.

Fuster, J. M. (1997). Network memory. *Trends in Neurosciences, 20*, 451–459.

Gabbard, G. O. (1994a). A response to Davies (but not the last word). *Psychoanalytic Dialogues, 4*, 509–510.

Gabbard, G. O. (1994b). Sexual excitement and countertransference love in the analyst. *Journal of the American Psychoanalytic Association, 42*, 1083–1106.

Gabbard, G. O. (1995). The early history of boundary violations. *Journal of the American Psychoanalytic Association, 43*, 1115–1136.

Gabbard, G. O. (1998). Commentary on paper by Jody Messler Davies. *Psychoanalytic Dialogues, 8*, 781–789.

Gabbard, G. O. (2001). Cyberpassion: E-Rotic transference on the Internet. *Psychoanalytic Quarterly, 70*, 719–737.

Gabbard, G. O., & Peltz, M. L. (2001). Speaking the unspeakable: Institutional reactions to boundary violations by training analysts. *Journal of the American Psychoanalytic Association, 49*, 659–673.

Gabbard, G. O., & Westen, D. (2003). Revisiting therapeutic action. *International Journal of Psychoanalysis, 84*, 823–841.

Gadamer, H.-G. (2004). *Truth and method* (2nd rev. ed.). Berkeley, CA: Continuum. (Original work published in 1975).

Galin, D. (1974). Implications for psychiatry of left and right cerebral specialization: A neurophysiological context for unconscious processes. *Archives of General Psychiatry, 31*, 572–583.

Gallagher, H. L., & Frith, C. D. (2003). Functional imaging of "theory of mind." *Trends in Cognitive Sciences, 7*, 77–83.

Gallese, V., Eagle, M. N., & Migone, P. (2007). Intentional attunement: Mirror neurons and the neural underpinnings of interpersonal relations. *Journal of the American Psychoanalytic Association, 55*, 131–176.

Gay, P. (1988). *Freud: A life for our time.* New York: W. W. Norton & Co.

Gazzaniga, M. S. (1998). *The mind's past.* Berkeley, CA: University of California Press.

Gazzaniga, M. S., Doron, K. W., & Funk, C. M. (2009). Looking toward the future: Perspectives on examining the architecture and function of the human brain as a complex system. In M. S. Gazzaniga (Ed.), *The cognitive neurosciences* (4th ed., pp. 1247–1254). Cambridge, MA: MIT Press.

Gifford, S. (1957). Transient disturbances in perception: Two psychoanalytic observations. *Journal of the American Psychoanalytic Association, 5*, 108–114.

Gill, M. M. (1976). Metapsychology is not psychology. In M. M. Gill & P. S. Holtzman (Eds.), *Psychology verses metapsychology: Essays in honor of George S. Klein* (pp. 71–105). New York: International Universities Press.

Gill, M. M. (1982). *Analysis of transference, volume I: Theory and technique.* New York: International Universities Press.

Gill, M. M. (1994). *Psychoanalysis in transition: A personal view.* Hillsdale, NJ: The Analytic Press.

Gill, M. M., & Holtzman, P. S. (Eds.). (1976). *Psychology versus metapsychology: Essays in honor of George S. Klein.* New York: International Universities Press.

Gilovich, T., & Griffin, D. (2002). Heuristics and biases: Then and now. In T. Gilovich, D. Griffin, & D. Kahneman (Eds.), *Heuristics and biases: The psychology of intuitive judgment* (pp. 1–18). Cambridge, UK: Cambridge University Press.

Gilovich, T., & Savitsky, K. (2002). Like goes with like: The role of representativeness in erroneous and pseudo-scientific beliefs. In T. Gilovich, D. Griffin, & D. Kahneman (Eds.), *Heuristics and biases: The psychology of intuitive judgment* (pp. 617–624). Cambridge, UK: Cambridge University Press. (Original work published in 1996).

Ginsburg, S. A., & Cohn, L. S. (2007). To coerce and be coerced. *Journal of the American Psychoanalytic Association, 55*, 55–79.

Glover, E. (1931). The therapeutic effect of inexact interpretation: A contribution to the theory of suggestion. *International Journal of Psychoanalysis, 12*, 397–411.

Goldman, D. (2007). Faking it. *Contemporary Psychoanalysis, 43*, 17–36.

Goldman, M., Marlow-O'Connor, M., Torres, I., & Carter, C. S. (2008). Diminished plasma oxytocin in schizophrenic patients with neuroendocrine dysfunction and emotional deficits. *Schizophrenia Research, 98*, 247–255.

Goldner, V. (1991). Toward a critical relational theory of gender. *Psychoanalytic Dialogues, 1*, 249–272.

Goldner, V. (2002). Relational theory and the postmodern turn. In S. Fairfield, L. Layton & C. Stack (Eds.), *Bringing the plague: Toward a postmodern psychoanalysis* (pp. 157–165). New York: Other Press.

Goodchild, P. (1996). *Deleuze and Guattari: An introduction to the politics of desire.* London: Sage Publications.

Goodheart, W. B. (1987). A clinical illustration. *Contemporary Psychoanalysis, 23*, 145–160.

Gottman, J. M. (1991). Chaos and regulated change in families: A metaphor for the study of transitions. In P. A. Cowan & E. M. Hetherington (Eds.), *Family transitions* (pp. 247–272). Hillsdale, NJ: Lawrence Erlbaum Associates.

Gottman, J. M., Murray, J. D., Swanson, C. C., Tyson, R., & Swanson, K. R. (2005). *The mathematics of marriage: Dynamic nonlinear models.* Cambridge, MA: MIT Press. (Original work published in 2002).

Grand, S. (2007). Reflections on intentionality, power and the mask: Discussion of papers by Margaret Crastnopol and Dodi Goldman. *Contemporary Psychoanalysis, 43*, 37–46.

Gray, P. (1990). The nature of therapeutic action in psychoanalysis. *Journal of the American Psychoanalytic Association, 38*, 1083–1096.

Green, H. (1967). "In praise of my doctor"—Frieda Fromm-Reichmann. *Contemporary Psychoanalysis, 4*, 73–77.

Greenberg, J. R. (1991). *Oedipus and beyond: A clinical theory.* Cambridge, MA: Harvard University Press.

Greenberg, J. R. (1999). Analytic authority and analytic restraint. *Contemporary Psychoanalysis, 35*, 25–41.

Greenberg, J. R. (2001). The analyst's participation: A new look. *Journal of the American Psychoanalytic Association, 49*, 359–381.

Greenson, R. R. (1967). *The technique and practice of psychoanalysis.* New York: International Universities Press.

Gregory, R. L. (1997). *Eye and brain: The psychology of seeing* (5th ed.). Princeton, NJ: Princeton University Press.

Grinstein, A. (1957). A specific defense met in psychoanalytic therapy—"Comes the knight in shining armor." *Journal of the American Psychoanalytic Association, 5*, 124–129.

Grotstein, J. S. (1990). The contribution of attachment theory and self-regulation theory to the therapeutic alliance. *Modern Psychoanalysis, 15*, 169–184.

Grubrich-Simitis, I. (1996). *Back to Freud's texts: Making silent documents speak* (P. Slotkin, Trans.). New Haven, CT: Yale University Press. (Original work published in 1993).

Grünbaum, A. (1984). *The foundations of psychoanalysis.* Berkeley, CA: University of California Press.

Gudjonsson, G. H. (1984). A new scale of interrogative suggestibility. *Personality and Individual Differences, 5*, 303–314.

Gutting, G. (2003). Foucault and the *History of Madness.* In G. Gutting (Ed.), *The Cambridge companion to Foucault* (2nd ed., pp. 49–73). Cambridge, UK: Cambridge University Press.

Hale Jr., N. G. (1995). *The rise and crisis of psychoanalysis in the United States: Freud and the Americans, 1917–1985.* New York: Oxford University Press.

Hari, R. (2007). Human mirroring systems: On assessing mind by reading brain and body during social interaction. In S. Bråten (Ed.), *On being moved: From mirror neurons to empathy* (pp. 89–99). Amsterdam: John Benjamins Publishing Company.

Harris, A. (1997). Aggression, envy, and ambition: Circulating tensions in women's psychic life. *Gender and Psychoanalysis, 2*, 291–325.

Harris, A. (2009). The socio-political recruitment of identities. *Psychoanalytic Dialogues, 19*, 138–147.

Harris, A. (2011). The relational tradition: Landscape and canon. *Journal of the American Psychoanalytic Association, 59*, 701–735.

Hartmann, H. (1958). *Ego psychology and the problem of adaptation* (D. Rapaport, Trans.). New York: International Universities Press. (Original work published in 1939).

Hartmann, H. (1964a). Comments on the psychoanalytic theory of the ego. In *Essays on ego psychology: Selected problems in psychoanalytic theory* (pp. 113–141). New York: International Universities Press. (Original work published in 1950).

Hartmann, H. (1964b). Understanding and explanation. In *Essays on ego psychology: Selected problems in psychoanalytic theory* (pp. 369–403). New York: International Universities Press. (Original work published in 1927).

Hassabis, D., & Maguire, E. A. (2007). Deconstructing episodic memory with construction. *Trends in Cognitive Sciences, 11*, 299–306.

Hatano, G., & Inagaki, K. (1986). Two courses of expertise. In H. Stevenson, H. Azuma, & K. Hakuta (Eds.), *Child development and education in Japan* (pp. 262–272). San Francisco: Freeman.

Hegel, G. W. (1969). *The phenomenology of mind* (J. B. Baillie, Trans.). New York: Harper Collins. (Original work published in 1807).

Heidegger, J. (2008). *Being and time* (J. Macquarrie & E. Robinson, Trans.). New York: Harper Perennial. (Original work published in 1928).

Hickok, G. (2008). Eight problems with the mirror neuron theory of action understanding in monkeys. *Journal of Cognitive Neuroscience, 21*, 1229–1243.

Hickok, G., & Hauser, M. (2010). (Mis)understanding mirror neurons. *Current Biology, 20*, R593–594.

Hoffman, I. Z. (1987). The value of uncertainty in psychoanalytic practice. *Contemporary Psychoanalysis, 23*, 205–214.

Hoffman, I. Z. (1996). The intimate and ironic authority of the psychoanalyst's presence. *Psychoanalytic Quarterly, 65*, 102–136.

Hoffman, I. Z. (1998). *Ritual and spontaneity in the psychoanalytic process: A dialectical-constructivist view.* Hillsdale, NJ: The Analytic Press.

Hoffman, I. Z. (2009). Doublethinking our way to "scientific" legitimacy: The desiccation of human experience. *Journal of the American Psychoanalytic Association, 57*, 1043–1069.

Holder, A. (1992). A historical-critical edition. In D. G. Ornston, Jr. (Ed.), *Translating Freud* (pp. 75–96). New Haven, CT: Yale University Press.

Holmes, J. (2010). *Exploring in security: Towards an attachment-informed psychoanalytic psychotherapy.* London: Routledge.

Hoorwitz, A. N. (1989). *Hypnotic methods in nonhypnotic therapies.* New York: Irvington Publishers Inc.

Iacoboni, M. (2007). Face to face: The neural basis of social mirroring and empathy. *Psychiatric Annals, 37*(4), 236–241.

Iacoboni, M., Woods, R. P., Brass, M., Bekkering, H., Mazziotta, J. C., & Rizzolatti, G. (1999). Cortical mechanisms of human imitation. *Science, 286*(5449), 2526–2528.

Issacharoff, A. (1977). A re-reply. *Contemporary Psychoanalysis, 13,* 125–127.

Jacobs, L. (2010). Truth is what matters: Commentary on paper by Philip A. Ringstrom. *Psychoanalytic Dialogues, 20,* 224–230.

Jacobson, E. (1957). Denial and repression. *Journal of the American Psychoanalytic Association, 5,* 61–92.

Jacobson, E. (1964). *The self and the object world.* New York: International Universities Press.

Jacquette, D. (Ed.). (2004a). *The Cambridge companion to Brentano.* Cambridge, UK: Cambridge University Press.

Jacquette, D. (2004b). Brentano's concept of intentionality. In D. Jacquette (Ed.), *The Cambridge companion to Brentano* (pp. 98–130). Cambridge, UK: Cambridge University Press.

James, W. (2007). *Principles of psychology* (Vol. 1). New York: Cosimo, Inc. (Original work published in 1893).

Janik, A., & Toulmin, S. (1996). *Wittgenstein's Vienna.* Chicago: Ivar R. Dee. (Original work published in 1973).

Jimenez, P. (1989). Some reflections on the practice of psychoanalysis in Chile today (From the point of view of the relationship between psychoanalysis and society). *International Review of Psychoanalysis, 16,* 493–504.

Johnston, W. M. (1972). *The Austrian mind: An intellectual and social history 1848–1938.* Berkeley, CA: University of California Press.

Kahneman, D. (2011). *Thinking, fast and slow.* New York: Farrar, Straus and Giroux.

Kahneman, D., Slovic, P., & Tversky, A. (Eds.). (1982). *Judgment under uncertainty: Heuristics and biases.* Cambridge, UK: Cambridge University Press.

Kahneman, D., & Tversky, A. (1982). Variants of uncertainty. *Cognition, 11,* 143–157.

Kandel, E. R. (2001). The molecular biology of memory storage: A dialogue between genes and synapses. *Science, 294,* 1030–1038.

Kandel, E. R., & Tauc, L. (1965). Mechanism of heterosynaptic facilitation in the giant cell of the abdominal ganglion of *Aplysia depilans. Journal of Physiology (London), 181,* 28–47.

Kantrowitz, J. (1997). A different perspective on the therapeutic process: The impact of the patient on the analyst. *Journal of the American Psychoanalytic Association, 45,* 127–153.

Kardiner, A. (1977). *My analysis with Freud.* New York: W. W. Norton & Co.

Kaufmann, W. (1988). *Hegel: A reinterpretation.* South Bend, IN: University of Notre Dame. (Original work published in 1966).

Kernberg, O. (1968). The treatment of patients with borderline personality organization. *International Journal of Psychoanalysis, 49,* 600–619.

Kernberg, O. (1994). Love in the analytic setting. *Journal of the American Psychoanalytic Association, 42,* 1137–1157.

Kernberg, O. (1996). The analyst's authority in the psychoanalytic situation. *Psychoanalytic Quarterly, 65,* 137–157.

Kesey, K. (2002). *One flew over the cuckoo's nest.* London: Penguin Books. (Original work published in 1962).

Kihlstrom, J. F. (2008). The domain of hypnosis, revisited. In M. R. Nash & A. J. Barnier (Eds.), *The Oxford handbook of hypnosis: Theory, research, and practice* (pp. 21–52). Oxford: Oxford University Press.

Kimball, D. R., & Holyoak, K. J. (2000). Transfer and expertise. In E. Tulving & F. I. M. Craik (Eds.), *The Oxford handbook of memory* (pp. 109–122). Oxford: Oxford University Press.

Kirshner, L. A. (2005). Rethinking desire: The objet petit a in Lacanian theory. *Journal of the American Psychoanalytic Association, 53,* 83–102.

Kirsner, D. (2000). *Unfree associations*. London: Process Press.

Kirsner, D. (2007). Fresh Freud: No longer lost in translation. *Psychoanalytic Psychology, 24*, 658–666.

Kirsner, D. (2009). *Unfree associations: Inside psychoanalytic institutes, updated edition*. Lanham, MD: Jason Aronson.

Klein, G. S. (1966). The several grades of memory. In M. L. Rudolph, L. M. Newman, M. Schur, & A. J. Solnit (Eds.), *Psychoanalysis—A general psychology: Essays in honor of Heinz Hartmann* (pp. 377–389). New York: International Universities Press.

Klein, G. S. (1970). *Perception, motives, and personality*. New York: Alfred A. Knopf.

Klein, G. S. (1976a). Freud's two theories of sexuality. In M. M. Gill & P. S. Holtzman (Eds.), *Psychology versus metapsychology: Psychoanalytic essays in honor of George S. Klein* (pp. 14–70). New York: International Universities Press. (Original work published in 1969).

Klein, G. S. (1976b). *Psychoanalytic theory*. New York: International Universities Press.

Klein, J. G. (2005). Five pitfalls in decisions about diagnosis and prescribing. *British Medical Journal, 330*, 781–783.

Kohler, L. (1984). On selfobject countertransference. *Annual of Psychoanalysis, 12*, 39–56.

Kohut, H. (1966). Forms and transformations of narcissism. *Journal of the American Psychoanalytic Association, 14*, 243–272.

Kohut, H. (1971). *The analysis of the self*. New York: International Universities Press.

Kohut, H. (1977). *The restoration of the self*. New York: International Universities Press.

Kohut, H. (1979). The two analyses of Mr. Z. *International Journal of Psychoanalysis, 60*, 3–27.

Kohut, H. (1984). *How does analysis cure?* (A. Goldberg, Ed.). Chicago: University of Chicago Press.

Kosfeld, M., Heinrichs, M., Zac, P. J., Fischbacher, U., & Fehr, E. (2005). Oxytocin increases trust in humans. *Nature, 435*, 673–676.

Kris, E. (1955). Neutralization and sublimation: Observations on young children. *Psychoanalytic Study of the Child, 10*, 30–46.

Kristensen, P., & Bjerkedal, T. (2007). Explaining the relation between birth order and intelligence. *Science, 316*, 1717.

Kupfermann, I., & Kandel, E. R. (1969). Neuronal controls of a behavioral response mediated by the abdominal ganglion of *Aplysia*. *Science, 164*, 847–850.

Labov, W., & Fanshel, D. (1977). *Therapeutic discourse: Psychotherapy as conversation*. New York: Academic Press.

Lacan, J. (1991a). *The ego in Freud's theory and in the technique of psychoanalysis (Seminar Book II)* (S. Tomaselli, Trans.). New York: W. W. Norton & Co. (Original work published in 1978).

Lacan, J. (1991b). *The four fundamental concepts of psychoanalysis (Seminar Book VIII)*. New York: W. W. Norton & Co. (Original work published in 1973).

Lacan, J. (2006a). *Écrits* (B. Fink, Trans.). New York: W. W. Norton & Co. (Original work published in 1966).

Lacan, J. (2006b). The direction of the treatment and the principles of its power. In *Écrits* (pp. 489–542). New York: W. W. Norton & Co.

Langs, R. (1986). Clinical issues arising from a new model of the mind. *Contemporary Psychoanalysis, 22*, 418–444.

Langs, R. (1987). Clarifying a new model of the mind. *Contemporary Psychoanalysis, 23*, 162–180.

Laplanche, J., & Pontalis, J. B. (1973). *The language of psycho-analysis* (D. Nicholson-Smith, Trans.). New York: W. W. Norton & Co. (Original work published in 1967).

Laszlo, E. (1996). *The systems view of the world: A holistic vision for our time*. Cresskill, NY: Hampton Press Inc. (Original work published in 1972).

Latour, B. (1987). *Science in action: How to follow scientists and engineers through society*. Cambridge, MA: Harvard University Press.

Latour, B. (1993). *We have never been modern* (C. Porter, Trans.). Cambridge, MA: Harvard University Press. (Original work published in 1991).

Latour, B. (1999). *Pandora's hope: Essays on the reality of science studies*. Cambridge, MA: Harvard University Press.

Latour, B., & Woolgar, S. (1986). *Laboratory life in the construction of scientific facts*. Princeton, NJ: Princeton University Press.

Layton, L. (2000). The psychopolitics of bisexuality. *Studies in Gender and Sexuality, 1*, 41–60.

Le nouveau petit Robert de la langue Française 2009. (2009). Paris: Le Robert.

Lear, J. (1998). *Love and its place in nature*. New Haven, CT: Yale University Press. (Original work published in 1990).

Leffert, M. (2003). Analysis and psychotherapy by telephone: Twenty years of clinical experience. *Journal of the American Psychoanalytic Association, 51*, 101–130.

Leffert, M. (2007a). A contemporary integration of modern and postmodern trends in psychoanalysis. *Journal of the American Psychoanalytic Association, 55*, 177–197.

Leffert, M. (2007b). Postmodernism and its impact on psychoanalysis. *Bulletin of the Menninger Clinic, 71*, 15–34.

Leffert, M. (2008). Complexity and postmodernism in contemporary theory of psychoanalytic change. *Journal of the American Academy of Psychoanalysis and Dynamic Psychiatry, 36*, 517–542.

Leffert, M. (2010a). *Contemporary psychoanalytic foundations: Postmodernism, complexity, and neuroscience*. New York: Routledge.

Leffert, M. (2010b). Commentary on "Returning to Freud" by Richard D. Chessick: Why one should (or shouldn't) read Freud. *Journal of the American Academy of Psychoanalysis and Dynamic Psychiatry, 39*, 348–357.

Leffert, M. (2011a). Commentary on "The rise and fall of the autochthonous self" by Richard D. Chessick: The self is alive and well and living at MoMA. *Journal of the American Academy of Psychoanalysis and Dynamic Psychiatry, 39*, 348–357.

Leffert, M. (2011b). The psychoanalysis and death of George Gershwin: An American tragedy. *Journal of the American Academy of Psychoanalysis and Dynamic Psychiatry, 39*, 420–451.

Leuzinger-Bohleber, M., & Target, M. (Eds.). (2001). *Outcomes of psychoanalytic treatment perspectives for therapists and researchers*. London: Whurr Publishers.

Levine, S. S. (2007). Nothing but the truth: Self-disclosure, self-revelation, and the persona of the analyst. *Journal of the American Psychoanalytic Association, 55*, 81–104.

Levy, J. (2009). Studying the interpretation of dreams in the company of analytic candidates. *Journal of the American Psychoanalytic Association, 57*, 847–870.

Levy, S. T., & Inderbitzin, L. B. (1989). Negativism and countertransference. *Journal of the American Psychoanalytic Association, 37*, 7–30.

Lichtenberg, J. D. (Ed.). (1997). New psychoanalytic perspectives on the treatment of sexual trauma. *Psychoanalytic Inquiry, 17*(3).

Lichtenberg, J. D. (Ed.). (2004). Problems of power in psychoanalytic institutions. *Psychoanalytic Inquiry, 24*(1).

Lichtenberg, J. D., & Galler, F. B. (1987). The fundamental rule: A study of current usage. *Journal of the American Psychoanalytic Association, 35*, 47–76.

Lindsay, R. C., Ross, D. F., Read, D. V., & Toglia, M. (Eds.). (2006–2007). *The handbook of eyewitness psychology: Vols I & II*. London: Psychology Press.

Lipton, S. D. (1977). Clinical observations on resistance to the transference. *International Journal of Psychoanalysis, 58*, 463–472.

Loewald, H. W. (1960). On the therapeutic action of psycho-analysis. *International Journal of Psychoanalysis, 41*, 16–33.

Loewald, H. W. (1988). *Sublimation: Inquiries into theoretical psychoanalysis*. New Haven, CT: Yale University Press.

Lukes, S. (2005). *Power a radical view* (2nd ed.). New York: Palgrave Macmillan.

Lyons, R. (2011). The spread of evidence-poor medicine via flawed social-network analysis. *Statistics, Politics, and Policy, 2*(1), 1–26.

Lyotard, J. (1988). *The differend: Phrases in dispute* (G. V. D. Abbeele, Trans.). Minneapolis: University of Minnesota Press. (Original work published in 1983).

Lyotard, J. (1993). *Libidinal economy* (I. H. Grant, Trans.). Bloomington, IN: Indiana University Press. (Original work published in 1974).

Mahony, P. J. (1987). *Freud as a writer: Expanded edition.* New Haven, CT: Yale University Press.

Main, M. (1991). Metacognitive knowledge, metacognitive monitoring, and singular (coherent) vs. multiple (incoherent) model of attachment. In C. M. Parkes, J. Stevenson-Hinde, & P. Marris (Eds.), *Attachment across the life cycle* (pp. 126–159). London: Routledge.

Main, M., Kaplan, N., & Cassidy, J. (1985). Security in infancy, childhood, and adulthood: A move to the level of representation. *Monographs of the Society for Research in Child Development, 50,* 66–104.

Malabou, C., & Derrida, J. (2004). *Counterpath* (D. Wills, Trans.). Stanford, CA: Stanford University Press. (Original work published in 1999).

Malmgren, R. D., Stouffer, D. B., Motter, A. E., & Amaral, L. A. N. (2008). A Poissonian explanation for heavy tails in e-mail communication. *Proceedings of the National Academy of Science, 105,* 18153–18158.

Marcus, D. M., & "Hope" (2007). *Taking risks from the unconscious: A psychoanalysis as experienced from both sides of the couch.* Lanham, MD: Jason Aronson.

Marion, R. (1999). *The edge of organization: Chaos and complexity theories of formal social systems.* Thousand Oaks, CA: Sage Publications.

Markowitsch, H. J. (2000). Neuroanatomy of memory. In E. Tulving & F. I. M. Craik (Eds.), *The Oxford handbook of memory* (pp. 465–484). Oxford: Oxford University Press.

Mayes, A. R. (2000). Selective memory disorders. In E. Tulving & F. I. M. Craik (Eds.), *The Oxford handbook of memory* (pp. 427–440). Oxford: Oxford University Press.

McClelland, J. L., & Rumelhart, D. E. (1986). *Parallel distributed processing* (Vol. 2). Cambridge, MA: MIT Press.

McGowan, J. (1991). *Postmodernism and its critics.* Ithaca, NY: Cornell University Press.

McGrath, W. J. (1986). *Freud's discovery of psychoanalysis: The politics of hysteria.* Ithaca, NY: Cornell University Press.

Mednick, S. C., Christakis, N. A., & Fowler, J. H. (2010). The spread of sleep loss influences drug use in adolescent networks. *PloS ONE, 5,* e9775.

Meehl, P. (1954). *Clinical versus statistical prediction.* Minneapolis: University of Minnesota Press.

Menand, L. (2010, March 1). A critic at large: Psychotherapy under siege. *The New Yorker, 86,* 68–74.

Merriam-Webster's Collegiate Dictionary. (2004). (Eleventh ed.). Springfield, MA: Merriam-Webster Inc.

Mitchell, S. A. (1988). *Relational concepts in psychoanalysis.* Cambridge, MA: Harvard University Press.

Mitchell, S. A. (1992a). Commentary on Trop and Stolorow's "Defense Analysis in Self Psychology." *Psychoanalytic Dialogues, 2,* 443–453.

Mitchell, S. A. (1992b). Introduction. *Psychoanalytic Dialogues, 2,* 279–285.

Mitchell, S. A. (1998). The analyst's knowledge and authority. *Psychoanalytic Quarterly, 67,* 1–31.

Mitchell, S. A. (2002). *Can love last? The fate of romance over time.* New York: W. W. Norton & Co.

Molnar-Szakacs, I., & Arzy, S. (2009). Searching for an integrated self-representation. *Communicative and Integrative Biology, 2,* 365–367.

Morris, B. (2008). *1948: A history of the first Arab–Israeli War.* New Haven, CT: Yale University Press.

Moulton, R. (1977). Woman with double lives. *Contemporary Psychoanalysis, 13,* 64–84.

Nacht, S. (1962a). The curative factors in psycho-analysis. *International Journal of Psychoanalysis, 43,* 206–211.

Nacht, S. (1962b). The curative factors in psycho-analysis—Contributions to discussion. *International Journal of Psychoanalysis, 43,* 233.

Nader, K. (2009). Reconsolidation: A possible bridge between cognitive and neuroscientific views of memory. In M. S. Gazzaniga (Ed.), *The cognitive neurosciences* (4th ed., pp. 691–703). Cambridge, MA: MIT Press.

Natterson, J. M. (2003). Love in psychotherapy. *Psychoanalytic Psychology, 20,* 509–521.

Neisser, U., & Libby, L. K. (2000). Remembering life experiences. In E. Tulving & F. I. M. Craik (Eds.), *The Oxford handbook of memory* (pp. 315–332). Oxford: Oxford University Press.

Nietzsche, F. (1969). *On the genealogy of morals* (W. Kaufmann, Trans.). New York: Vintage Books. (Original work published in 1887).

Nisbett, R. E., & Ross, L. (1980). *Human inference: Strategies and shortcomings of social judgment.* Englewood Cliffs, NJ: Prentice-Hall.

Nisbett, R. E., & Wilson, T. (1977). Telling more than we can know: Verbal reports on mental processes. *Psychological Review, 84*, 231–259.

Noel, H., & Nyhan, B. (2011). The "unfriending" problem: The consequences of homophily in friendship retention for causal estimates of social influence. *Social Networks, 33*, 211–218.

Norris, C. (2002). *Deconstruction theory and practice* (3rd ed.). London: Routledge.

Novick, J., & Novick, K. K. (2000). Love in the therapeutic alliance. *Journal of the American Psychoanalytic Association, 48*, 189–218.

Nyberg, L., & Cabeza, R. (2000). Brain imaging of memory. In E. Tulving & F. I. M. Craik (Eds.), *The Oxford handbook of memory* (pp. 501–519). Oxford: Oxford University Press.

Ofshe, R., & Watters, E. (1994). *Making monsters: False memories, psychotherapy, and sexual hysteria.* New York: Charles Scribner's.

Ogden, T. H. (1994). The analytic third: Working with intersubjective clinical facts. *International Journal of Psychoanalysis, 75*, 3–19.

Ogden, T. H. (1997). *Reverie and interpretation.* Northvale, NJ: Jason Aronson.

Ogden, T. H. (2003). The analytic third: Implications for psychoanalytic theory and technique. *Psychoanalytic Quarterly, 73*, 167–195.

Orne, M. (1970). Hypnosis, motivation, and the ecological validity of the psychological experiment. In W. Arnold & M. Page (Eds.), *Nebraska symposium on motivation, 1970 ed.* (pp. 187–205). Lincoln, NE: University of Nebraska Press.

Ornston, D. G., Jr. (1982). Strachey's influence: A preliminary report. *International Journal of Psychoanalysis, 63*, 409–426.

Ornston, D. G., Jr. (1985a). The invention of "cathexis" and Strachey's strategy. *International Review of Psychoanalysis, 12*, 391–398.

Ornston, D. G., Jr. (1985b). Freud's conception is different from Strachey's. *Journal of the American Psychoanalytic Association, 33*, 379–412.

Ornston, D. G., Jr. (Ed.). (1992a). *Translating Freud.* New Haven, CT: Yale University Press.

Ornston, D. G., Jr. (1992b). Alternatives to a *Standard edition.* In D. G. Ornston, Jr. (Ed.), *Translating Freud* (pp. 97–113). New Haven, CT: Yale University Press.

Palla, G., Barabási, A.-L., & Vicsek, T. (2007). Quantifying social group evolution. *Nature, 446*, 664–667.

Panksepp, J. (1998). *Affective neuroscience: The foundations of human and animal emotions.* Oxford: Oxford University Press.

Panksepp, J. (2008). The affective brain and core consciousness: How does neural activity generate emotional feelings? In M. Lewis, J. M. Haviland-Jones, & L. F. Barrett (Eds.), *Handbook of emotions* (3rd ed., pp. 47–67). New York: Guilford Press.

Panksepp, J. (2009). Brain emotional systems and qualities of mental life: From animal models of affect to implications for psychotherapeutics. In D. Fosha, D. J. Siegal, & M. Solomon (Eds.), *The healing power of emotion: Affective neuroscience, development, and clinical practice* (pp. 1–26). New York: W. W. Norton & Co.

Parish, M., & Eagle, M. N. (2003). Attachment to the therapist. *Psychoanalytic Psychology, 20*, 271–286.

Peabody, F. (1927). The care of the patient. *Journal of the American Medical Association, 88*, 877–882.

Pinsky, E. (2011). The Olympian delusion. *Journal of the American Psychoanalytic Association, 59*, 351–375.

Plato (2006). Symposium. In C. D. C. Reeve (Ed.), *Plato on love* (pp. 26–87). Indianapolis: Hackett Publishing Co.

Polsby, N. W. (1980). *Community power and political theory* (2nd ed.). New Haven, CT: Yale University Press. (Original work published in 1963).

Porges, S. W. (1998). Love: An emergent property of the mammalian autonomic nervous system. *Psychoneuroendocrinology, 23*, 837–861.

Porges, S. W. (2009). Reciprocal influences between body and brain in the perception and expression of affect: A polyvagal perspective. In D. Fosha, D. J. Siegal, & M. Solomon (Eds.), *The healing power of emotion: Affective neuroscience, development, and clinical practice* (pp. 27–54). New York: W. W. Norton & Co.

Psychoanalytic Electronic Publishing. (2010). PEP Archive 1 version 10 (1871–2007).

Pulver, S. E. (1987). The manifest dream in psychoanalysis: A clarification. *Journal of the American Psychoanalytic Association, 35*, 99–118.

Pulver, S. E. (2003). On the astonishing clinical irrelevance of neuroscience. *Journal of the American Psychoanalytic Association, 51*, 755–772.

Rachman, A. W. (1997). *Sándor Ferenczi: The psychotherapist of tenderness and passion*. Northvale, NJ: Jason Aronson.

Rapaport, D. (1956). *The psychoanalytic theory of consciousness and the study of dreams*. Unpublished lecture, Detroit Psychoanalytic Society.

Rapaport, D. (1967). *A theoretical analysis of the superego concept* (M. M. Gill, Ed.). New York: Basic Books. (Original work published in 1957).

Rapaport, D., & Gill, M. M. (1959). The points of view and assumptions of metapsychology. *International Journal of Psychoanalysis, 40*, 153–162.

Ravasz, E., & Barabási, A.-L. (2003). Hierarchical organization in complex networks. *Physical Review E.67*, 026112.

Reeder, J. (2004). *Hate and love in psychoanalytical institutions*. New York: Other Press.

Renik, O. (1993). Analytic interaction: Conceptualizing technique in light of the analyst's irreducible subjectivity. *Psychoanalytic Quarterly, 62*, 553–571.

Ringo, J. L., Doty, R. W., Demeter, S., & Simard, P. Y. (1994). Time is of the essence: A conjecture that hemispheric specialization arises from interhemispheric conduction delay. *Cerebral Cortex, 4*, 331–343.

Ringstrom, P. A. (2010). Meeting Mitchell's challenge: A comparison of relational psychoanalysis and intersubjective systems theory. *Psychoanalytic Dialogues, 20*, 196–218.

Risse, G. L., & Gazzaniga, M. S. (1978). Well-kept secrets of the right hemisphere: A carotid amytal study of restricted memory transfer. *Neurology, 28*, 487–495.

Rorty, R. (1979). *Philosophy and the mirror of nature*. Princeton, NJ: Princeton University Press.

Rorty, R. (1982). *Consequences of pragmatism: Essays 1972–1980*. Minneapolis: University of Minnesota Press.

Rorty, R. (1989). *Contingency, irony, and solidarity*. Cambridge, UK: Cambridge University Press.

Rosenblatt, A. D., & Thickstun, J. (1970). A study of the concept of psychic energy. *International Journal of Psychoanalysis, 51*, 265–278.

Rosenblatt, A. D., & Thickstun, J. T. (1977a). Energy, information, and motivation: A revision of psychoanalytic theory. *Journal of the American Psychoanalytic Association, 25*, 537–558.

Rosenblatt, A. D., & Thickstun, J. T. (1977b). *Modern psychoanalytic concepts in a general psychology*. New York: International Universities Press.

Rosenquist, J. N., Murabito, J., Fowler, J. H., & Christakis, N. A. (2010). The spread of alcohol consumption behavior in a large social network. *Annals of Internal Medicine, 152*, 426–433.

Rosten, L. (1961). *Captain Newman, M.D.* New York: Harper & Brothers.

Rubins, J. L. (1967). The neurotic personality and certain sexual perversions. *Contemporary Psychoanalysis, 4*, 53–72.

Rumelhart, D. E., & McClelland, J. L. (1986). *Parallel distributed processing* (Vol. 1). Cambridge, MA: MIT Press.

Said, E. W. (1979). *Orientalism*. New York: Vintage Books.

Said, E. W. (1994). *Culture and imperialism*. New York: Vintage Books.

Said, E. W. (2001a). *Power, politics, and culture: Interviews with Edward Said* (G. Viswanathan, Ed.). New York: Vintage Books.

Said, E. W. (2001b). Language, history, and the production of knowledge, interview with Gauri Viswanathan. In G. Viswanathan (Ed.), *Power, politics, and culture: Interviews with Edward Said* (pp. 262–279). New York: Vintage Books. (Original work published in 1996).

Sandler, J. (1983). Reflections on some relations between psychoanalytic concepts and psychoanalytic practice. *International Journal of Psychoanalysis, 64*, 35–45.

Sato, W., & Aoki, S. (2006). Right hemisphere dominance in processing unconscious emotion. *Brain and Cognition, 62*, 261–266.

Schachtel, E. (1959). *Metamorphosis*. New York: Basic Books.

Schacter, D. L. (1996). *Searching for memory*. New York: Basic Books.

Schacter, D. L. (2001). *The seven sins of memory*. Boston: Houghton Mifflin Company.

Schacter, D. L., Addis, D. R., & Buckner, R. L. (2008). Episodic simulation of future events concepts, data, and applications. *Annals of the New York Academy of Science, 1124*, 39–60.

Schacter, D. L., Wagner, A. D., & Buckner, R. L. (2000). Memory systems of 1999. In E. Tulving & F. I. M. Craik (Eds.), *The Oxford handbook of memory* (pp. 627–643). Oxford: Oxford University Press.

Schafer, R. (1997). *The contemporary Kleinians of London*. Madison, CT: International Universities Press.

Schecter, M. (2007). The patient's experience of validation in psychoanalytic treatment. *Journal of the American Psychoanalytic Association, 55*, 105–130.

Schimel, J. L. (1977). The consequences of predicting disaster. *Contemporary Psychoanalysis, 13*, 94–101.

Schooler, J. W., & Eich, E. (2000). Memory for emotional events. In E. Tulving & F. I. M. Craik (Eds.), *The Oxford handbook of memory* (pp. 379–392). Oxford: Oxford University Press.

Schore, A. N. (1994). *Affect regulation and the origin of the self*. Hillside, NJ: Lawrence Erlbaum Associates.

Schore, A. N. (2002). Neuropsychoanalysis, attachment theory, and trauma research: Implications for self psychology. *Psychoanalytic Inquiry, 22*, 433–484.

Schore, A. N. (2003a). *Affect dysregulation and disorders of the self*. New York: W. W. Norton & Co.

Schore, A. N. (2003b). *Affect regulation and the repair of the self*. New York: W. W. Norton & Co.

Schore, A. N. (2009). Right-brain affect regulation: An essential mechanism of development, trauma, dissociation, and psychotherapy. In D. Fosha, D. J. Siegal, & M. Solomon (Eds.), *The healing power of emotion: Affective neuroscience, development, and clinical practice* (pp. 112–144). New York: W. W. Norton & Co.

Schore, A. N. (2011). The right brain implicit self lies at the core of psychoanalysis. *Psychoanalytic Dialogues, 21*, 75–100.

Schore, J. R., & Schore, A. N. (2007). Modern attachment theory: The central role of affect regulation in development and treatment. *Clinical Social Work Journal, 36*, 9–20.

Schorske, C. E. (1980). *Fin-de-siècle Vienna*. New York: Alfred A. Knopf.

Schur, M. (1972). *Freud: Living and dying*. New York: International Universities Press.

Searles, H. F. (1959). Oedipal love in the counter transference. *International Journal of Psychoanalysis, 40*, 180–190.

Segal, H. (1962). The curative factors in psycho-analysis: Contributions to discussion. *International Journal of Psychoanalysis, 43*, 232–233.

Shalizi, C. R., & Thomas, A. C. (2011). Homophily and contagion are generically confounded in observational social network studies. *Sociological Methods and Research, 40*, 211–239.

Shane, M. G., & Shane, M. (2001). The attachment motivational system as a guide to an effective therapeutic process. *Psychoanalytic Inquiry, 21*, 675–687.

Shapiro, S. A. (2000). Publications of Benjamin Wolstein. *Contemporary Psychoanalysis, 36*, 361–367.

Sharpe, E. F. (1968). The analysand. The analytic task. General procedure. Errors avoidable by beginners. In M. Brierley (Ed.), *Collected papers on psycho-analysis* (pp. 22–37). London: Hogarth Press. (Original work published in 1950 [1930]).

Shobe, K. K., & Kihlstrom, J. F. (2002). Interrogative suggestibility and "memory work." In M. L. Eisen, J. Quas, & G. S. Goodman (Eds.), *Memory and suggestibility in the forensic interview* (pp. 309–327). Mahwah, NJ: Lawrence Erlbaum Associates.

Shrager, Y., & Squire, L. R. (2009). Medial temporal lobe function and human memory. In M. S. Gazzaniga (Ed.), *The cognitive neurosciences* (4th ed., pp. 675–702). Cambridge, MA: MIT Press.

Silverman, D. K. (2003). Theorizing in the shadow of Foucault: Facets of female sexuality. *Psychoanalytic Dialogues, 13*, 243–272.

Silverstein, S. M., & Silverstein, M. A. (1990). Freud and hypnosis: The development of the interactionist perspective. *Annual of Psychoanalysis, 18*, 175–194.

Simon, E. (1987). A new model of the mind (a symposium)—Forbidden transitions. *Contemporary Psychoanalysis, 23*, 122–130.

Simon, H. A. (1956). Rational choice and the structure of the environment. *Psychological Review, 63*, 129–138.

Slade, A. (1999). Attachment theory and research: Implications for the theory and practice of individual psychotherapy with adults. In J. Cassidy & P. R. Shaver (Eds.), *Handbook of attachment: Theory, research, and clinical applications* (pp. 575–594). New York: Guilford Press.

Sperling, O. E. (1957). A psychoanalytic study of hypnagogic hallucinations. *Journal of the American Psychoanalytic Association, 5*, 115–123.

Spezzano, C. (1998). Listening and interpreting—How relational analysts kill time between disclosures and enactments: Commentary on papers by Bromberg and by Greenberg. *Psychoanalytic Dialogues, 8*, 237–246.

Spreng, R. N., Mar, R. A., & Kim, A. S. N. (2008). The common neural basis of autobiographical memory, prospection, navigation, theory of mind, and the default mode: A quantitative meta-analysis. *Journal of Cognitive Neuroscience, 21*, 489–510.

Steiner, R. (1987). A world wide international trademark of genuineness? Some observations on the history of the English translation of the work of Sigmund Freud, focusing mainly on his technical terms. *International Review of Psychoanalysis, 14*, 33–102.

Stern, D. B. (1997). *Unformulated experience: From dissociation to imagination in psychoanalysis.* Hillsdale, NJ: The Analytic Press.

Stern, D. B. (2002). What you first know: Construction and deconstruction in relational psychoanalysis. In S. Fairfield, L. Layton, & C. Stack (Eds.), *Bringing the plague: Toward a postmodern psychoanalysis* (pp. 167–194). New York: Other Press.

Stern, D. B. (2003). Commentary on "Psychoanalytic discourse at the turn of our century: A plea for a measure of humility." *Journal of the American Psychoanalytic Association, 51*(Suppl.), 98–108.

Stern, D. N. (1985). *The interpersonal world of the infant.* New York: Basic Books.

Stern, D. N., Sander, L. W., Nahum, J. P., Harrison, A. M., Lyons-Ruth, K., Morgan, A. C., et al. (1998). Non-interpretive mechanisms in psychoanalytic therapy: The "something more" than interpretation. *International Journal of Psychoanalysis, 79*, 903–921.

Stolorow, R. D. (2011). *World, affectivity, trauma.* New York: Routledge.

Stolorow, R. D., & Atwood, G. E. (1992). *Contexts of being.* Hillsdale, NJ: The Analytic Press.

Stolorow, R. D., Atwood, G. E., & Brandchaft, B. (1994). *The intersubjective perspective.* Northvale, NJ: Jason Aronson.

Stolorow, R. D., Orange, D., & Atwood, G. E. (2002). *Worlds of experience: Interweaving philosophical and clinical dimensions in psychoanalysis.* New York: Basic Books.

Strachey, J. (1934). The nature of the therapeutic action of psycho-analysis. *International Journal of Psychoanalysis, 15*, 127–159.

Strachey, J. (1961). Appendix A. In *The standard edition of the complete psychological works of Sigmund Freud* (Vol. 19, pp. 60–62). London: Hogarth Press.

Strachey, J. (1966a). General preface. In *The standard edition of the complete psychological works of Sigmund Freud* (Vol. 1, pp. xiii–xxvi). London: Hogarth Press.

Strachey, J. (1966b). Editor's note to *Beyond the pleasure principle.* In *The standard edition of the complete psychological works of Sigmund Freud* (Vol. 18, pp. 3–6). London: Hogarth Press.

Szasz, T. S. (1961). *The myth of mental illness: Foundations of a theory of personal conduct.* New York: Hoeber-Harper.

Szasz, T. S. (1969). *The ethics of psychoanalysis the theory and method of autonomous psychotherapy.* New York: Dell. (Original work published in 1965).

Szasz, T. S. (1997). *The manufacture of madness: A comparative study of the inquisition and the mental health movement.* Syracuse, NY: Syracuse University Press. (Original work published in 1970).

Tannert, C., Elvers, H.-D., & Jandrig, B. (2007, October 8). The ethics of uncertainty: In the light of possible dangers, research becomes a moral duty. *EMBO Reports*, 892–896.

Tasso, A. F., & Perez, N. A. (2008). Parsing everyday suggestibility: What does it tell us about hypnosis? In M. R. Nash & A. J. Barnier (Eds.), *The Oxford handbook of hypnosis: Theory, research, and practice* (pp. 283–309). Oxford: Oxford University Press.

Tausk, V. (1933). On the origin of the "influencing machine" in schizophrenia. *Psychoanalytic Quarterly, 2*, 519–556.

Teicholz, J. G. (1999). *Kohut, Loewald and the postmoderns.* Hillsdale, NJ: The Analytic Press.

Tessman, L. H. (2003). *The analyst's analyst within.* Hillsdale, NJ: The Analytic Press.

The Oxford English dictionary. (1989). (2nd ed.). Oxford: Clarendon Press.

Tilly, C. (1991). Domination, resistance, compliance … discourse. *Sociological Forum, 6*(3), 593–602.

Timms, E. (1989). *Karl Kraus apocalyptical satirist: Culture and catastrophe in Hapsburg Vienna.* New Haven, CT: Yale University Press. (Original work published in 1986).

Tintner, J. (2007). Bypassing barriers to change? Bariatric surgery, case material. *Contemporary Psychoanalysis, 43*, 121–134.

Trumble, W. R. (2007). *Shorter Oxford English dictionary* (6th ed.). Oxford: Oxford University Press.

Tulving, E. (2003). Memory and consciousness. In B. J. Baars, W. P. Banks, & J. B. Newman (Eds.), *Essential sources in the scientific study of consciousness.* Cambridge, MA: MIT Press. (Original work published in 1985).

Tulving, E., Kapur, S., Craik, F. I. M., Moscovitch, M., & Houle, S. (1994). Hemispheric encoding/retrieval asymmetry in episodic memory: Positron emission tomography findings. *Proceedings of the National Academy of Science, 91*, 2016–2020.

Tutte, J. C. (2004). The concept of psychical trauma: A bridge in interdisciplinary space. *International Journal of Psychoanalysis, 85*, 897–921.

Tversky, A., & Kahneman, D. (1982). Belief in the law of small numbers. In D. Kahneman, P. Slovic, & A. Tversky (Eds.), *Judgment under uncertainty: Heuristics and biases* (pp. 23–31). Cambridge, UK: Cambridge University Press. (Original work published in 1971).

Uddin, L. Q., Iacoboni, M., Lange, C., & Keenan, J. P. (2007). The self and social cognition: The role of cortical midline structures and mirror neurons. *Trends in Cognitive Sciences, 11*, 153–157.

Vivona, J. M. (2009). Leaping from brain to mind: A critique of mirror neuron explanations of countertransference. *Journal of the American Psychoanalytic Association, 57*, 525–550.

von Bertalanffy, L. (1968). *General systems theory: Foundations, development, applications.* New York: George Brazilier.

von Senden, M. (1960). *Space and sight: The perception of space and shape in the congenitally blind before and after operation* (S. Schweppe, Trans.). London: Methuen & Co. (Original work published in 1932).

Wallerstein, R. S., & Nemetz, S. J. (1979). Conceptualizing the nature of the therapeutic action of psychoanalytic psychotherapy. *Journal of the American Psychoanalytic Association, 27*, 127–144.

Wallin, D. J. (2007). *Attachment in psychotherapy.* New York: Guilford Press.

Walton, J. (1997). Re-placing race in (white) psychoanalytic discourse: founding narratives in feminism. In E. Abel, B. Christian, & H. Moglen (Eds.), *Female subjects in black and white: Race, psychoanalysis, feminism* (pp. 223–252). Berkeley, CA: University of California Press.

Wheeler, J. A., & Zurek, H. (1983). *Quantum theory and measurement.* Princeton, NJ: Princeton University Press.

Whitaker, R. (2010). *Anatomy of an epidemic: Magic bullets, psychiatric drugs, and the astonishing rise of mental illness in America.* New York: Crown Publishers.

Williams, M. (1987). Reconstruction of an early seduction and its aftereffects. *Journal of the American Psychoanalytic Association, 35,* 145–163.

Willingham, D. B., & Preuss, L. (1995). The death of implicit memory. *Psyche, 2,* 15.

Winnicott, D. W. (1955). Metapsychological and clinical aspects of regression within the psycho-analytical set-up. *International Journal of Psychoanalysis, 36,* 16–26.

Winnicott, D. W. (1975a). *Through paediatrics to psycho-analysis.* New York: Basic Books.

Winnicott, D. W. (1975b). Anxiety associated with insecurity. In *Through paediatrics to psycho-analysis* (pp. 97–100). New York: Basic Books. (Original work published in 1952).

Winnicott, D. W. (1975c). Primitive emotional development. In *Through paediatrics to psycho-analysis* (pp. 145–156). New York: Basic Books. (Original work published in 1945).

Winnicott, D. W. (1989). On the basis for self in body. In C. Winnicott, R. Shepherd, & M. Davis (Eds.), *Psycho-analytic explorations* (pp. 261–283). Cambridge, MA: Harvard University Press. (Original work published in 1971).

Wittels, F. (1924). *Sigmund Freud.* New York: Dodd-Mead.

Wittenberg, E. G. (1987). Clinical innovations and theoretical controversy. *Contemporary Psychoanalysis, 23,* 183–198.

Wohlberg, J. W. (1997). Sexual abuse in the therapeutic setting: What do victims really want? *Psychoanalytic Inquiry, 17,* 329–348.

Wolstein, B. (1977a). Psychology, metapsychology, and the evolving American school. *Contemporary Psychoanalysis, 13,* 128–154.

Wolstein, B. (1977b). Expanding the interpretive range of psychoanalytic therapy: A critical metamorphosis of its structure of inquiry. *Contemporary Psychoanalysis, 13,* 209–232.

Wolstein, B. (1977c). Countertransference, counterresistance, counteranxiety: The anxiety of influence and the uniqueness of curiosity. *Contemporary Psychoanalysis, 13,* 16–29.

Yalom, I. D. (1996). *Lying on the couch: A novel.* New York: Basic Books.

Yalom, I. D., & Elkin, G. (1974). *Every day gets a little bit closer: A twice-told therapy.* New York: Basic Books.

Zeddies, T. J. (2001). On the wall or in the ointment? The psychoanalytic community as a third presence in the consulting room. *Contemporary Psychoanalysis, 37,* 133–147.

Zeeman, E. C. (1987a). *Catastrophe theory: Selected papers 1972–1977.* Reading, MA: Addison-Wesley.

Zeeman, E. C. (1987b). Brain modeling. In *Catastrophe theory: Selected papers 1972–1977* (pp. 287–292). Reading, MA: Addison-Wesley. (Original work published in 1976).

Zola, S. M., & Squire, L. R. (2000). The medial temporal lobe and the hippocampus. In E. Tulving & F. I. M. Craik (Eds.), *The Oxford handbook of memory* (pp. 485–500). Oxford: Oxford University Press.

Zweig, S. (1964). *The world of yesterday: An autobiography of Stefan Zweig.* Lincoln: University of Nebraska Press. (Original work published in 1943).

Author Index

Subject Index